CULTURAL POETICS IN ARCHAIC GREECE

CULTURAL POETICS
IN ARCHAIC GREECE

Cult, Performance, Politics

Edited by

CAROL DOUGHERTY

LESLIE KURKE

New York   Oxford

Oxford University Press

1998

Oxford New York
Athens Auckland Bangkok Bogota Bombay
Buenos Aires Calcutta Cape Town Dar es Salaam
Delhi Florence Hong Kong Istanbul Karachi
Kuala Lumpur Madras Madrid Melbourne
Mexico City Nairobi Paris Singapore
Taipei Tokyo Toronto Warsaw

and associated companies in
Berlin Ibadan

Library of Congress Cataloging-in-Publication Data
Cultural poetics in archaic Greece : cult, performance, politics /
[edited by] Carol Dougherty and Leslie Kurke.
p. cm.
Originally published: Cambridge : Cambridge University Press, 1993.
Based on a conference at Wellesley College in October 1990.
ISBN 0-19-512415-4 (pbk.)
1. Greece—Civilization—To 146 B.C.—Congresses.
I. Dougherty, Carol. II. Kurke, Leslie.
DF222.C85 1998
938—dc21 98-10745

1 3 5 7 9 8 6 4 2

Printed in the United States of America
on acid-free paper

Contents

List of Illustrations   *page* vii
Acknowledgments   ix
Abbreviations   xi
List of Contributors   xv

I   Introduction   I
    Carol Dougherty and Leslie Kurke

PART ONE: THE USES OF THE PAST

2   Poetics of Power: The Interpretation of Ritual Action in Archaic
    Greece   15
    Ian Morris

3   The Archaeology of Ancestors   46
    Carla Antonaccio

PART TWO: POLITICS AND PERFORMANCE

4   Divine Selection: Epiphany and Politics in Archaic Greece   73
    Rebecca H. Sinos

5   Hipparchos and the Rhapsodes   92
    H. A. Shapiro

6   The Seven Sages as Performers of Wisdom   108
    Richard P. Martin

CONTENTS

PART THREE: NEGOTIATING CIVIC CRISIS

7 The Economy of *Kudos*   131
   Leslie Kurke

8 Hero Cult and Politics in Herodotus: The Bones of Orestes   164
   Deborah Boedeker

9 It's Murder to Found a Colony   178
   Carol Dougherty

PART FOUR: THE END OF AN ERA

10 Thucydides' Solonian Reflections   201
    Andrew Szegedy-Maszak

11 The Athenian Revolution of 508/7 B.C.E.: Violence, Authority,
    and the Origins of Democracy   215
    Josiah Ober

    Bibliography   233
    Index   261

Illustrations

1   Mainland Greece: distribution of Iron Age/archaic tomb cult, incorporating reuse, eleventh to fifth century, B.C.E.   *page* 49
2   Berbati Tomb III: cross section showing Iron Age reuse   50
3   Asine: Barbouna area, circular platforms near eighth-century necropolis   51
4   Mycenae: circular platform in chamber tomb next to Grave Circle B   53
5   Sparta (Therapne): Menelaion   54
6   Mycenae: Cyclopean bridge and shrine retaining wall south of acropolis (Agamemnoneion)   55
7   Lakonia and Messenia: distribution of Iron Age/archaic tomb and hero cult   56
8   Attika and Euboia: distribution of Iron Age/archaic tomb and hero cult   58
9   Kerameikos (Athens): *tritopatreion* boundary wall and *horos*   59
10 Argolid: distribution of Iron Age/archaic tomb and hero cult   60
11 Leto on the chariot with Hermes standing in front, Apollo and Artemis at the side: black-figure amphora by the Rycroft Painter   74
12 Departing warrior taking leave of his family: black-figure amphora Near Group E   75
13 Gods accompanying the bride and groom in their procession: black-figure hydria by the Antimenes Painter   76
14 Women with baskets escorting the bride and groom: black-figure amphora Near Group E   77
15 Chariot outfitted with pillows; on the reverse, the groom leading the bride on foot: red-figure krater by the Painter of the Athens Wedding   78
16 Athena mounting the chariot beside Herakles: black-figure hydria by the Priam Painter   81

17 Athena awakening Theseus from his bridal bed: red-figure
   lekythos Near the Pan Painter   82
18 Aulode and accompanist: black-figure amphora of Panathenaic
   shape, ca. 550 B.C.E.   94
19 Aulete: black-figure amphora of Panathenaic shape, ca. 550–540
   B.C.E.   94
20 Kithara player between Panathenaic columns: black-figure neck
   amphora, 540–530 B.C.E.   95
21 Aulode: red-figure neck amphora (Side A), ca. 500–490 B.C.E.   96
22 Flute player: Side B of Figure 21   97
23 Aulode and accompanist: black-figure neck amphora (Side A),
   ca. 500 B.C.E.   98
24 Aulode and accompanist: Side B of Figure 23   99
25 Rhapsode: black-figure amphora of Panathenaic shape, 520–500
   B.C.E.   100
26 Athena between columns: black-figure amphora of Panathenaic
   shape (Side A), ca. 540 B.C.E.   101
27 Rhapsode: Side B of Figure 26   102
28 Kitharode: black-figure pelike, ca. 500 B.C.E.   103
29 Herald announcing the victor in the horse race, as a youth
   approaches with tripod and crown: black-figure amphora of
   Panathenaic shape, ca. 570 B.C.E.   143
30 Crowning of athletic victor wreathed in fillets: black-figure
   amphora of Panathenaic shape   145

Acknowledgments

IT HAS BEEN a long process from the conception, planning, and orchestration of the original conference at Wellesley College in October 1990 to the transformation of the proceedings into a volume, and we have incurred many debts of gratitude along the way. Thanks, first, to two conspicuous absent presences at the conference – W. R. Connor and Gregory Nagy – who have always given us their support but, more important, have served as the guiding intellectual forces behind this endeavor.

For the financial assistance that made the conference possible, we thank the Wellesley departments of Art History, History, and Greek and Latin, the Mary Horton Lecture Fund, and the Wesleyan Department of Classics. Pat Bois, secretary of the Wellesley Department of Greek and Latin, deserves special mention. Without her organizational skill, attention to detail, and irrepressible good nature, the conference would never have come off. Thanks also to the faculty, students, and staff at Wellesley who offered crucial support and help before and during the conference – especially Robin Akert, Pat Berman, Randall Colaizzi, Katherine Geffcken, Gregory Gómez, Miranda Marvin, Lisa Maurizio, Guy Rogers, and Ray Starr. We owe a particular debt of gratitude to Susan Taylor, director of the Wellesley College Art Museum, for organizing an exhibit to coincide with the conference and for offering us the use of the Museum Sculpture Court. And for their abiding interest and genial hospitality, we thank Mary Lefkowitz and Hugh Lloyd-Jones. Finally, we owe the greatest debt to those (speakers and audience alike) who participated in the conference and made it such a stimulating experience; thanks especially to our moderators, Deborah Boedeker, Mary Lefkowitz, and Emily Vermeule, and to our speakers, Carla Antonaccio, Richard P. Martin, Ian Morris, Josiah Ober, H. Alan Shapiro, Rebecca H. Sinos, and Andrew Szegedy-Maszak.

Many others have earned our gratitude for their help in transforming the conference into a book. Renewed thanks to all our contributors for their unflagging patience and good humor (not to mention their conscientiousness) through the long metamorphosis. Richard Martin kindly offered advice at every stage of the planning and read the book prospectus and introduction. Thanks to Berkeley colleagues Tom Habinek and Ron Stroud for guidance on conference volumes and technical details respectively; to Carla Antonnacio, for long-distance archaeological help from Athens; and to Andrew Garrett, for his unstinting interest in formatting issues. For their assistance in the preparation of the manuscript, we thank Roger Travis, Jr., and Naomi Rood, who contributed their share of insights and good humor as well. For financial support, we are indebted to the UC Berkeley Committee on Research, and crucially to Wellesley College for funding a year's leave and thereby making possible collaborative work in Berkeley. Finally, warm thanks to the anonymous readers for Cambridge University Press and to Beatrice Rehl, fine arts editor at Cambridge, for her steadfast support and enthusiasm about the volume from the very beginning.

Abbreviations

The abbreviations of ancient authors and titles are as listed in the *Oxford Classical Dictionary*, 2d ed. Other abbreviations are as follows:

AA	*Archäologischer Anzeiger*
AAA	*Athens Annuals of Archaeology*
ABV	J. D. Beazley, *Attic Black-Figure Vase-Painters*
AC	*L'Antiquité Classique*
AE	*Archaiologike Ephemeris*
AHR	*American Historical Review*
AION ArchStAnt	*Annali dell' Instituto universitario orientale di Napoli*, Dipartimento di studi del' mondo classico e del Mediterraneo antico, Sezione di archeologia e storia antica
AJA	*American Journal of Archaeology*
AJAH	*American Journal of Ancient History*
AJP	*American Journal of Philology*
AM	*Mitteilungen des Deutschen Archäiologischen Instituts*, Athenische Abteilung
AmAnt	*American Antiquity*
Annales ESC	*Annales (Economie, Sociétés, Civilisations)*
AntJ	*The Antiquaries Journal* (Society of Antiquaries of London)
AntK	*Antike Kunst*
AR	*Archaeological Reports*
ArchDelt	*Archaiologikon Deltion*
ARV²	J. D. Beazley, *Attic Red-Figure Vase-Painters*, 2d ed.
ASAA	*Annuario della Scuola Archeologica di Atene* a delle Missioni Italiane in Oriente
ASNP	*Annali della Scuola Normale Superiore di Pisa*, Classe di Lettere e Filosofia
BABesch	*Bulletin Antieke Beschaving*

BCH	*Bulletin de Correspondance Héllenique*
BICS	*Bulletin of the Institute of Classical Studies*
BSA	*Annual of the British School of Athens*
C & M	*Classica et Medievalia*
CA	*Classical Antiquity*
CAH[2]	*Cambridge Ancient History*, 2d ed.
CEG	*Carmina Epigraphica Graeca*, vols. I and 2, ed. P. A. Hansen
CJ	*Classical Journal*
CP	*Classical Philology*
CQ	*Classical Quarterly*
CRDAC	*Centro ricerche e documentazione sull' antichità classica. Atti*
CSCA	*California Studies in Classical Antiquity*
CVA	*Corpus Vasorum Antiquorum*
CW	*Classical World*
DK	*Die Fragmente der Vorsokratiker*, 6th ed., ed. H. Diels and W. Kranz
EMC/CV	*Echos du Monde Classique/Classical Views*
FGrH	*Die Fragmente der Griechischen Historiker*, ed. F. Jacoby
GRBS	*Greek, Roman, and Byzantine Studies*
HSCP	*Harvard Studies in Classical Philology*
HTR	*Harvard Theological Review*
JdI	*Jahrbuch des Deutschen Archäologischen Instituts*
JHS	*Journal of Hellenic Studies*
LakSpoud	*Lakonikai Spoudai* (= *Laconian Studies*)
LCM	*Liverpool Classical Monthly*
LSJ	*Greek–English Lexicon*, 9th ed., ed. H. G. Liddell, R. Scott, and H. S. Jones
MH	*Museum Helveticum*
Nauck[2]	*Tragicorum Graecorum Fragmenta*, 2d ed., ed. A. Nauck.
OAth	*Opuscula Atheniensia* (Acta Inst. Athen. Regni Sueciae)
ÖJh	*Jahreshefte des Österreichischen Archäologischen Instituts in Wien*
PAE	*Praktika of the Archaeological Society in Athens*
PMG	*Poetae Melici Graeci*, ed. D. L. Page
PP	*La Parola del Passato*
QUCC	*Quaderni Urbinati di Cultura Classica*
RA	*Revue Archéologique*
RE	Pauly-Wissowa, *Real-Enzyklopädie der klassischen Altertumswissenschaft*
REA	*Revue des Études Anciennes*
REG	*Revue des Études Grecques*
RhM	*Rheinisches Museum*
SEG	*Supplementum Epigraphicum Graecum*
SIG	*Sylloge Inscriptionum Graecarum*
SIMA	*Studies in Mediterranean Archaeology*

SO	*Symbolae Osloenses*
TAPA	*Transactions of the American Philological Association*
V	*Sappho et Alcaeus*, ed. E.-M. Voigt
W	*Iambi et Elegi Graeci*, 2 vols., ed. M. L. West
ZPE	*Zeitschrift für Papyrologie und Epigraphik*

Contributors

CARLA ANTONACCIO is Assistant Professor of Classics at Wesleyan University in Connecticut. She is co-director of the Morgantina Expedition in Sicily and has excavated in Greece, Cyprus, and Sicily. Her interests include the archaeology of ethnicity and gender, state formation, and trade and exchange in prehistory. Her essay in this volume previews her new book, *An Archaeology of Ancestors: Hero and Tomb Cult in Early Greece* (Rowman & Littlefield, 1993).

DEBORAH BOEDEKER is co-director of the Center for Hellenic Studies in Washington, D.C., and Professor of Classics at Brown University. Her publications include *Aphrodite's Entry into Greek Epic* (Brill, 1974), *Descent from Heaven: Images of Dew in Greek Poetry and Religion* (Scholar's Press, 1984), and articles on Sappho, Hesiod, Homer, and Herodotus. She organized a conference entitled "Herodotus and the Invention of History" and edited the proceedings for a special issue of *Arethusa* (1987). Besides her current project on hero cult in Herodotus, she is working on Greek tragedy, particularly Euripides' *Medea*.

CAROL DOUGHERTY is Assistant Professor of Greek and Latin at Wellesley College. Her primary interests are oral poetics, ethnography, and cultural studies and literature of archaic and classical Greece. She is the author of *The Poetics of Colonization: From City to Text in Archaic Greece* (Oxford University Press, 1993) and of several articles on colonial discourse and Greek poetry. Future projects include Ion of Chios and the intellectual history of early-fifth-century Athens and a study of ethnographic and exploration literature of archaic/classical Greece.

LESLIE KURKE is Assistant Professor of Classics and Comparative Literature at the University of California at Berkeley. She specializes in Greek literature and cultural history. She is the author of *The Traffic in Praise: Pindar and the Poetics of Social Economy* (Cornell University Press, 1991) and articles on Pindar, Alkaios, Theognis, and Herodotus. She is currently working on the ideological contestation of real and symbolic economies in archaic Greece.

RICHARD P. MARTIN is Associate Professor of Classics at Princeton University. His primary interests are Homer, Celtic studies, poetics, folklore, and Greek religion and mythology. He is the author of *The Language of Heroes: Poetry and Performance in the "Iliad"* (Cornell University Press, 1989) and the editor of a new edition of Bulfinch's *Mythology*. He is currently engaged in two projects: a book about Telemachus (*The Trickster's Son*) and a book on the Greek wisdom tradition (*Acts of Wisdom*).

IAN MORRIS is Associate Professor of History and Classics at the University of Chicago. He works at the intersection of archaeology, history, and anthropology and participates in archaeological fieldwork in Greece. He is the author of *Burial in Ancient Society* (Cambridge University Press, 1987) and *Death Ritual and Social Structure in Classical Antiquity* (Cambridge University Press, 1992) and the editor of *Classical Greece: Ancient Histories and Modern Archaeologies* (Cambridge University Press, 1993). He is currently working on a book entitled *The Archaeology of Democracy*.

JOSIAH OBER is Professor of Greek History at Princeton University. He is the author of *Fortress Attica* (Brill, 1985), *Mass and Elite in Democratic Athens* (Princeton University Press, 1989), *The Anatomy of Error* (with B. S. Strauss, St. Martin's Press, 1990), and articles on Greek history, archaeology, and political philosophy. He is currently writing a book on Athenian critics of popular rule, a study of the interplay between several key political texts and the ideological context of late-fifth- and fourth-century Athens.

H. A. SHAPIRO is Associate Professor of Humanities at Stevens Institute of Technology. He is a former Fellow of the American School of Classical Studies and the Alexander von Humboldt-Stiftung. He specializes in the iconography of Attic vase painting, and his publications include *Art and Cult under the Tyrants in Athens* (P. von Zabern, 1989) and *Personifications in Greek Art* (Akanthus-Verlag, 1992).

REBECCA H. SINOS is Professor of Classics at Amherst College. She has published articles on Greek lyric poetry, vase paintings, and rituals. She is co-author, with John Oakley, of *The Wedding in Ancient Athens* (University of Wisconsin Press, 1993).

ANDREW SZEGEDY-MASZAK is Jane A. Seney Professor of Greek at Wesleyan University in Connecticut. His interests range from Theophrastus and the Greek lawgivers to the history of photography of classical sites. He has organized photo exhibitions at the Davison Museum at Wesleyan, the Tampa Museum of Art, and the J. Paul Getty Museum and is currently working on a book about the representation of classical sites in nineteenth-century photography and travel narrative.

CHAPTER ONE

Introduction

Carol Dougherty and Leslie Kurke

GERALD ELSE once described the sixth century B.C.E. as the "histrionic period of Athenian history."[1] He coined the phrase to sketch the background for the beginnings of tragedy, but in a certain sense it can stand as an emblem for the entire archaic period throughout Greece. The archaic age (broadly defined as the period stretching from the eighth century B.C.E. to the time of the Persian Wars) has remained peculiarly recalcitrant for those attempting to reconstruct its history and culture. Much poorer in contemporary literary and archeological evidence than the classical era, the earlier period compels researchers to turn to later traditions and to different kinds of evidence for the work of reconstruction. As Else's phrase implies, much of the tradition provides us with a very odd view indeed: not the "straight" version of history and politics that Thucydides promises for the classical period, but a fanciful and often fragmentary concatenation of ritual and playacting.

And yet the need to make sense of the archaic age is particularly urgent. Dubbed by Anthony Snodgrass the "age of experiment," the archaic period was a truly revolutionary age that witnessed the emergence of the city-state, the reintroduction of writing and the slow spread of literacy, the codification of the Homeric poems and the trend toward Panhellenism, the rise to prominence of the Delphic oracle, the surge of the Greek colonial movement, the establishment of the Panhellenic games, the age of tyrants, and the beginnings of democracy.[2] How did a traditional society come to grips with these momentous changes and sources of instability? The question is an important one, for taken together, the developments of the archaic period altered the way the Greeks constructed their world. Everything that defines the Greeks of the classical period as peculiarly Greek – their institutions, laws and customs, and even their sense of themselves – has its roots in the archaic period. If we are to understand what makes the Greeks "different," what makes them unique, we must develop the tools to make sense of the archaic age.

With this need in mind, it is worth considering again Else's characterization. It captures something of the historian's frustration: as if a modern reporter were to focus her camera on a street performer while somewhere else, beyond the frame, a military coup were taking place. Indeed, many discussions of Herodotus' version of events express exasperation at his willful or incompetent reportage, his focus on the marginal and the histrionic rather than the "realities" of power. But perhaps Else's thumbnail sketch can lead us in a different direction, urging us to take the Greeks' playacting seriously. That is to say, perhaps Herodotus and other reporters of the archaic period focused their attention on the right objects (if only we know how to read them); perhaps the military coup takes place *through* the ritualized drama of the performance in the street. As W. R. Connor persuasively argues in an article that has influenced many of the chapters in this volume, we must view ritual and ceremony "as part of the symbolic expression of civic concerns and as a difficult to read but ultimately eloquent text about the nature of civic life."[3]

It is our contention that the archaic period is in a sense "predisciplinary," that politics, religion, and economics as separate spheres are the invention of a later age. The Greeks of the archaic period, like other members of traditional societies, took for granted the complete interpenetration of these spheres. The predisciplinary nature of the archaic period, in turn, requires from scholars a complementary *inter*disciplinary approach: only by combining the methods and subject matter of history, philology, art history, and archaeology (subfields that are still relatively autonomous within the field of classics) can we constitute the "text" of the archaic period and read it aright. The symposium, "Cultural Poetics in Archaic Greece: Tyranny, Cult, and Civic Ideology," held at Wellesley College on October 20, 1990, was an attempt to do just that. Our aim was to set up a dialogue among scholars within the various disciplines, all working on the archaic period. Insofar as that dialogue was achieved, we hope that the present volume will make a contribution to an interdisciplinary cultural history of archaic Greece.

"Ritualized drama," "eloquent text" – these are not the traditional metaphors used to describe ancient society. These phrases reveal our debt, not only to a range of subdisciplines within classics, but also to theoretical paradigms drawn from other fields. Indeed, it may be that the moment is propitious for the development and application of new methods to the archaic period, for there is a widespread tendency toward breaking down disciplinary boundaries beyond the field of classics.[4] Anthropologists, historians, and literary theorists are actively borrowing from one another, and this interdisciplinary ferment has generated a number of new approaches well suited to the peculiarities of the archaic period and the fragmentary state of our evidence.[5] Anthropology supplies a framework for studying archaic culture in all its complex texture, while literary theory offers other models for reading the archaic text.

In trying to "think with" the Greeks of the archaic period in addition to thinking about them, we have been influenced by Clifford Geertz, a self-described "meanings-and-symbols ethnographer," who looks for cultural significance in the particulars, in the seemingly idiosyncratic rituals and practices a society uses to help construct its own cultural identity.[6] In an essay discussing the nature of anthropological understanding, Geertz explains just what he sets out to do when studying another culture:

In all three of the societies I have studied intensively, Javanese, Balinese, and Moroccan, I have been concerned, among other things, with attempting to determine how the people who live there define themselves as persons, what goes into the idea they have (but, as I say, only half-realize they have) of what a self, Javanese, Balinese, or Moroccan style, is. And in each case, I have tried to get at this most intimate of notions not by imagining myself someone else, a rice peasant or a tribal sheikh, and then seeing what I thought, but by searching out and analyzing the symbolic forms – words, images, institutions, behaviors – in terms of which, in each place, people actually represented themselves to themselves and to one another.[7]

Geertz discovers, for example, what being a Balinese is "really like" through his careful (and highly stylized) analysis of a public spectacle – the cockfight. He defines the cockfight as a sociological entity, a "focused gathering" (Goffman's term), and shows how closely allied cockfighting and its attendant rituals and equipment are to important principles of Balinese culture. Temple festivals are preceded by cockfights; cockfights serve as collective responses to natural disasters such as illness, volcanic eruptions, and crop failure; they even provide the Balinese with metaphors for heaven and hell: "The Balinese compare the former to the mood of a man whose cock has just won, the latter to that of a man whose cock has just lost."[8] The cockfight, in Geertz's analysis, reproduces the social matrix of the Balinese; the various and continually shifting political and social relationships among the different kinship groups in Bali are played out through the elaborate betting rituals that comprise the very heart of the cockfight. For Geertz, the cockfight is an art form, and as such it "renders ordinary, everyday experience comprehensible by presenting it in terms of acts and objects which have had their practical consequences removed and been reduced (or, if you prefer, raised) to the level of sheer appearances, where their meaning can be more powerfully articulated and more exactly perceived."[9] This kind of contextual analysis can help us interpret the rituals, spectacles, and ceremonies of archaic Greek culture. Of course, given the fragmentary state of our evidence, our task is somewhat more complicated: it is as if we have only the cockfight from which to reconstruct the encircling context of Balinese culture. Still, Geertz's method – especially his emphasis on the particulars, on "local knowledge" – offers us a way to derive the larger system of culture from the fragments that remain.

Yet as scholars in the fields of history and anthropology have already acknowledged, Geertz's elegant systematizations of culture require some qualifications. In constructing culture as a "web of signification," this approach runs the risk of being too static, of ignoring important questions of historical and political change.[10] Given the complex, rapidly changing character of archaic Greece, we find it necessary to complicate Geertz's static model with a mode of analysis sensitive to historical contingencies and power inequalities. Marshall Sahlins's work on Captain Cook's arrival in Hawaii and its historical and cultural aftermath provides a model for interpretive anthropology within a historical framework; he advocates a "structural, historical anthropology" that sets a culture's "structure" (its received cultural categories) in a dialectical relationship with historical events.[11] The structure will inform the way individual events are initially understood: thus, as Sahlins argues, the Hawaiians interpreted the arrival of Captain Cook in 1778 within an established mythical framework as the annual return of Lono, the Hawaiian fertility god, from Kahiki. In this context, Cook served as a "historical metaphor of a mythical reality."[12] Hence (and this is abundantly true for our Greek material as well) a mythical reality is continually reproduced and reinforced as it orders and structures new historical phenomena within a preexisting system.

But the opposite is also true; this is not a static model of endless, unchanging repetition and reproduction. Instead, historical events in turn alter the Hawaiians' received cultural categories, modifying their structure. Thus Sahlins maps the ways in which the interaction of British and Hawaiians caused the Hawaiians to rethink and reorder their cultural categories: the arrival of the British and the introduction of commerce generated new relationships between men and women, chiefs and commoners. Sahlins describes

> the historical stress put upon the entire Hawaiian scheme of social distinctions, together with its cosmological values. The categories were redefined by their differential relationships to the European presence. . . . No matter that the motivation for the differential responses of men and women or commoners and chiefs to the foreigners was altogether Hawaiian. The content picked up in the experience meant that the relationships between them would never be the same. . . . The structure, as a set of relationships among relationships, is transformed.[13]

Sahlins's model provides a way to account for historical change and transformation within a cultural continuum.[14] His work on the Hawaiian response to European contact can help us answer the question we posed earlier about the strategies by which archaic Greeks responded to and accommodated epochal changes in their society. One way a traditional culture deals with social crisis is by continually reevaluating and renegotiating the relationships among categories – without abandoning the categories themselves. "The more things remain the same," as Sahlins inverts the familiar adage, "the more they change."[15]

In addition to recognizing the "continuous and reciprocal movement between the practice of the structure and the structure of the practice," Sahlins's approach allows for a pluralistic and differentially interested view of culture. His Hawaiians do not act as a homogeneous body, but differently as men, women, commoners, and chiefs. This is a good corrective to the tendency to overgeneralize and to miss the multiplicity of voices and points of view within any one culture – another criticism that has recently been leveled at Geertz's brand of interpretative anthropology.[16] Keeping this objection in mind, we can still talk about "the Greeks" as a cultural entity with shared beliefs and customs as long as we particularize our analysis whenever possible and focus on the specific subgroups of archaic Greek society that comprise the whole: the aristocracy, the demos, tyrants, Ionians, Dorians, those who lived in the country or the city.[17] These groups may espouse competing paradigms of the good, and so burial rituals or wedding ceremonies, for example, may mean (*in addition* to what they "mean" to the culture as a whole) different things at the same time to different subgroups.[18] Those with power will be more likely to stage ritual events, and they may well interpret them in a different way than the politically and economically disempowered. This is not to say that the elite cynically manipulate ritual to promote their ends. Rituals and religious ceremonies are inseparable from what we now call politics, subject to negotiation from both above and below. The staging metaphor reminds us that any drama includes an audience that participates in the action and so forces us to look beyond the elite, the powerful, those on the stage.

Thus we derive our interest in "ritualized drama" from the field of anthropology; with "eloquent text," we move to the influence of literary criticism and theory. In general, the use of language and textuality as operative metaphors for cultural productions stems from a renewed concern with representation in all its forms. Literary critics have denied that there is any world of objective facts to which language gives us simple, unobstructed access – we are always enmeshed in systems of representation that problematize and obfuscate the real as much as they reflect it. The subject of study, then, is always already a construct, a set of representations that must be analyzed as such. That we have nothing but a set of "texts" (in the broadest sense) is even more true of past cultures than of contemporary ones (and this is perhaps why this claim has begun to have an impact on historians).[19] Starting from the premise of our entrapment in textuality, literary criticism then offers methods and strategies for fine textual analysis. It teaches us to look for the shaping influence of traditional narrative patterns and the audience's generic expectations; it leads us to appreciate the ways in which a text's meaning and effects are engendered by the language of tropes and figures.

Many literary critics combine an awareness of the rhetorical complexities of texts with an interest in exposing the power relations that work through and inform them. In this respect, they have been profoundly affected by Michel Foucault's claim that everything is political: that language and knowledge, like everything else in culture, are not separate, disinterested spheres exempt from the play of differential power relations, but are discourses generated and structured by those relations.[20] In particular, we have found congenial the practices of the New Historicism (or what Stephen Greenblatt would prefer to call "cultural poetics"). This approach, starting from an emphasis on representation and power relations, offers a new way of conceptualizing the relation of art to society. Cultural poetics rejects the privileging or bracketing of a self-contained realm of art within society, which an old-fashioned historical approach to literature maintains, with its carefully articulated foreground and backdrop, the text and its context. Instead, this approach sees texts as sites for the circulation of cultural energy and for the ongoing negotiation of power relations within society.[21] In practice, this method entails a level of local attention to detail that makes it less schematic even than Sahlins's model of cultural change; thus the New Historicists may detect a struggle of different discourses within a single text or anecdote. Furthermore, given its interest in representation, New Historicism recognizes that not only events can alter the "structure" in conjuncture – language itself and other acts of signification are potential sites for cultural change. Thus the negotiation of power relations that the New Historicists locate in texts is a constant two-way process between text and audience, representation and social structure.

This postulated model has a corollary: we must view all acts of representation together and read them against one another – thus the well-known New Historicist penchant for reading anecdotes, private journals, medical treatises, maps, broadsheets, miniatures, and *Wunderkämmer,* all against canonical, high literary texts.[22] Such an approach is very well suited to the study of the archaic period, where we must read and use everything we have – often including evidence embedded in much later sources. The use of later sources makes our task doubly complicated, but it is precisely techniques learned from literary practice that may assist us. That is to say, there is some justification for mining later sources (as we must, given the exiguousness of actual archaic evidence) if we can identify metaphors or systems of signification that correspond to archaic ones and that are often anomalous or obscure within the text in which they are embedded. For example, much later texts record (though they do not seem to understand) the special power of an Olympic victor in his victory crown or the murderous background of a colonial founder.

It is no accident that this catholic approach to representation was developed in Renaissance studies, with particular application to Renaissance drama, since in this period theatrical scripts were not segregated from other texts as "literary" but were instead embedded in occasion and performance setting. The same holds true for the archaic period and makes the application of New Historicist models particularly appropriate: archaic texts are often scripts for ritual performance (e.g., epinikia, paians, parthenia), records of such performances (e.g., the figures on the Dipylon vase, Herodotus' story of Peisistratos and Phye), or the means of reenacting ritual (e.g., dedications and inscriptions).[23] In a sense, this concept of art as necessarily and profoundly interactive with its social "frame" inverts (and thereby complements) Geertz's theoretical model. Geertz teaches us to read ritual as art; the New Historicists would have us see art as ritual. We feel that the ongoing oscillation between these two models – between the neatness of Geertz's decipherable codes and the messiness of New Historicist "negotiations" – can produce a profounder understanding of the archaic period and its remains.

The essays in this volume are concerned with the past – in at least three senses. At the most obvious level, we study the archaic period at a distance of more than two and a half millennia. Because of this enormous gulf, there is an urgent need for us to understand as well our own scholarly past and the constraints it imposes on the methods we use and the questions we ask of the period. Finally, we are interested in the ways in which the Greeks of the archaic period used their own deeper past – the cultural pluperfect, as it were. Ian Morris's essay, "Poetics of Power," critically examines all three of these levels of the past. It is Morris's contention that unless we understand the intellectual and theoretical trends that shaped the approaches to ritual still current in ancient history, we are doomed to repeat the errors of our scholarly ancestors. Thus Morris chronicles the development and competition in the preceding century of various models of ritual activity, which he terms the sociological, the psychological, and (in this century) the cultural. Each method, according to Morris, has its limitations; only by combining them and by broadening the base of the evidence we use can we eke out enough data from the archaic period and do justice to its predisciplinary nature. In the final sections of the essay, Morris examines in light of his theoretical remarks the relations of a particular set of Greeks to their dead and their past. In a wide-ranging survey of Athenian cult and burial practices, Morris summarizes the archaeological evidence for the Athenian "turn inward" in the first half of the seventh century B.C.E. Supplementing his sociological analysis of this phenomenon in *Burial and Ancient Society* (1987), Morris insists that the political and economic are inseparable in this period from the religious and that we must read this withdrawal as religious revival as well as political conservatism.

Carla Antonaccio's essay, "The Archaeology of Ancestors," shares with Morris's a concern with the archaic Greeks' use of the dead and the past within a contemporary "contest of paradigms."[24] Any society's relationship with its dead – the rituals it invokes to commemorate their absence and mark their continued presence – participates in a larger system of negotiation with and through the past. Thus both essays assume that the past within a traditional culture is a limited symbolic resource – a site of contestation among different groups and different communities. In the archaic Greeks' relations to different categories of ancestor, Antonaccio sees the lines of contest drawn. In clarifying the distinctions between "tomb cult" and "hero cult" for the Iron Age and early archaic Greece, she uses both textual and material evidence to uncover the complex but inextricable relations among burial practices, kinship structures, and political development for three different geographical regions in the archaic period. While hero cults help a city forge a connection to figures of the heroic past, tomb cults are concerned with ancestors in a more immediate sense, as a way to structure kinship and leadership relations within the polis. Antonaccio provides insight into how different city-states negotiated different relationships with their past for the sake of competing versions of the present.

The archaic Greeks performed rituals for the dead, but they also staged performances on a grander scale as a forum for debating the past. Thus with Rebecca Sinos's "Divine Selection," we modulate from the use of the past to the prevalent mode of performance, of communal drama, as a means of social and political negotiation within the archaic period. Any performance entails both actors and audience, but ritual performances, such as epiphanies, processions, and cult ceremonies, complicate the relationship between performer and spectator: a drama may be performed for a multiplicity of audiences (each of which may interpret the spectacle in a different way), but even more important, *as spectators* the members of the audience play an important role in the communal drama.

Perhaps one of the best-known performance pieces of the archaic period is Peisistratos' grand entry into Athens on a chariot, led by Athena herself. Herodotus, our source for this episode, is very careful to let us know that this alleged goddess was in reality a tall and beautiful woman from Paiania named Phye, and in so doing he articulates at least two different audiences for the spectacle: the Athenians watching the procession and his own audience, for whom such a charade seems "by far the silliest thing" ever done. Sinos's essay investigates the competing receptions of this Phye performance by exploring the meaning of its constituent elements. Drawing upon literary sources, cult practices, and vase paintings, she recontextualizes for a modern audience the significance of the chariot, of marriage and victory processions, and of divine epiphanies within the archaic period. Each of these elements helps evoke a symbolic landscape comparable to that of the epic poems – a time and place where gods and mortals mingle, where a god's aid to a hero is emblematic of his superior skills. Sinos suggests then that the Peisistratos and Phye episode be read as the restaging of a heroic past within a contemporary context; it is a communal drama that allows both Peisistratos and the Athenians to negotiate political power from a ritual space shared by mortals and gods.

Alan Shapiro's essay, "Hipparchos and the Rhapsodes," reviews another kind of performance – that of the rhapsodes at the Panathenaic festival – together with its larger social and political context. The Panathenaia was perhaps the single most important ceremony in the Athenian religious calendar, and Shapiro reminds us of the complete interpenetration of religion, politics, and poetry within this celebration of Athenian civic identity. *Mousikoi agōnes,* alongside the athletic games, were a distinctive feature of the Panathenaic festival, and rhapsodes competed with one another in singing material drawn from the epic cycle. Working from textual sources as well as evidence from vase painting, Shapiro articulates the role of Hipparchos, tyrant of Athens, in confining the rhapsodic repertoire to the *Iliad* and the *Odyssey.* The tyrant's restriction of performance represents another way of controlling the heroic past in an ever-volatile present and reminds us of the continued political importance of these literary texts.

Poetry, performance, and politics are again intertwined in the following essay, "The Seven Sages as Performers of Wisdom," by Richard Martin. While we may never be able to discover the historical facts behind the Seven Sages, Martin shows that the traditions that surround and survive the sages are themselves valuable for an understanding of what it means to be wise in the archaic period: a sage is at once a poet, a performer, and a politician. Drawing upon his previous work on speech acts in the *Iliad,* Martin shows that sages operate in an agonistic performance context not unlike that of the Homeric heroes.[25] Competition, in fact, is built into their identity as sages, and for this reason "*there had to be an idealized corporate body of sages. . . . One wise man doesn't work.*" Comparative ethnographic evidence confirms this composite profile of the sages and indicates that in traditional societies, such as archaic Greece, advising and decision making were, in fact, conducted in ritual, performance contexts.

In the figures of the sages, we also see a traditional society responding to upheaval – particularly in the form of civic crisis. We have already emphasized the transitional nature of the archaic period: new paradigms that emerge in the wake of such developments as writing, coinage, colonization, tyranny, and emergent Panhellenism are achieved only through strategies designed to accommodate change within the structure of the polis. The following three essays describe three different kinds of response to civic crisis in the archaic period. Yet in all three cases, existing narrative patterns, metaphors, and religious practices are used to fashion a productive relationship between a powerful individual (victor, hero, or city founder) and the community at large. This is not to say that this is merely the manipulation of religion by an individual leader. All three essays underscore the inseparability of the two spheres of religion and politics, especially in the context of change. It is precisely this interaction of political development with religious stability that recalls Sahlins's motto "The more things stay the same, the more they change."

Leslie Kurke's essay, "The Economy of *Kudos*," sets out to discover the meaning of *kudos* in an epinikian context. Combining epinikian poetry with more concrete evidence from the victory ceremony itself, Kurke suggests that *kudos* is talismanic power that the victor acquires by his victory. A victor's reentry into his city provides the context for sharing his talismanic power with the community. In certain cases of civic crisis, the privileged status of the victorious athlete is extended to heroic honors, and this is what explains the small group of "hero-athletes" that clusters in the late sixth and early fifth centuries. In this brief window of time, we see the intersection of conditions of civic crisis with an aristocratic bid for renewed talismanic authority within the polis. Thus Kurke locates the phenomenon within the context of shifting power relations among classes in this politically tumultuous period.

The talismanic power associated with an athletic victor is not unlike that invested in the bones of a hero, as Deborah Boedeker demonstrates in "Hero Cult and Politics in Herodotus." As the essays of Antonaccio and Morris also make clear, hero cults are very much a part of the development of a polis; they help define and reflect its geographical, political, and ideological nature. Rejecting the prevalent but purely propagandistic reading of the bones of Orestes episode as a ploy of Sparta's foreign policy, Boedeker argues for the internal importance of Orestes in mid-sixth-century Sparta. Within Sparta, the cult of Orestes helps transcend aristocratic family interests; his return "embodies Sparta's communal claim to the inheritance of the Pelopids" and reflects a political ideology of equality. Finally, Boedeker suggests that this particular narrative pattern – crisis, oracular consultation, translation of heroic bones, resolution – in turn shapes the way Herodotus tells the history of Sparta in his own text.

A closely related narrative pattern informs the telling of colonial tales as well. Carol Dougherty, in "It's Murder to Found a Colony," explores overseas colonization as yet another response to civic crisis in archaic Greece. Land shortages, drought, political stasis, and other factors combined to force a large number of Greek cities to send colonial expeditions overseas. Yet these motives are often suppressed, and in their place many colonies memorialize their founders as murderers. In an effort to explain this phenomenon, Dougherty suggests that Delphic Apollo's important civic role as a source of purification in cases of homicide provides the Greeks with a metaphor, a conceptual analogy, for describing colonization. Both institutions expel the dangerous element to preserve the rest of society; both create order where there once was chaos; both depend upon Delphic Apollo. The analogy then generates the narrative pattern in which the ritually charged power of the purified murderer, like that of the victorious athlete or dead hero, is channeled into the founding of a new city.

The last two essays approach the archaic period from the vantage point of the fifth century; they reflect upon the period after the fact and at its moment of transition. As the Greeks move into the classical period, the archaic age, itself a time of crisis and innovation, acquires the prestige of the past, available for the interpretation and definition of a new present. For this reason, it is worth asking how the Greeks of the classical period characterized and represented the archaic period to themselves – what continued to be useful amid the events and concerns of the fifth century?

While Richard Martin approaches Solon in his role as one of the Seven Sages, part of a corporate body of wise men in the archaic world, Andrew Szegedy-Maszak looks at how Solon plays at home, in Athens. While acknowledging that the sage is conspicuously absent from Thucydides' fifth-century historical record, Szegedy-Maszak identifies a repertoire of gestures, allusions, and resonances that would be recognized by a contemporary audience as Solonian. Both the use of *eunomia* (a term closely identified with Solon) and the presentation of Pericles as a fifth-century embodiment of Solon show how powerful his persona and political ideology continued to be in shaping Athens' civic identity. Szegedy-Maszak's careful reading of the traces of Solon in Thucydides show once again how models of the past continually inform representations of the present. For Thucydides, the continued presence of Solon as part of Athenian cultural memory helps the historian structure his own understanding of Athenian politics as a series of paired oppositions: *eunomia/isonomia:* Solon/Kleisthenes: Pericles/Kleon.

Josiah Ober's essay, "The Athenian Revolution of 508/7 B.C.E.," also focuses on Athens and investigates what for many historians marks the end of the archaic period – the reforms of Kleisthenes in 508/7 B.C.E. While most narrative accounts center on Kleisthenes as the inventor of democracy at Athens, Ober challenges this "great man" theory of historical causation and brings to light the key role played by the people, the demos, in these epochal events. In constructing the siege of Kleomenes on the Acropolis as a leaderless mass riot, Ober describes a moment that is both the end and the culmination of the "histrionic period of Athenian history." This event represents a moment of radical discontinuity in that the demos has achieved a new level of political self-awareness and has chosen to act for itself. Yet there are also striking continuities with the archaic period as characterized by the other essay in the volume: this is still history as theater, but theater turned on its head. The demos, normally the audience, has become the actor, while Kleisthenes, the noble leader, has become the spectator skilled in interpreting the signifying gesture of revolutionary action. Kleisthenes' response – the reforms that authorize the people's continued political involvement – then resumes the negotiation enacted through social drama. It is in a way fitting that this final exchange of power, which altered forever the balance of political authority in Athens, stands as the last act of our new history of the archaic period.

NOTES

1. Else 1957: 36.
2. On the profound developments of the archaic period in general, see Austin and Vidal-Naquet 1977; Snodgrass 1980a.
3. Connor 1987: 41.
4. Of course, we are also indebted to the many classicists who have already brought interdisciplinary approaches to the study of ancient material: J. Carter, W. R. Connor,

M. Detienne, L. Gernet, S. Humphreys, N. Loraux, G. Nagy, C. Renfrew, J.-P. Vernant, P. Vidal-Naquet, J. J. Winkler, F. I. Zeitlin, to name just a few.

5. For examples of what Geertz terms "blurred genres" among the disciplines, see Geertz 1983. See also Greenblatt 1980; Darnton 1985; Hunt 1989; Veeser 1989.

6. For the idea of "thinking with" a culture, see Geertz 1973: 23; for his self-characterization as "meanings-and-symbols ethnographer," see Geertz 1983: 69; on the importance of the particulars, see Geertz 1983: 43.

7. Geertz 1983: 58.

8. Geertz 1973: 421.

9. Geertz 1973: 443.

10. See Geertz 1973: 5: "Believing, with Max Weber, that man is an animal suspended in webs of significance he himself has spun, I take culture to be those webs, and the analysis of it to be therefore not an experimental science in search of law but an interpretive one in search of meaning." For objections to this static model, see Crapanzano 1986; Biersack 1989. As Biersack points out, "Geertz's cultural analysis is as static as any structuralism. . . . Time is merely another mode of displacement, a further estrangement. Meaning is described, never derived" (80).

11. Sahlins 1981, 1985.

12. Sahlins 1981: 11.

13. Sahlins 1981: 37.

14. Sahlins's model for transformation within a structural system is very similar to another theoretical framework more familiar to many classicists (which also allows for innovation within a traditional format) – oral formulaic theory. In a sense, our aim is to apply a flexible model of innovation within tradition beyond the literary sphere to cultural phenomena.

15. Sahlins 1981: 7.

16. See, e.g., Crapanzano 1986, who objects to Geertz's tendency to talk about an entire culture as if it were of a single mind. In his discussion of the cockfight, for example, Geertz never specifies *which* Balinese he means. Roger Keesing 1987: 161–2 (quoted in Biersack 1989: 81) raises similar questions about power and prestige: "Cultures are webs of mystification as well as signification. We need to ask who *creates* and who *defines* cultural meanings, and to what ends."

17. Cf. Sahlins 1981: 3–8: "The continuities of cultural categories as modes of interpretation and action," what Sahlins calls "structures of the *longue durée*," are always being revalued and renegotiated by individual members of the community as they, in turn, mutually determine their relationship to one another. Sahlins takes his term "structures of the *longue durée*" from Fernand Braudel (1958). He derives his view of community as a "whole having many parts, which are thus comprehended as mutually determining," from Kant (*Critique of Pure Reason*). It is important to note that the act of determination is a mutual one, moving in both directions, not just from the top down.

18. Bourdieu 1977: 106–14 also reminds us of the dangers of investing too heavily in theories of cultural coherence. The analyst, by gathering more information than can be mastered by any single informant, gains what Bourdieu calls a "privilege of totalization." He can apprehend a logic of the system that any partial view would miss. The danger of this totalizing view is that it can make *theoretically* impossible things that are in fact *practically* possible. Since symbolic objects and practices can enter (without contradiction) into successive relationships from different points of view, our analysis of those symbolic actions must try to allow for such multiplicity, variation, and difference. See also V. Turner 1974: 14 for comments on how coherent wholes are achieved through the contest of conflicting paradigms.

19. See Hunt 1989: 16–17.
20. See, e.g., the formulation of Foucault 1977: 27: "Perhaps we should abandon the belief that power makes mad and that, by the same token, the renunciation of power is one of the conditions of knowledge. We should admit rather that power produces knowledge . . . ; that power and knowledge directly imply one another; that there is no power relation without the correlative constitution of a field of knowledge, nor any knowledge that does not presuppose and constitute at the same time power relations."
21. For examples, see Greenblatt 1980, 1988a, 1988b; Veeser 1989. These notions of circulation and negotiation reveal the New Historicists' debt to Bourdieu – in particular, to his concept of "symbolic capital" (for which, see Bourdieu 1977, 1984).
22. For examples, see the essays of Greenblatt, Montrose, Mullaney, Fumerton, and Helgerson collected in Greenblatt 1988a; see also Greenblatt 1988b: 66–93 and the remarks of Fineman in Veeser 1989.
23. There are, of course, differences as well as similarities between the Renaissance and the archaic period so that we cannot adopt New Historicism wholesale as the "solution" to the problems of the archaic period. One element characteristic of New Historicism that we very much doubt will catch on in classics is the fetishization of the weird – the commitment to the decentering force of the bizarre anecdote. Given the exiguousness of our evidence, classicists will probably always remain more invested in reconstructing a normative version of history than in subverting it with the strange and "marginal" moment. For critiques of New Historicism from various perspectives, see Fox-Genovese, Graff, Lentricchia, Newton, Pecora, Terdiman, B. Thomas, and Spivak in Veeser 1989; see also Rée 1991; B. Thomas 1991.
24. For the phrase "contest of paradigms," see V. Turner 1974: 14.
25. Martin 1989.

PART ONE

The Uses of the Past

CHAPTER TWO

Poetics of Power

The Interpretation of Ritual Action
in Archaic Greece

Ian Morris

IRIS MURDOCH, in her novel *The Nice and the Good,* comments that "there are certain areas of scholarship, early Greek history is one . . . where the scantiness of the evidence sets a special challenge to the disciplined mind. It is a game with very few pieces, where the skill of the player lies in complicating the rules."[1] It is hard to disagree with her, and since most of the very few pieces with which the archaic Greek historian plays were produced by or for rituals,[2] we might expect these historians to spend a great deal of their time discussing the ways in which they have complicated the "rules" of ritual. But on the whole, they do not.[3] In this essay I argue that analysis of theoretical and historiographic issues is not a deflection of energies from the "real job" of looking at the actual evidence, but is itself part of the process of defining what our evidence is and what it is evidence for.

I identify three main perspectives in the history of research into Greek ritual in English-language scholarship.[4] I call these the *sociological,* the *psychological,* and the *cultural.*[5] I examine their origins and historical development, beginning in the mid-nineteenth century with the emergence of sociological theories, which explained ritual behavior as a reflection of an underlying social structure. Until about 1918, proponents of this view were locked in debate with other scholars who assumed that rituals were prior to the rest of society and determined the form of other institutions. I call this group of historians "ritualists." Their views were seen as a powerful alternative to sociological theorizing among those scholars who were interested in generalizing about religious behavior, but after 1918 this argument virtually disappeared. During this period another point of view was gaining popularity, the idea that rituals were largely autonomous from the rest of society, telling us solely about ancient beliefs. This I call the psychological method. Its roots lie partly in an alternative conception of the "scientific" role of the historian as a collector of data as opposed to a high-level theorist and partly in an ideological reaction to the political implications of Marxism, the most rigorous form of sociological analysis. Within classics, debate subsided after 1918, and psychologists dominated the field virtually without challenge until the 1970s. In the subjects that have come to be known as the social sciences, however, conservative scholars responded to Marxism by developing functionalism, a model of the world that allowed them to be every bit as "scientific" as the Marxists and to continue to formulate general sociological models without challenging the legitimacy of capitalism. Ritual and belief were seen as being determined by more fundamental forces, but as simultaneously playing a beneficial role in contributing to the stability of society. By about 1970 functionalism was being rejected by most social scientists, but at that point it began to be discovered by classicists, particularly in archaeology. In the 1980s a third perspective began to gain popularity. This, the cultural, is more complex and harder to define. The variant I discuss draws on poststructuralist literary theory to decenter in radical fashion the subject of analysis, producing interpretations of rituals that blur the distinctions between the modern interpreter, the ancient sources, and the ancient actors themselves.

In each case what historians have treated as evidence and what they have assumed that it is evidence for have been determined by nonempirical assumptions – in the historiographer Hayden White's words, by a "prefigurative act [that] is *poetic* inasmuch as it is precognitive and precritical in the economy of the historian's own consciousness."[6] Practicing historians often feel they can safely go on with their work without worrying too much about such theoretical debates, and they may frequently be right. Peter Novick, a leading protagonist in the renewed arguments among Americanists over the nature of historical objectivity, points out that even such an apparently central issue may have little impact on the way historians actually interpret the past: "If two historians, one a 'nihilist' relativist and the other a dyed-in-the-wool objectivist, set out to produce a history of the Civil War, or a biography of George Washington, there is nothing about their 'relativism' or 'objectivism' *per se* that would lead them to do their research differently, frame their analysis differently, or, indeed, prevent their writing *identical* accounts."[7] But in this essay I will try to show that if three historians set out to analyze the rituals of archaic Greece, one writing in the psychological mode, one in the sociological, and one in the cultural, *everything* about their accounts would be different.

In the main part of the essay I analyze the history of these approaches, hoping to clarify their limitations. We can transcend the restrictions imposed on us by fin-de-siècle academic conflicts only by making theoretical discussion a basic part of the analysis of ritual. I then return to my opening point, the relationship between the specific evidence we have from archaic Greece and our wider understanding of general questions of ritual process. I do not offer yet another grand theory of ritual or simply suggest that open-mindedness will solve all our problems. Instead, I provide a brief case study of Athens in the seventh century, arguing that by taking a broader approach to defining the relationships between ritual and other kinds of behavior we can combine many of the strengths of the three approaches without reproducing their weaknesses.

THE BATTLE FOR RITUAL, 1860–1920

The study of ancient religion changed dramatically in the second half of the nineteenth century. In the early part of the century, higher education had been dominated by clergymen, who on the whole embraced a static ideal of knowledge. As T. W. Heyck puts it, "Everything worth knowing and teaching had been established long before, either by the ancients or the great mathematicians."[8] But from the 1860s on a new idea took hold, that of the university as a place where new knowledge was produced by professional academics.[9] The study of religion gradually changed from something that united all branches of knowledge into just one more academic "discipline." Oxford established an honors school in theology in 1870 and Cambridge a theological tripos in 1871, and religion was dropped from the curricula of other formative subjects.[10]

The modern disciplines took shape as professional scholars tried to define themselves as scientists who could provide something the older generation of clergymen and men of letters did not. Historians found two main ways to do this. The first was to respond directly to the great intellectual crisis of the mid-nineteenth century. An 1851 article in the popular journal *The Economist* is fairly typical of the dominant middle-class outlook in this period:

> It is not too much to say that, in wealth, in the arts of life, in the discoveries of science and their application to the comfort, the health, the safety, and the capabilities of man, in public and private morality, in the diffusion if not in the advancement of knowledge, in the sense of social charity and justice, in religious freedom and in political wisdom, – the period of the last fifty years has carried us forward faster and further than any other half-century in modern times.[11]

Thinkers of all political persuasions felt the need to explain this by uniting every aspect of human life within some single framework, accounting for changes in any one part through its connections to the whole.[12] As Philip Abrams explains, this "was probably the first generation of human beings ever to have experienced within the span of their own lifetime socially induced change of a totally transformative nature – change which could not be identified, explained, and accommodated as a limited historical variation within the encompassing order of the past."[13]

The second main strategy for professionalizing historians in both the United States and Britain was to reject the first approach as representing merely a mechanistic attempt to create a pseudoscience of society and to embrace instead what they saw as a genuinely scientific method of positivist fact gathering. For J. A. Froude, a leading figure in the "Oxford school" of historiography, "history itself depends on exact knowledge, on the same minute, impartial, discriminating observation and analysis of particulars which is equally the basis of science,"[14] but not on the generalizations that writers like Auguste Comte and Buckley saw as the essence of scientific history. The notion of the "contribution" rather than the overarching theory came to be seen as the goal of the historian. Another Oxford historian, J. R. Green, wrote to a geologist friend in 1862, "If I could advance History, if you could advance Science, by a single fact . . . I am sure we could both willingly lose all thought of ourselves, and be content to remain obscure, and it may be poor. But knowledge is great riches."[15] On both sides of the Atlantic, the detailed research in primary sources characteristic of German *Wissenschaft* was seized upon to define scientific history, but the metaphysical generalizations that were so important in German scholarship were ignored. When John Seeley, Regius Professor at Cambridge from 1869 to 1882, argued that science involved theorizing as well as conscientious research, he came to be stigmatized as the leader of a "thoughts without facts" school.[16]

I must now introduce two further distinctions. The first concerns primarily the generalizing historians of religion, who should be split into two groups: those who argued that religion and ritual were epiphenomenal to the real workings of society, their forms being determined by deeper forces, usually economic; and those who argued that religion and ritual themselves determined the forms of other institutions and ideas, and that social progress was caused by changes in beliefs. The first group I call the "sociologists of religion," and the second the "ritualists." The ritualists' views were extremely important in the late nineteenth century, particularly within classics, but have had less long-term influence than the sociologists'. My second distinction was made by the anthropologist Edward Evans-Pritchard and mainly concerns the particularizing rather than the generalizing historians. Evans-Pritchard divided treatments of religion into two types, which he called "intellectualist" and "emotionalist."[17] The intellectualists were most interested in tracing the evolution in belief systems from polytheism to a universal and unified concept of the divine that foreshadowed monotheism, while the emotionalists liked to look for the links between the Greek gods and "primitive" religion, full of totems and taboos. The former often emphasized religion and ritual as precursors of scientific thought; the latter were fascinated by the emotional turmoil it was assumed must be produced in those taking part in primitive rites.[18]

Classicists were prominent in theoretical debates over the interpretation of religion before the First World War. Before about 1880, they frequently made contributions to generalizing theories, but almost always on the ritualist side. Fustel de Cou- langes's 1864 book *La cité antique* was particularly influential.[19] Fustel was a leading light in the reactionary Catholic circles around the empress Eugénie. Ferociously anti-German, he rejected all methods pioneered by the philologists across the Rhine and wrote a polemical tract that completely ignored current classical scholarship. He argued that all Indo-European societies were founded on ancestor cult and that this cult, focused on a family tomb outside each house, had caused Greek and Roman society to be based on agnatic descent. The whole history of the classical world became the story of the conflict between this kinship principle and emerging political forces. This struggle periodically came to a head in revolution, which was always bad. Fustel wanted to show that the family and individual private property had always been the twin pillars of European civilization, even though this forced him to undermine his own argument repeatedly and to torture the source material into providing strange answers to his questions. Nevertheless, as Sally Humphreys comments, the book "has had, for a thoroughly self-contradictory argument, a remarkably successful career."[20] Fustel was widely read throughout the rest of the century and was translated into English as early as 1873. He had an enormous influence, in Britain as well as France.[21]

One element of Fustel's argument, that rituals shaped other institutions, was developed independently and taken further still by W. Robertson Smith, a prominent biblical scholar. His career reveals even more clearly than Fustel's the tensions between organized religion and religious scholarship. The son of a Scottish Free Church secessionist minister, he took the Chair of Hebrew and Old Testament Exegesis in the Free Church College of Aberdeen in 1870 at the age of just twenty-four, but between 1875 and 1881 found himself repeatedly on trial for heresy in the Free Church's courts.[22] Smith's main interest lay in the institutions of the ancient Hebrews and pre-Islamic Bedouins. He argued in his *Lectures on the Religion of the Semites*[23] that the earliest Semitic rituals had shaped their social institutions. He adopted from his friend John F. McLennan[24] a unilineal evolutionary model and used it to show that all Semites had once been totemic and had gone through a stage of matrilineal institutions before reaching their textually attested patrilineal systems. Smith's arguments overlapped with Fustel's,[25] but he introduced a novelty by arguing that ritual was also prior to belief. He claimed that the earliest religions lacked creeds and dogmas. Instead, "they consisted entirely of institutions and practices." Rituals, he suggested, were more stable through time than the beliefs invented to explain them.[26]

Between the 1880s and 1910s there was a gradual shift among historians of classical religion from the generalizing to the fact-grubbing conception of the science. I would identify an intermediate stage in which many classicists were still eager to convert their knowledge of ancient polytheism into part of a general theory, but did not want to make such powerful claims for rituals as did Fustel and Smith. Increasingly, classicists were defining individual religious belief as the most interesting topic for research. In these years the psychological approach to classical ritual and religion took shape, emphasizing the actors' personal beliefs as the only element worth serious study. Max Müller, professor of Sanskrit at Oxford, was one of the leading classical scholars of the day. He was instrumental in the rise of a solar theory of religion. He argued that once the Infinite had been thought of, it could be talked about only by analogy with the most magnificent aspects of the known world, such as the sun and moon. After a while these lost their metaphorical sense and began to be treated as gods in their own right. Thus *nomina* became *numina;* as Müller put it, religion was a "disease of language."[27] Everything from the story of Apollo and Daphne to the Trojan War was reduced to a solar myth. This seems rather odd a century later, and indeed some found it so at the time; one student published a pamphlet arguing that Müller himself was a solar myth.[28] But like Fustel, Müller was enormously influential. His prestige was such that he declined a knighthood because he had already received higher honors from other European states. Müller's contemporaries in British classics included Andrew Lang, R. R. Marett, A. E. Crawley, and James Frazer,[29] all of whom moved easily between Greek and "primitive" religion. There were serious differences among these scholars, but all shared an interest in accounting for the origins of religion and its development through various stages to polytheism and finally monotheism; and as the First World War neared, a gradual trend toward granting religious belief a certain amount of autonomy from other social institutions can be seen in their work.

While classicists had been drifting toward particularism and intellectualism, an alternative sociological approach to ritual had grown out of the midcentury generalizing historical sciences. The "sociological" perspective can be traced back to

Aristotle, who observed that the gods were ruled by a king because the human societies that invented the gods used to be ruled by kings, and Karl Marx, who emerged as the leading theorist of socialism in the 1860s, indeed had a Ph.D. from Berlin in Greek philosophy.[30] But there was little enthusiasm for his approach within the academy, and I know of no examples of sociological interpretations of Greek ritual before the Second World War. The liberal associations that Greece had had in the days of Humboldt and George Grote had disappeared, and the politically subversive implications of the sociological theory of ritual may have been important in limiting its impact on classicists around 1900.[31]

Marx himself wrote little about ritual, apparently feeling that the Young Hegelians had already dealt with the religious question.[32] His contribution lay in his claims that economic and institutional structures determined intellectual superstructures, including ritual. In his 1859 "Preface" he spelled out his assumptions with the greatest clarity:

> A distinction should always be made between the material transformation of the economic conditions of production, which can be determined with the precision of natural science, and the legal, political, religious, aesthetic, or philosophic – in short, ideological forms in which men become conscious of this conflict and fight it out. Just as our opinion of an individual is not based on what he thinks of himself, so can we not judge of such a period of transformation by its own consciousness; on the contrary, this consciousness must be explained rather from the contradictions of material life.[33]

Ritual was thus uninteresting in itself, except as a mirror of deeper changes in society. The massive scholarship of classicists was, from a Marxist perspective, worse than a waste of time: it was a product of bourgeois false consciousness, drawing attention away from class conflict, the real motor of history. Marx claimed to have identified the scientific laws of history and to have shown how material factors determined human behavior.[34] But bourgeois social scientists were unwilling to leave Marxists in possession of a monopoly on scientific materialism. The sociological interpretations of ritual that emerged in the last years of the century were often implicit rebuttals to Marx, providing ways for liberal thinkers to hold theories that were just as scientific and materialist. Emile Durkheim, whose *Les formes élémentaires de la vie religieuse* appeared in 1912, was by far the most important figure in this movement.[35] Durkheim, the son of a rabbi, for a while also attended rabbinical school and was later a student of Fustel. He argued that rituals created social solidarity and that this was more important than people's beliefs; in fact, religion was really a way of worshiping the social order itself. Durkheim was strongly opposed to communism and developed a radically different theory of the future of society, which he liked to call socialism.[36] He was even more successful than Müller had been; contemporaries caustically remarked that the Third Republic's educational policy was a form of "State Durkheimianism."[37]

Between about 1910 and 1940, a series of grand systematizations of Durkheim's ideas drove both particularist and ritualist theories from the field in the social sciences. In the United States, Talcott Parsons created an anti-Marxist blend of

Max Weber, Durkheim, and Vilfredo Pareto, arguing that institutions and rituals interlock to maintain the equilibrium of societies, adjusting themselves to restore the balance if exogenous forces threaten the system.[38] Alfred Radcliffe-Brown established theoretical functionalism in British anthropology. He was sympathetic to Marxism, but treated rituals as Parsons did: personal beliefs were mere cultural details. What mattered was social structure, how ritual reinforced stability. It would be hard to improve on Radcliffe-Brown's lucid summary of his position:

> Stated in the simplest possible terms the theory is that an orderly life amongst human beings depends upon the presence in the minds of the members of a society of certain sentiments, which control the relation of the individual in his behaviour to others. Rites can be seen to be the regulated symbolic expressions of certain sentiments. Rites can therefore be shown to have a specific social function when, and to the extent that, they have for their effect to regulate, maintain and transmit from one generation to another sentiments on which the constitution of society depends.[39]

To the extent that rituals regulated sentiments, they were worth study; when they could not be shown to act as a form of social control, they were not. To the functionalist, ritual was a good thing, providing the glue for a social contract that rendered Rousseau's unnecessary; to Marxists it was the same but bad, providing ideologies that blinded the people to the real conditions of their existence.[40] Ernest Gellner's more jaundiced view of functionalism exposes some of its limitations:

> The idea was that a tribal society has a certain structure or organisation, each part of which imposed such pressures and sanctions on the individuals within it as to ensure that they behaved in a way that sustained that structure, and so on forever, or at any rate for quite a long time. Structure was important, a matter of serious concern for men (inside the society or among investigators). Culture [including ritual and religion], on the other hand, was relatively ephemeral, accidental, epiphenomenal, and altogether suitable for women (inside the society or among investigators). Structure was, for instance, whom one could marry; culture was what the bride wore.[41]

Cultural details – including personal beliefs – were largely banished from legitimate discourse within the social sciences after the 1920s, but this had very little impact in classics. Instead, arguments went on exclusively within a psychological framework and came down largely to confrontations between emotionalist/comparativist and intellectualist/positivist views. Around 1900 a group of young scholars, later known as the Cambridge school, began to challenge the ideas about Greek religion held by scholars of Müller's generation. Their leader, Jane Harrison, explained that "we Hellenists were, in truth, at that time a 'people who sat in darkness,' but we were soon to see a great light, two great lights – archaeology, anthropology. Classics were turning in their long sleep. Old men began to see visions, young men to dream dreams."[42] Some of the school's leading figures proclaimed Durkheim as an influence; Francis Cornford borrowed his terminology, appealing to the collective consciousness of ancient Athens, and Gilbert Murray suggested that "the real religion of the fifth century was . . . a devotion to the City.''[43] However, as Evans-Pritchard notes, their Durkheimianism was only skin deep. Their main inspirations were Smith, Frazer, and Fustel. Harrison explained archaic and classical Greek rituals in terms of beliefs in fertility spirits and argued from them that there had been an evolution from matri- to patrilineal descent in Greece.[44]

The most important opponent of the Cambridge school's emotionalism was Lewis Farnell, an Oxford classicist whose alternative to the corn-spirit approach followed the path marked out a generation earlier by the Oxford school in British history. Farnell was a prolific scholar who dwelled in enormous detail on the particulars of Greek rituals and myths, in search of the Hellenic sense of religious purity.[45] By 1920 the Cambridge school's approach would have looked distinctly old-fashioned to functionalist anthropologists, and there was a clear opportunity for younger classicists to adapt Durkheim (or even Marx) and produce a sociological interpretation of ritual that would challenge both Farnell and Harrison. However, that did not happen. Instead, the psychological dispute between the emotionalists and the intellectualists was resolved so decisively in the latter's favor that *all* social scientific borrowings in classics fell into disrepute. Paul Shorey's comments in the 1920s on Murray's *Four Stages of Greek Religion* tar all comparativists with the same brush, damning "the anthropological Hellenism of Sir James Frazer, the irrational, semi-sentimental, Polynesian, free-verse, sex-freedom Hellenism of all the gushing geysers of 'rapturous rubbish' about the Greek spirit.''[46] As Moses Finley put it, "The Cambridge School . . . had become a pejorative by-word, shorthand for 'the dreadful consequences of the straying by Hellenists into the slime of anthropological Hellenism, not only of the Frazer variety but equally of all other schools of anthropology.' ''[47] Consequently, Parsons, Radcliffe-Brown, and the triumph of the sociological interpretation of ritual had minimal results. Those who had taken Durkheim to heart before the war were marginalized; even in France, Durkheimianism was not acceptable in classics, and its chief proponent, Louis Gernet, spent most of his career in virtual academic exile in Algeria.[48]

The scale of the Cambridge school's collapse has never been adequately explained. Both internal and external factors seem to have been involved. Harrison's lack of empirical rigor left her open to constant factual correction, which was undoubtedly important. So too were the personalities of the protagonists. After 1918 Harrison despaired of the West, left England for a long period, and became obsessed with Russian mysticism. Murray involved himself in the League of Nations and, though he continued to publish, seemed to have lost his prewar commitment. Farnell, in contrast, rose to become vice-chancellor of Oxford, and from that eminence, with his main opponents routed, he continued to pour out detailed accounts of what Greek rituals told us about Greek beliefs.[49] The Cambridge school's attachment to evolutionism and a "bits-and-pieces" comparativism no doubt isolated it from the more dynamic researchers in the social sciences, who were moving toward functionalism, while the similarity between Farnell's epistemology and that of the Oxford school of British history must have reinforced his credibility. For the next generation, the only legitimate way to study Greek ritual was in psychological and intellectualist terms.

PSYCHOLOGICAL RITUALS, 1920–90

Farnell's success rendered the relationships between ritual and most other institutions unproblematic: there were none. The assumption that ancient rituals tell us about ancient beliefs – in John Gould's words, about "religion as a system of explanation and response and as constituting a complex statement about what the world of experience is like"[50] – soon became a matter of common sense, and thus beyond serious challenge. Scholars of ritual drew a line between the realm of belief and a separate, reified society, which was seen as somehow disconnected from ritual and religion. Religion became an autonomous sphere, for both the analyst and the ancient Greeks who were imagined within this framework. One of the best examples is Louis Moulinier's massively detailed account of archaic and classical Greek concepts of pollution. On its own terms, this book is difficult to fault; but as Jean-Pierre Vernant pointed out, from the perspective of a social historian it is a failure. Moulinier did not try to find a social logic behind Greek concepts of pollution, which remained discrete "beliefs" without a unifying theme.[51] We are all familiar with the most common result of psychological assumptions, which lead historians to write books on Greek history that treat politics, warfare, economics, and so on as major categories of analysis, but relegate religion and ritual to a chapter of their own, away from "real" events.

This is obviously an arbitrary division. W. Robert Connor's study of the formula *hiera kai hosia* shows this, demonstrating how Athenians would not even have understood our distinction between "sacred" and "secular."[52] The psychological perspective forces historians to start from the assumption that ritual and politics *must* be separate and that rituals *only* tell us about belief. The many cases where religious belief and secular action are blurred then cause a problem. This is usually resolved by what we might call the propagandistic fallacy – identifying a deliberate and culpable intrusion of politics into the sacred. Episodes as diverse as Epimenides' purification of Athens, Peisistratos' Athena ruse, the vogues for Heracles and Theseus in Attic vase painting, and the use of the bones of heroes by various statesmen are regularly described in these terms.[53]

Obviously there were people who manipulated ritual to further their own interests. This is precisely how Herodotus saw the Alkmeonids' manipulation of the Delphic oracle to persuade Kleomenes to expel Hippias from Athens and Isagoras' cynical reuse of a century-old curse to have Sparta expel the Alkmeonids themselves, both around 510 B.C.E.[54] But that does not make it the only way to understand ancient religion, and as a general model of ritual the rigid separation of politics and religion is limiting and neglects much of our evidence. This is true of some of the best-known incidents in ancient history. Even the trial of Socrates must be rewritten if we break down the barriers between ritual and politics. Some historians believe that Socrates was in trouble because of his idiosyncratic beliefs; others, that he was on trial for his involvement with the Thirty; others still blame the baseness of the Athenian demos. But none of them have been able to explain how the two halves of Anytos and Meletos' accusation – that Socrates refused to worship the gods recognized by the city and that he was corrupting the youth – fit together. In another recent paper Connor shows that Socrates' religious ideas should be seen as part of a wider, Lakonizing critique of Athenian religion, ritual, society, and politics in which young aristocrats were particularly prominent. Once we abandon the psychological separation of religion from the rest of society, the difficulties disappear.[55]

The classic case of the inability of psychological approaches to account for the facts is the Greek cult of Roman emperors. There are many problems involved in believing that when the worthies of cities in the Eastern Empire erected statues of *theos Sebastos* they thought that Augustus was literally a god. Glen Bowersock suggested that the phenomenon says "little about the religious life of the Hellenic peoples but much about their ways of diplomacy," whereas Arthur Darby Nock was typical of another large group of scholars in trying to rescue the cult as "religion" by arguing that "there were no doubt moments of intense emotion."[56] Simon Price, the son of an Anglican minister, has perceptively pointed out that all these approaches are "covertly Christianizing."[57] The psychologists assume that rituals tell us about personal belief; when they clearly do not, then something is wrong with the ancient ritual, not with the modern analysis. By narrowing the focus to belief as the only phenomenon to be explained, historians of Greek religion have produced some monuments of scholarship, but at the cost of denying us the possibility of using our major sources of evidence from archaic Greece, the texts and artifacts produced in or for ritual, to examine any other aspects of society.

THE RETURN OF SOCIOLOGICAL RITUALS, 1950–90

A few English-speaking classicists flirted with anthropology in the years between 1920 and 1950,[58] but the return of sociological theory was linked to the appearance of Moses Finley's first two books. Finley had enjoyed an exposure to social theory that was unique among ancient historians. After obtaining an M.A. in public law and working as an assistant to Westermann in Roman legal studies, Finley was employed from 1937 to 1939 at Horkheimer's Institut für Sozialforschung in New York. From 1948 to 1954 he was closely linked with Karl Polanyi's graduate student group at Columbia University. His Ph.D., which was published in 1952 as *Studies in Land and Credit in Ancient Athens,* was heavily influenced by the Institut's debates with Marxism. Many of his analytical categories came from Max Weber, who had rejected the division of Greek life into separate "economic" or "political" spheres. Finley sought to show that Athenian lending and borrowing were as much political and social as financial operations.[59] In 1954 he published his seminal *The World of Odysseus,* treating Homer as a source for social history and interpreting the ritualized gift exchanges that play such a prominent part in heroic etiquette in terms of Marcel Mauss's discussion of similar phenomena among the Maori. His few footnotes to modern works include references to Bronislaw Malinowski and Radcliffe-Brown.[60]

Finley himself had little interest in Greek religion, preferring to concentrate on what Humphreys has called the "logic of institutions."[61] Even in this area, his work on Homer was more admired than imitated until the 1980s.[62] When sociological analyses of Greek rituals did begin to appear in the 1960s, they focused mainly on the classical period, where the sources are fuller. They also owed as much to

Parisian structuralism and neo-Marxism as to Finley's Weberian methods. Gernet's return to Paris in 1947 was vitally important in reintroducing Durkheimian approaches to the mainstream of French classics. Humphreys suggests that his sociological interests (as well as his bizarre dress sense) contributed to his image "as a sort of Rip van Winkle."[63] Two main strands can be seen in Gernet's work. The first went back to Frazer: Gernet wanted to identify stratified traces of earlier historical stages within accounts of classical religion. The second was his commitment to Durkheimian sociology. His treatment of Fustel typifies his methods: he accepted Fustel's belief that it was possible to reconstruct the prehistory of Greek ritual but followed Durkheim in asserting that Fustel's primeval ancestor worship must have been preceded by an earlier stage of collective worship of the dead.[64] He had very few students, but one of these few was Jean-Pierre Vernant, who since the 1950s has combined Durkheim's ideas with those of Marx and Lévi-Strauss in a series of pioneering studies of archaic myth. Vernant was also a student of the psychologist Ignacy Meyerson, and he was able to appeal to a wide range of interests. At one point he linked Hesiod with Georges Dumézil, at another he explained the myth–logic connecting rituals of Hermes and Hestia, and on other occasions still he used marriage and purification rituals to expose the social structure of the polis and offered neo-Marxist interpretations of the ancient Greek class struggle.[65] Vernant became the leader of a dynamic school of thought in Paris, and some of his followers, particularly Marcel Detienne, Nicole Loraux, and Pierre Vidal-Naquet, leaned further toward sociological interpretations.[66] Developments in postwar French Marxism, particularly the drift away from class conflict as the central dynamic, made these theoretical accommodations easier than they would have been in Gernet's time.[67] Structuralists, functionalists, and neo-Marxists often treat rituals in broadly similar ways, at least when viewed against the background of psychological interpretations. By the mid-1970s the new French work was winning audiences in Britain and the United States, and syntheses with functionalist anthropology were appearing, although the classical period continued to receive greater attention than the archaic.[68] However, it is important not to exaggerate the scale of the sociological turn. James Redfield suggests:

> In the generation before my own . . . M. I. Finley, Arnaldo Momigliano, J. P. Vernant, Michael Jameson . . . reached the highest levels of the profession; they were accepted as classicists and admired as theorists. Yet at the same time they were not (at least in the English-speaking world) models to the profession. If Finley wanted to read Malinowski and Karl Polanyi, if Vernant wanted to read Mauss and Lévi-Strauss, that was, so to speak, *their problem;* theorists of this kind did not become an integral part of education in the classics.[69]

The most significant movement toward sociological interpretations of archaic rituals in the 1970s came from archaeologists. There were two main reasons for this. The first was the nature of their data: it had long been recognized, as in Hawkes's infamous "ladder of archaeological inference," that religious beliefs could be examined through artifacts only by making wild and unwarranted leaps of faith about the "meaning" of specific objects.[70] Archaeologists had to choose between accepting a subsidiary role as the providers of material to illustrate text-based accounts of ancient religion or abandoning psychological methods altogether. Most were content with the former, but not all.

The second reason was the spread into Aegean prehistory of ideas drawn from the New Archaeology of the 1960s. Rejecting psychological methods with a vehemence rarely found in classics, a growing number of North American and Northwest European archaeologists stressed, as the subject of analysis, society viewed as an interacting system and put special emphasis on ecological forces.[71] Their methods were generally ahistorical and favored extreme materialist reductionism,[72] but when deployed skillfully they produced radical reinterpretations of the Greek Bronze Age.[73] In the early 1960s Chester Starr had constructed a sociological interpretation of Dark Age and archaic Greece drawing mainly on the archaeological evidence, but in the 1970s this was transformed in detail and sophistication by Anthony Snodgrass, who, often working with the techniques of the prehistorians, explained eighth-century changes in sanctuaries, burials, hero cult, and art as reflections of the rise of the polis.[74] As happened with Vernant, some of Snodgrass's students in the 1980s departed even more sharply from psychological methods, borrowing from comparative anthropology, Marxism, functionalism, and quantitative methods.[75]

All these approaches abandon the basic assumptions of psychological treatments of ritual to look at how rituals maintain social power. To varying degrees the sociologists gloss over the meaningful content of symbolism so that they can explain its general context. But in some ways they, as much as the psychologists, remain trapped in the debates of the late nineteenth century. Both approaches are reductionist, and both assume a gap between the rituals under study and some distinct "social reality" outside them. For the psychological historian, "society" is something external and irrelevant to belief; for the sociologist, rituals reflect the structure of a reified social system.[76]

CULTURAL RITUALS, 1985–

Charles Tilly identifies a group of "pernicious postulates" that nineteenth-century scholarship beqeathed to us and that underlie both psychological and sociological methods.[77] The first serious break with these came in the 1960s. For more than a generation, functionalist anthropology had provided the paradigm for research into the human condition. According to Vincent Pecora, its "first-hand experience with much that seems to lie outside the 'West' automatically endows [its] work with a privileged vantage on activities – such as 'theory' or 'interpretation' – whose obvious culture-boundedness haunts every modern critic . . . anthropology is the quintessential post-Hegelian enterprise: it seems to promise, through the ability to understand the other, a clearer definition of self."[78] But in the mid-sixties, anthropology lost its dominant position to literary theory, and even within its own ranks the unifying force of the old notions of social structure and culture has disappeared.[79] A broad range of new approaches to ritual emerged, but by far the most original was a group of perspectives drawing heavily on poststructuralist literary theory. Categorizing the various dimensions of this broad movement has proved to be extremely difficult, and by no means all its strands are equally well represented within classical studies. In this section I concentrate on just one part of the tradition, which I refer to as the "cultural" approach to archaic Greek ritual.

Two figures must be singled out if we are to understand the implications of this shift for classicists. The first is the French critic Michel Foucault, who attacked the totalizing aims that had been bequeathed to social history by the nineteenth-century assumption that all institutions and ideas must be interlocked and reducible to a single underlying pattern. "A total description," he said, "draws all phenomena around a single center – a principle, a meaning, a world-view, an overall shape," such as the reductionist concept of social structure that gives meaning to sociological approaches to ritual. In its place, Foucault proposed a "general history," which, "on the contrary, would deploy the space of dispersion."[80] Foucault adamantly refused to "explain" culture by reducing it to a deeper structure. This basic idea of the decentering of the subject of analysis – fragmenting it and denying the possibility of a single dominant interpretation – runs through most poststructuralist work. Jean-François Lyotard, the author of a treatise that is often considered the manifesto of postmodernism, argues that "the society of the future falls less within the province of a Newtonian anthropology (such as structuralism or systems theory) than a pragmatics of language particles. There are many different language games – a heterogeneity of elements. They only give rise to institutions in patches – local determinism." The breakdown of the subject of analysis is accompanied by a retreat from grand unifying themes or, as Lyotard puts it, an "incredulity toward meta-narratives."[81]

Clifford Geertz's anthropological writings have had almost as much influence on attempts to deconstruct the unified social subject of 1950s social science. Geertz argues that he is attacking a "gift of the nineteenth century, that 'symbolic' opposes to 'real' as fanciful to sober, figurative to literal, obscure to plain, aesthetic to practical, mystical to mundane, and decorative to substantial." Geertz, like Foucault, rejects the principles of both psychological and sociological analysis, and overcomes the separation of ritual and reified society by collapsing the two, producing, as he says, "a poetics of power, not a mechanics."[82] Geertz recognizes a danger that "cultural analysis . . . will lose touch with the hard surfaces of life – with the political, economic, stratificatory realities within which men are everywhere contained."[83] Some critics feel that this is precisely what has happened. Roger Keesing claims that "where feminists and Marxists find oppression, symbolists find meaning"; Ronald Walters, that "the tendency [of Geertz's position] is to reinforce the impulse to burrow in and not to try to connect the dots."[84]

Some see in cultural assumptions a left-wing plot; others, the ideology of the latest phase of capitalism.[85] One result can be history writing, like Lyotard's vision, fragmenting the past into isolated local knowledges, emphasizing the private worlds of those excluded from the centralizing realm of public power – of women, children, the elderly, the mad, and other "marginal" groups. W. Robert Connor and Brook Manville both note that the decline of interest in Greek citizenship may be part of this tendency.[86]

Poststructuralist analysis has had important effects on Greek historiography – for example, stimulating more sophisticated approaches to representation and a shift in the focus of ritual studies from the autonomous individual to the *oikos*.[87] But there have also been more radical attempts to collapse the analyst, the author of a source, the actors performing an ancient ritual, the spectators, and the readers of the modern account into one another and into the act of representation itself. This is the strongest form of cultural analysis. Most historians have kept their distance from such methods, pinning a perhaps exaggerated faith to the primacy of discrete "evidence" that always remains distinct from the analyst and the act of analysis;[88] but anthropologists, perhaps because of their generally greater consciousness of the extent to which they themselves create "evidence" in the process of conducting ethnography, have been more eager to problematize their stance as creators of supposedly authoritative texts. The analyses they produce often read more like literary criticism than the work of earlier generations of anthropologists, with the complexity and richness of a reading counting for more in validating an argument than the way it illuminates some assumed social "reality," whether an institutional structure or a set of individually held religious beliefs. White argues that post-structuralist historiography does not substitute textuality for reality, but merely changes the nature of textual emplotment. The new cultural poetics focuses attention on different aspects of the past from those singled out by the "codelike" approach of the materialists – "whence," White concludes, "their interest in what appears to be the episodic, anecdotal, contingent, exotic, abjected, or simply unnecessary parts of the historical record."[89] But traditional historians, used to totalizing approaches, find the new ideas disturbing – Novick suggests that for them "the locution [postmodernism] is symbolic of a circumstance of chaos, confusion, and crisis, in which everyone has a strong suspicion that conventional norms are no longer viable, but no one has a clear sense of what is in the making."[90] Even Geertz, frequently hailed by culturalists as a venerable ancestor, seems surprised by the handwringing intensity of a genre that accepts no distinction between the author and any external subject: "The question is, of course, how anyone who believes all this can write anything at all, much less go so far as to publish it."[91]

The best way to illustrate the culturalist approach to ritual is to take an example from archaic Greece. Applications within classics are still rare, but Robin Osborne has provided two extremely important studies of vase painting and sculpture from archaic Athenian funerals.[92] His work circumvents the reductionism of the psychological and sociological methods, and promises to be the starting point for a whole new way of looking at archaic art. In his account of the Polyphemos vase, used as a coffin for a child at Eleusis a little before 650, he argues that the Gorgons on its belly draw the viewer into a debate, as "the whole question of who is subject and what is object, of seeing and being seen, is reopened," and that "the whole vase is a construal of death, a discussion of the nature of death as sensory deprivation. Death comes when the visual world closes in on you, when you yourself are to be seen in a pot." He contrasts this with the Dipylon vase, an Athenian grave marker pot of about 760 B.C.E.,[93] of which he says, "This is life and death as seen from the outside by others, not explored as individual expressions demanding to be comprehended."[94] This is at once a theory of beliefs about death and a theory of changing ideas of community, transcending the limitations of both psychological and sociological analysis. Osborne develops a fascinating account of social changes in the seventh century, arguing that his approach "may be the lifeline enabling history to be written out of archaeology" for seventh-century Attika.[95] This claim is valid, but only, I think, if we are prepared to forget most of the questions that interest nonculturalists. Rightly or wrongly, we have constructed archaic Athenian history as a discourse of social conflict, tracing an evolution from Kylon to Kleisthenes. Perhaps we have let the literary sources dictate our questions; but Osborne's approach rules these questions out of bounds[96] and renders rituals far less interesting for most archaic historians than the sociological method, for all its shortcomings.[97] Deciding among theoretical positions on the basis of their "interest" will hardly be satisfactory to most historians, but if nothing else, it should be safe to assume that we will want to adopt a perspective that gets less from our evidence only if there are compelling reasons to do so.

Osborne's papers exemplify the profound challenge that culturalism can pose to traditional historiography and for this reason deserve detailed comment. Their underlying premise, the dissolution of boundaries between social structure, actors, representation, and the modern historian, presents the greatest difficulty. It is never clear whose interpretations of ritual Osborne is discussing. If the Dipylon vase is "death seen from the outside," are we to conceive of this as the painter's view? Or the patron's? Or a wider social group's, or even a metaphysical "collective unconscious"? Or purely Osborne's own? The strategy of the social historian is normally to assume that both the producers and the consumers of images are located within cultural systems that inform their interpretations of what they are doing, simultaneously constraining and enabling the creation of meaning. Some interpretations can therefore be shown to be definitely wrong if they are anachronistic or ignore the social context.[98]

The Dipylon vase is crucial to the contrast between the eighth and seventh centuries that Osborne makes in his 1988 paper. It was found in 1871 in a small cemetery under modern Peiraios Street in Athens.[99] This cemetery produced a spectacular haul of giant pots with scenes of funerals and battles.[100] In spite of a century of new excavations, about three-quarters of the fifty known Late Geometric Athenian funerary paintings and twenty-two battle scenes come from this cemetery. Nearly all of them belong to the style called Late Geometric Ia, conventionally dated to a single decade, from about 760 to 750 (see note 93). They were the products of an artist conventionally known as the Dipylon Master and a very small group of painters working in his style.[101] Part of this concentration may simply be the result of different processes of postdepositional disturbance; many of the Dipylon graves were preserved under a fifth-century tumulus, while the nearby cemetery on Kriezi Street, which has produced a handful of marker vases with figured scenes, is known only through rescue digs, that of 1968 conducted entirely at nighttime.[102] However, this cannot account for the whole pattern. Even before the 1871 dig, the Dipylon cemetery had produced remarkable scenes, and the meticulous Kerameikos excavation recovered countless fragments of destroyed grave markers, but nothing that could compare to the Dipylon cemetery. The only other major form of Late Geometric figured art, the thin gold diadem with impressed decoration, makes its appearance at roughly the same time as the Dipylon Master's paintings. Ten of the thirty-five examples found in Athens are from the Dipylon graveyard, with a further fourteen cases from the nearby Kerameikos and Kriezi Street cemeteries.[103] For reasons that remain to be discovered, the users of a small group of cemeteries on the northwest edge of Athens around 750 B.C.E. had an interest in figured art that went far beyond what we find anywhere else in Greece.

The Dipylon vase's spatial context is, then, important for its interpretation. The users of this small cemetery, or the painters they commissioned, were creating images that set their burials apart from those of other Athenians. The importance of this becomes clearer when we look at the paintings in their ritual context. Almost 90 percent of the known Athenian adult burials from the previous three centuries were cremations.[104] Just at the point that the Dipylon paintings began, the Athenians switched over to inhumation. The new rite was part of a package of changes in burial customs, including the appearance of oversized grave cuttings, more varied pottery and metal grave goods, in some cases much richer grave goods, and an explosion in artistic motifs.[105] The Dipylon cemetery was at the forefront of changes in taste around 760 B.C.E., and many of the characteristic features of Athenian Late Geometric burial make their first appearance here. The funerary scenes on pots like the Dipylon vase drew attention to the act of burial and thereby to the novelty of what the users of this cemetery were doing,[106] leading the way in rituals that cut ties to the Athenian past and at the same time reached out to a wider Greek community, where inhumation had been the norm throughout the Dark Age (1100–750 B.C.E.). But during the Late Geometric Ib pottery phase (ca. 750–735) the Dipylon cemetery was already losing its symbolic leadership, as most Athenians adopted the rites associated with inhumation, and control over the definition of ritual seems to have passed to the users of the nearby Kerameikos cemetery.[107]

The rituals that produced the Dipylon vase must be understood in a wide social context. The use of funerary scenes divided the Athenians, marking off a small group who were particularly eager to embrace a new symbolic order. This new order also set its users off from the Athenian past of cremation and extreme care over the selection of a small number of objects to be placed in the grave.[108] Snodgrass has added another dimension to the associations of these scenes, arguing that in the eighth century they evoked a generalized aura of the age of heroes, linking the users of the Dipylon cemetery to a glorious past, which, by implication, other Athenians did not have.[109] This interpretation depends partly on the messages triggered by a single motif, the so-called Dipylon shield. Sixteen paintings from the Dipylon cemetery show battles between men carrying this type of shield and men with round shields. In thirteen cases the men carrying Dipylon shields are defeated, and in the other three they look like they are on the verge of losing the fight. No painting shows Dipylon shields in use on both sides or their users winning. The idea that these scenes evoked heroic stories is not universally accepted,[110] and Snodgrass has sought a compromise position, arguing that "the painters . . . were trying to characterize the users of these shields in some way, at least when it came to combat, and that their meaning was intelligible at least in the small circle of their known customers. . . . What I am suggesting is not that the content of these scenes need therefore be heroic; but that they are likely to have a narrative content of some kind."[111] Even if the content of both the battle and the funeral scenes was intended by painter, patron, and viewers as strictly contemporary, the users of the

Dipylon cemetery were still, for a decade or so, associating themselves in their monumental art with a story peculiarly their own. They set themselves apart from (and most likely above) other Athenians, rejecting local burial traditions in favor of Panhellenic rites and advertising the fact through their ostentatious use of funerary scenes. Their rituals may have evoked complex and contradictory responses. If, as Snodgrass first suggested, their paintings looked back to a heroic age, that message may have been subverted by the use of inhumation rites, which severed their links with the Athenian past;[112] alternatively, developing another idea of Snodgrass's, inhumation itself may have had associations going back beyond the heroes of Troy and Thebes, who cremated their dead, to still earlier races.[113] Collapsing all perspectives – painter, burier, ancient viewer, modern art historian – into a single interpretation, as Osborne does, destroys much of the historical significance of this evidence. Before discussing ideas of community, we have to consider whose ideas they were, in precisely what rituals they were created, and how these rituals were understood by those who did not share these symbols. The Dipylon iconography may well represent death as communal, but perhaps in the sense that those who buried their dead here felt that the loss of one of their number was an event implicating the whole of Athens, just as the death of a hero or his kinsfolk would affect all whom he protected.

The comparison with the Polyphemos vase throws us into a very different but equally complex and divided context. The Dipylon vase was part of a veritable forest of funeral and battle scenes that sprang up in the 750s in one small cemetery; the Polyphemos vase, in contrast, acted as a coffin for a child at Eleusis roughly a century later. More than one hundred such child pot burials are known from seventh-century Attika, but no more than half a dozen of them were in pots decorated with narrative mythical scenes. The other examples all date about a generation later, around the time of the Nessos Painter.[114] The handful of burials were scattered all over Attika: three in Eleusis, one or two in Phaleron, and one from Mt. Imittos.[115] Significantly, no example comes from Athens, although the Nessos Painter's name vase, which is iconographically somewhat similar to the Polyphemos vase, showing Gorgons and a scene of Herakles killing Nessos, was probably an offering over an adult grave on Peiraios Street.

The social functions of figured scenes on vases had changed dramatically between 750 and 650 B.C.E. Funeral scenes had a revival in the final decades of the eighth century, but the distribution of finds is markedly different from the mid-eighth-century situation, with a much higher proportion coming from the countryside. Some rural workshops also played a major role in production, and Kenneth Sheedy has argued that the Dipylon tradition had ''fossilized'' and that at least one painter was looking to Egypt for a new twist on the old theme.[116] This regionalism was paralleled in other aspects of burial customs, which were more diverse in the last two decades of the eighth century than at any other time in Attic history. This variability has rarely been discussed,[117] but it forms a striking contrast with the uniformity we find after 700. There were virtually no exceptions to the new rite of primary cremation with tumulus for adults and inhumation in a Subgeometric or plain pot for children. The occasional use of a pot with a narrative scene, however, does distinguish the countryside from Athens. James Whitley argues that seventh-century Athenians were very careful in deciding in which situations it was appropriate to use Protoattic pottery.[118] Orientalizing art may have been just as politically engaged as the narrative scenes of the eighth century, and subtle variations in its use may tell us a great deal about the relationships between Athens and the countryside.

If we are to compare the Dipylon vase and the Polyphemos vase and to understand the rituals that caused them to enter the archaeological record, we have to ask what made this small group of people who buried their dead around what is now Peiraios Street and these few children from small towns in the Attic countryside so special. That means that we have to break down "meaning" in more traditional ways. Unlike the Dipylon vase, the Polyphemos vase was buried underground, severely restricting the range of people it could engage in discussions about death. Are we to think that the painter saw it as a construal of death? Probably not; we do not know what the pot was originally made for, but it probably was not commissioned for the burial, since a hole had to be cut in it to insert the body. Perhaps the child's parents chose it from the vases they had around the house because it seemed rather suitable; or perhaps the punning link between the Gorgons and death is entirely fortuitous. It certainly has no archaic Greek parallels. This, of course, does not disprove Osborne's arguments, but there is no way for nonculturalists to use them without first having to ask a series of unanswerable questions. Nor does the cultural approach to ritual provide compelling advantages that make it worth abandoning the older questions. Osborne offers an intriguing poetics of archaic ritual and overcomes the separation between sociology and psychology that plagued earlier approaches; but in so doing he succumbs to the "ever-present" danger that Geertz noted and loses contact with the hard surfaces of life. The approach ends up being every bit as reductionist as earlier all-embracing theories. The hard surfaces of seventh-century Attic society were excessively hard, and social conflict, whether along class or regional lines (or along gender lines, on which our literary sources are silent), should be at the heart of any history of the period. An approach in which ritual, our main source of evidence, cannot help us understand the profound structural transformations of these years must be judged unsuccessful.

EARLY ARCHAIC ATHENS

Few of us consciously choose to be a culturalist, an intellectualist, or anything else; one way of looking at rituals – or, usually, one blend of these three ingredients – simply seems the best way to do things. To some extent our attitudes are based on our feelings about the correct distances between classics and other disciplines; to some extent, on the attitudes of those who taught us or argued with us in graduate school; and to some extent, on our social and political ideals. Each way of looking at ritual explains part of the evidence well, but at the cost of downplaying other parts.

I am not going to conclude by unleashing another grand theory of religion, or by simply following Lyotard's arguments and leaving scholars to play their own language games, ruling nothing out of bounds and forgetting no possibilities. The desire not to draw lines and not to close off any avenue simply paralyzes analysis.

As Stanley Fish concludes, "You cannot not forget; you cannot not exclude; you cannot refuse boundaries and distinctions."[119]

Instead, I return to my starting point, the relationship between the way we prefigure the study of ritual and the evidence we have from archaic Greece. I believe the only way to produce accounts of archaic rituals that are at least in principle satisfactory within all three perspectives is to try more seriously to combine archaeological and textual sources so that a richer picture can be built up. Generally, archaic historians rely on the very few texts, drawing on artifacts in a bits-and-pieces method, picking out the outstanding or the supposedly typical case for illustrative material.[120] The sheer quantity of the archaeological record, for all its obscurities and ambiguities, lets us expand our study of rituals by identifying temporal and spatial changes that the texts cannot reach. I am skeptical about the chances of a broader approach to ritual unless we emphasize a broader range of evidence. In understanding the limits of our theoretical assumptions our problem is historiographic; in transcending them, it is empirical.

I illustrate this argument with a summary interpretation of the rituals of early archaic Attika. In a way this is a bad choice for a case study, since the textual sources are so poor that there is wide agreement on the need to rely on artifacts, but looking at the better-documented late sixth century would raise too many issues for the scope of this essay. Seventh-century Attika also allows me to continue the discussion I began in the preceding section.

To understand the seventh century we must always begin in the eighth; and to understand Attika, it is best to begin outside it. In most areas of Greece, all rituals for which we have evidence changed radically in the eighth century. It seems that Corinthia was at the forefront of these changes. To judge from recent excavations at Isthmia, where a simple open-air cult involving fire had been going on since the eleventh century, Dark Age religion in Corinthia was much like that known from the rest of Greece.[121] Distinct temples, with *temenē*, large altars, and vast numbers of votives, including metal objects, appear all over Greece by 700,[122] but the Corinthians seem to have been among the leaders on the mainland, perhaps establishing the first temple to Hera at Perachora as early as 800. This also established the "religious bipolarity" that François de Polignac sees as a defining feature of the polis, with a major sanctuary near a frontier (in this case, the Megarian border) balancing a cult center in the main settlement. Corinth was also prominent in the development of monumental stone architecture for temples, and perhaps even in stoneworking techniques. By 700 at least one part of the settlement was laid out in a regular fashion, and there may have been one or more defensive walls. Around 800 there was a dramatic increase in the grave goods placed in some Corinthian graves. By 775 the first large extramural cemeteries were being laid out; by 750 the increase in grave goods had been reversed, ending up in the seventh century well below even the levels of the ninth century, and intramural burials had stopped. Corinthian wealth was probably not waning in the eighth century, but a new symbolic system of large, poor, homogeneous "citizen" cemeteries had been established.[123]

Ritual changes began slightly later in neighboring Argos. The number and diversity of graves and the richness of the goods placed in some of them increased suddenly around 750 and continued to grow until 700. A new type of adult grave appeared after 725, a simple cylindrical pithos with few or no grave goods. After 700 rich cist graves disappeared almost completely, as did intramural adult burials and grave goods. As at Corinth, large, simple, and poor "citizen" cemeteries outside the town were characteristic of the seventh-century polis. Changes in sanctuaries also followed the Corinthian model, with the appearance of substantial stone temples both inside the town and outside it, near Mycenae, during the seventh century. The building of the Heraion is often interpreted as part of a policy of consolidating the Argive plain under the political control of Argos itself, and it has recently been argued that Argive ceramics indicate the same process of centralization in the late eighth century.[124]

At first Athens was heavily involved in this pattern. In the second quarter of the eighth century variability in burials started to increase. The Dark Age custom of cremation for adults, which had set Attika apart from its neighbors, began to be replaced by inhumation; after 750, grave goods escalated, the number of burials increased dramatically, and inhumation was almost the only rite in use. By 700 intramural cemeteries were going out of style, and rich grave goods had begun to decline at Athens itself, although they continued to be used until 700 at some rural sites. Cemeteries were beginning to be walled off, and simple temples appeared, with abundant cheap votive offerings and a few more expensive ones.[125]

Up to this point, the story at Athens is very much like that at Corinth and Argos. In *Burial and Ancient Society*[126] I argued that the ritual changes in all three poleis were part of a huge social transformation. In the simple rituals of the Dark Age I saw a social structure that divided people into two groups, which, following the usage of the early Greek poets, I called the *agathoi* (good people) and *kakoi* (bad people), with the latter being excluded from full membership of the community. I interpreted the group-oriented rituals that appeared in the eighth century as the manifestation of a new idea of society in which all free-born men were at least in a vague sense equal citizens. Obviously this notion underwent substantial changes over the next three centuries, and the "citizens" of eighth-century Corinth or Athens may have had little more power than those in the Ithakan Assembly in *Odyssey,* Book 2; but all the same, around 750 B.C.E. we see the emergence of a recognizably "classical Greek" kind of society, whereas before that date no such notion of the polis as a community of citizens had existed.

One of the weaknesses of this argument is its exclusively sociological approach. By changing from cremation to inhumation and adopting new kinds of sacrifice, the Athenians had certainly joined in a general set of symbolic acts that made them part of the rise of the "Greek" city-state; but they had also changed the nature of their most basic religious practices. One of the reasons I avoided discussion of the meaningful content of the new symbols of the eighth century was that the task of attributing such meanings to archaeological data usually involves arbitrary assumptions that cannot be justified. It is much more difficult than most historians seem to realize to assert that a find means that Greeks held specific religious beliefs. Even defining what "belief" should consist of as an abstract category is often impossible.[127] But some suggestions seem reasonable. When the Athenians decided around 750 that the dead should be left to rot rather than be burned and that the gods needed physical homes, walled *temenē,* and abundant but cheap votives, they were giving up practices their ancestors had followed for three hundred years, in favor of belonging to a wider Greek *koinē*. This implies at least some modifications of the concept of the divine. Herodotus thought that Homer and Hesiod "created for the Greeks their theogony" (2.53), and it seems quite likely that these years saw a new fusion of beliefs derived from the Dark Age and earlier times, the Near East, and original eighth-century ideas.[128] A set of Panhellenic rituals and beliefs was emerging and being codified, in much the same way that Gregory Nagy suggests that heroic poetry united Greeks in this period by being relevant to all poleis but specific to none.[129] To label this as either a social or a religious change, as if these were rigid and mutually exclusive categories, would be to miss the point. New relationships within the community – the disappearance of the gulf between the *kakoi* and *agathoi* – simultaneously meant new relationships between mortals and immortals, living and dead, the community and its heroes. It must also have involved a serious reassessment of the relationships between men and women, but here the evidence is more difficult to interpret.[130]

What makes seventh-century Athens remarkable is that this community abandoned *to hellenikon,* the new "Greekness" of the late eighth century, in what seems to have been an attempt to re-create the vanished world of the Dark Age. The Athenians did not go on to elaborate de Polignac's bipolar religious orientation or to develop monumental stone temples. Their seventh-century temples are hardly more impressive than contemporary houses, and even small villages in the Aegean islands boasted more imposing sanctuaries than Athens. Their votive offerings, both within Attika and at the Panhellenic sanctuaries, grew poorer at this point, just as those of other Greek states escalated. There is no evidence during most of the seventh century for Athenian involvement in Panhellenic games, hoplite warfare, colonization, or a host of other "Greek" activities.[131] Attic sanctuaries and funerals, and probably the city of Athens itself, would have looked distinctly old-fashioned to a Corinthian or Argive visitor around 650. The reversion to cremation was another change in rituals that looked back to the past. Nicholas Coldstream identifies a similar change in Attic vase painting: "It appears, then, that during the late eighth century the men of Attika were contracting out of their enterprises abroad, and transforming themselves into a quiet inward-looking people."[132]

In *Burial and Ancient Society* I interpreted this as an attempt to return to the stratified society of the Dark Age, but it is self-evidently just as much a religious revival. Athens shared the Olympian pantheon in the seventh century and was tied into the Panhellenic myth cycles through the Homeric *Hymn to Demeter;* but if, as is widely assumed (following Robertson Smith), taking part in rituals was a major component of ancient "belief," then the Athenians obviously did go in their own direction. Examining the theological implications of this change is not an alternative to the sociological perspective. It simply fills out the picture. Walter Burkert and Vernant have pointed out that Homeric cremation parallels in many ways the structure of animal sacrifice,[133] and returning to this rite for the disposal of the dead can hardly have been without religious meaning. The *psyche* normally left the body immediately upon death.[134] Cremation need not have had any major impact on concepts of Hades, but the rite still combined the piety of animal sacrifice with the evocation of the age of heroes, as well as recalling the Athenians' own history –

if indeed these categories were ever actually separated – by returning to practices abandoned a mere two generations earlier. Athenian rituals were backward- and inward-looking, creating a religious world in imitation of the simpler times of the Dark Age, when the gods did not need massive stone houses or bronze cauldrons, and the dead were engulfed in flames in a peculiarly Athenian style rather than left to rot as in other states.[135]

The Athenian experiment in turning the clock back did not, of course, succeed. By 640 we can see signs that the strict simplicity of Athenian ritual was breaking up. Much larger grave mounds were coming into use, and *kouroi* were being set up above a few graves by 600.[136] The first monumental stone altar on the Acropolis probably dates to the closing years of the seventh century, with the Old Temple of Athena just a little later.[137]

Once again the religious and the social have to be fused in our analyses. According to Aristotle (*Ath. Pol.* 5.1), in the late seventh century "the many were enslaved to the few, and the people (ὁ δῆμος) rose against the notables (τοῖς γνωρίμοις)." The division of Athens into a ruling elite and a mass of dependent peasants was more like the social organization of the Dark Age or of *ethnē* like Thessaly than like contemporary poleis such as Corinth and Argos. In the late seventh century there were at least two attempts to bring the Athenian political system back into line with "typical" Greek practices, which I believe have to be linked to the contemporary process whereby the simple rituals of seventh-century Athens once more came into line with the practices of its neighbors. It is hard to say much about the later of these, the law code of Drakon, perhaps passed in 621. It could be seen as an attempt to modernize Athens, but the sources are even more problematic than those for the reforms of Solon.[138] A few years earlier, possibly in 636 or 632, Kylon had tried to make himself tyrant of Athens. Although the sources for this event all date from at least two hundred years after the fact, they have a certain coherence. According to Thucydides, Kylon seized the Acropolis with the backing of troops provided by his father-in-law Theagenes, who was tyrant of Megara.[139] Thucydides links the coup with religious festivals at all stages. Kylon checked his plan with Delphi and was told to stage his rising during the great festival of Zeus. He assumed this to mean the Olympic games, but after his failure the oracle was interpreted to have been referring to the Diasia, which, Thucydides tells us, "takes place outside the city, and the whole people make a number of sacrifices not including blood sacrifices, but traditional offerings of the country."[140] The evidence is much poorer than that for links between politics and religion in 399, but the idea that by juxtaposing a tyrannical coup – a modernizing act in isolated seventh-century Athens – with a traditional festival Kylon would have succeeded raises the intriguing possibility that at least some Athenians, even if not Kylon himself, perceived the problems of the 630s to be as much religious as sociopolitical. Kylon's ritual entanglements continued with his supplication at the altar on the Acropolis and ultimate betrayal and murder at the altars of the Furies. Even that was not enough; the bones of the Alkmeonids who had slaughtered Kylon's men were subsequently exhumed, and as part of this act Epimenides the Cretan was brought in to purify the city.[141] The exhumation must have taken place some time after Kylon's coup, which puts Epimenides' visit very close to Solon's reforms in 594, and perhaps even means that the two should be linked.[142] Aristotle, Plutarch, and other late accounts of Solon emphasize his political and economic reforms. The fragments said to be from his law codes are also mainly constitutional rather than religious, but again we are at the mercy of ancient selectors writing in the aftermath of Solon's rise to prominence as a political symbol at the end of the fifth century, which may distort the picture.[143] None of these late accounts inspires confidence, but most modern writers have followed their example, treating Solon as a social, economic, and political reformer and looking at the constant references to religion in his poems as a matter of literary style, to be distinguished from their "real" content. This is perhaps a mistake; Solon seems to have seen the problems of Athens in the 590s as ones that involved the gods as much as mortals.

After Solon, Athens moved back into the Greek mainstream in ritual practices and in what we know of its constitutional history. By the time of Peisistratos' first coup in 561 a swing back to inhumation was under way, expensive dedications were becoming common on the Acropolis,[144] and the Panathenaic games had been established. A late source associates Peisistratos with the foundation of the games in 566. This is questionable, but he and his sons did carry out a major building program that transformed Athens and sanctuaries all around Attika.[145] It is often suggested that the tyrants played a decisive role in turning Athens into a "modern" polis,[146] and ritual was very much a part of this. By 500 B.C.E. the visitor to Athens would have found the city far more like other leading poleis than it had been in 650. It was certainly not "typical" in any sense, but its unusualness now lay in a new aggressive democratic ethos rather than in a backward-looking mentality.[147] The historical origins of this ethos are to be sought as much in the transformations of ritual in the eighth through the sixth centuries as in political, economic, or social forces as traditionally defined; and it is only by transcending the limitations of the psychological, sociological, and cultural perspectives on ritual that we can hope to do this.

CONCLUSION

I have argued that the study of archaic Greek ritual was, from the 1920s until the 1970s, virtually cut off from the influence of nonclassical disciplines. This stifled debate. In the 1970s, when a few scholars interested in Weber, French anthropology, or prehistoric archaeology tried out alternative ways of looking at the evidence, it was all too easy for the majority of historians to marginalize them as merely trendy and to assume that they would soon disappear as completely as the Cambridge school. That now seems unlikely to happen.

By developing greater historical awareness about our own practices, we can come to terms with their limits and can identify ways to capitalize on their strengths. Changes in theoretical positions often lead to changes in our sense of the evidence itself. We cannot understand the rituals of sixth- and fifth-century Athens without putting them into a long historical context, going back to the massive changes of the eighth century and the subsequent reaction around 700, nor without seeing Athens in its Panhellenic context. To do this we have to combine archaeological and textual evidence in new ways.

NOTES

1. Murdoch 1968: 165. Historians of early Greece will recognize that this quotation has been used before, by Starr 1977: 18.
2. Defining "ritual" is notoriously difficult (for attempts, see, e.g., Goody 1961; G. Lewis 1980: 6–38; La Fontaine 1985: 11–18; Kertzer 1988: 8–12). Observers and participants often dispute marginal cases of what is or is not ritual, but in any culture there is a central field where all intuitively know that they are in its presence. This is as true of scholars reading accounts of archaic Greece as of any other group. Since all the examples I discuss in this essay belong to this central field, and I think that few, if any, historians would wish to challenge them on definitional grounds, I will not attempt any exclusive formulation here.
3. There are, of course, some exceptions to this statement. Bremmer's volume of essays, *Interpretations of Greek Mythology* (1987), starts from the assumption that theoretical differences are important; and Helene Foley 1985: 30–64 provides a valuable account of approaches to the interpretation of sacrifice in Athenian tragedy. Robertson's recent reviews of books on Greek religion (1990b, 1991) also contain useful comments on methods and approaches.
4. I limit myself to English-language research because trying to be comprehensive, particularly by including discussions of the highly varied continental European traditions, would produce an unacceptably long and unnecessarily complex essay. I therefore venture into continental scholarship only on the (rather numerous) occasions when it has had a significant impact on the Anglo-American work.
5. I take the first two terms from Evans-Pritchard 1965: 4, and the third from White 1989: 294. These three modes of thought do not exhaust all possible ways of looking at rituals, but most work dealing specifically with archaic Greece can be subsumed within them. The major exception is the approach developed by Walter Burkert, who argues that the Swiss folklorist Karl Meuli 1975 [1946] developed "a concept of ritual 'custom' which is practically identical with the biological definition" (1979: 37) and goes on to offer a synthesis of sociobiology, folklore, and philology as an alternative to older methods of analysis. He combines sociological and psychological elements, but his interest in tracing ritual behavior back to paleolithic roots has much in common with nineteenth-century evolutionism. Overall, he has had little influence on the theoretical development of studies of ritual in the United States and Britain, although his massive erudition has rightly won him many admirers (Burkert 1966, 1979, 1983, 1985). See also H. Foley 1985: 46–56.
6. White 1973: 31, emphasis in original.
7. Novick 1991: 700, emphasis in original.
8. Heyck 1982: 73.
9. See particularly Gilbert 1965; Rothblatt 1968; Stone 1975; Bledstein 1976; Heyck 1982: 81–154; Engel 1983; Weisz 1983; Levine 1986; Novick 1988: 47–60; Ross 1991.
10. Chadwick 1970: 450–2.
11. "The First Half of the Nineteenth Century," *The Economist* 9 (1851), 57–8, cited from the text in Goldstein and Boyer 1988: 98–9.
12. See Heyck 1982; Bowler 1989.
13. Abrams 1972: 22.
14. Froude 1871: 462. The Oxford school was first defined in Gooch's classic study (1913).
15. Quoted in Heyck 1982: 144.
16. For Britain, see Heyck 1982: 133–43; for the United States, Novick 1988: 24–31.

17. Evans-Pritchard 1965: 4. He attributes the terms to Wilhelm Schmidt.
18. Vernant 1991: 271 suggests that the two lines of thought were of roughly equal importance in French classical scholarship around 1900; the situation in Britain and the United States needs further research.
19. Fustel de Coulanges 1864.
20. Humphreys 1980: 96. See also Momigliano 1977: 325–43; Momigliano and Humphreys 1980.
21. F. M. Turner 1981: 121, 258–9, on British classicists; British sociology also owed much to Fustel, and Spencer (e.g., 1882: 440) shared many of his ideas.
22. Smith's career has not been adequately studied. See Evans-Pritchard 1981: 69–81; M. Smith 1991.
23. W. R. Smith 1889.
24. McLennan 1876, 1885. See M. Smith 1991: 253–5.
25. Smith also paralleled Fustel in his cavalier use of evidence; see Evans-Pritchard 1965: 51–3, 1981: 71–80.
26. W. R. Smith 1889: 23–31, quotation from 16. Maine 1883: 116 developed some rather similar arguments.
27. Müller 1878, 1882; Evans-Pritchard 1965: 20–3; F. M. Turner 1981: 104–15.
28. Dorson 1974: 55 n. 22.
29. See Frazer 1890; Lang 1898; Crawley 1902; Marett 1909; also, discussions in Evans-Pritchard 1965: 31–8; F. M. Turner 1981: 77–186; Bremmer 1987; Ackerman 1975, 1987, 1991.
30. Arist. *Pol.* 1.1252b27–8, with Burkert 1985: 247. On Marx, see McLellan 1973.
31. See F. M. Turner 1981: 244–63.
32. Marx 1977a [1844].
33. Marx 1977b [1859].
34. See particularly Cohen 1978.
35. Durkheim 1912.
36. See Giddens 1977: 49–62; R. A. Jones 1991.
37. Giddens 1977: 19.
38. Parsons 1937; see Ross 1991.
39. Radcliffe-Brown 1952: 157; cf. Kuper 1983: 36–68.
40. Abercrombie, Hill, and Turner 1980: 7–58. Evans-Pritchard 1965: 77 also stresses the overlap between Marxist and Durkheimian approaches to religion.
41. Gellner 1985: 135–6.
42. Harrison 1965 [1921]: 342–3. However, F. M. Turner 1981: 116–17 shows that we should not exaggerate the break between Victorian approaches to Greek religion and the Cambridge school. The school's formation is usually dated to August 24, 1900, when Harrison sent an admiring letter to Murray (printed in Stewart 1959: 30).
43. G. Murray 1912: 99; Cornford 1912 (with Wood 1990); cf. Evans-Pritchard 1965: 73. Humphreys 1978: 96 gives examples of Cornford's and Harrison's uses of Durkheimian schemes and draws attention to the two rather hostile reviews in Durkheim's *Année sociologique* (David 1913a, 1913b).
44. Harrison 1903, 1912; see Ackerman 1972; F. M. Turner 1981: 115–28; Peacock 1988. A. B. Cook, admittedly a somehat marginal member of the group (Ackerman 1991a: 1 n. 2), actually collaborated with Frazer (Ackerman 1987: 197–200). I have not yet seen Robert Ackerman's new book *The Myth and Ritual School: J. G. Frazer and the Cambridge Ritualists* (1991b). Schlesier 1990 summarizes Harrison's main arguments about ritual.
45. E.g., Farnell 1896–1909, 1912. Harrison had other bitter enemies, as the hostile

responses to her work show; see Ackerman 1991: 4; Africa 1991: 29–32. Harrison's correspondence with Murray reveals an intense personal antipathy between her and Farnell (F. M. Turner 1981: 129–30). Unfortunately, she burned her own collection of letters in 1922. For samples of surviving correspondence, see Ackerman 1971; Stewart 1959.

46. Quoted in M. I. Finley 1975: 102–3. Shorey was intellectually and politically conservative, but was by no means excessively so by the standards of contemporary classicists. He even had a youthful fascination with Herbert Spencer's sociology, which he claimed to have lost after he read Plato as an undergraduate at Harvard in the 1870s (Kopff 1990: 447).

47. M. I. Finley 1975: 103. Fowler 1991 gives a more balanced evaluation of Murray's book.

48. Humphreys 1978: 76–106; Vernant 1981. Vernant identifies a group of classicists in France around 1900 "who, rejecting the dual and contrary facileness of survival and prefiguration, decided to keep strictly to Greek facts" (1991: 271), much as Farnell did; however, other than suggesting that Müller and Frazer brought comparative studies into some disrepute (1991: 276), he does not explain this development.

49. See Harrison 1921; Farnell 1934; F. M. Turner 1981: 129–34. Africa 1991: 32–3 gives samples of the devastating attacks on Harrison's lack of accuracy.

50. Gould 1985: 14.

51. Moulinier 1952; Vernant 1980: 110–29.

52. Connor 1988b; cf. Vernant 1991: 273.

53. Epimenides: Forrest 1956; contra, Robertson 1978. Peisistratos: see articles cited and challenged in Connor 1987: 42–7, R. M. Cook 1987, and Boardman's reply (1989); see also Sinos, Chapter 4, this volume. Vase painting: Boardman 1972, 1975, 1978, 1982, 1984, 1986, 1989 (with bibliography of criticisms); cf. Shapiro 1989. Boardman's arguments have won wide acceptance. Heroes' bones: e.g., Andrewes 1957: 58–61 (Kleisthenes of Sikyon); see also Boedeker, Chapter 8, this volume.

54. Hdt. 5.63.1, 5.70.2. The main elements are repeated in Arist. *Ath. Pol.* 19.2–4, 20.2. The curse was used yet again in the diplomatic exchanges between Athens and Sparta in 432/1 (Thuc. 1.126–8). The Spartans' notorious gullibility about religion – largely a product of the difficulties their social structure created for the legitimation of political decisions – is discussed in Hodkinson 1983. For further cases of the manipulation of oracles by or against Spartans, see Hdt. 5.90–1, 123, 6.66, 74–5, 84; Thuc. 6.53, 59, 8.16; Philochorus *FGrH* IIIB 328 F 115; Isoc. 15.232, 16.25; Arist. *Ath. Pol.* 19; Diod. 14.13.2–8; Plut., *Lys.* 25, 26; *Mor.* 403B; Paus. 3.4.5–6.

55. The charges appear in Diog. Laert. 2.40; Pl. *Apol.* 24b; Xen. *Mem.* 1.1.1; *Apol.* 10. Brickhouse and Smith 1988 review the range of interpretations; and see Connor 1991 and Garland 1992: 136–51. The evidence for religious reform is, however, open to numerous interpretations; see Robertson 1990a and P. J. Rhodes 1991.

56. Bowersock 1965: 112; Nock 1972: 843.

57. Price 1984: 10.

58. As M. I. Finley 1975: 103–5 points out, Dodds, Kirk, and particularly Parry were all interested in anthropology, but none of them adopted a particularly sociological approach.

59. See M. I. Finley 1952; Shaw and Saller 1981. Finley's approach is extended in Millett 1991.

60. M. I. Finley 1978: 23, 64 (Malinowski); 105 (Radcliffe-Brown); 145 (Mauss).

61. On the paradox of Weber's great interest in Greek society and economics and his neglect of Greece in his work on the sociology of religion, see Vernant 1991: 274.

Finley published very little on religion or ritual besides his classic study of the sociology of Spartan rituals (1968) and a brief introduction to a book on religion (1985). On Finley's approach to the logic of institutions, see Humphreys 1978: 24–6. The neglect of ritual, what Weber called the "religious unmusicality" of the social scientist, was very common from the 1930s to the 1960s; Victor Turner even speaks of "the reluctance I felt at first to collect ritual data" (1969: 7) in the 1950s in the face of its studied neglect by his elders.

62. E.g., Donlan 1981, 1982, 1989a, 1989b; Qviller 1981; Redfield 1983, 1986. The only major development of Finley's work on ritual aspects of the gift is by one of Finley's students, Gabriel Herman (1987), who has studied ritualized friendship in the classical and Hellenistic periods.

63. Humphreys 1978: 80.

64. Gernet 1932 with Humphreys 1978: 80–3.

65. See particularly Vernant's own comments on his influences (1991: 291) and the essays collected in translation in Vernant 1980, 1983, 1991; Vernant and Vidal-Naquet 1981; Detienne and Vernant 1989. The translation of the bulk of Vernant's papers into English in the 1980s has increased his influence enormously.

66. See Detienne 1981b, 1986a, 1986b; Loraux 1981, 1986; Vidal-Naquet 1986.

67. See A. Hirsch 1981; Anderson 1983.

68. E.g., studies of hoplite warfare (Detienne 1968; Vidal-Naquet 1968; Cartledge 1977; Connor 1988a; Hanson 1989, 1991), sacrifice (Burkert 1983; H. Foley 1985; M. H. Jameson 1986, 1988; Detienne and Vernant 1989), and Athenian dramatic festivals (Cartledge 1985; Euben 1986; Connor 1989a; Winkler and Zeitlin 1990). One important exception to the focus on the fifth and fourth centuries is Redfield's treatment of purification rituals in Homer (1975).

69. Redfield 1991: 11.

70. Hawkes 1954; cf. I. Morris 1992: 17–21.

71. See particularly, on the historical dimensions, Binford and Binford 1968; Clarke 1968; Binford 1972, with Trigger 1989: 289–328.

72. M. I. Finley 1975: 87–93; Hodder 1991b.

73. E.g., Renfrew 1972.

74. Starr 1961; Snodgrass 1971, 1980a, 1980b, 1982, 1986, 1988a.

75. E.g., Gallant 1982; Morgan 1990; Morgan and Whitelaw 1991; I. Morris 1987, 1988, 1989a, 1989b, 1992; Whitley 1988, 1991a, 1991b, 1993. I discuss the work of Osborne (1988, 1989), another Snodgrass student, at length later.

76. Bloch 1986: 1–11, 175–87.

77. Tilly 1984.

78. Pecora 1989: 245.

79. Kuper 1983: 206–10; Geertz 1988; Hunt 1989; Senjak 1990; Manganaro 1990.

80. Foucault 1972: 9–10. See also Sheridan 1980: 113–63; Eribon 1991: 187–223.

81. Lyotard 1984: xxiii.

82. Geertz 1980: 135, 123. Geertz 1973: 361 says that he developed his semiotic approach to culture as a way to avoid the reductionism of both Hegelian and Marxist methods.

83. Geertz 1973: 30.

84. Keesing 1987: 166; Walters 1980: 551.

85. For a sample of the debates, see Kellner 1989; Veeser 1989; Hoesterey 1991; F. Jameson 1991.

86. Connor 1989b; Manville 1990: ix–xi; cf. Connor 1985: 1–14. To some extent, Marxist historians like E. P. Thompson (1963) have similar aims in their attempts to write "history from below," and much of Finley's Weberian work on antiquity concentrated

on slavery (e.g., M. I. Finley 1980); but in both cases the overall aim remains totalizing and structural.

87. E.g., Goldhill 1986; Kurke 1991.
88. The virulent response to White's *Metahistory* (1973), frequently perceived as saying that the only grounds for choosing among rival accounts of the past are aesthetic or moral, illustrates this feeling well (see Novick 1988: 600–3). The most important movement away from historical empiricism is perhaps represented by the self-styled "New Cultural Historians" (see Hunt 1989).
89. White 1989: 301.
90. Novick 1988: 524; cf. Berkhofer 1988; Ankersmit 1989. The implications and existence of such chaos and confusion are discussed in Kloppenberg 1989; Hollinger 1991; Megill 1991; Novick 1991.
91. Geertz 1988: 96, speaking of Rabinow 1977; Crapanzano 1980; Dwyer 1982.
92. Osborne 1988, 1989. Osborne has also examined the Athenian Acropolis in the classical period in similar ways (1984, 1987).
93. I follow the absolute dates proposed by Coldstream (1968). I accept that there are certain problems with the ceramic chronology of the eighth and seventh centuries (I. Morris 1987: 10–18, 156–67). However, although we cannot treat an archaeological "date" like 760 as corresponding to a real calendar year – even the most optimistic assessments (e.g., R. M. Cook 1969) concede that we must allow a good twenty-five years' elasticity in the absolute chronology – Coldstream's chronology provides an excellent relative system, and the intervals of time between the Late Geometric Ia painters, whom he places around 760–750, and those of Late Geometric IIb, whom he puts around 720–700, can hardly have been fewer than fifty or more than seventy-five years. James et al.'s attempt (1991a) to downdate Late Geometric pottery into the seventh century is unconvincing; see also James et al. 1991b.
94. Osborne 1988: 4–5.
95. Osborne 1989: 322.
96. Cf. Fox-Genovese 1989; Pecora 1989.
97. The cultural approach also rules out all feminist approaches that focus on exploitative relationships (see MacKinnon 1989: 3–80).
98. See Preziosi 1989: 49. Osborne 1991: 273 has also urged the need for "allowing the artist back in" while preserving the insights of a consumer-oriented perspective, but this concern has not been prominent in his treatments of archaic funerary art.
99. Brückner and Pernice 1893: 101–41.
100. Most of the material is published in Villard 1954.
101. For the workshops and painters involved, see Coldstream 1968: 29–33. The material is collected very usefully and analyzed in Ahlberg 1971a, 1971b. Athenian giant marker vases go back at least to 900 B.C.E., with Kerameikos grs. G 1 and 2 (Kübler 1954: 209–12), and funerary paintings had begun by 850 (Kerameikos gr. G 43, Kübler 1954, pls. 22, 146). However, the Dipylon vase stands at the head of the most numerous and most impressive series of funerary scenes, which runs from 760 to 700 (see Whitley 1991b: 137–43).
102. Brückner and Pernice 1893: 91; Alexandri 1968: 20–2.
103. On the early digs on Peiraios Street, see Poulsen 1905: 10–12. Boardman 1988: 174 n. 6 points out that there are many Late Geometric marker vases in museum collections without known provenances. These may diminish Peiraios Street's numerical dominance, but it is also possible that many of these vases themselves came from illicit digs on Peiraios Street. The gold bands are collected in Ohly 1953; see the remarks in Whitley 1991b: 143–4.

104. I. Morris 1987: 60–1, 120–5; Whitley 1991b: 97–137.

105. I. Morris 1987: 58–9, 81–2, 125–28; Whitley 1991b: 137–62.

106. Brückner and Pernice 1893: 104–7 were unsure whether the Dipylon vase (Athens NM 804) belonged with gr. 2 or gr. 4. Gr. 4 contained a sword, and since NM 804 is a belly-handled amphora, conventionally used as a female symbol for more than five hundred years (Boardman 1988), the vase should probably go with gr. 2. This was a primary cremation, which raises the interesting but insoluble problem of whether we should see the grave assemblage as a continuation of the Dark Age primary cremation tradition best exemplified in the important Areopagus plot (I. Morris 1987: 124), as a transitional stage between Middle Geometric urn cremations and Late Geometric inhumations, as a precursor of the seventh-century primary cremations, or as a rite reserved for a few exceptional burials (e.g., the remarkable Erechtheiou Street gr. θ 2 [Brouskari 1979]).

107. I. Morris forthcoming.

108. See Whitley 1991b: 116–36.

109. Snodgrass 1980a: 48–58, 1980b; cf. Coldstream 1968: 349–51. See also Antonaccio, Chapter 3, this volume.

110. E.g., Carter 1972, who disagrees with the version in Webster 1955; Boardman 1983.

111. Snodgrass 1987: 153; cf. Coldstream 1974: 395. Compromise has also been sought by Hurwit 1985b.

112. The eighth-century noblemen who used the Dipylon cemetery would then be creating the same kinds of ideas as those de Polignac 1984: 147 sees in late-eighth-century notions of the hero – "these heroes are located at the meeting point of two worlds, of two ideologies, of two sets of military and political values. The hero plays the role of the first and last champion of the polis."

113. Snodgrass 1987: 158–64.

114. The standard account of Protoattic painting is still J. M. Cook 1934–5, although a radically different argument, assigning Middle Protoattic to Aigina, has been advanced by S. P. Morris 1984. On the Nessos Painter, see Ohly 1961; Hurwit 1985a: 176–9.

115. Eleusis, West Cemetery gr. Γ 6 (Polyphemos grave): Mylonas 1975: 91–2, with Mylonas 1958 and S. P. Morris 1984: 43–6; gr. Z 10, Mylonas 1975, 251–3. Eleusis, South Cemetery gr. 6: Skias 1912: 32–3. Phaleron: gr. 18, R. S. Young 1942: 35–6, and possibly a second grave published by Couve 1893. Mt. Imittos: Böhlau 1887: 43–4.

116. Rombos 1988: 77–91, 357–68, for the Trachones and Thorikos workshops. Sheedy 1990: 132–46.

117. I. Morris 1987: 195, forthcoming.

118. Whitley 1993.

119. Fish 1989: 311.

120. I. Morris 1992: 8–29. There are a few more archaeological treatments of archaic rituals, but these tend to ignore broader questions. Simon's brief methodological statement (1983: 3) is probably fairly representative of classical archaeologists' feelings.

121. Gebhard and Hemans 1992: 9–22.

122. Coldstream 1977: 317–40; Snodgrass 1980a: 49–65; Hägg, Marinatos, and Nordquist 1988. On the weakness of the high dates advanced by excavators for many sanctuaries, see Snodgrass 1971: 394–401.

123. On Corinthian expansion, Morgan 1988. On the sanctuaries, Salmon 1972; Robinson 1976; de Polignac 1984: 86–9. Graves: Salmon 1984: 45–52; I. Morris 1987: 185–6. The main evidence comes from the North Cemetery (Blegen, Palmer, and Young 1964), which may have been unusually poor in the seventh century; the chance find

of an Early Protocorinthian grave (Weinberg 1974) is distinctly richer. However, the overall impression of a major decline in grave wealth since the early eighth century remains clear, although, as Morgan 1988 shows, from about 800 on the Corinthians were very active in pursuing new metal sources. Metalwork: Brookes 1981, with a different picture in R. F. Rhodes 1987. Planning: C. K. Williams 1982.

124. On the burials, see Courbin 1974; Hägg 1974, with Courbin's review (1977); Hägg 1983a; I. Morris 1987: 183–5. More details are provided in A. Foley 1988. Urbanization: Aupert 1982; Hägg 1982. Ceramics: Morgan and Whitelaw 1991.

125. For details, see I. Morris 1987, 1989a: 313–20, with references. The elaborate bronze tripod dedications of the late eighth century are discussed in Touloupa 1972, and smaller bronze figurines in Weber 1974. Some of these small late-eighth-century figurines have been found at Delphi (Morgan 1990: 140–1). The best-known sanctuaries are at the Academy (Stavropoullos 1958), Eleusis (Travlos 1983), Lathouresa (Lauter 1985b), the Agora (Burr 1933), Mt. Imittos (Langdon 1976), and Mt. Tourkovouni (Lauter 1985a).

126. I. Morris 1987.

127. I. Morris 1992: 17–24.

128. As argued by Burkert 1985: 47–53.

129. Nagy 1979, 1990b.

130. I. Morris 1988, 1989a. On gender, Whitley 1991b: 157–9, 195; for examples of the problems of analysis, Gero and Conkey 1991.

131. Stone temples: Mallwitz 1981. Seventh-century houses: H. A. Thompson 1940: 6–7; Bingen 1965: 20–3, 1968a: 25–36, 1968b: 31–49; Servais 1968: 9–19; Lauter 1985b; Mazarakis 1987. Temples in the islands: e.g., Boardman 1967; Cambitoglou et al. 1971, 1988; Schilardi 1988. Athletics: Kyle 1987: ch. 1; Morgan 1990: 207–12. Warfare: Frost 1984, with Connor 1988a. Colonization: Viviers 1987.

132. Coldstream 1968: 361.

133. Burkert 1983: 48–58; Vernant 1989: 38–41.

134. Bremmer 1983.

135. I explore these ideas more fully in I. Morris forthcoming.

136. I. Morris 1987: 128–37, 152–5.

137. Plommer 1960; Iakovides 1962: 62–5; Nylander 1962: 52–7; Preisshofen 1977; Schneider and Höcker 1990: 74–102.

138. *IG* i³ 104; Andoc. 1.83; Arist. *Ath. Pol.* 4; Plut. *Sol.* 17. *Ath. Pol.* 4 is the fullest account, but it seems highly unreliable and is likely to be a late interpolation (P. J. Rhodes 1981: 85–8, 108–18).

139. Thuc. 1.126. A similar story appears in Hdt. 5.71, who says only that he "won to himself an association of young men his own age." Lambert 1986 attempts to reconcile the contradictions between the two accounts of Kylon's coup.

140. M. H. Jameson 1965: 167–72 points out that Thucydides' reference to the Diasia makes most sense if there was an alternative story in circulation in the late fifth century, in which Kylon did launch his coup during the Athenian festival.

141. Epimenides is mentioned in Arist. *Ath. Pol.* 1; Plut. *Sol.* 12.

142. However, P. J. Rhodes 1981: 83 suggests that "the link [of Epimenides] with Solon is a later fiction . . . and dates in the 590's for Epimenides' purification are derived from that function."

143. See Ruschenbusch 1966. Several sources (Dem. 43.62; Cic. *Leg.* 2.64; Plut. *Sol.* 21) do say that Solon passed laws restraining the scale of funerals. Aeschines 3.108 also has Solon propose the motion that led to the First Sacred War around 590 B.C.E.; on the difficulties here see Robertson 1978.

144. Raubitschek 1949.
145. *FGrH* 334 F 4. Kyle 1987: 28–9 provides a good example of the propagandistic fallacy in arguing that Peisistratos not only established the games but also used them as a springboard for his coup five years later. On the building campaign, see Kolb 1977; Angiolillo 1983; Shapiro 1989.
146. E.g., Andrewes 1982; Frost 1985.
147. See particularly Hdt. 5.78; Ober, Chapter 11, this volume.

CHAPTER THREE

The Archaeology of Ancestors

Carla Antonaccio

> . . . the tendency [is] to try to transform what was a living person and is now a decaying cadaver into something permanent and stable – mummy, monument or memory, ash, ancestor or angel. Broadly speaking, there seem to be three main ways of accomplishing this. The deceased may become identified with some stable material object, usually a part of, receptacle for or representation of his or her own body; he or she may be reincorporated into society as an ancestor or by reincarnation; or he or she may start a new life in the world of the dead. These alternatives are not by any means mutually exclusive; they frequently coexist in a somewhat loose and apparently inconsistent articulation.[1]

THERE are many studies on Greek burial practices, but little on the transformation process after death described here by Sally Humphreys. We might add to her list of transformations, but we would have to agree that the various possibilities not only may be difficult to sort out, but may in fact function together. This essay examines a variant of one model – whereby society reincorporates the dead as ancestors – for Iron Age and early archaic Greece.

My approach combines textual and material evidence for Greek kinship, burial, and cult practices to arrive at an "archaeology of ancestors," keeping in mind the functional overlap alluded to by Humphreys. My method has much in common with a contextual approach to archaeological evidence (a variant of postprocessual archaeology articulated in particular by Ian Hodder) that is well-suited to protohistoric and early historic Greek society. Briefly put, in contextual archaeology "other worlds of meaning, other historical contexts with their unique frameworks of meaning, can be understood through an examination of material culture."[2] This approach considers the relationship of archaeology to history, a major concern for classical archaeology, and it is aware of the pitfalls in interpreting ritual (identified by Morris, Chapter 2, this volume). By emphasizing the context of ritual action and its traces in the material record, a contextual approach opens new possibilities for understanding meaning. In this essay, context includes regional comparison, the occurrence of similar artifact types in different ritual spheres, the preserved literary record, and various historical frameworks (political, economic, social).[3]

DEFINITIONS

The Greeks used the term "ancestors" (*progonoi*) to refer to their forebears: immediate kin still remembered by the living or fictive heroes – founders and others who served as starting points for an imagined or symbolic descent for a family (*oikos*) or community. Heroes in their various manifestations have received much attention; ancestors, although they are nearly ubiquitous in Greek literature, are scarcely mentioned. In discussing the Greeks I use the term "ancestors" in an inclusive sense: I mean to go beyond both the mythical or legendary founders of lineages or communities and our own notions of the Greeks' cultural and historical ancestors (the Mycenaeans). I focus on the ancestors implied in Greek kinship structures as practiced and as revealed by the archaeological record.

Both literary and archaeological evidence for the recognition and veneration of ancestors – either divine and corporate or human and private – are fragmentary and difficult to interpret. But since we have to work with Greek notions of kinship, real or imagined, this is where we begin. Usually, discussions of Greek kinship focus on the developed political structures of ideal kinship described in written sources of historical Greece. These have been accepted as the original basis for social organization, dating from the period after the collapse of Bronze Age, palace-based authority.[4] Furthermore, many studies of early Greek religion featured a strong presumption of the importance of genealogy and ancestral veneration as the basis of property and inheritance.[5] But Sally Humphreys, who views Greek society from a comparative anthropological perspective, has observed that Greek kinship (unlike many other systems) was not in fact determined by genealogy. In archaic and classical Athens, kinship relations

> do not show the processes of fission and fusion characteristic of the segmentary lineage system as a political organism. They are administrative (and military) divisions. . . . In anthropological terminology tribes, trittyes and phratries are patrilineal clans and sub-clans made up not of lineages but of individual households [*oikoi*] and associations with a mixed basis of recruitment.[6]

Consequently, since personal ancestors do not determine the rights or obligations of members of the polis (city-state),[7] an ancestor worship that consistently determines and articulates the relations of living and dead does not figure prominently. Nonetheless, everyone has progenitors, everyone disposes of the dead, and the *oikos* (household) is basic to Greek society.[8] So by "ancestor," I designate the archaeological remains of the dead, both recent and remote.

Rather than "ancestor cult," the Greeks articulated relationships between the living and the dead with "cult of the dead," "tomb cult," and "hero cult." The use of these terms in the scholarship varies greatly, and until recently "tomb cult" and "hero cult" were conflated. The following discussion is meant to establish their usage in this essay. Even the basic term "cult" is not consistently understood.

Emile Durkheim defined it as "not a simple group of ritual precautions which a man is held to take in certain circumstances; it is a system of diverse rites, festivals, and ceremonies which all have this characteristic, that they reappear periodically."[9] Thus a cult, as opposed to a rite or ritual performed occasionally, entails repeated actions at regular intervals. But while the "cult" in hero cult may fit comfortably into this definition, the Greek cult of the dead and ancestor cult, as archaeology has shown, do not (see later). So in spite of the promiscuous application of the term "cult," its meaning varies in Greek practice. Durkheim's definition applies to Greek cults of gods and heroes, but other "cults" also comprise patterned, if occasional, action without the regular repetition and permanence of Durkheim's definition.

Although the "cult of the dead" and "ancestor cult" tend to merge in anthropological discussion, the two should be separated.[10] "Cult of the dead" encompasses the mortuary rituals of mourning, funeral, and disposal that take place at or near the time of death. "Ancestor cult," in contrast, often continues long after death; the dead have a definitive effect on the survivors and this may entail the transformation of the deceased into an impersonal entity.[11] But we should also appreciate, with Jack Goody, the potential complexities of ancestor cult: "Even in ancestor worship in the strict sense, the relationship of the living to the dead has a number of modalities that must be disentangled if we are to establish any correlations between religious systems and other aspects of the social order."[12] We turn next to the Greek systems in detail.

Tomb Cult

For the Greeks, Lewis Farnell used the term "tendance" – family visits to tombs of kin to remember or mourn individuals – to distinguish the cult of the dead from worship of ancestors. In the same vein, Humphreys says, "The cult of the dead was a memorial-cult, rather than ancestor-*worship*."[13] Farnell's "tendance" and Humphrey's use of "cult of the dead" (and "tomb cult") correspond to what I call "tomb cult." Originally, tomb cult described family visits in the classical period to tombs after the burial for the purpose of making offerings of food, garlands, and the like.[14] It followed the mortuary rituals immediately after death, but extended them in time *without* reincorporating the dead as permanent members of a genealogical system. Tomb cult had little depth in time, tended to be irregular, and gradually tapered off. As observed, if Durkheim's definition of "cult" is applied, "tomb cult" comes up short. Yet a structured pattern of action can be identified in the record; it is of short duration, but not entirely random or spontaneous.

In the classical period, tomb cult also encompassed a concern with placing the dead, not just tending graves. The newly deceased were buried with immediate lineal forebears to create a burial group based on close kinship; funerary iconography and inscriptions reinforced the ideal of family solidarity.[15] Yet these burial groups had little depth in time, extending to only a few generations.

This essay adopts the classical notion of tomb cult and traces analogous practices in the Iron Age and archaic period, directed both at Mycenaean tombs of centuries before and at contemporary burials (Figure 1). I argue that tomb cult at Mycenaean

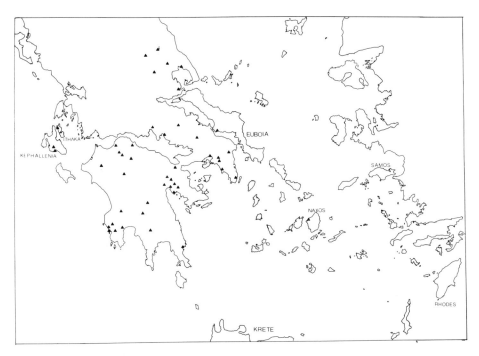

Figure 1. Mainland Greece: distribution of Iron Age/archaic tomb cult, incorporating reuse, eleventh to fifth century B.C.E.

tombs was neither hero cult nor strictly votive. Instead, it articulated a claim of kinship between the practitioners and those long dead, both in contemporary tomb cult (or tendance) and in tomb cult at Bronze Age tombs. But the Bronze Age ancestors did not serve as reference points in a pedigree or genealogy; like the close kin of burying groups, their relation to the living was more immediate and destined to be short-lived since the *oikos* was chronologically shallow.

A close connection between living and dead is to be found not only in tomb cult, but in occasional Iron Age (and later) reuse of Bronze Age tombs for burials. Though not a routine practice, a clear pattern of reuse from the eleventh century on emerges. It has been little remarked, however, because reuse is simply dismissed out of hand as the exploitation of a convenient hole in the ground.[16] I consider this reuse as an aspect of tomb cult. Such funerary reuse may occur in the same prehistoric cemetery as tomb cult, although not always. A clear example is a collapsed Mycenaean chamber tomb at Berbati in the Argolid; it received a Middle Geometric burial, dating to the later ninth century (Figure 2).[17] There is no question that burial, not worship, was the aim; rich ceramic offerings accompanied the skeleton of a young woman. Such cases constitute a deliberate choice to associate one's own with ancient dead, and a pattern of such reuse can be isolated in chamber and tholos tombs at many sites.[18]

There is a further connection between contemporary funerary ritual and votive

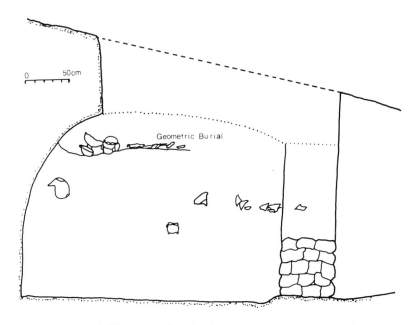

Figure 2. Berbati Tomb III: cross section showing Iron Age reuse. (After Säflund 1965: fig. 17.)

deposits and burials at Mycenaean tombs. In Iron Age cemeteries at Asine in the Argolid and Grotta on the island of Naxos, low circular platforms constructed of large pebbles were built over or near contemporary graves and used for varying lengths of time at ritual meals (Figure 3).[19] They were too small and low to the ground for diners to have gathered around to eat; they were not hearths, since there is no trace of burning on them. Ash, bone, and pottery were deposited and indicate their use as offering tables. This tendance of recently deceased ancestors in Iron Age burial grounds and the tomb cult aimed at the Mycenaeans are explicitly connected, for in the Late Geometric period, a circular platform was constructed not at a contemporary burial, but in a Bronze Age chamber tomb next to Grave Circle B at Mycenae itself (Figure 4).[20] (Alan Wace found quantities of Geometric material in nearby tholos tombs named for Klytemnaistra and Aigisthos, which together with similar evidence from the other seven tholoi and some chamber tombs have been considered evidence for hero cult. Burials, however, continued in the area from Late Helladic III:C until Late Geometric so that the area's function as a cemetery was retained. Continuing burials were again deliberately located near earlier tombs.)[21] Other circular platforms of the Iron Age associated with Mycenaean tombs occur at Prosymna and Argos.[22] Thus the recent dead and the Mycenaean dead received the same treatment in the Iron Age and seem to have been similarly regarded as ancestors. Furthermore, analogous structures also turn up in certain domestic contexts. In the earlier Iron Age, so-called chieftains' houses (e.g., Unit IV at Nichoria, the burial building at Lefkandi) also featured these circular platforms,

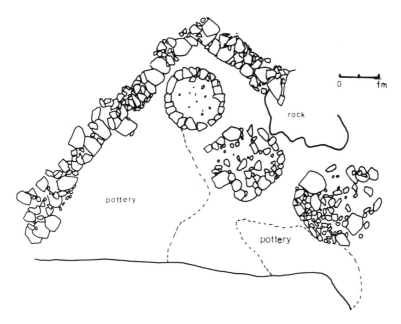

Figure 3. Asine: Barbouna area, circular platforms near eighth-century necropolis. (After Hägg 1983a: fig. 1.)

probably part of ritual feasting within a settlement context to consolidate and maintain the power of community leaders. The occasion, scale, and location differ from the activities at the tombs, but feasting fosters group solidarity and provides a context for social display and cohesion in both cases.[23]

The so-called heroön at Lefkandi in Euboia deserves special consideration in this context. Although its excavators call this building, constructed around 1000 B.C.E. in the Toumba burial ground of the Protogeometric period, a "center of hero-cult," little about the building supports this interpretation.[24] The man and woman buried beneath the building were unquestionably at the apex of their society, but to speak of heroization is misleading. In this respect, the excavators were unduly influenced by the role of heroes in epic poetry. The apsidal building, about 15 meters wide and 45 meters long, seems to have been built as a sort of mortuary chapel: drinking pottery, storage pithoi in the apse, and a circular platform in the east portion of the building all indicate that funerary meals took place inside.[25] Beneath its floor were found a sacrifice of horses and an heirloom bronze cauldron containing a male cremation and a female inhumation with gold jewelry – all aspects of social display within the context of competition and control. The structure was deliberately buried shortly after the burials, but not immediately; pottery from the building indicates its use over perhaps fifty years. Most important of all, the tumulus that covered the building became the focal point not for cult but for a cemetery, which continued in use for two centuries; the tumulus itself was undisturbed, and any observances directed at the two original burials were discontinued when the building was buried.[26]

51

If anything, Toumba shows how Iron Age ritual could utilize the dead to structure group relations through feasting and the placement of later burials. It is not known how the burials made in the cemetery after the creation of the tumulus were related to the original pair. But the tumulus provided a focus for a burying group that ultimately included dozens of individuals, some of whom were laid to rest with similar offerings, many imported from Attika, Thessaly, Cyprus, Egypt, and the Near East. The burial offerings reinforced the solidarity of the group; their close relation to the original pair has been confirmed by recent finds of another pair of horses and another double burial.[27] All this suggests that the structure at Lefkandi was a center for tomb cult as I am defining it here, rather than a heroön.

Hero Cult

Hero cult is distinct from tomb cult. Hero cult is more Durkheimian than tomb cult; it finds formal expression in scheduled ritual action at specific locations, including processions, sacrifice, and games, and is often emphasized by the construction of a monument such as a naiskos and/or altar. The recipient is expressly identified by name (even if simply as "the hero") on inscribed offerings and/or in literary descriptions of the cult. Participation involves corporate effort and is regular and relatively permanent, extending over centuries in many instances.

Heroes as a category are notoriously difficult to define, since they vary over time and from region to region. At the very least, a hero is by definition neither an Olympian god nor an ordinary mortal (though figures like Herakles stretch these limits). Heroes are in the first instance human, although they may have divine parentage. After death or disappearance, they continue to be physically powerful and if disturbed must be propitiated; myth and epic maintain their memory. In some communities like Athens (and poetic traditions like Hesiod), some heroes were like "lesser gods" and did not have specific names or stories.[28] But all were utilized as corporate ancestors; different groups or individuals in Greek society (genē, phratries, entire communities) traced their origins to a hero. On the other hand, in funerary ideology the deceased ordinarily did not join the ranks of heroes (until the Hellenistic period, at any rate). One early exception was the founders of colonies; in this case, historical individuals became heroes (archēgetai) after death and their tombs became shrines.[29] I will return to this later.

Until recently, the inquiry into hero cult's origins conflated it with Iron Age tomb cult. The term "hero cult" was used to designate not only formal, ongoing cults of named (especially epic) figures but also the deposits of votive offerings in Bronze Age tombs, especially during the late eighth century B.C.E.[30] Thus Erwin Rohde invoked a "cult of ancestors" as the older stratum and basis for the transformed practices of hero cult, assuming familial and religious continuity between the Bronze Age and historic periods that archaeology fails to confirm.[31] Lewis Farnell and Nicholas Coldstream have taken both phenomena, tomb and hero cult, to be hero cult and associated it with the composition and circulation of the Homeric poems in the second half of the eighth century B.C.E.[32] According to this view, mainland Greeks of the late Iron Age, having lost their Bronze Age past, were reintroduced to it through Ionian epic poetry and thereby inspired to venerate the Mycenaean

Figure 4. Mycenae: circular platform in chamber tomb next to Grave Circle B. (Photograph from Mylonas 1972: vol. 2, pl. 5a, b. Reproduced by permission of the Archaeological Society of Athens.)

Figure 5. Sparta (Therapne): Menelaion.

tombs all around them as the tombs of epic heroes (and their ancestors). Indeed, the entire late protohistorical–early archaic period has been described as the "age of Homer," a Panhellenic "Greek Renaissance" that rediscovered the late Bronze Age or the "heroic age."[33] In fact, Homeric epic has conditioned scholars' own identification of the Mycenaeans as heroes and influenced the interpretation of post-Mycenaean ritual activity at Mycenaean tombs. There is, however, no evidence that the ancients viewed the Mycenaeans as heroes. Recently, several archaeologists have advanced the long-standing discussion of hero cult by distinguishing between hero cult and the votive deposits in Mycenaean tombs.[34] The practice of placing votives in Mycenaean tombs now comes under the rubric "tomb cult," as discussed earlier. I differ, however, from Ian Morris and Susan Alcock, who do not use the term "tomb cult" to suggest that kinship played a role, as I do, but merely to distinguish it from hero cult.[35]

Hero cults as they are defined here begin to be archaeologically visible in the late eighth or early seventh century. The Menelaion at Sparta provides the clearest early case; the identification of a shrine of Agamemnon at Mycenae has been questioned (Figures 5 and 6).[36] A deposit of votives at Sklavochori, near Amyklai in Lakonia, may be connected with the later cult of Agamemnon and Kassandra mentioned by Pausanias; it contains material as early as the Late Geometric period but is concentrated in the sixth century.[37] There was cult activity on the island of Ithaka in a cave at Polis, but the only early reference connecting it with the hero

Figure 6. Mycenae: Cyclopean bridge and shrine retaining wall south of acropolis (Agamemnoneion).

Odysseus is *Odyssey* 13, describing how the hero and Athena hide his Phaiakian gifts in a cave. Because bronze tripods figure among the gifts in the poem and also among the offerings at the cave, the link would seem clear. However, early inscribed dedications at the Polis cave are addressed to Athena and to the Nymphs, while Odysseus is recorded only from the late Hellenistic period in an inscription on one of many terra-cotta votive masks.[38]

It is striking that, contrary to expectations based on copious written references to hero cult, none of these early cults was connected with actual tombs, either in the late Iron Age or in the better-known archaic and classical periods. Tomb cult, in contrast, did take place at actual tombs; unlike the more durable hero cults, the visits to a given tomb were in nearly all cases restricted, often to a single instance.[39] The recipients remained anonymous, and there was no monumental construction. Though a concentration of this activity occurs in the later eighth century, as is now well known, intrusions into Bronze Age tombs in fact occurred from the eleventh century (Protogeometric) onward.

REGIONAL SURVEY

The remainder of this essay concentrates on three areas at the end of the Iron Age and into the archaic period: Lakonia and Messenia, Attika, and the Argolid (Figures 7–9). All three areas provide both written and archaeological evidence for consid-

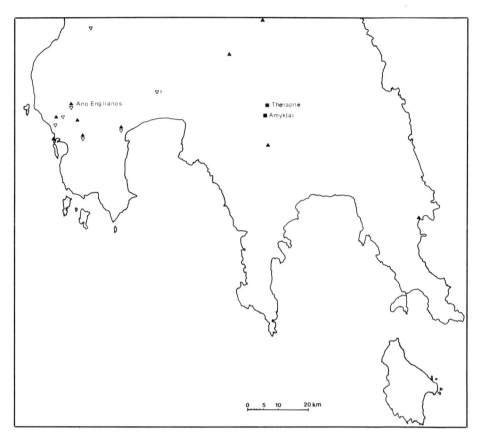

Figure 7. Lakonia and Messenia: distribution of Iron Age/archaic tomb and hero cult. Square indicates site of hero cult; triangle, tomb cult; inverted triangle, reuse.

eration and include instances of both tomb and hero cult. Furthermore, since all three regions were important in both the Bronze Age and archaic period, their contrasting records may usefully be compared.[40] Though I have selected these three areas for their records and their later historical significance, it is important to keep in mind that tomb cult was a Panhellenic phenomenon (Figure 1). Panhellenism entailed the rise of interstate sanctuaries and competitions, the spread of art styles and of a literary culture, and can be taken as evidence of communication among the elites of several states.[41] Though the search for a single explanation for tomb and hero cult is liable to charges of uniformitarianism, the wide scope of the phenomena and the persistence of tomb cult command attention.[42] Any consideration of tomb and hero cult must be comprehensive, taking account of their distribution over space and time, but it must also acknowledge the variations in the record — regional, temporal, and ideological.

Lakonia and Messenia

In Lakonia, very few tombs of any period are known (Figure 7). At Epidauros Limera, a Late Helladic rock-cut tholos tomb held a Protogeometric jug along with the Bronze Age grave goods. This artifact bears witness to a visit made centuries after the construction and primary use of the tomb. The site of Synoikismos (Palaiochoria on the Arcadia border) and Pellanes (on the north Eurotas River) provide other examples.[43] The tomb cults are early Dark Age and perhaps represent an attempt to maintain a link with the Bronze Age into the ensuing period. Adjacent and closely related Messenia furnishes many more examples of tomb cult than Sparta; before the end of the eighth century, tomb cult is well attested in tumuli, tholoi, and chamber tombs at Papoulia, Akourthi, Volimidia, and Voidokoilia.[44] Historical sources report Spartan aggression against Messenia, culminating in the Messenian Wars, which began in the eighth century. Tomb cult in Messenia could reflect this outside pressure and represent a search for group identity and cohesion. However, some very early reuse in Messenia parallels the situation at Sparta, and the Messenian Wars should not dictate an explanation of tomb cult as a national act of defiance.

Yet perhaps the earliest bona fide hero cult, to Menelaos (and Helen), is located at the major Lakonian Bronze Age settlement of Therapne above the Eurotas, a short distance from Sparta itself (Figure 5).[45] Construction of the Menelaion has been claimed to mark victory in the struggle with Messenia. The cult originated simply, with votive deposits directly on the ruins, but its formalization with the construction of the Old Menelaion surely represents a corporate effort. A hero cult of Menelaos, the epic king of Sparta, located on the site of the most important Bronze Age settlement in Lakonia, suggests that Sparta found this cult pattern best suited to express its political and social ideology, at least at the close of the Iron Age. However, written sources refer not only to Helen and Menelaos worshiped at Therapne, but also to the Dioskouroi, Helen's divine brothers.[46] Lakonia's stone and terra-cotta "hero reliefs" are well known, and it has been suggested that they are connected with the Dioskouroi and worship of Spartan kings.[47] As mentioned, a cult located at Sklavochori near Amyklai, possibly devoted in the classical period at least to Agamemnon and Kassandra, had its origins in the Iron Age; all that is known of it is the votive dump containing thousands of terra-cotta plaques and figurines. At Amyklai itself, another hero cult, of Hyakinthos, is an especially difficult subject; a Mycenaean cult had existed on the site, although there is probably an unbridgeable gap to the Iron Age. Hyakinthos is not an epic hero, and there does not seem to be a Mycenaean grave on the site. This is in any case a hero cult, not a case of tomb cult that had a name attached to it.[48]

Attika

There are clear instances of tomb cult in Attika at Aliki Glyphada, Menidhi, Eleusis, and Thorikos, as well as evidence of reuse at Eleusis, Athens, and perhaps Marathon (Figure 8).[49] This contrasts with the larger number at Messenia, the few instances

Figure 8. Attika and Euboia: distribution of Iron Age/archaic tomb and hero cult. Squares indicate site of hero cult; triangles, tomb cult; inverted triangle, reuse.

in Lakonia, and, as will be seen shortly, the large number from Argos. In addition, several enclosures that appear in the Athenian Agora and Kerameikos in the sixth and fifth centuries stand near or mark off earlier anonymous graves (Figure 9). These stone monuments, often triangular in plan, compare best to the well-known so-called heroön at the West Gate of Eretria on Euboia, but in the Kerameikos, inscriptions identify the monument as a *tritopatreion*. Although it does not enclose any graves, it is located at the intersection of the Sacred Way and the Street of Tombs in the middle of a burial ground and refers specifically to *tritopatreis*, "ancestors," rather than heroes.[50]

In Attika, we have no archaeological evidence for early named hero shrines; written sources, however, suggest it is possible that a Theseion existed before Kimon

Figure 9. Kerameikos (Athens): *tritopatreion* boundary wall and *horos*.

brought Theseus' purported remains to Athens in the early fifth century.[51] Attika is famously home to myriad local heroes, often reifications like the hero Echetlos, who rose up at Marathon to aid the Athenians and whose name derives from ἐχέτλης, ''plow,'' or nameless ciphers associated with a deme or kin group.[52] As Ferguson, Nock, and Kearns have all discussed, however, Attic hero cults never seem to have been focused on a tomb. Though we could speculate that either the Menidhi tholos or the Thorikos chamber tomb might have been the object of a hero cult, this is not reflected in any of the documents pertaining to Attic religion or specified by the offerings.[53]

Argolid

Finally, the Argolid provides a wealth of complexity (Figure 10). Tomb cult was most widely practiced in the Argolid, though research in this region relative to others has been extensive and may skew our perceptions. Still, it does seem probable that the density of settlement and relative continuity of habitation on Bronze Age sites played a role in tomb cult frequency. Tomb cult was practiced at Mycenae, Prosymna, Dendra, and Asine as well as Argos; tombs were reused at Asine, Argos, Dendra, Prosymna, Mycenae, and Berbati in the Argolid.[54] Many settlements were

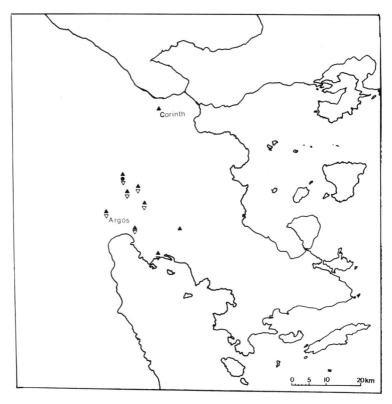

Figure 10. Argolid: distribution of Iron Age/archaic tomb and hero cult. Circle indicates site of hero cult; triangles, tomb cult; inverted triangles, reuse.

located very close to one another, as in the Bronze Age. Argos was competing with several other communities within the plain during the Iron Age, including Mycenae, Tiryns, and Asine, as well as with communities outside, like Sparta in Lakonia. Even in the fifth century Argos still struggled to control the entire plain.[55] In the Argolid, tomb cult appears to have staked out territory and delineated boundaries between communities, for intensive tomb cult and tomb reuse at Mycenae and at Prosymna occurred at the limits of the plain, just before the foundation of the Argive Heraion at the Bronze Age site of Prosymna.[56] Although there are instances of reuse at both sites, little direct evidence for habitation in the area complements the burials, so we cannot say for certain who was burying at Prosymna at this time.[57]

Near the end of the Iron Age, a stone's throw away from the chamber tombs, the construction of the Old Temple at the Heraion (which I date together with the Old Temple terrace to the second half of the seventh century) symbolized the hegemony of Argos in the Argolid. This move paralleled the foundation and location of the Menelaion – and possibly also responded to it – drawing our attention to the wider audience of hero cult beyond the immediate community.[58] Thus in Argos, the Heraion may be seen as the functional equivalent of hero cult elsewhere, for Argos certainly had its epic and local heroes, and if the sanctuary was designed to legitimate Argive hegemony, we might expect to find one of these. It may be, however, that Argos in particular chose Hera because of her associations with the Argive elite and also as part of a general trend toward Olympian sanctuaries.[59] At Athens, of course, it was Athena who dominated the Acropolis at the heart of the city; other Argive communities, like Tiryns and Mycenae, also worshiped Athena.[60] For such communities this might be an act of self-definition in contrast to the Argive Hera, but it is important to recognize that Hera, Herakles, Zeus, and Ares were also worshiped at Tiryns and Mycenae, although dating the different cults and assessing their relative importance are difficult.[61]

Survey Summary

The frequency of tomb cults varies in date, number, and location for the three regions. The differences among Argos, Athens, and Lakonia in these activities depend on differences in power relations within these regions and competition among their communities as they emerged and developed in the late Iron Age and early archaic period. In Lakonia, an atypical polis, the scarcity of data perhaps renders statistics meaningless: there was almost no tomb cult, but then, few tombs are known. By contrast, Lakonians founded the early hero cult at the Menelaion. Sparta's political and power relations were anomalous in Greece, and its use of heroic ideology may be specifically designed to legitimize the dual kingship, a system that did not characterize the other areas under discussion. (Many cases involving purported "hero bones" involve Sparta; see later in this section and Boedeker, Chapter 8, this volume.) Neighboring Messenia provides a wealth of evidence in contrast to Lakonia: a strong record of tomb cult (including reuse), which reflects the continuity of at least some of the population and the importance of the region after the close of the Bronze Age. The decline of these activities at the close of the eighth century may relate to the Spartan conquest of the region in the Messenian Wars. Tomb cult reemerged, along with hero cults like those of Messene that specifically expressed the identity of the region, after the liberation of Messenia in the fourth century.[62] Thus tomb cult might have been an expression of resistance (e.g., in Messenia on the eve of Spartan domination), but might also be indicative of competition among groups within a community (see later).

In Attika votive tomb cults were relatively rare, while reuse of prehistoric tombs was relatively frequent. However, these relative frequencies are misleading, because there were only a total of three (rural) tomb cults, while reuse occurred in the cemeteries that saw burials acccumulate over long periods of time (e.g., the West Cemetery at Eleusis). One view links tomb cult in Attika to population increase in the eighth century, the argument being that offerings in the tombs were made by new settlers seeking to lay claim to empty land.[63] Another sees a reaction of the old communities of Attika to such incursions and an expression of resistance to the growing importance of Athens.[64] Both theories are based on incomplete counts of the frequency of tomb cult in Attika and Athens and do not recognize the significance of reuse. But the comparative rarity of Attic tomb cults and relative frequency of hero cults in the archaic period may indicate that the inhabitants of Attika did not find tomb cult a particularly useful way to articulate their conflicts or emergent social structures. Although tomb cult would seem well suited to reinforce the proverbial Attic claim of autochthony, the claim may have been sufficiently established without it. Hero cult, however, was clearly crucial for the Athenians in the archaic and classical periods.

In the Argolid, there was a greater balance between tomb cult and the reuse of tombs. There were also many more examples than in any other region save Messenia, in part at least for the reasons already noted. The known tomb cults and the reuse of tombs, combined with the development of sanctuaries on the borders of growing communities, were functions of the intense competition and conflict on the plain.[65] We must also allow for similar actions having different functions in different contexts since communication between communities from one region to another might produce apparent uniformity of practice without uniformity of meaning.[66]

While there is a plethora of evidence for tomb cult, we must acknowledge the rarity of true hero cults in the late Iron Age. Their geographical distribution is also peculiar; they were found at Sparta, only possibly at Mycenae and Ithaka. In other words, there is no certain case of hero cult as defined here except for the Menelaion at Sparta. Though a polis, Sparta was unique; it had hereditary kingship, a non-nucleated pattern of settlement, and rigid distinctions among the three groups of *homoioi, perioikoi,* and *helotai.*[67] These unique features, especially the dual kingship, may help account for the prominence of hero cult in Sparta. Moreover, since social groups were distinct, there was less room to negotiate tensions over prestige through something like tomb cult.

It appears, then, that early hero cults really belong in the seventh century and later (rather than the eighth century) and that they were not connected with major poleis as one would expect were they a significant part of a Panhellenic system of shared values and structures early on. Even the evidence for heroes at state or interstate sanctuaries devoted to Olympian deities is not clear-cut; for example, the Pelopeion, said to be the burial mound of the hero Pelops at Olympia, does not have a Bronze Age or even Iron Age pedigree, but seems to be a creation of the archaic period.[68] Nor are hero cults connected with tombs, as one would expect if they were predicated on physical remains or relics that "bound" the hero to a place. Rather, the examples given here are associated with Bronze Age habitation or cult sites. Thus to a certain extent the rise of epic heroes' cults, widely accepted as a prominent feature of the later eighth century B.C.E., is a mirage.

If this is so, how do we reconcile the archaeological and literary evidence? After all, the traffic in heroes' relics figures prominently in several ancient authors. Written accounts of the relations and strategies among poleis in the archaic period record episodes involving Athens, Sparta, and Argos in which the bones or other relics of heroes of myth are acquired, stolen, or transferred.[69] These reports, combined with the emphasis on the bones of dead warrior-heroes in epic poetry, led Rohde and others to conclude that the power of a hero was invested in his bones. Since the bones were located in tombs, it followed that the tomb was the center of hero cult.[70] It might seem, then, that the cult of relics provides a link between hero and tomb cult, but there are in fact relatively few recorded cases of relic mongering, although they have received wide attention in the scholarship.[71] And for all the emphasis on the possession of a hero's bones, the bodily relics themselves seldom figured in the practice of cult; they were not displayed, carried in procession, or made accessible to participants. Furthermore, the cult of heroes as depicted in written sources involved only purported graves. Findspots, when disclosed, did not include actual Bronze Age tombs (chamber or tholoi). Even the celebrated bones of Orestes, discovered by a blacksmith digging a well in Tegea, were found contained in a coffin in a cist or pit grave, not in a Bronze Age tomb.[72]

Moreover, the evidence of tomb cult, which *does* involve prehistoric tombs, shows that ancient burials were not disturbed or removed; in many cases the roofs of chamber or tholos tombs had fallen in, making the original floor levels, and hence the bones, inaccessible. Though it is possible that objects recovered from Bronze Age tombs would have been claimed as heroic relics, this does not seem to have occurred. When "heirlooms" do turn up in later contexts, these contexts are funerary, not sacral. In fact, some artifacts found when ancient burials were disturbed became new grave gifts; others seem to have been held as prized possessions and consigned to the grave at the appropriate time.[73]

Thus the traffic in relics described in our sources appears distinct from tomb cult, for it involves the fabrication of antiques, even though authentic Bronze Age remains were known. In the same way, hero cult is not predicated on actual tombs, though such tombs were clearly available. Both hero cult and the traffic in relics go hand in hand with fictional genealogies and other fabricated links with the past. While tomb cult involves actual remains of the Bronze Age, hero cult and the traffic in relics are deliberate and "state-supported" forgeries; they may compete with or complement tomb cult activity.[74] One does not replace the other since they are concurrent. But insofar as both cult practices deal with the dead (and hence with ancestors, even if fictitious), they are related.

CONCLUSION

We return to kinship and the dead. Previously, scholars have assumed that kinship determined much about Greek burials, especially their location and grouping. But there are several problems in deriving burial practice from kinship structures (which are largely deduced from the literary evidence). First, as Ian Morris has shown, our archaeological evidence is fragmentary and may not represent a full population.[75] Second, limited reuse of burial sites seems to be linked to a three-generation genealogical memory[76] – both point to a shallow time depth within lineage structures. *Tritopatores* or *tritopatreis,* the "third fathers" (great-grandfathers, ancestors), known at Athens and elsewhere in the archaic period and later, represent this symbolic three-generation limit. François Bourriot observes that the three-sided form of the Kerameikos *tritopatreion,* and the other triangular monuments, directly expresses this limit.[77] As many have pointed out, there was little if any trace of regular veneration at tombs anywhere from the Bronze Age to the classical period, a fact that undermines the written ideology of ancestral tombs and their veneration. In fact, little continuous observance of long duration took place at family tombs even in the supposedly conservative, autochthonous, and genealogically minded polis of the Athenians. Athenian funerary conservatism was an invention of the late classical period, as Sally Humphreys has demonstrated.[78]

Third, Denis Roussel and François Bourriot have shown that the kinship terms of tribe and *genos* are not of hoary antiquity, but rather are structures of the polis and hence relatively recent.[79] Iron Age kingship has been reexamined as well, and it has been shown that political power at this time was achieved, not inherited.[80] In anthropological terms, *basileis* are "big men," leaders whose position depends on their ability to attract and keep followers through personal talent, feasting, and gift giving. Such a position is only partly heritable, and a "big man" is only a *primus inter pares*.[81] Furthermore, "big men" were not confined to the early Iron Age. In the archaic period as well, *basileus,* tyrant, and aristocratic politician were all big men; political power in the Greek polis was never either strictly inherited nor easily shared.[82] Thus claims of descent from heroes did not reflect real kinship relations, but constituted a legitimating device that allowed such individuals to forge links with the past in a civic context. For the "rise of the state" in Greece entailed the appearance of formal structures of authority, but not classes or castes that had exclusive access to them. It is for this reason that tomb and hero cult endured even after the rise of the polis. The emergence of formal offices, the rise and fall of tyrannies, and major interstate conflicts did not eradicate tomb cult or hero cult.

Within the polis, hero cult functioned to create a fictitious kinship that may have served individuals and families. It paralleled social display and epic poetry as means of legitimating social and economic inequality. The divinely supported aristocracy of Homer's poems – their values, actions, and institutions – both expressed and were structured by the current dominant ideology.[83] The cults of epic heroes can be seen as part of that ideology: their worship confirmed social realities for those in power, who claimed them as ancestors. Hero cults may also have contributed to the self-definition of a community both in relation to itself and in relation to its peers, friends or foes. *Archēgetai* functioned in this way; they were used at Athens not only by Kleisthenes to focus new allegiances but also as the fictional ancestors of the *genē* that controlled priesthoods and claimed political power.[84] They also functioned as city founders in colonies; here historical figures were transformed through the extraordinary circumstances of the foundation of new communities. In either case, hero cult served the group.

In the regions surveyed here, tomb cult coexisted with hero cult, but they were practiced at different locations, using different forms. Such reuse and rituals, however, need not exclusively support the claims of the *aristoi,* as has recently been argued by Ian Morris.[85] For example, although the ninth-century burial at Berbati is extraordinarily rich, attempted self-legitimation by the *aristoi* does not make sense of such practices as simple burials (including those of children) in the entryways of Mycenaean tombs or the extreme modesty of many offerings.[86] The demos could be claiming its own ancestors by such a strategy, perhaps in imitation of or competition with funerary ritual used by other groups in the community. The struggle for ancestors may have been part of the widening of formal burial privileges in the late eighth century (though this may not apply to all communities, and certainly not equally).[87] It preceded the beginnings of hero cult and continued apace. The two were distinct practices.

Tomb cult did not constitute continuous long-term ''ancestor worship'' connected with graves. Though tomb cult peaked in the later eighth century, it did not spring up de novo at that time, nor did it end with the establishment of the polis, which settled a supposed ''crisis of sovereignty'' at the end of the Iron Age.[88] The offerings in the tombs comprise a continuing but circumscribed practice with a wide distribution, paralleling contemporary funerary rituals, especially in the offering of pottery and consumption of meals. Furthermore, veneration of the dead with graveside meals and offerings of pottery, small terra-cottas, and bronzes went hand in hand with the reuse of tombs, both Bronze Age and more recent (as discussed earlier). Both offerings and the reuse of tombs for different types of burials suggest a range of users and practitioners.[89] Claimed as ancestors of the people burying in the area during later times, the ancient dead may have been adopted by both the *aristoi* and the demos in competing or complementary strategies that enabled them to define themselves in relation to their own and other communities.

The archaic and classical Greeks, says Sally Humphreys, ''hoped to achieve for the dead . . . perpetual remembrance, by strangers as well as kin. The dead did not become ancestors (they had no effect on the lives of their descendents and were not reincorporated into society to serve as focal points in the genealogical definition of social relationships): they became *monuments*.''[90] This perhaps sums up the distinctive nature of ancestors for Greek society in contrast to others, but this essay has drawn attention to ways in which the dead were reincorporated and did have an effect on the lives of their descendants.[91] Greeks in different communities manipulated the dead in the material record and in the collective fabricated memory of myth and epic to create ancestors when none existed. This too is a form of monumentalization; it creates stability in the face of change and provides the space in which to enact and contest claims to power and authority.

NOTES

With apologies to Susan Alcock and Ian Morris. I would like to thank E. Bobrick, D. Charles, C. Dougherty, L. Kurke, and I. Morris for help of various sorts, which is not to implicate them in the results.

1. Humphreys 1981: 268.
2. Hodder 1987: 10; see also Hodder 1986a and, in general on ''postprocessual'' archaeology (i.e., post-''New Archaeology''), Hodder 1986b; and recently, Hodder 1991b.
3. Cf. Brady 1991: 4, who describes a ''poetics of anthropology'' that seeks to explore the ''intellectual and analytic implications of redefining and expanding the role of a broadly conceived poetics relative to the scientist thinking that has dominated anthropology for more than a century.'' Morris, Chapter 2, this volume, considers the New Historicism and a contextual approach to archaic Athenian ritual in the material record.
4. See later in this essay for work that strongly challenges the antiquity of these structures.
5. E.g., Rohde 1920.
6. Humphreys 1983b: 195; see also later in this essay. ''Clans'' here must be understood as a term of anthropological analysis, not a simple matter: ''Clan has been defined as 1) any unilineal descent group, 2) a matrilineal descent group, and 3) a residential group consisting of the consanguineal members of one sex, their spouses, and their unmarried siblings'' (Schusky 1972: 88). This author goes on to define clan as ''a compromise

kin group based on a rule of residence and a rule of descent. A unilocal rule of residence combines with a unilinear rule of descent. Some affinal relatives are included and some consanguineal kinsmen excluded. . . . The clan is a grouping composed of a number of lineages" (90). Note also Humphreys's use of *oikos,* meaning "household," without the clannish connotations of "house" (as in House of Atreus). The work of Fustel de Coulanges, which stresses the importance of descent for inheritance and land tenure, though important, is based on false notions of ancestor cult. I have to thank Ian Morris for access to Morris 1991a before publication. See also the important article by Humphreys 1980.

7. On this term see I. Morris 1991b; also the subject of a massive study by M. Sakellariou 1989.

8. The *oikos* has recently been considered by Cavanagh (1991: 98–105), who discusses "genealogical shallowness in the family [*oikos*]" (100). But I cannot agree with his statement that (for rural populations) "ancestral pedigrees were a charter: in Greek, as in many traditional societies, the genealogical model was the means whereby the individual established his place in a free society. No one would advertise the aspects of fission or failure of lineage" (103). See further later.

9. Quoted by Goody 1962: 18.

10. E.g., Durkheim defined "cult of ancestors" as follows: "There is no cult of the ancestors except where sacrifices are made on the tombs from time to time, when libations are poured there on certain more or less specific dates, or when festivals are regularly celebrated in honor of the dead" (Durkheim 1915 [1912], quoted by Goody 1962: 18). This definition contradicts his usual definition of cult, and Jack Goody observes that Durkheim "fails to distinguish between ancestor worship and the cult of the dead, a distinction of some importance in the analysis of these institutions." Goody himself stipulates that worship "in which the living and the dead are kin one of another, for that we shall reserve the phrase 'ancestor worship' " (Goody 1962: 381; this statement appears in a discussion of the difference between Chinese ancestor worship and Christian worship of saints).

11. Goody 1962: 379.

12. Goody 1962: 381.

13. Farnell 1921: 343; Humphreys 1983b: 13.

14. See Humphreys 1980; Garland 1985: ch. 5.

15. Humphreys 1980 and R. Thomas 1990 for Athens; generalizing risks "Athenocentrism," but there is some evidence from other communities as well; see later. One obvious exception to this emphasis on family is the practice of burying war dead together, either on the battlefield (e.g., Marathon) or at the city.

16. Cf. Snodgrass 1971: 193; Coldstream 1976.

17. Chamber Tomb III: Säflund 1965: 35–7, 81–90, 655–75, and figs. 17, 18; see also Coldstream 1968: 118 and pl. 24 b–d.

18. See Antonaccio 1993.

19. Asine: Frödin and Persson 1938: 135–6, 426–7, and figs. 118–118a; Hägg 1983c. Naxos: Lambrinoudakis 1983, 1984, 1985, 1987.

20. Papademetriou 1952: 467 and fig. 34; Mylonas 1972–3: 18 and pl. 5 a,b (here Figure 4).

21. Antonaccio 1993; A. Foley 1988: 42–3, 51.

22. Courbin 1966: 5–6 (Argos, near Deiras tomb XIX); A. Foley 1988: 152; Antonaccio 1993 (Prosymna Tomb L).

23. Nichoria: McDonald et al. 1983: 27–30 and fig. 2-18, pls. 2-25, 2-27; see also Mazarakis 1985, Fagerström 1988. Feasting: O. Murray 1980; Antonaccio 1993.

24. Popham 1981–2, 1983: 19; Popham et al. 1982a, 1982b, 1988–9; Touchais 1982;

Calligas 1984–5, 1988; Mazarakis 1985: 6–9; Sackett 1986 and personal communication; Catling and Lemos 1990. I am indebted to Hugh Sackett for many details and permission to cite his information.

25. Antonaccio 1993. The excavators' sequence of events has been recently challenged by Whitley 1991a: 350 1991b: 185–6, but he himself offers no additional evidence to support his assertion; there is no evidence that the Protogeometric building was in a habitation area or that Toumba was ever anything other than a cemetery.

26. See the illustrations in Popham et al. 1982a and Popham 1981–2, 1983, and the plan and section in Catling and Lemos 1990. The excavators suggested that three cuttings in the rock to the east of the tumulus were meant to hold a monumental tripod cauldron; if so, this would be a possible indication of cult on the site.

27. Popham et al. 1988–9: Tombs 68 and 49 (two inhumations).

28. Ferguson 1944; Nock 1944; Hes. *Op.* 106–25.

29. Of course, historical figures in the fifth century also were heroized, e.g., Brasidas (though as a founder). But these are not the ordinary dead, like Epikteta on Thera, who provided for a memorial cult to her heroized family ca. 200 B.C.E. See Farnell 1921: 313, 361–72; Rohde 1920: 172 with n. 126 and 526 with n. 17; Humphreys 1980: 122.

30. The locus classicus is Coldstream 1976; see also Blegen 1937a and an important paper by Snodgrass 1982 as well as Antonaccio 1993 for other bibliography.

31. Rohde 1920: 123, 125; Blegen 1937a.

32. Farnell 1921; Coldstream 1976.

33. The most extensive exposition of this point of view is Hägg 1983a; on Panhellenism, see Nagy 1979: 7–10, 14, and Coldstream 1977, now to be considered in light of Morgan 1990: e.g., 147.

34. I. Morris 1988; Snodgrass 1988a; Whitley 1988; Antonaccio 1993.

35. Adopted by me from Humphreys 1980. Used also by Garland 1985; Morris 1988; Alcock 1991.

36. Menelaion: Droop et al. 1908–9; H. Catling 1975, 1976, 1977a, 1977b, 1983, 1992; R. Catling 1986; Cavanagh and Laxton 1984. Literary evidence: Wide 1893; Farnell 1921: 323–4. Agamemnoneion: R. M. Cook 1953a, 1953b; Marinatos 1953: 87–8; Hägg 1987; A. Foley 1988: 51, 145. I share Marinatos's skepticism of the dedication of this shrine to Agamemnon in the archaic period, now joined by that of Morgan and Whitelaw 1991: 89; the epigraphic evidence is at least fourth century. The famous sherd found by Schliemann "above" Grave Circle A at Mycenae and inscribed "το Hερooς εμ[ι" (*IG* iv 495), first of all, does not name a specific hero; second, has no context and is at least fifth century in date; and last, may be directed at Perseus, known to be worshiped near the citadel (for material on Perseus see Jeffery 1990: 173, cat. no. 6 and pl. 31.6; M. H. Jameson 1990).

37. See Salapata 1990a, 1990b; *ArchDelt* 1956: 100–4, 1960: 167–73; cf. 1957: 12–13; 1958: 548–51; Cartledge 1979: 112, 139.

38. Benton 1934–5, 1936, 1938–9; *Ody.* 13.345–65. See Heubeck and Hoekstra 1989: 177 on ll. 217–18 (tripods given by Phaiakian *basileis*), 170 on l. 97 (cave) and "local knowledge," which may have influenced Homer or the epic tradition. See also Lamberton 1983.

39. An exception to the rule of short duration is the famous Menidhi tholos in Attica (see later). In the Roman period, a monument base was constructed in the so-called Treasury of Minyas at Orchomenos in Boiotia, but is connected with Hera and/or a Roman imperial cult: Schliemann 1881: 19–25; Schachter 1981: 242; P. Wallace 1985; Antonaccio 1993.

40. Other locations: Arcadia, Corinthia, Phokis, Boiotia, Kephallenia, Euboia. Whitley 1988 focuses on comparing Attika and the Argolid, but does not consider Lakonia (or Mes-

senia, except in a brief addendum). His analysis of his limited catalog of examples does not distinguish between hero cult and tomb cult. The claim that "the practice of placing offerings in Mycenaean tombs ... begins in the late eighth-century (and not before)" (174) is incorrect. We also differ in our conclusions (see later).

41. Snodgrass 1986.
42. See esp. I. Morris 1988: 758.
43. Epidauros Limera: Vanderpool 1955; Demakopoulou 1968. Synoikismos: Waterhouse and Hope Simpson 1961: 130 n. 119. Pellanes: Waterhouse and Hope Simpson 1961: 125 (and display in the Sparta Museum).
44. Korres 1977, 1981–2; Chatzis 1981–2; Coulson 1988; Antonaccio 1993.
45. See note 36.
46. Alcm. fr. 14b (Page); Hdt. 6.61.19–21; Paus. 19.7–20 and n. 9. Dioskouroi: Alcm. fr. 7 *PMG;* Wide 1893: 309–25; Cartledge 1988; Parker 1988.
47. Tod and Wace 1906: 102–13. The terra-cotta plaques from Sklavochori (Amyklai) are discussed by Salapata 1990a, 1990b.
48. For Amyklai, see esp. Demakopoulou 1982. The relationship of this cult to the later historical one or the nature of Hyakinthos (whose cult companion is Apollo) is beyond the scope of this essay; see Antonaccio 1993 with further references.
49. There is no tomb cult at the large chamber tomb cemetery at Perati on the Attic coast. For Attika: Coldstream 1976: 11–12; Hägg 1987; Whitley 1988: 176–8; Antonaccio 1993. I discount such evidence as the "heroön of the Seven against Thebes" in Eleusis and the "local hero" Akademos: the former is not a shrine, but an instance of reuse; the latter is based on a sherd with restored graffito naming the hero, found in the Agora (see Antonaccio 1993).
50. Agora: Lalonde 1968. Eretria: Bérard 1970, 1978, 1982; C. Krause 1972, 1981; Auberson and Schefold 1973; Rolley 1974; Martin 1975; Altherr-Charon and Bérard 1978. I will return to *tritopatreis* and *archēgetai* later.
51. Theseion: Pfister 1909–12: 198–206; see Shapiro 1989: 142–5 here and later on heroes' relics.
52. Paus. 1.15.4 for Echetlos, not to mention the heroes Marathon and Theseus. See Kron 1976; Kearns 1989: app. 1. See also Ferguson 1944; Nock 1944. Kleisthenes' Attic *eponymoi* are not heroes, actually, but *archēgetai,* on which more later.
53. Ferguson 1944; Nock 1944; Kearns 1989. See Hägg 1987 and Devillers 1988 on the votive offerings. The lack of inscriptions is especially striking in tomb cult; divine recipients were often named on votives, and even anonymous heroes were specified.
54. Antonaccio 1993; A. Foley 1988:151–3 ("hero cult"); see also her ch. 2 for eighth- and seventh-century burials.
55. Morgan and Whitelaw 1991.
56. de Polignac 1984 refers to "balissage" by means of sanctuary foundations. Whitley 1988: 179–80, extends this to include tomb cult, though on the basis of different reasoning; see Antonaccio 1992.
57. A. Foley 1988: 45–6, 52 makes the improbable suggestion that Mycenae was abandoned as a settlement in this period and was used only ceremonially.
58. Antonaccio 1992; see also Morgan 1990: 85–9. I have called into question the "Agamemnoneion," but whether or not this shrine was devoted to Agamemnon from the eighth century, its foundation outside the settlement, on the road to Prosymna and the Heraion, represents a boundary-marking strategy. The foundation of a shrine to Enyalios northwest of the citadel reinforced the claim on the road to the Corinthia.
59. Wright 1982 emphasizes the heroic connections of Hera, the patroness of epic's Argive

heroes, and explicitly connects the choice of deity to the cult of "heroic" tombs at Prosymna. But Wright does not consider how the Heraion is part of a pattern of extramural sanctuaries that grew up around developing poleis (as detailed by de Polignac 1984).

60. Tiryns: Jantzen 1975; A. Foley 1988: 143; Jeffery 1990: 150, cat. no. 9. Mycenae: Wace 1949: 84–6.

61. Hera: *IG* iv 492 (Mycenae), Jameson et al. 1975 (Tiryns); A. Foley 1988: 145–7. Boundary stone: Jeffery 1990: 174, cat. no. 4 (c. 475).

62. See, e.g., Paus. 4.1.1–4.1.3 and 4.31.11; Alcock 1991.

63. Snodgrass 1982.

64. Whitley 1988: 178.

65. Morgan and Whitelaw 1991; Antonaccio 1992.

66. Morris 1988: 756–8. See Appadurai 1981 for an example of variable pasts in Indian Hindu temples and communities.

67. There were *thētes* at Athens and seemingly similar groups elsewhere, but these were not permanently disenfranchised as at Sparta.

68. Adler et al. 1892: 65–7; 1897: 73; Dörpfeld 1935: 122–3; Mallwitz 1972: 133–7, 1988; H. V. Herrmann 1980: 59–74. See H. Catling 1988, French 1989–90, 1990–1, Kyrieleis 1992, and Protonotariou-Deilaki 1992 for recent excavations at the Pelopeion that so far seem to confirm this view. Other sanctuaries (e.g., Nemea and Isthmia) provide no compelling evidence for Iron Age hero cult, though continuing research may change this.

69. Pfister 1909–12 remains the most comprehensive study of this phenomenon; see also Boedeker, Chapter 8, this volume. For the medieval cult of saints' relics, see Geary 1978.

70. Rohde 1920: 121–4; Nagy 1979: 116.

71. Pfister 1909–12: 196–238 (e.g., Orestes, Tisamenos, Theseus, Rhesos).

72. In several instances, supposed hero remains are described as gigantic bones; this fits with the frequently expressed belief that heroes, their deeds, and their weapons were bigger than those of the present day. But most often, ancient sources identify huge bones as the remains of giants, or even of mythical monsters, not of heroes (see Pfister 1909–12: 425–8, 507–8). It is clear from many of the texts that these bones were fossils. A recently published fossil hippo bone from the Heraion on Samos perhaps exemplifies this (Reese 1985; Hainsworth 1987; Kyrieleis 1987: 220 and fig. 9; Leighton 1989; Mayor 1989; I am indebted to Adrienne Mayor for access to her work on the folklore of fossil bones in the Mediterranean and additional references). In fact, where findspots are mentioned, they are geologically appropriate for fossils in most cases.

73. See Benson 1970 for a study of prehistoric artifacts in historical contexts, and Overbeck 1980 for the "recycling" of Bronze Age grave goods. See also the twelfth-century bronze cauldron used as an ash urn in the tenth-century cremation at Toumba.

74. Although the term "polis" and the "rise of the polis" are confidently discussed, I am not certain we are dealing with states as such in the Iron Age. I have used "community" to get around the problem elsewhere in the essay, but the cult of relics belongs to the archaic and classical periods, when Greek communities certainly had attained state-level function. See I. Morris 1991b, though his assertion that "rural hero cults [*sic*] were also important in polis religion" (37, citing Whitley 1988) is puzzling.

75. I. Morris 1987.

76. Bourriot 1976: 1178; also on the limits, even in cemeteries like the much- and long-used Kerameikos, see Humphreys 1980, 1983b: 13–14, also discussed by Cavanagh 1991: 98–100.

77. Bourriot 1976: 1135–46 (Athens and Delos). See Kearns 1989: 76–7, who considers them specifically connected mostly, though not exclusively, with phratries rather than *genē*.

78. Humphreys 1980: 268. The exception is Naxos, where we find long-term tomb cult at early Iron Age graves located in a former Mycenaean settlement area (like the Menidhi tholos in Attika).

79. Bourriot 1976; Roussel 1976. See also Kearns 1989: 64–79.

80. Drews 1983 suggests that "chief" is a more apt translation for *basileus* than is "king."

81. See, besides Drews 1983, Qviller 1981 and van der Vliet 1986. I. Morris 1991b: 40–4 discusses hierarchy in Iron Age communities, arguing for state-level function. However, his argument abstracts the degree of hierarchy from (very uncertain) population levels and does not cite work more recent than Drews's. Goody observes in a footnote (1962: 382 n. 1) that "a pedigree, as distinct from a genealogy, traces a line of filiation. . . . it is a charter to office and to other rights; the longer the pedigree, the more imposing and the more effective it is as a device for legitimizing both the office and the office holder." He also points out that this is affected by literacy (388).

82. Contra, Whitley 1991a: 352; cf. Whitley 1991b: 184–6.

83. I. Morris 1986.

84. Kearns 1985.

85. "By making dedications at [Bronze Age] tombs, the peasantry was in part offering support for the dominance of the agathoi" (I. Morris 1987: 194), "in part," because the rest of the motivation was to claim ownership of the land by association with ancestral tombs. See also I. Morris 1988.

86. E.g., Mycenae T. 533 (seventh century): Wace 1932: 114, 117 and figs. 47–9, pl. 56; see also Coldstream 1968: 147 and n. 5.

87. See I. Morris 1987.

88. See Vernant 1982: 38–48 for the "crisis of sovereignty." The argument rests on the notion that the collapse of Iron Age kingship supposedly precipitated the crisis; it was seriously undermined by Drews 1983. See also Qviller 1981.

89. I. Morris 1988 points to the ambiguity or polyvalence of tomb cults, though his definitions of "tomb" and "hero cult" are rather different from mine.

90. Humphreys 1981: 269–70 (following Maurice Freedman).

91. There is no room here to pursue several important issues: the relationship of tomb location to land tenure, cults of founders in the colonies, and the deformation of hero and tomb cult over time into the classical and hellenistic periods. See, e.g., on land tenure, I. Morris 1991a; founders, Malkin 1987 and Dougherty, Chapter 9, this volume; the heroization of athletic victors, Kurke, Chapter 7, this volume; tomb cult after the classical period, Alcock 1991.

PART TWO

Politics and Performance

Divine Selection

Epiphany and Politics in Archaic Greece

Rebecca H. Sinos

AFTER Peisistratos was driven from Athens, he formed an alliance with Megakles, to be sealed by his marriage to Megakles' daughter, and the two of them devised a plan to ensure Peisistratos' acceptance among the Athenians. Herodotus describes their scheme as follows (1.60):

> In the village Paiania there was a woman named Phye, who was nearly six feet tall, and quite beautiful as well. They fitted this woman out in full armor and had her mount a chariot and pose in a most striking attitude, and then drove into the city, preceded by messengers who said, as they had been instructed, when they reached the city, "Athenians! Receive and welcome Peisistratos, since Athena herself has honored him especially of all men, and is bringing him back to her own acropolis." They spread these things throughout the city, and soon the story had reached the outlying districts that Athena was bringing Peisistratos back, and the city's inhabitants, convinced that the woman was the goddess herself, offered prayers to this mortal woman and welcomed Peisistratos back.

Herodotus prefaces this story with the comment that this contrivance was "by far the silliest thing, in my opinion" and that one would have expected better of the Athenians. Most modern scholars seem to agree, and some even question that the incident ever happened, calling the story a "legend" or "folktale" and sometimes suggesting possible origins for it.[1] But whether or not the story actually happened as Herodotus tells it, all the ancient authors who refer to this incident accept it as historic.[2] For the ancient Greeks, apparently, it was not difficult to believe that Peisistratos staged such a procession and that the Athenians accepted him into their city as a result of his performance. Their belief may well be as important to our understanding of ancient political life as would be proof of the historicity of Peisistratos' procession. It requires us to take the performance seriously, as a ceremony that was understood by the ancient audience even if its significance is not easily grasped today.

This essay investigates the ancient audience's reception of this performance by

Figure 11. Leto on the chariot with Hermes standing in front, Apollo and Artemis at the side. Black-figure amphora by the Rycroft Painter. Worcester, Massachusetts, Worcester Museum of Art 1956.83. (Photo courtesy of the museum.)

exploring the meaning of its constituent elements. In Herodotus' description there seem to be three important parts to the tyrant's entry – the chariot procession, the young woman dressed as Athena, and the messengers who preceded the procession. The presence of the messengers suggests that the visual display was not sufficient in itself to communicate fully to the Athenians the message the tyrant wanted to convey. Still, the appearance presented by the tyrant and his goddess-like companion was part of the message and undoubtedly important to the Athenians' reception of it. To understand the meaning of this display, we must examine the role of imitation of the gods among the ancient Greeks and also try to reconstruct the ancient perception of chariot processions by considering the range of contexts in which they belonged. Chariots were used in processions both in rituals honoring the gods and in celebrations honoring human victors.[3] They also appear in art, most frequently in black-figure vase paintings, whose iconography can tell us much about the symbolic value of this vehicle. All of these subjects have something to offer to our inquiry, though here we can survey them only briefly.

Figure 12. Departing warrior taking leave of his family. Black-figure amphora Near Group E (Group of Vatican 347). Rome, Vatican 353. (Photo courtesy of the museum.)

BLACK-FIGURE PROCESSION SCENES

Black-figure scenes depicting chariot processions are highly conventional and thus can be discussed generally by type.[4] Sometimes they depict a traveling god (Figure 11);[5] in art as well as in literature, chariots are the usual form of transportation of the gods.[6] Mortals ride in chariots in depictions of wedding processions and warriors' departures, and in both cases the scenes seem to float between human and divine levels.

In the black-figure scenes of warriors, a warrior dressed in hoplite armor and carrying a hoplite shield stands in a chariot beside a charioteer, facing to the right (Figure 12).[7] There is some variety in the figures who surround the horses and chariot; usually they include women, sometimes holding children, and an old man, the family members whom the warrior is leaving behind. Another hoplite warrior usually stands or walks beside the horses.

The incongruity of these elements has long been noticed – why is a hoplite soldier standing in a chariot? This vehicle has nothing to do with the hoplite mode of

75

Figure 13. Gods accompanying the bride and groom in their procession. Black-figure hydria by the Antimenes Painter. London, British Museum 1843.11–3.83 (B340). (Photo courtesy of the Trustees of the British Museum.)

fighting or transportation to battle.[8] Instead, the chariot connects the hoplite soldier to the heroes of epic, suggesting a heroic ideal that inspired and exalted hoplite warriors even though their warfare was different in kind from Homer's.[9] The ancient battlefield was certainly a place where men seem to have left the mundane world and entered a heroic one, rising to the level represented to the Greeks by Homer's poetic account of heroic achievement. The chariot in these scenes effects this comparison between the hoplite soldier and his epic counterpart, uplifting the human activity by connecting it with a mythic paradigm.

Scenes of wedding processions use the chariot in much the same way. The great majority of black-figure wedding scenes depict the bride and groom standing in a horse-drawn chariot. Again there is some variety in the accompanying figures; sometimes they have the attributes of gods (Figure 13)[10] and sometimes they appear to be mortals, such as women carrying baskets, which may have contained the bride's trousseau (Figure 14).[11] But there is no evidence that the chariot was actually used for this purpose in real life; lexicographers who provide detailed information about the wedding ritual always describe the vehicle used in the procession as a cart, such as the *eussōtros apēnē* (cart with good wheels) used in the wedding procession in the pseudo-Hesiodic *Shield* (l. 273).[12] Why, then, do the vases almost

Figure 14. Women with baskets escorting the bride and groom. Black-figure amphora Near Group E (Group of London B174). London, British Museum 1868.6–10.2 (B174). (Photo courtesy of the Trustees of the British Museum.)

always depict the bride and groom in a chariot procession? These scenes cannot be meant to be realistic. One telling red-figure vase, in fact, depicts a chariot being outfitted with pillows, a strange image that conflates reality with the symbolism of the chariot scene; in real life, these pillows would have been useful for a bride and groom as they sat in a cart (Figure 15).[13] In wedding scenes depicting the bride and groom on a chariot, this vehicle gives the scene a higher status. The bride and groom stand in the pose of gods or heroes (cf. Figure 11).[14] Thus the chariot links the couple to the sphere of the gods and heroes, functioning in the same way as songs performed for the wedding that honor the bride and groom by calling them *makarioi*, ''blessed,'' and by comparing them to specific gods or heroes.[15]

The other regular occasion for the performance of songs to honor a mortal was the celebration of a victory in the games. Here chariots appear not only in vase paintings of the victor, but also in the actual ritual of the victor's return, which was celebrated with splendor befitting a god. Pindar mentions the burning of incense (*Nem.* 11.6) and exhorts the people to receive the victor using language also found in descriptions of divine arrival.[16] A vehicle is not always mentioned, but it is clear

77

Figure 15. Chariot outfitted with pillows; on the reverse, the groom leading the bride on foot. Red-figure krater by the Painter of the Athens Wedding. Athens, National Museum 1388. (After *AE* 1905: pls. 6 and 7.)

that at least sometimes the victor rode into the city standing in a chariot (*Ol.* 4.8–12).[17] The impression he made is clear from Lucian's description of a victor standing before a crowd, *isotheos,* ''godlike'' (*Anach.* 10). Leslie Kurke's persuasive discussion of the victor's talismanic power demonstrates the force behind the imagery of these rituals of return; underlying descriptions of the victor as godlike is a belief that he has attained a measure of divine favor and power beyond other men. In this case, the heightened status that the ritual of reentry celebrates will endure beyond the ritual itself.

In all of these contexts, artistic or real, the chariot procession effects a dissolution of the normal boundaries that distinguish mortals from gods or heroes. Peisistratos undoubtedly had this in mind when he chose the format of a chariot procession for his entry into Athens. By riding a chariot into the city, he presented the superhuman image seen in vase paintings of warriors and weddings and in the ritual entry of a victor returning to his city. But this was not the full extent of Peisistratos' display. The most eye-catching part of his procession was undoubtedly the young woman dressed as Athena.

EPIPHANY

Peisistratos' staging of an epiphany of Athena must be viewed against the busy background of phenomena in ancient Greece attesting the entry of gods and heroes into the mortal realm.[18] The appearance of Aphrodite in the *Homeric Hymn* to this goddess, "immortal beauty gleaming from her cheeks," Sappho's depiction of Aphrodite with her divine smile (1 V), and the surge of awe before the epiphany of Dionysus in Euripides' *Bacchae* are just a few of many unforgettable descriptions of epiphanies in Greek literature. These passages not only attest but also probably furthered belief in epiphany by providing full descriptions that might have served as paradigms for future encounters in life as well as literature.[19] Inscriptions as well as historical accounts make it clear that manifestations of divine or heroic presence were more than a poetic conceit.

Historic examples of epiphanies are clustered in contexts outside the routine world of humanity. One of the settings in which gods or heroes appear most frequently is the battlefield.[20] Herodotus himself provides several examples. In his description of the Battle of Marathon, for example, he mentions a tall soldier in hoplite armor with a beard spreading all over his shield. The man who saw this apparition lived to tell it, but was blinded (6.117). Plutarch adds to Herodotus' account that several Athenians saw their ancestral hero Theseus fighting at the head of the army (*Thes.* 35). Before the Battle of Salamis, there were several portents at Delphi when the Persians came through; the sacred weapons mysteriously moved from their storage place within and appeared in front of the temple, and thunderbolts and pinnacles of rock from Parnassus came crashing down on the Persians as they reached the sanctuary of Athena below (8.37). As they were fleeing, two soldiers of superhuman size (local heroes, according to the Delphians) joined the Delphians in savage pursuit (8.38–9). During the Battle of Salamis, the shape of a woman appeared and exhorted the Greeks, calling out loud enough for the entire fleet to hear her (8.84.2).

Later on in the fifth century, at the Battle of Koroneia, an inscription from the Kerameikos blames a demigod who fought against them for the defeat and death of Athenian men (Peek 1955, I. no. 17). We hear of several epiphanies of the Dioskouroi from various periods; they appeared often enough that a Spartan king could fake their epiphany easily enough, as reported by Polyaenus, referring to a fifth-century battle in Arcadia (1.41.1):[21]

> Archidamos inspired the Spartans with courage by setting up an altar in the night, decking it with the most brilliant armor, and leading two horses around it. When dawn came, the captains saw the new armor and the tracks of the two horses and the altar that appeared of its own accord, and they proclaimed that the Dioskouroi had come to fight as allies. The soldiers took courage with this inspiration and fought nobly, and they beat the Arcadians.

As in Homer, divine assistance should be seen as a sign not of human weakness and need but of the privilege of divine favoritism. Perhaps the heroic achievements of warriors were thought to create an environment where gods and mortals might mingle more freely.

Cult is the other context in which epiphanies are attested most frequently. Healing cults furnish particularly abundant evidence. Apparently the "healing hand" of Asklepios was not a metaphor for his treatment from beyond, but a reference to the actual divine touch that could cure an ailment. The Edelsteins' collection of testimonia for Asklepios and his sanctuaries contains many examples of dedications thanking Asklepios for his help, which mention the god's healing hand or direct application of drugs.[22] Even the appearance of the god in a dream might indicate his actual epiphany, as one account on a papyrus from Oxyrhynchos makes clear (*P. Oxy.* xi.1381, Edelstein 331). It describes a young man in the sanctuary of Asklepios at Memphis, lying ill in bed, with his mother at his side. As she sat, she saw a figure appear, taller than human size, wrapped in white cloth and holding a book in his right hand. After looking at the boy two or three times from head to foot, he disappeared. After this, the boy was cured. When his mother woke him, she did not need to tell him about the divine visit, for he had seen it in a dream.

Thus one might meet with a god by entering his sacred space. Other inscriptions found in sanctuaries record the foundation of a cult, a temple, or offerings in response to an epiphany, which might take place in a sanctuary or elsewhere. An inscription from Ephesus of the second century C.E. mentions the altars and temples dedicated to Artemis because of her conspicuous epiphanies (*enargeis epiphaneiai, SIG* ii 867). At Magnesia-on-the-Maeander, in 220 B.C.E., Artemis Leukophryne is said to have appeared to her priestess; as a result, games were founded in her honor (*SIG* ii 557). Herodotus mentions Pan's appearance to the runner Pheidippides, complaining that he had not been honored at Athens. The Athenians responded by building him a shrine under the Acropolis and founding an annual festival in his honor, with sacrifices and a torch race (6.105). Here the god's epiphany to prompt the foundation of a shrine and ritual observance is somewhat like the role given to Athena in Peisistratos' procession, where the goddess is presented as seeking to found Peisistratos' leadership in her city.

ATHENA AS POMPOS

Within this general context of divine display, Peisistratos' specific intent, of course, was to create the illusion of divine sponsorship. A close parallel for this image of divine support is the scene on Polyneikes' shield in Aeschylus' *Seven Against Thebes*. On the shield is depicted "a woman modestly leading a man, all in gold, dressed as a warrior. She says that she is *Dike,* and the inscription reads: I will bring this man home, and he will have his city and will walk in his ancestral home" (645–8).

The image on this shield reproduces an old motif of a divine guide leading a chosen man. It is a tradition seen in the *Odyssey* when Athena leads Odysseus to the palace of the Phaiakians, and it is alluded to earlier in the same work when Athena sends to Penelope an image in a dream to comfort her, telling her that Odysseus has Athena as his *pompos.*[23]

Figure 16. Athena mounting the chariot beside Herakles. Black-figure hydria by the Priam Painter. Madison, Wisconsin, Elvehjem Museum 68.14.1. (Photo courtesy of the museum.)

In Athens, the image of this goddess serving as *pompos* for a hero occurs with some frequency in sixth-century vase paintings of Athena leading Herakles in a chariot; the goal of their procession is Olympus, the ultimate home for this hero (Figure 16).[24] These vase paintings have been linked specifically to Peisistratos' procession by John Boardman, who suggests that the images were meant to allude to Peisistratos' entry into Athens and are thus political propaganda.[25] Our sources for Peisistratos' procession, however, do not make this connection explicit; there is no indication that Peisistratos dressed as Herakles.[26] It is more likely that the scene of Athena escorting Herakles simply reproduces the old tradition that attributes to the goddess of Athens the role of escort or guide for select men, of whom Herakles is the most conspicuous example.

Athena also assists a hero with closer ties to Athens, Theseus. In a vase painting of about 470 B.C.E, she is rousing Theseus from where he sleeps beside Ariadne; their union has just been consummated, as Maidenhood flits away from the peaceful bride, who is sleeping soundly with the help of Hypnos perched on her head (Figure 17).[27] The hero gestures to Athena as if remonstrating as she leans over him, but

Figure 17. Athena awakening Theseus from his bridal bed. Red-figure lekythos Near the Pan Painter. Taranto, Museo Archeologico Nazionale IG 4545. (After *ÖJh* 41 [1954]: 78–9, figs. 47 and 48.)

the ancient viewer knew the outcome just as we do. Theseus will leave Ariadne and go to Athens to assume the leadership of the city, just as Athena wants him to do.

The story of Phye and Peisistratos shows Peisistratos trying to portray himself as heir to the tradition to which this vase painting belongs.[28] As a favorite of Athena, Peisistratos steps into the shoes of such exalted heroes as Herakles and Theseus.[29] And the divine connections he manifests in this way are similar to those that gave authority to many political figures in archaic Greece, according to Plutarch.[30] In his *Life of Numa,* Plutarch suggests that we should believe the claims that Greek and Roman kings and lawgivers such as Zaleukos, Minos, Zoroaster, Numa, and Lykourgos had divine favor, since such rulers and lawgivers were the men with whom gods would most want to associate in order to teach and advise them (4.7). And if instead there is truth in the other account of these men, that since they had capricious multitudes to manage and great innovations in government to introduce they pretended to have divine sanction, which sanction was the salvation of the citizens to whom they made this pretense, then "there is no disgrace in that either" (4.8).

This passage serves as a useful corrective to modern suspicions that Peisistratos' arbitrary staging of the impersonation of Athena was impious.[31] Apparently there were many precedents for a leader persuading his people that his rule had divine support. Representing himself as Athena's candidate for ruler of Athens, Peisistratos was attempting to join the ranks of other distinguished rulers who presented their laws and reforms as the will of the gods. The Athenians' reaction to his procession indicates their understanding of this imagery.

RE-CREATING EPIPHANY

Peisistratos' success in receiving a favorable reaction from the Athenians was due not only to their understanding of the connections his processions evoked, but also to the fact that they were familiar with ritual impersonation.[32] From inscriptions as well as other literary texts we learn of many other examples of ritual impersonations of the gods.[33] Those that re-create the image of a god riding on a chariot come close indeed to the image represented by Peisistratos. There is an example in Herodotus' account of the people of Libya. One of the peoples near the coast celebrated a local goddess with a procession in which the best-looking girl was dressed in Greek armor and a Corinthian helmet, then stood on a chariot and led around the lake in a circle (4.180). Whatever was intended by the people performing this ritual, Herodotus equates their goddess with Athena, apparently seeing in this procession an attempt to imitate the Greek goddess. It seems that he is familiar with the practice of ceremonial representations of gods. Similarly, in Pausanias' description of Patrai, he mentions a festival to Artemis called the Laphria, involving a procession in which the virgin priestess of Artemis rode on a chariot drawn by deer (7.18.7). Thus Peisistratos' presentation of Phye dressed as Athena seems to make use of a pattern familiar from ritual.

What was the role of the audience present at these ritual re-creations of divinity? This question may shed light on the Athenians' reaction to Peisistratos' procession, and in an illuminating article on civic rituals in sixth-century Athens, W.R. Connor has identified a passage that suggests an answer.[34] Near the beginning of his novel, Xenophon of Ephesus describes a procession in which Anthia, the heroine of the story, dresses as Artemis to lead a band of young women in honor of the goddess. She wears a fawn skin draped over a purple chiton, a quiver hanging from one shoulder, carries a bow and javelins, and dogs follow along with her as she goes. The Ephesians often saw her in this guise, and when they did they "bowed down as if to Artemis. And this time, too, when Anthia came into view the whole crowd cried out, and there were various things said by the spectators. Some of them asserted with vehemence that she was the goddess, others that she was a replica fashioned by the goddess. But all did obeisance to her and bowed down and called her parents blessed" (1.2.7).

Comparing this passage to Peisistratos' performance, Connor suggests that in both cases it is not a question of duping the audience, but rather of their playful participation in a shared drama: "They know perfectly well this girl is a human, but they delight in her beauty and express that delight by their responses."[35] His view of the onlookers as participating in the drama rather than being manipulated by a deceptive disguise is an important advance in our understanding of this sort of ritual. As he points out, such rituals allowed for two-way communication, since the crowd's reaction appears to be uncoerced. But his description of the audience's playful attitude seems to assume that throughout these rituals the playacting is transparent, that there is a clear distinction between the human being playing the role and the deity being portrayed. This is not necessarily what the Ephesians' actions suggest. When they see this girl in costume they honor her as a goddess, as if the ritual transcends reality by the symbolic power of the procession. This must be the ideal and expected reaction to the ritual representation of a god. It suggests a blurring of the boundaries between actor and god, thus uniting mortals and gods, a goal of many rituals of worship.[36] The whole community participating in the illusion is transformed by the experience of divine presence.

TRANSCENDING TIME

To explore further the nature of the transformation of audience as well as performer, let us consider an example of symbolic transformation in religious ritual today, the divine liturgy of the Eastern Orthodox Church. Father Alexander Schmemann has described beautifully the symbolism of the liturgy, which is as a whole "a symbolic representation of the earthly life of Christ."[37] He goes on to explain, however, that there is one moment when "the symbolism disappears and is replaced by 'realism.' When dealing with the transformation of the bread and wine into the Body and Blood of Christ, the term 'symbolic' is out of order and sounds heretical." Thus inherent in the ritual are what we might call different levels of symbolism, some to be distinguished from the things they represent and some identical to them, the "realism" to which Father Schmemann refers.

As the liturgy is performed, it is difficult to distinguish just where symbolism ends and reality begins. At one point before the actual transformation of the bread and wine, the priest goes behind the altar and the choir sings the words of the angels quoted in Isaiah and Revelations. Father Schmemann explains, "The liturgical function of this mention . . . is to certify that the Church has entered its heavenly dimension, has *ascended into heaven*. It indicates that we are now at the Throne of God, where the angels eternally sing 'Holy, Holy, Holy.' "[38] And at this point, the priest is transformed. He turns to face the congregation, raises his hand, and says, "Peace be with you all," thus speaking the words of God to the church. The reading of the Gospel and the ceremony of the Eucharist follow upon this entry into heaven.

Two points in this description present parallels that are suggestive for the ancient material. The first is the role of the members of the congregation. As silent witnesses, they constitute an audience for the drama enacted before them. Nevertheless, they too experience this ascension to heaven, which the very structure of the church represents all around them.[39] The ancient rituals we have considered seem to involve the audience similarly. It is quite different in a theater, where the divisions between audience and actors are clearly laid out, and only the chorus serves as the audience for the action within the dramatic time and space; the spectators do not enter into it. In other rituals, there is no such division between audience and actors. Those who witness the spectacle are not passive receivers of the drama, but participants as well. The transformation, then, is not only of the bridal couple, or the warrior, or the person dressed as a god. In the time and space of the ritual performance, the audience, too, enters into the illusion. For example, if the bride and groom are like Hera and Zeus, then those who escort them in the procession are like the other gods at the divine wedding.[40] And the spectacle of Athena escorting Peisistratos to Athens honors not only the tyrant, but also the Athenians who witness Athena in their midst.

The second point in the liturgy that may suggest a way of understanding some ancient rituals is the nature of the transformation that brings together the worshipers and God. God does not descend from heaven to enter the community of worshipers; instead, the community is lifted up to enter the kingdom of God. This concept simply extends the separation of the group from the mundane sphere that is fundamental to most ritual occasions. The separation, in this case, is not only spatial but also temporal. Thus in the fourteenth-century *Commentary on the Divine Liturgy* by Nicholas Cabasilas, the teachings of the Orthodox faith concerning the sacrament of Holy Communion are stated as follows (32): "In the first place, that this sacrifice is not a mere figure or symbol but a true sacrifice; secondly, that it is not the bread which is sacrificed, but the very Body of Christ; *thirdly, that the Lamb of God was sacrificed once only, for all time* (emphasis mine)."[41] In leaving the world of humanity to enter the kingdom of heaven, the worshipers also leave historic time and enter into the eternal time of God.

I suggest that the ancient Greek rituals that connect mortals to heroes or gods, presenting the bride and groom as gods or heroes, or a costumed mortal as a god, do not show gods or heroes entering our world, but rather create the illusion that those witnessing the spectacle have been removed from their mundane world and have left historic time in order to experience the heroic past, the time of myth, when gods and humans mingled more freely than they do in our world. Diodorus describes explicitly such ritual re-creation of a past age in speaking of Bacchic rituals, in which he says women "act the part of the Maenads who were of old the companions of the god" (4.3.3). Also suggesting re-creation of the mythic past is the use by worshipers of names of mythic figures; we learn from Pausanias that the *korai parthenoi*, "virgin girls," who serve as priestesses at the sanctuary of the Leukippides at Sparta are called "Leukippides," "the same as the goddesses" (3.16.1).[42]

These passages suggest that in some rituals the usual boundaries between mortals and gods were transcended by effecting a reentry into the world of gods and heroes that is the subject of Greek myth. By re-creating the figures of myth in ritual performance, the assembled community could transcend the usual boundaries between mortals and gods much as in the black-figure vase paintings that link the mortal and divine spheres iconographically. Not only some ceremonies honoring the gods, but also other ritual activities such as weddings, warfare, and competition in the games seem to take place in a "heroic time" that is blatantly evoked by the mythic exempla called forth in songs or speeches associated with these activities.

It is this ritual time and space that Peisistratos effectively created with his chariot procession into Athens.

HERODOTUS AND PEISISTRATOS

The ritual precedents for a heroic illusion such as Peisistratos created suggest that he did not so much deceive the Athenians as create a heroic model that they willingly accepted.[43] Why, then, does Herodotus criticize their foolishness? Herodotus' comment is one of the many instances in which he seems to insist on his own ability to judge events by rational standards.[44] Also, he must have enjoyed this opportunity for a joke at the expense of the intellectualism of the Athenians, "said to be first of all the Greeks in wisdom (*sophia*)" (1.61), who no doubt thought of themselves in those terms, too. But he does not criticize the Athenians for their stupidity in falling for either of the other two stratagems employed by Peisistratos to establish his rule, neither of which inspire confidence in the Athenians' judgment.[45] As for rationalism, it seems to be selective. Throughout his work he accepts many manifestations of divinity, especially in the books describing the Greeks battling Persians, but also in many other contexts.[46] In his books on Egypt, for example, he mentions without comment the local legend of epiphanies of Perseus in the town of Chemmis in the district of Thebes, leaving on occasion as a sign his three-foot-long sandal (2.91). Further on in his account of Egypt, he accepts an epiphany of the sacred cow Apis when Cambyses arrived at Memphis (3.27). He reports a miraculous epiphany of Helen at Therapne without comment; at the shrine of Helen, a woman appeared, looked at the homely baby girl who had been brought there every day, stroked her head, and from that day the child grew more and more beautiful. Later, when the child had become a woman, Herodotus tells of the visit of a phantom in the form of her husband, wearing the wreath of the hero Astrabakos (6.61.2–5). He also reports that a Greek man who lived at Paios was said to have received Kastor and Polydeukes under his own roof (6.127). And he cites several incidents of epiphany during the Persian Wars, as I have already mentioned.

It is true that the epiphany of Athena staged by Peisistratos re-creates a divine appearance of greater stature than any of the others reported by Herodotus. But I think that Herodotus' rationalism is not the only reason for his comment on Peisistratos' performance, nor is it a sufficient explanation for his singling out of this particular incident. Herodotus describes Peisistratos' entry into Athens in the context of Croesus' inquiries at Athens and Sparta, gathering information as to which side was stronger so that he could make an alliance for his expanding empire. Immediately after we learn about the situation at Athens, Herodotus goes on to Sparta. In the section on Sparta he makes two general points – the government there had been put on a sound basis by Lykourgos, and the Spartans were now in command of much of the Peloponnesus. In conveying these points, Herodotus tells stories that paint the Spartans in conspicuous contrast to his account of the Athenians. This does not seem to me coincidental. Herodotus has chosen his details in order to present opposing pictures of the cities that were powerful not only at the time of Croesus' inquiry, but in his own day as well.

Herodotus begins his description of affairs at Sparta with a story about Lykourgos' rise to power. This change to good government that Lykourgos accomplished began, according to Herodotus, with his visit to the Delphic oracle, where he was greeted with an acclamation of his favored status in the eyes of Zeus and all the gods and told by the Pythia that she was inclined to believe that he himself was a god (1.65)![47] Here we have a situation opposite to that described at Athens, where Peisistratos presents himself as escorted by Athena. This contrast makes clear one result of Herodotus' emphasis on the foolishness of the performance; by insisting that the spectacle of Peisistratos' divine support was no more than folly, Herodotus draws attention to the episode's falsity. He leaves no doubt that this tyrant did *not* have divine sponsorship, despite his ultimate success in securing power in Athens.

Thus the Athenians are clearly free agents in their decision to accept the tyrant; there is no divine will or coercion at work in his entry into their city. By making clear the absence of divine sponsorship for the tyrant, Herodotus makes it very apparent that the Athenians accepted his manifestation of divine support simply because they wanted to believe in the illusion he presented to them. Their folly is simply their willingness to enter into the heroic world that Peisistratos' ruse conjures up for them. And this willingness to take on a heroic role marks them throughout Herodotus' work.

Later on in the *Histories,* Herodotus again expresses his opinion of the Athenians' judgment, while describing their reception of the proposal of Aristagoras of Miletus. Aristagoras comes to Athens hoping to persuade the Athenians to send ships to help the Ionian Greeks in their struggles with Persia. The incident presents interesting parallels and contrasts to Herodotus' description of the Athenians in Book 1. There, too, the general context is the Greeks' alliance with the East, but while in Book 1 Herodotus depicts the Athenians by describing their situation internally, in Book 5 we see them responding to an outsider's proposal for their involvement abroad. As did Croesus in Book 1, Aristagoras first goes to Sparta, the most powerful state in Greece at the time. But while in Book 1 Sparta accepts Croesus' offer, in Book 5, the Spartan king Kleomenes refuses the enticement of Eastern wealth (5.49–51). Thus Aristagoras comes to Athens. Mirroring Book 1, in which Croesus' interest in alliance prompts Herodotus' description of Peisistratos' rule, at the point of Aristagoras' arrival in Book 5 Herodotus describes the expulsion of the tyrants (5.55–65).[48] Having won freedom, Athens was now a more powerful city than it had been at the time of Croesus' inquiry. And when Aristagoras presents his arguments at Athens, he succeeds in persuading the Athenians to send ships to Ionia. We don't know which of Aristagoras' arguments persuaded them, but the last one mentioned is the plea that the Athenians defend their fellow Ionians, since Miletus was founded by Athenian settlers. Herodotus comments, "Apparently it is easier to impose upon a crowd than upon an individual, for Aristagoras, who had failed to impose upon Kleomenes, succeeded with thirty thousand Athenians" (5.97.2).[49] He goes on to state, "These ships were the beginning of trouble for both Greece and for other peoples."

Herodotus' comments here have been interpreted as an indication that the growing power of Athens has corrupted its judgment, so that we see the corrupting effect of power on a city just as it corrupts individual tyrants and kings.[50] But have things really changed at Athens? My answer would be no. The Athenians, who were so ready to see themselves as the objects of Athena's special interest that they were receptive to Peisistratos' re-creation of heroic splendor, are just as ready to take on an endeavor that the Spartans have rejected as impractical and in which, in fact, they will not succeed. But perhaps their ultimate victory in the Persian Wars stems from their ability to transcend practicality, to conceive of themselves as heroes capable of the impossible.

We have no doubt about how the Athenians will respond when they receive yet other overtures from the East, from the Persian king. They were governed by tyrants not because of slavishness but because of their heroic aspirations; they have more confidence than they should in taking on ventures that are beyond their capability; and they will never submit to the terms of a foreign despot in order to avoid the risk of battle, even against tremendous odds. They would be far more likely to take on the role of oppressor themselves, as Herodotus knew.[51]

In describing Peisistratos' entry into Athens, Herodotus draws our attention to the Athenian reaction to his performance and presents our first view of the Athenian people. To those familiar with the symbolism inherent in this pageantry, the Athenians' reaction can be understood as a willingness to enter into the heroic image presented by the man and goddess standing on the chariot. Their cooperation with Peisistratos' reenactment of a hero's entrance is the first indication in the *Histories* of their character. The Athenians' willingness to take risks and assume a hero's role sometimes leads them into difficulties, but it also leads them to free Greece from the Persian threat and become the true heroes of the Persian Wars, of whom Herodotus claims, "To say that the Athenians were the saviors of Greece would not miss the truth" (7.139.5).

NOTES

I am grateful for the advice and encouragement of Deborah Boedeker, Diskin Clay, Carol Dougherty, Leslie Kurke, Lisa Maurizio, Kurt Raaflaub, Emily Vermeule, Rev. Dr. Haralambos Vulopas, and the anonymous reviewers for Cambridge University Press.

1. Beloch 1890 argues that the Phye story grew from a battle fought near the sanctuary of Athena at Pallene. Rose 1940: 81 suggests two steps in the development of the story: first, believers in divine support for Peisistratos' "Golden Age" created a pious version that told of the actual goddess leading in the hero; later, skeptics explained this story as a fraud. Moon 1983: 101 calls the Phye incident a folktale, but does not speculate about its origin.
2. Arist. *Ath. Pol.* 14.4; Kleidemos *FGrH* 323 F 15 (= Ath. 13.609); Polyaenus *Strat.* 1.21.1.
3. Pfuhl 1900; Nilsson 1951b; Bömer 1952.
4. I have discussed the iconography of chariot processions more fully in "Godlike Men: A Discussion of the Murlo Procession Frieze," in DePuma and Penny Small forthcoming.
5. *ABV* 335.5bis; *Para* 148; *Addenda* 91.
6. For vase paintings of gods riding chariots, see Metzger 1975. Literary examples are common, e.g., Sappho 1.8–9; *Hymn. Hom. Cer.* 19; Eur. *Ion* 1528, *Tro.* 856.
7. *ABV* 138.2.
8. Boardman 1983: 28–9 argues that chariots need not recall the past, since they continued

to be used for ceremonial processions and racing, and suggests that they even had a role in battle. In sixth-century Athens, however, the complete lack of evidence makes the latter very unlikely, and it is also unlikely that Attic vase painters had in mind the military practices of the Lydians and other Easterners when they depicted hoplite warriors on a chariot. As for processions and racing, chariots used in these contexts may well have embodied a heroic image.

9. Bazant 1983; he also notes the presence in these scenes of throwing spears as opposed to the hoplite thrusting spear.

10. *ABV* 267.9; *Addenda* 69.

11. *ABV* 141.1; *Addenda* 38.

12. Pollux 19.33; Hesychius s.v. *klinis;* Photius *Lex.*1.246; Naber s.v. *zeugos hēmionikon ē boeikon* (cf. *Souda* s.v.); also Paus. 9.3.1–2. There is a fine depiction of such a cart on a lekythos by the Amasis Painter in the Metropolitan Museum, New York, 56.11.1, published by Bothmer 1960.

13. *ARV*² 1317.1; *Para* 478; *Addenda* 363; see Perdrizet 1905. On the incongruity of pillows in a chariot, see Lorimer 1903: 132 n 2.

14. Krauskopf 1977: 27–8. See also Sutton 1981: 166–8 for a useful discussion of the iconography of these scenes. I examine the subject at greater length in a forthcoming study together with J. Oakley, *The Wedding in Ancient Athens.* The absence of evidence for the actual use of the chariot in the wedding procession does not, of course, preclude the possibility that it was used occasionally; if so, its symbolic function must have been the same as in the vase paintings, to present the couple in a heroic pose.

15. Mangelsdorff 1913; Hague 1983; Seaford 1987; Contiades-Tsitsoni 1990.

16. Crotty 1982: 198–209; cf. Kleinknecht 1937: 296; Pfister 1924: 312.

17. Cf. Plut. *Quaest. conv.* 2.5.2. On the ceremonies celebrating the victor's arrival, see Slater 1984 and Kurke, Chapter 7, this volume.

18. Pfister 1924; Pax 1962; van Straten 1976; Pritchett 1979; Versnel 1987; Fox 1989.

19. Fox 1989: 164 puts it well: "Between life and literature, there was not a divide but a mutual relationship, in which the one, as so often, enhanced the other."

20. Pritchett 1979: 11–46. For a modern parallel, see Fox 1989: 121.

21. For other examples, see, e.g., Plut. *Lys.* 12.1; Paus. 4.16.5; Diod. 8.32.

22. Sources compiled in Edelstein 1945: vol. 1; their discussion, however, rationalizes far too much, in my view.

23. Else 1957: 36–7, pointing to Athena's role in *Od.* 24; Connor 1987: 43 also mentions Stein's comparison of Peisistratos' procession to Athena and Diomedes in *Il.* 5 (in his commentary on Herodotus 1.60).

24. *ABV* 333.26bis; *Para* 146; *Addenda* 90.

25. Boardman 1972; refuted by Moon 1983 and Cook 1987. In response Boardman (1989) argues cogently that the prominence of Herakles in sixth-century art attests to the choice of this hero to represent the leaders of Athens. But while Peisistratos' procession may have recalled Athena's escort of Herakles, it is not specific enough to recall that image alone, to the exclusion of other heroic processions.

26. Connor 1987: 43.

27. *ARV*² 560.5, 1659; *Para* 388; *Addenda* 259; see Simon 1954.

28. See Snodgrass 1980a: 114–15; after citing Peisistratos' performance as an example of political propaganda "blatant to the point of absurdity," he points out that such activity "could be presented as a reversion to older ways."

29. Connor 1987: 45–6 notes the description of Phye as *parabates* in *Ath. Pol.* and Kleidemos and suggests that Peisistratos might be reversing the pattern of an ancient ritual of

kingship by having Athena act in the role that a king would have taken. Since Herodotus does not mention this detail, however, it seems that he did not interpret the procession in this way.

30. For various rulers' adoption of divine costume, see Connor 1987: 45. Lavelle 1991 suggests that Peisistratos' extraordinary intelligence may have been perceived as a sign of divine patronage.

31. E.g., Moon 1983: 101.

32. Back 1883; Connor 1987: 43–5.

33. See also *SIG* ii 736, at Andania; the regulations concerning dress stipulate that "the women who must be dressed in the manner of the gods are to wear the clothing that the priests specify." At Pellene the priestess of Athena is said to have worn a helmet and carried a shield, presenting such a convincing image of the goddess that enemy forces that saw her on the city's acropolis fled (Polyaenus, *Strat.* 8.59). Burkert 1985: 97, 100, 186, mentions several other cases in which priests or priestesses resemble the god or goddess they serve, including the priest of Apollo Ismenios at Thebes (Paus. 9.10.4), the priestess of Hera at Argos (Hdt. 1.31), and the priest of Demeter in Pheneos in Arcadia (Paus. 8.15.3). The minutes of the Athenian cult group called the Iobacchoi stipulate the division of portions from the sacrifice among various officials, including not only a priest, vice-priest, arch-bacchus, and treasurer, but also Dionysus, Kore, Palaimon, Aphrodite, and Proteurhythmos, names that are to be apportioned by lot among the members (*SIG* iii 1109); we do not know what taking one of these names involved, but it seems likely that there was some kind of role playing.

34. Connor 1987: 44.

35. Connor 1987: 44.

36. This is not to overlook the demarcations between human and divine such as are drawn in the sacrificial ritual, but only to suggest that these divisions are made within the newly constituted group of gods and mortals that has been created by the ritual.

37. Schmemann 1990: 103.

38. Schmemann 1990: 107.

39. There is a concise account of the traditional arrangement of the icons in Baggley 1988: 89–95.

40. See Rösler 1980.

41. Cabasilas 1960: 81.

42. Cf. Paus. 3.13.7. On the Leukippides and their role in cult, see Calame 1977: 1.323–33. Nagy argues that the two choral leaders in Alkman 1 imitate the Leukippides (1990b: esp. 345–9).

43. On the audience's cooperation, see Connor 1987: 44, 46, 50.

44. For Herodotus' place among fifth-century thinkers, see Hunter 1982. On his penchant for rationalism, see Rose 1940.

45. Note Solon's judgment of the first time Peisistratos seized control, by cutting himself and his mules and pretending that he had been injured by an enemy and needed a bodyguard: "Peisistratos was wiser than some men and braver than others – wiser than those who did not recognize that he would install himself as tyrant and braver than those who knew but did not speak out" (*Ath. Pol.* 14.2). Herodotus expresses no opinion of this incident.

46. See Lloyd 1979: 29–32.

47. Cf. the description of Darius' ascension to power as a result of a clever trick – but to the accompaniment of lightning and a clap of thunder, a sign from heaven ensuring the god's support for his rule (3.86).

48. Here we see most clearly the connection between Herodotus' treatment of the tyranny

at Athens and his larger theme of the struggle of the Greeks against the tyranny (in a broader sense) of the Persians. On the importance of the theme of tyranny to Herodotus' work as a whole, see Lanza 1977: 33–4.

49. Translation by de Sélincourt 1954.
50. Stahl 1983.
51. See Raaflaub 1987 on the influence of the post–Persian War events of the fifth century on Herodotus' treatment of history. Herodotus does note a change in the Athenians' behavior after they gained their freedom: according to him, tyranny had kept them from realizing their potential (5.78). Their underlying character, however, endured. Cf. the Samians, 4.142–3.

CHAPTER FIVE

Hipparchos and the Rhapsodes

H. A. Shapiro

T HIS essay deals with two conspicuous and disparate features of archaic Greece, tyrants and epic poetry, at a key moment when the two intersect. It is a rare instance in which not simply is a tyrant recorded as the patron of one or another famous poet, but the tyrant seems to have played a direct role in determining the form and shape of poems as they have come down to us – and not just any poems, but the Homeric *Iliad* and *Odyssey*. I propose to bring to bear some modest iconographical evidence on this nexus of thorny problems: Who were these rhapsodes of the sixth century? What exactly did they do at the Panathenaic festival in Athens, and when did they start doing it? And what did they contribute to the shaping of our *Iliad* and *Odyssey?*

The main text related to my topic is well known, and I will present it briefly as a prologue to the evidence from vase painting. It occurs in a dialogue named *Hipparchos,* after the son of the tyrant Peisistratos and co-tyrant himself, with his brother Hippias, from the death of their father in 528. The dialogue has come down to us in the corpus of Plato; opinion nowadays generally considers it not by Plato, but by someone writing perhaps a generation after Plato's death, still well within the fourth century.[1] Though nominally a discussion of *to philokerdes* (love of profit) between Socrates and an unnamed interlocutor, the dialogue becomes, in the middle section, a kind of encomium of the enlightened tyrant Hipparchos. Here we learn, among other things, of Hipparchos' strong literary bent (a judgment confirmed by Arist. *Ath. Pol.* 18.1), manifested in the celebrated poets he brought to Athens (Anakreon and Simonides), as well as the verses he himself composed to be carved on herms set up as road signs in the Attic countryside. Judging from the two examples quoted in the dialogue (229a–b), Simonides and Anakreon had no cause to fear Hipparchos as a rival.

The section of the dialogue that particularly concerns us deals with recitations by rhapsodes at the Panathenaia:

καὶ τὰ Ὁμήρου ἔπη πρῶτος ἐκόμισεν εἰς τὴν γῆν ταυτηνί, καὶ ἠνάγκασε τοὺς ῥαψῳδοὺς Παναθηναίοις ἐξ ὑπολήψεως ἐφεξῆς αὐτὰ διιέναι, ὥσπερ νῦν ἔτι οἴδε ποιοῦσι·

He who first brought the poems of Homer to this land and compelled the rhapsodes at the Panathenaia to go through them in order, each taking up the cue, as they still do now. (228b)

Essentially the same story is told by Diogenes Laertius (1.57), only substituting Solon for Hipparchos. Modern critics tend to favor Hipparchos, not only because the author of the dialogue is much earlier and seems generally knowledgeable, but because the dual tradition seems to illustrate two well-known phenomena in Athenian historiography: Peisistratos and his sons are denied credit for anything good that happened in the sixth century, and Solon is credited with practically everything.[2]

Assuming the veracity of this testimonium about Hipparchos, we are still left with at least three unresolved questions. Did Hipparchos introduce these rhapsodic contests, or did he simply lay down new rules for an existing competition? If the latter, when did rhapsodes first compete in Athens, and what did they perform before Hipparchos' rule? Finally, did Hipparchos' activity as a kind of minister of culture begin only after his father's death in 528 (though presumably after 546, when Peisistratos finally secured his power)?[3]

I come now to the vases. But before looking specifically for rhapsodes, it is worth setting them in the wider context of the *mousikoi agōnes* that formed, alongside the athletic games, a significant part of the program at the Greater Panathenaia.[4] Indeed, it was these musical contests – and in particular the rhapsodes – that most set Athens apart from the games at the four great Panhellenic centers.[5]

A well-known fourth-century inscription lists prizes for four types of musical competition[6] – for aulodes, who sang to the accompaniment of the flute; for auletes, or lone flute players; for kitharodes, who sang while accompanying themselves on the kithara; and for kitharists, who played but did not sing. With the help of fairly abundant vase paintings we can affirm that all four contests were already on the program in the sixth century (Figures 18–20).[7] Flutists and aulodes appear a few years earlier than kithara players, that is, by the middle of the sixth century, if not slightly before. We recognize immediately the festive and colorful costume of the flutist.[8] There are two strong indicators that these scenes do indeed depict contests at the Panathenaia, and not simply concerts or informal performances. One is the *bēma,* or podium on which competitors regularly stood. The other is the shape of the vase on which many of these scenes occur, a smaller-scale imitation of the distinctive form of amphora that, filled with olive oil, was the prize in the athletic contests.[9] Victorious musicians were awarded prizes other than oil (in the fourth century, gold or silver; in the sixth, perhaps bronze tripods) – hence no official prize amphora (so designated by inscription) depicts a musical event.[10] These pseudo-Panathenaics could have been made as commemorative items for the winners, their friends, and families.[11]

Given the early date of several of the vases depicting musical contests, about 550, I think it is a reasonable inference that all four musical contests were introduced

Figure 18. Aulode and accompanist. Black-figure amphora of Panathenaic shape, ca. 550 B.C.E. London, British Museum B141. (Photo courtesy of the Trustees of the British Museum.)

Figure 19. Aulete. Black-figure amphora of Panathenaic shape, ca. 550–540 B.C.E. Austin, Texas, Archer M. Huntington Museum, University of Texas, 1980.32. (Photo courtesy of the museum.)

Figure 20. Kithara player between Panathenaic columns. Black-figure neck amphora, 540–530 B.C.E. London, British Museum B260. (Photo courtesy of the Trustees of the British Museum.)

with the major reorganization of the Panathenaia in the year 566.[12] When we turn to the rhapsodes, however, the evidence is diappointingly scarce. The most recent discussion of the subject that I know of lists only four examples,[13] and there are none that I am aware of that have been put forward by other scholars.

Of these four, the one most often cited and illustrated in discussions of rhapsodes is also the most problematical (Figures 21 and 22).[14] The date of this vase, a neck amphora in the British Museum, is not long after 500, and it is attributed to the Kleophrades Painter, perhaps the greatest master of his time. The putative rhapsode, a mature, bearded man clad in a simple but dignified himation, stands on a low *bēma*. The knotty stick he holds out could well be taken to be the *rhabdos* that some sources claim was the origin of the word "rhapsode."[15] We now know this is a *Volksetymologie* (the real derivation from *rhaptein,* one who stitches together a song),[16] but it is still quite possible that the *rhabdos* was a regular attribute of the rhapsode, a token of his itinerant career.

He is in the midst of a performance, the words spilling from his mouth: ὧδέ ποτ' ἐν Τίρυνθι (Once upon a time in Tiryns). Here lies the first problem, for

Figure 21. Aulode. Red-figure neck amphora (Side A), ca. 500–490 B.C.E. London, British Museum E270. (Photo courtesy of the Trustees of the British Museum.)

the verse is clearly not from Homer, as we should have expected of a true rhapsode.[17] Did rhapsodes in fact perform material other than the two Homeric poems? The question arises in Plato's *Ion,* and Socrates' questioning implies that they sometimes did, though in the end Ion insists that Homer is quite enough for him (531a). In any event, Plato's dialogue is more than a century later than our vase, and as I shall argue below, in the archaic period it is more likely that rhapsodes limited themselves to Homer – at least at the Panathenaia.[18]

A more troubling feature of the Kleophrades Painter's amphora is the splendid flute player on the other side. Are these two separate scenes, two events, or one, simply spread out over both sides of the vase, as was often the Kleophrades Painter's practice?[19] His colleague, the Berlin Painter, did this even more often, as on his famous amphora in New York, where the kitharode and his trainer (or perhaps a judge) are similarly separated from one another.[20] If the two sides of the London amphora form a single scene, as I believe, then our "rhapsode" is rather an aulode, for there is no indication that rhapsodes performed to musical accompaniment.[21] Again I would claim that Plato's Ion, whose skill in playing the kithara is mentioned

96

Figure 22. Flute player. Side B of Figure 21. (Photo courtesy of the Trustees of the British Museum.)

(540d–e), is not a reliable guide to the ways of the archaic rhapsode. It is true that vases of this period not infrequently combine two separate competitions, such as aulode and kitharode (Figures 23 and 24),[22] so that we might have taken the Kleophrades Painter's two performers for an aulete and a rhapsode. But the vases with two events always make it clear, through the presence of spectators, that there are two self-contained scenes, while the Kleophrades Painter's is most naturally read as one.[23]

I would prefer, then, to exclude the Kleophrades Painter's vase from the ranks of those depicting rhapsodes, even if those ranks are becoming rather thin. A slightly later vase by the Harrow Painter is also problematical.[24] There is no *rhabdos* – except that of the listener – and the arm wrapped up in the cloak of the performer is odd, for we would expect that the rhapsode used hand gesture to dramatize his recitation.[25] This man looks more like an orator, of the sort we see in fourth-century and Hellenistic sculpture (though admittedly political life is generally not a subject for Attic vase painting).

This leaves us with only two rhapsodes that are indisputable. Both are in black

97

Figure 23. Aulode and accompanist. Black-figure neck amphora (Side A), ca. 500 B.C.E. London, British Museum B188. (Photo courtesy of the Trustees of the British Museum.)

figure of the last decade of the sixth century. An amphora in Oldenburg is Panathenaic in shape – a promising start (Figure 25).[26] The performer holds a stick, as do his listeners, but the rhapsode's is distinctive, with a curved handle. He stands on a *bēma,* and there is no musical accompaniment. The scene on a pelike in Dunedin is in principle very close.[27] The shape is, of course, not Panathenaic, but black-figure pelikai show an astonishing predilection for musical subjects and others with Panathenaic associations.[28]

These two rhapsodes provide welcome confirmation of the rhapsodic competitions ascribed to Hipparchos, though they are too late in date to help clarify any of the questions concerning the origin of such contests and the role of the tyrant. At this point I would like to introduce my own candidate for the earliest known rhapsode. The vase is now in the National Gallery at Liverpool (Figures 26 and 27) and was once part of a remarkable collection, limited to Panathenaic amphoras, at Norwich Castle.[29] Its date is about 540.

Recently I illustrated a detail of Side A,[30] but the rhapsode on Side B has remained unpublished but for a tiny drawing reproduced by Eduard Gerhard in 1843 and an

Figure 24. Aulode and accompanist. Side B of Figure 23. (Photo courtesy of the Trustees of the British Museum.)

illustration in a small brochure, rather difficult of access, prepared for the Liverpool Public Museums in 1956, on the occasion of the acquisition of the Norwich Castle Panathenaic amphoras.[31]

The shape is Panathenaic, but it is not a prize amphora, rather "pseudo-Panathenaic." On the obverse, a striding Athena of Promachos type appears between two columns. Most unusually, the columns are topped not by the cocks of the prize amphoras, but by panthers. Konrad Schauenburg has demonstrated the wide variety of animals and inanimate objects (e.g., cauldrons) that may be substituted for the cocks, but this is the only instance of panthers of which I am aware.[32] In general it seems that these substitutions represent, in addition to artistic fantasy, a deliberate statement that the vase, though superficially similar, is not trying to pass itself off as a prize amphora.

The performer on the reverse is a mature man leaning on a staff. As in the two later scenes of rhapsodes, his listeners are both bearded men as well. Only the *bēma* is lacking, but this can be paralleled on several vases with musical *agōnes* (Figure 28).[33] The absence of the *bēma* has perhaps obscured the recognition of

99

Figure 25. Rhapsode. Black-figure amphora of Panathenaic shape, 520–500 B.C.E. Old-enburg, Stadtmuseum. (Photo courtesy of the museum.)

the rhapsode. Dietrich von Bothmer, for example, recently wrote of the scene, "Between the two that are seated, a third draped man leans on a stick and seems to talk to the man on the right who smells a flower."[34] But in light of the purely Panathenaic context, indicated by both the shape and the Athena and columns on Side A, it is difficult to see what else this man could be if not a rhapsode.

A small detail provides confirmation that this is an excerpt from an *agōn,* the flower in the hand of the listener at the right. It looks at first like an unarticulated blob of glaze, but comparison with many other vases reveals that it must be a flower, a regular attribute of the audience at Panathenaic musical contests and similar performances. These flowers have often been thought particularly to characterize the elegant and effete *jeunesse dorée* of early red figure.[35] But they occur earlier, and as Bothmer has already seen, the best parallel for our vase is one in the collection of the late Norbert Schimmel (recently bequeathed to the Metropolitan Museum), showing an aulodic contest.[36] As in Liverpool, there are two bearded listeners seated on *diphroi;* one holds a round object that may be a fruit, and the other sniffs a flower.

Figure 26. Athena between columns. Black-figure amphora of Panathenaic shape (Side A), ca. 540 B.C.E. Liverpool, National Gallery 56.19.18. (Photo courtesy of the museum.)

The pose of the Liverpool rhapsode is somewhat different from those of his two later colleagues. They both have head held high, in midperformance, whereas he looks down, as if at a pause, gathering himself to resume the recitation. Such pauses for dramatic effect were no doubt part of the performance, as we can infer from Plato's Ion, who describes to Socrates some of the gestures and other techniques he uses to hold the audience's attention and to heighten emotions (535c–e).[37]

Both the shape and figure style of the Liverpool amphora place it in the third quarter of the sixth century. In 1958, H. R. W. Smith suggested an attribution to the Swing Painter, which was evidently not accepted by Beazley and is not mentioned by Elke Böhr in her monograph on the painter.[38] With the help of the new Schimmel amphora and another in Geneva, Bothmer has convincingly argued for an attribution to the Princeton Painter.[39]

What, then, are the implications of this vase for the issues raised at the outset? We may conclude, first of all, with some certainty that performances by rhapsodes at the Panathenaia did take place before Hipparchos introduced the so-called Pan-

Figure 27. Rhapsode. Side B of Figure 26. (Photo courtesy of the museum.)

Figure 28. Kitharode. Black-figure pelike, ca. 500 B.C.E. Kassel, Staatliche Kunstsamm-lungen T.675. (Photo courtesy of the museum.)

athenaic rule.⁴⁰ Whether or not they were on the program from 566, along with the musicians and singers, is impossible to say on the basis of a single vase of ca. 540, but I would be inclined to think they were. Certainly the date is not unimaginably early, when we recall the famous story in Herodotus (5.67) of how Kleisthenes of Sikyon banned rhapsodic performances there during his war with Argos, about 600. There is, further, evidence that rhapsodic contests were held in the archaic period at Brauron, the region in which the family of Peisistratos was based.⁴¹

What did the rhapsodes recite before Hipparchos implemented his rule? My guess would be that they performed material from various parts of the epic cycle that were attributed, whether correctly or not, to Homer. A passage in Aelian's *Varia Historia* (13.14) on the "rhapsodes of old" (*hoi palaioi*) makes it clear that they thought of the stories not so much as parts of lengthy poems but as discrete episodes: *Aristeia tou Agamemnonos; Ta athla epi Patroklou;* and so on. As early as about 580, the Athenian vase painter Sophilos evidently knew such designations, for he used *Patroklou athla* as the title for a picture.⁴² Episodes from our *Iliad* and *Odyssey* could have been on the program, but *need* not have been.

Returning to the pseudo-Platonic *Hipparchos,* I think the key element is the *first* half of the statement: "Hipparchos first brought the Homeric poems to Athens."[43] Where did he get them? – most likely from the Homeridai on Chios.[44] When we consider that among knowledgeable fifth-century writers like Thucydides and Herodotus, there was still much confusion about who wrote which parts of the epic cycle,[45] this was perhaps the principal intent of Hipparchos' action, to establish once and for all that only these two poems, *Iliad* and *Odyssey,* were genuine works of Homer. Beyond that, the texts of each poem that Hipparchos received established the correct ordering of the many episodes that were already well known. This is not so obvious in either poem – in the *Iliad* because so much takes place in a short span of time and many battle episodes could come earlier or later without affecting the overall structure; in the *Odyssey* because of the complex flashback technique employed by the poet.

Hipparchos' Panathenaic rule thus meant both a narrowing of the repertoire of the rhapsode and more emphasis on rote memorization, with no freedom, say, to "stitch together" episodes in different ways. This reconstruction is in keeping with that advanced recently in a brilliant paper by Walter Burkert, in which he sees the rhapsode becoming increasingly professionalized in the course of the sixth century, desperately trying to turn the Homeric poems into "classics" in order to compete with the newer and more appealing musical genres of choral and monodic lyric.[46]

In addition, the evolution of rhapsodic performance suggested here is more or less consistent with the mythological repertoire of Attic vase painting in the sixth century. In the middle and third quarter of the century, there was a burst of interest in epic subjects, but it focused on a small number of favorite episodes, the kind that might have formed the subject for a single recitation: how the three goddesses came to Paris on Mt. Ida; how Odysseus' men were turned to swine by Circe, then saved by Odysseus himself; how the young prince Troilos fell victim to Achilles' ambush so that Troy might be taken; how the great city of Priam fell on that fateful night.[47] *Iliad* and *Odyssey* did not yet have the imprimatur of genuine Homer, so they got no special treatment in the choice of subject, either by rhapsodes or painters, but neither were they entirely neglected. Only from the 520s, then, in the wake of Hipparchos' activity, did many new Iliadic subjects – and a few from the *Odyssey* – enter the painters' repertoire.[48]

The historian Raphael Sealey once suggested that one motive for Hipparchos' Panathenaic rule was to counter the tendency of earlier rhapsodes to recite only a few favorite episodes, the ones that were sure-fire crowd pleasers, omitting many others.[49] According to Sealey, the new rules ensured that in the course of a three-day festival the audience would hear the entire *Iliad* and *Odyssey* in the correct order.[50] We cannot be certain that this is really what happened, but this intriguing theory is consistent with what we hear, in the dialogue named for him, of Hipparchos' almost paternalistic concern for the education and edification of the Athenians. His herms, for example, not only offered little elegiac hexameter tidbits for the moral improvement of the citizenry, but performed a useful civic function as roadmarkers.[51] His regulation of the rhapsodes may not have done much for freedom of artistic expression, but it did ensure that all Athenians got their regular dose of Homer and got it in a way they were sure to enjoy.

NOTES

1. See Leisegang 1950: 2367.

2. See Ruschenbusch 1966: 53–8. On the two traditions see also Herington 1985: 86.

3. On the vexed problem of the chronology of Peisistratos' tyrannies and exiles, I follow the reconstruction of Andrewes 1982: 400. The Battle of Pallene, and with it the establishment of Peisistratos' third and lasting period in power, occurred in 546.

4. For the athletic contests at the Panathenaia see Kyle 1987: esp. 36–9, 178–94. For the *mousikoi agōnes* there is no systematic modern study, but much useful information and good discussion in Herington 1985: esp. apps. 1–4. The most useful earlier studies are Davison 1958 supplemented by Davison 1962. The most recent discussion that touches on all the *mousikoi agōnes* is Tiverios 1989.

5. On the locations where rhapsodic contests are attested see Kannicht 1989: 40. They include Delos, Sikyon, and Epidauros, along with Athens.

6. *IG* ii–iii² 2311. On this inscription see most recently Johnston 1987.

7. Lists are given by Davison 1958: 41 and Abel 1969. I treat these scenes in detail in Shapiro 1992.

8. More complete and up-to-date lists of auletes and aulodes are given by Vos 1986.

9. On these so-called pseudo-Panathenaics see Webster 1972: 64; Böhr 1982: 18, 62 n. 112.

10. There is one apparent exception (Leningrad 17295; *ABV* 410.2), but it belongs to the early years of the Peloponnesian War, when there was no doubt a shortage of gold and silver for contest prizes.

11. See Webster 1972: 159–60.

12. Among the earliest vases are, for aulodes, a neck amphora, London B 141; *CVA* (British Museum 1) pl. 6, 1b (here Figure 18); for auletes, a neck amphora, Austin (Texas) 1980.32; *CVA* (Castle Ashby) pl. 15, 6 (here Figure 19); for kitharodes, amphora, London B 139; *CVA* (British Museum 1) pl. 5, 3 and the neck amphora London B260 (not in *ABV*) (here Figure 20).

13. Vos 1986: 121.

14. London E270; *ARV²* 183, 15.

15. See Burkert 1987: 48.

16. See most recently Nagy 1989: 7. Among earlier studies devoted to the problem see especially Patzer 1962; Tarditi 1968a. The close association of rhapsodes with agonistic contests like the Panathenaia is stressed by Else 1957.

17. See Herington 1985: 14, who notes the problem. Herington suggests that the line could come from an epic on Tydeus or his son Diomedes, who in Homer are lords of Tiryns. An alternative would be Herakles, who is closely associated with Tiryns in legend.

18. For the poets other than Homer that rhapsodes are known to have performed (though not at the Panathenaia) see Herington 1985: 174–5.

19. Cf. the neck amphora New York 13.233; *ARV²* 183, 13; Richter and Hall (1936) pls. 14–15, depicting the Struggle for the Tripod. Apollo is on one side of the vase, Herakles on the other.

20. New York 56.171.38; *ARV²* 197, 3; Beazley 1922: 72–3 and pl. 2. Cf. the amphora, also by the Berlin Painter, recently acquired by the Metropolitan Museum, New York 1985.11.5; *Recent Acquisitions* 1985–6, 9. Here too a kitharode performs on one side, while a young listener stands on the other.

21. See Burkert 1987: 48 and Herington 1985: 10 on rhapsody as "unaccompanied delivery of stichic verse." See most recently A. Ford 1988: 303: "It was the solo presentation, in public, of a poetic text without musical accompaniment."

22. E.g., the alabastron Harvard 2397; Shapiro 1989: 47 and pl. 22d–e. Cf. the pelike in Sydney (see note 33) with an aulete on one side, a kitharode on the other.

23. See Herington 1985: 14, who also argues against the interpretation of the figure as a rhapsode, but suggests rather a private performance by an amateur.

24. Louvre G 222; *ARV²* 272,7; *CVA* (Louvre 6) pl. 42, 6.

25. This is the implication of Pl. *Ion* 535c on the powerful emotional impact of the recitation on the performer himself.

26. Oldenburg, Stadtmuseum; *Oldenburger Stadtmuseum, Städtische Kunstsammlungen: Griechische Vasen und Terakotten* (1978) no. 13.

27. Dunedin E 48.226; *ABV* 386, 12; *CVA* (New Zealand 1) pl. 17. I have recently illustrated and briefly discussed this and the Oldenburg vase in Shapiro 1989: 46 and pl. 22 a–c.

28. See the catalog of black-figure pelikai in von Bothmer 1951: 42–4. About one-third of those listed have a musical element.

29. On the vases at Norwich Castle see Vermeule and von Bothmer 1959: 165.

30. Shapiro 1989: pl. 15b.

31. Gerhard 1843: pl. B, 27–8; Tankard 1956: no. 8.

32. Schauenburg 1979: 68–70.

33. E.g., the black-figure amphora of Panathenaic shape once in the Hope Collection, Manchester III H52: Tillyard 1923: pl. 5, 27; a black-figure pelike, Sydney 47.07; described by Trendall 1948: 282; another black-figure pelike, Kassel T.675; *AA* 1966, 102; here Figure 28.

34. Bothmer in Chamay and von Bothmer 1987: 65.

35. The best examples are in the work of the Andokides Painter, e.g., the amphora Louvre G1; *ARV²* 3, 2; *CVA* (Louvre 5) pl. 25, 3.

36. New York 1989.281.89; Bothmer in Chamay and von Bothmer 1987: pls. 8, 3 and 9, 1–2.

37. The head lowered in concentration also occurs in some later depictions of kitharodes, e.g., on the amphora New York 1985.11.5 (see note 20).

38. Böhr 1982.

39. Bothmer in Chamay and von Bothmer 1987: 65. It may also be relevant that the Princeton Painter elsewhere shows a keen interest in subjects related to the Panathenaia and the cult of Athena, e.g., his amphora of Panathenaic shape, New York 53.11.1; *ABV* 298.5; Shapiro 1989: pl. 14b, showing Athena Promachos between worshipers.

40. This was conjectured already, but without evidence, by Davison 1958: 39 and earlier still by Zschietschmann 1930: 57–9 and Sealey 1957: 343.

41. Hesychius, s.v. Βραυρωνίοις. The association of Peisistratos with rhapsodes at both Brauron and Athens is made by Scheliha 1987: 49, but is very tenuous. On the rhapsodes at Brauron see most recently Hamilton 1989: 460.

42. Athens NM 15499; *ABV* 39, 16; Bakir 1981: pls. 6–7.

43. This, of course, contradicts another ancient tradition (e.g., Cic. *De Or.* 3.137) that credited the elder tyrant Peisistratos with "collecting" the Homeric poems. On the "Peisistratid recension" see Davison 1955; Lesky 1978. Just when Hipparchos implemented his rule is impossible to infer from the sources, but I would agree with Johansen 1967: 238, that it was probably ca. 520.

44. See Burkert 1987: 49.

45. E.g., Herodotus (4.32) accepted, with some hesitation, that Homer wrote the *Epigonoi*, but rejected Homer's authorship of the *Kypria* (2.117). Thucydides (3.104) accepted the *Hymn to Apollo* as a genuine work of Homer.

46. Burkert 1987. For another view of the problem of the rhapsode's creativity or lack of

it see Gentili 1988: 6–18. For the notion that a skilled rhapsode at the Panathenaia might be responsible for verses later recognized as interpolations see Kirk 1985: 207.

47. On these subjects in vase painting see Schefold 1978: esp. 184–8 (Judgment of Paris); 266–71 (Circe); 203–8 (Troilos); 254–60 (Iliupersis).

48. Johansen 1967: 225–6 shows that the early red-figure painter Oltos was a major innovator, introducing new *Iliad* scenes to vase painting in the years ca. 520–500. Johansen, too, saw the rhapsodic contests introduced by Hipparchos as the crucial influence on the vase painters, but he assumed that such contests did not exist before the late 520s.

49. Sealey 1957. See also Scheliha 1987: 48.

50. Burkert 1987: 50 doubts that the poems were performed in their entirety.

51. On the herms see Shapiro 1989: 125–6.

CHAPTER SIX

The Seven Sages as Performers of Wisdom

Richard P. Martin

NATURE, culture, gender, myth, East, West, truth – the degree to which these concepts are not transcendent universals but are socially constructed has finally hit us. Cultural anthropology will mold the shape of classical studies for this generation. This is an exciting but also difficult situation: to be fully and honestly philologists, we must now learn our Geertz along with Greek, absorb Lienhardt as well as Latin, undertake ethnography after epigraphy. It is with the help of such comparative studies that this essay examines just one aspect of a particular and complex Greek construction, the notion of ''wisdom.''

One way to get a clearer view of this concept in any society is to ask informants, ''Who is called wise?'' Had the question been put to a Greek in classical times, he or she would probably and properly have replied: ''The Wise Men.'' The answer is so simple indeed that most investigators of early Greek philosophy or society skip right over it. What can these ''sages'' (*sophoi*), usually numbered seven, these figments of folklore and garbled history, possibly tell us about the influential notion of ''wisdom'' as we see it articulated in early Greek culture? At best, they seem to copy the strategies of Odysseus, Palamedes, Sisyphus, and other traditional masters of ''cunning intelligence.'' At worst, their exploits come off sounding like bits out of the late antique joke book *Philogelos*. What makes them different from these creatures of myth or humorous fiction? What truth can we hope to extract from their stories?[1]

My preliminary answer is that we will not discover the positivist's dream of a ''historical'' occurrence, ''wie es eigentlich gewesen ist,'' what ''really'' went on. What we *can* find is the truth of historical *representations*. We might glimpse the way in which the Greeks themselves thought things happened and pictured to themselves the ideal by which they then judged the real. The method I am using, if applied to U.S. culture, would be equivalent to analyzing what use people have made of, say, the idealized Abraham Lincoln – from party politics to pennies, toymaking to car selling. I submit that there are interpretable cultural values embedded in the ''Lincoln tradition.'' In the same way, there are interpretable aspects of the Seven Sages wisdom tradition. To be sure, the traditions about the masters of wisdom make questionable use of historical facts and political programs, and mine the Greek poetic heritage as well as religious propaganda for material, all of which are then projected onto the figure of the *sophos*. But a sufficiently informed angle on such a rich and neglected store of material can tell us about the mentality of an ancient society. It may even suggest hitherto unnoticed ways in which some institutions in that society came to take their well-known shape. A workable combination of historical and structuralist analyses, avoiding the extremes of Lévi-Straussian abstraction without falling prey to the dangers of positivism, seems to me the best starting point for this sort of project.[2]

To most the names of four or five of the Seven Sages of Greece are familiar. In fact, the chances of naming seven are actually better than one might think. The accumulation of lists that survive from antiquity offers at least seventeen names of people who qualify for inclusion in a list of the "original" seven. Leophantus, son of Gorgiadas, Epimenides the Cretan, Anacharsis the Scythian, Myson, Pythagoras, Pherekydes, Lasos of Hermione, Aristodemos, Pamphylos, Akousilaos, son of Kabas (or Skabras) of Argos – these characters pass in and out of the line-ups like the names of young right-handers brought up for a stint from the farm team. Then there are the names one can rely on season after season: the sages Solon, Thales, Pittakos, Bias, Chilon, Kleoboulos, and Periander.[3]

Rather than argue for a certain list to the exclusion of others, I would like to review some of the traditions that come down to us concerning the most frequently named wise men. The information comes from a variety of sources, from Hipponax through Stobaeus, but most of it can be found in the longest and most coherent collection, Book I of Diogenes Laertius. This industrious compiler, who cites the names of two hundred authors and three hundred books he used, probably lived in the third century C.E. – more than eight hundred years after the era of the Seven Sages he discusses. But before dismissing the doxographer out of hand, we should realize that Diogenes merits some faith, precisely because he *is* such an unimaginative hack. He borrows at will from writers who borrowed from others, so that his information in many cases goes back to the much more scholarly productions of the Hellenistic period, or even to logographers of the fourth or fifth century B.C.E. – in other words, he has a claim to know valid old traditions along with much other miscellaneous information. We can orient ourselves, at least, using his list.[4]

Diogenes begins with Thales of Miletus, whose traditional dates are from approximately 624 to 545 B.C.E. In the view of Aristotle, two centuries later, Thales was the founder of Ionian natural philosophy (*Metaph.* 983b21). His opinions – among them that all is made of water, and that the earth is like a piece of wood swimming on water – are often cited as evidence for his scientific bent. It is worth recalling, however, that from a quite early period, in the fifth century at least, he also had a reputation as the original absent-minded professor.[5] Diogenes Laertius tells that

> once, when he was taken out of doors by an old woman in order that he
> might observe the stars, he fell into a ditch, and his cry for help drew from
> the old woman the retort, "How can you expect to know all about the heavens,

Thales, when you cannot even see what is just before your feet?'' (Diog. Laert. 1.34; all translations from Hicks 1925)

By some accounts Thales was the first to study astronomy, the first to predict eclipses of the sun and to fix the solstices, to maintain the immortality of the soul, to determine the sun's course from solstice to solstice, and ''according to some the first to declare the size of the sun to be one seven hundred and twentieth part of the solar circle, and the size of the moon to be the same fraction of the lunar circle. He was the first to give the last day of the month the name of Thirtieth, and the first, some say, to discuss physical problems'' (Diog. Laert. 1.23–4).[6]

According to Diogenes, some authorities said that he married and had a son Kybisthos; others that he remained unmarried and adopted his sister's son and that when he was asked why he had no children of his own he replied ''because he loved children.'' The story is told that, when his mother tried to force him to marry, he objected that it was too soon, and when she pressed him again later in life, he said that it was too late (Diog. Laert. 1.26).

I have quoted Diogenes at some length here to give you an idea of the hodgepodge he writes. We can turn, more briefly, to the second sage. Again, we are meant to think of all seven as contemporaries. It has to be that way if we follow several stories I shall discuss a bit later.

Solon, known primarily to history as a lawmaker and reformer, was chief archon of Athens in 594 B.C.E. This creates havoc with chronology in Herodotus, as is well known. It is highly unlikely that Solon ever met Croesus. Solon is supposed to have died in Cyprus at the age of eighty. He is credited – as are others – with the apothegm *Mēden agan* – ''nothing in excess.''[7]

More obscure is the figure of Chilon, son of Damagetas, a Spartan who served as ephor in 565. Chilon was an old man when Aesop the fable writer was in his prime, we are told – not much help for chronology. According to one source, his death took place at Pisa, just after he had congratulated his son on an Olympic victory in boxing. Diogenes Laertius says, ''It was due to excess of joy coupled with the weakness of a man stricken in years. And all present [at the Olympic games] joined in the funeral procession'' (1.72).[8]

Number four in our list, Pittakos, was a native of Mytilene. He supposedly helped the brothers of the poet Alkaios overthrow Melanchros, tyrant of Lesbos. He lived from about 650 to 570. For ten years he served as *aisymnētēs* – a term we should perhaps translate as ''public arbitrator.''[9]

Bias, the son of Teutames, our fifth sage, was born at Priene, not far from Miletus in Ionia. Some said he came from a wealthy family, others that he was a laborer in a wealthy man's house. He was best known for arguing legal cases, so much so that he died with his boots on. It is worth quoting Diogenes here:

> This was the manner of his death. He had been pleading in defence of some client in spite of his great age. When he had finished speaking, he reclined his head on his grandson's bosom. The opposing counsel made a speech, the judges voted and gave their verdict in favour of the client of Bias, who, when the court rose, was found dead in his grandson's arms. The city gave him a magnificent funeral. (Diog. Laert. 1.83–4)[10]

There are other intriguing tidbits about Bias. He said he would rather decide a dispute between two of his enemies than between two of his friends; for in the latter case he would be certain to make one of his friends his enemy, but in the former case he would make one of his enemies his friend. Asked what occupation gives a man most pleasure, he replied, "Making money." His favorite apothegm is "Most men are bad" – perhaps another gem from his courtroom experience (Diog. Laert. 1.87).

Kleoboulos came from Lindus in the island of Rhodes (and thus was yet another sage from the eastern Aegean). Some say that he traced his descent back to Herakles, that he was distinguished for strength and beauty and was acquainted with Egyptian philosophy. He had a daughter, Kleobuline, charmingly portrayed in Plutarch (*Mor.* 148c), who was known for posing riddles in hexameters. His apothegm was "Moderation is best" (Diog. Laert. 1.89–91).[11]

Sage number seven, Periander, was tyrant of Corinth from 625 to 585 B.C.E. The family traced its descent back to Herakles as well. Through his wife's family (also involved in tyranny) he had connections with absolute rulers in most of the central Peloponnese. The story went that "he killed his wife by throwing a footstool at her when he was angry, or by a kick, when she was pregnant, having been egged on by the slanderous tales of concubines whom he afterwards burnt alive." When the son whose name was Lykophron grieved for his mother, Periander banished him to Corcyra. Later, as an old man, he sent for the son, but the Corcyraeans put him to death before he could set sail. Enraged at this, Periander dispatched the sons of the Corcyraeans to the Lydian king Alyattes to make eunuchs of them, but when the ship touched at Samos, they took sanctuary in the temple of Hera and were saved by the Samians. Periander lost heart and died at the age of eighty (Diog. Laert. 1.94–5).

The sort of activities that mark Periander's career come as something of a shock after the mildly intellectual pursuits of his fellow sages in the traditional tales. It is not surprising that even the ancients felt this. Some scholars in antiquity distinguished two Perianders, one a tyrant, the other a sage. Neanthes of Kyzikos said the two Perianders were near relations. Aristotle (according to Diogenes) maintained that the Corinthian Periander was the sage, while Plato denied this. Perhaps not unfittingly, Periander's apothegm was *Meletē to pan* – "Practice makes perfect" (Diog. Laert. 1.98–9).[12]

To round out the picture of the sages that we get from ancient traditions, we should include a few figures whose names come up in one or another list of the seven less often but still more than once. Anacharsis the Scythian was said to be brother of the king of Scythia. His mother was a Greek, and for that reason he spoke both languages, the sources say. He wrote on the institutions of the Greeks and the Scythians, dealing with simplicity of life and military affairs. Coincidentally, he was a houseguest of Solon in Athens. Again, Diogenes offers the pithiest version:

After a while Anacharsis returned to Scythia, where, owing to his enthusiasm for everything Greek, he was supposed to be subverting the national institutions, and was killed by his brother while they were out hunting together. When struck by the arrow he exclaimed, "My reputation carried me safe through Greece, but the envy it excited at home has been my ruin." In some accounts it is said that he was slain while performing Greek rites.

According to some he was the inventor of the anchor and the potter's wheel (Diog. Laert. 1.101–2).[13]

Anacharsis was an inveterate visitor. The next less commonly cited sage, Myson, once received the Scythian. Myson lived in Chen – a town that might have been in any one of half a dozen different regions, as far as ancient scholars could make out. His father was said to be a tyrant. We are told that, when Anacharsis inquired if there was anyone wiser than himself, the Pythian priestess named Myson. His curiosity aroused, Anacharsis went to the village in summertime, found Myson fitting a share to a plough, and said, "Myson, this is not the season for the plough." "It *is* just the time to repair it" was the reply (Diog. Laert. 1.106–7). Plato substituted Myson for the despicable Periander in his list of the Seven Sages (*Prt.* 343a).[14]

Of the others on the lists that Diogenes knows, I will discuss Epimenides when the time comes. It is clear that much pushing and shoving of favorite sons, old enemies, and politically or philosophically correct names has shaped these sage lists over centuries. The historian perhaps dreams of finding the "right" list, the earliest notation that will enable us to identify an exclusive set of Seven Sages. It could be that an early document will yet appear, a list contemporary with the very sages it purports to canonize. After all, it was only in October 1966 that French archaeologists discovered at Ai-Khanum in Afghanistan, site of an ancient Greco-Bactrian city, an important missing piece of the sages puzzle: a poetic inscription on a stele base which confirms that a list of 147 sayings of the Seven Sages, a list known up until then only from very late literary sources such as the Byzantine scholar Stobaeus, was extant in the third century B.C.E. and purported to be an exact copy, by the Peripatetic Klearchos of Soli, of a list inscribed in Apollo's temple at Delphi.[15] Of course, I still wonder what we would then do if an "authoritative" list showed up. In a way, the project I am engaged in is to take what I see as the next step even in the absence of such a list. That is, I want to know *why* one is considered a sage, not just who are the sages. And I think I can do this on the basis of the evidence we have.

But this notion faces stiff resistance. I am thinking especially of the most recent full-scale examination of the question of the sages. In a monograph published in 1985, on the sages and early Greek chronology, the German historian Detlev Fehling claims to have shown conclusively that the Seven Sages never existed as a group even in oral traditions. Fehling asserts that Plato in the fourth century B.C.E. invented the whole idea and wrote about it for the first time in the *Protagoras*. Plato, argues Fehling, never lets on that he is inventing the notion, because that is the last thing Plato wants to do when he makes things up. When referring to Solon as one of the Seven Sages in his dialogue the *Timaeus*, Plato is citing his own invention, again without acknowledging it – so Fehling says. He has to concede that we have the names of most of the so-called Seven Sages attested in literature from the sixth century on, long before Plato. But, he says, these were simply that – names of "wise men" figures cited randomly, without any indication that they were members of a canonical set in the early Greek mind. He cites the disparate activities of the sage figures – from democratic reformer to tyrant, scientist to misanthrope – in order to suggest that Plato was yoking together an odd assortment of fellows he had come to know about by reading Herodotus and early poetry.[16]

Now the larger question raised by Fehling's work is important for anyone occupied with literary or historical studies. Are we entitled to believe that certain institutions or conventions existed before the first explicit mention is made of them in the documents we have? Can we extrapolate from the evidence available to us? Can we reconstruct backward? Comparative linguists would immediately say yes. But we might want to be cautious in taking linguistics as our model. Traditional tales do not have the same arbitrary nature as the linguistic sign; the possibilities for borrowing or the intrusion of universals are increased. Rather than appealing to "distinctive features," I will take a homier analogy to show in what follows that certain traits, certain recurring themes, in the stories of the sages allow us to extrapolate and to reconstruct a world in which the existence of a *group* of Seven Sages, long before Plato's era, makes good sense. Consider the composite sketches of criminals made by police artists, constructed from distinct bits and pieces – an eyebrow like this, a chin like that – as remembered perhaps indistinctly by the victim. I have combed through the sages' dossiers to find features that recur – I will not call them "motifemes" or anything more technical, since I am not promoting any one type of narratological analysis. I will call them "features," then – three of which stand out. First, the sages are poets; second, they are involved in politics; and, third, they are performers. After a brief survey of each feature, I will attempt to show what picture emerges from their combination.

First let us consider poetry. We read in Diogenes that Thales wrote an inscription on a gold cup that he dedicated to the god Apollo at Didyma in Ionia. Diogenes got his information from Callimachus, a fairly reliable Hellenistic source. Of course, the information comes to us in a Callimachean, poetic version (from the first *Iamb*). It is the Alexandrian, not the Milesian, who wrote:

Θάλης με τῷ μεδεῦντι Νείλεω δήμου
δίδωσι τοῦτο δὶς λαβὼν ἀριστῆον. (Diog. Laert. 1.29)

Thales gives me to the ruler of the people of Neleus, having gotten this prize twice.

But Thales is at least *represented* as having dedicated an object with a poetic inscription, of a type elsewhere attested in verse.[17] Another representation of this sage as writer follows from the attribution of the *Nautical Astrology* (Ναυτικὴ ἀστρολογία) to Thales.[18] No fragments survive; the title seems to indicate this was a poem resembling that attributed to Hesiod.[19] Thales' writings are said by one Lobon of Argos (third century B.C.E.) to have run to some two hundred lines – clearly he represented them as poetic. Diogenes quotes a *skolion*, one of the "songs still sung" (ᾀδομένων) attributed to Thales: "Many words do not declare an understanding heart. Seek one sole wisdom. Choose one sole good. For thou wilt check the tongues of chatterers prating without end" (Diog. Laert. 1.35).

Theodor Bergk printed these verses, and those attributed in Diogenes to other sages, under the individuals' names; at the other extreme, Fehling thinks Diogenes Laertius made up not only the verses but even the character "Lobon." Wilamowitz believed they came from a lost *Septem Sapientium Convivium* of the fifth century B.C.E., an opinion reported by Hugh Lloyd-Jones and Peter Parsons, who, however, remark, "The skolia appear redolent of the Hellenistic age," and assign them to the mysterious Lobon himself (*Supp. Hell.* nos. 521–6). West opts for a lost fourth-century source.[20] I see nothing in the actual diction of Thales' *skolion* or the others to distinguish these from such classical examples as *PMG* 911–12 (from Ar. *Vesp.* 1225–6, 1239–47):[21]

οὐδεὶς πώποτ' ἀνὴρ ἔγεντ' 'Αθήναις (*PMG* 911)

There was never a man in Athens

οὐκ ἔστιν ἀλωπεκίζειν
οὐδ' ἀμφοτέροισι γίγνεσθαι φίλον. (*PMG* 912a)

It's not good to play the fox, nor to be a friend to both sides.

χρήματα καὶ βίαν Κλειταγόρᾳ τε κἀμοὶ μετὰ Θετταλῶν.
(*PMG* 912b)

O the money and the power of Kleitagora and myself among the Thessalians.

Forgery is not the issue here; no matter who wrote the verses, we must admit that a number of sources took pains to *portray* Thales (and the others) as a poet.

Solon's poetry – or again, what is said to be his – survives, mostly by quotation in Plutarch and Aristotle.[22] It is worth noting that Solon also played the part of poetic critic. He criticized the verses of the poet Mimnermos, which praised death at sixty, and ordered instead: "Sing like this: may an 80-year-old fate take me." In all, Solon is said to have written more than five thousand lines of verse (Diog. Laert. 1.61).

The more obscure sages also get credited by Diogenes with having written poetry. Even though we do not have the remains of this verse, it is worth noting that Anaximenes (Diog. Laert. 1.40) had already observed that all the sages applied themselves to composing poetry.[23] Chilon wrote a poem in elegiac meter about two hundred lines long; perhaps it was in this that he declared that "the excellence of a man is to divine the future so far as it can be grasped" (Diog. Laert. 1.68). Pittakos wrote songs, some of which Diogenes quotes. Recall, also, that one of his sayings, perhaps from a poem, "It is hard to be good," was incorporated into another poem by the fifth-century writer Simonides (*PMG* 542). It is the discussion of what this saying means that prompts Plato's famous mention of the Seven Sages in the *Protagoras*.

Pittakos, we are told, also wrote six hundred lines in elegiac couplets, all lost, and a prose work, *On Laws*, for the use of the citizens (Diog. Laert. 1.78). Bias wrote a poem of two thousand lines on Ionia and the manner of rendering it prosperous. Kleoboulos was the author of thousands of lines of songs and riddles. Diogenes quotes several, including the inscription on the tomb of Midas:

χαλκῆ παρθένος εἰμί, Μίδα δ' ἐπὶ σήματι κεῖμαι.
ἔστ' ἂν ὕδωρ τε νάῃ καὶ δένδρεα μακρὰ τεθήλῃ,
ἠέλιός τ' ἀνιὼν λάμπῃ, λαμπρά τε σελήνη,
καὶ ποταμοί γε ῥέωσιν, ἀνακλύζῃ δὲ θάλασσα,
αὐτοῦ τῇδε μένουσα πολυκλαύτῳ ἐπὶ τύμβῳ,
ἀγγελέω παριοῦσι, Μίδας ὅτι τῇδε τέθαπται.

(Diog. Laert. 1.89–90)

I am a maiden of bronze and I rest upon Midas' tomb.
So long as water shall flow and tall trees grow, and the
sun and the bright moon, and rivers shall run and the sea
wash the shore, here abiding on his tear-sprinkled tomb
I shall tell the passers-by – Midas is buried here.

On the grounds of poetic diction as also from its archaic mode of direct address to the passerby, we can place this epitaph squarely in the sixth century.[24] Again, the slightly later poet Simonides knew and criticized this poem of a sage:

Who, if he trusts his wits, will praise Kleoboulos the dweller of Lindos for opposing the strength of a column to everflowing rivers, the flowers of spring, the flame of the sun, and the golden moon and the eddies of the sea? But all things fall short of the might of the gods; even mortal hands break marble in pieces; this is a fool's devising.[25]

We might not expect that the bloodthirsty Periander would indulge in verse composition. But he is represented as writing a didactic poem (*hypothēkai*) of two thousand lines. Unfortunately, this poem, required reading for would-be despots, is lost.[26] Finally, Anacharsis is said to have written "on the institutions of the Greeks and the Scythians, dealing with simplicity of life and military matters, a poem of 800 lines" (Diog. Laert. 1.101). Notice that only the mysterious Myson of Chen is not said to have composed verses.

When we turn to the second feature, involvement in politics, a similar scatter pattern appears. Five sages have this trait. Diogenes tells us that Thales advised the Milesians not to ally themselves with Croesus, the king of Lydia, and that the sage took part in politics before turning to the study of nature (Diog. Laert. 1.29, 1.23). He cites another source, Heraklides, who says that Thales kept aloof from politics (1.25); a third says that he lived with the tyrant of Miletus, Thrasyboulos (1.27). I shall return to this complex picture later. To continue with the dossier – Solon was preeminently political. The story goes that the Athenians would have gladly had him as tyrant but he refused (Diog. Laert. 1.49). Like Solon, Pittakos laid down his office after a period of successful political organizing that included ordering the Mytilenean constitution.[27] Chilon, as ephor, was involved in the political structure of Sparta.[28] Periander was a tyrant. Bias is remembered by Herodotus as the one who proposed that Ionians band together and emigrate to Sardinia. Thales also proposed Ionian federation at the Panionion, Herodotus notes (1.170).

It is the third feature, the sages as performers, which applies to all the characters I have mentioned thus far. By performance, I mean a public enactment, about important matters, in word or gesture, employing conventions and open to scrutiny and criticism, especially criticism of style. Performance can include what we call art. But as can be shown by the ethnographic record, it can also include such things as formalized greetings exchanged by chieftains, rituals, insult duels, and the recitation of genealogies. Some megaperformances involve several of these smaller types.[29]

This definition of performance can be found in the work of social anthropologists and sociolinguists. I am thinking especially of the work done by Richard Bauman and Michael Herzfeld, going back, on one hand, to the sociology of Erving Goffman and, on the other, to such diverse sources as Edward Sapir, William Labov, and Roman Jakobson.[30] With this social definition in mind, let us survey the traditional evidence about the sages. I draw attention first to the stories of *nonverbal* actions that "say" a great deal to an audience. Some of these read like the stories from Japanese literature about Zen masters – they provide a flash of illumination, if not *satori*. Others sound like clever ploys that demonstrate a point as they display the sage's sagacity. Thus Thales, in order to show how easy it is to grow rich, and foreseeing that it would be a good season for olives, rented all the oil mills and so amassed a fortune, we are told (Arist. *Pol.* 1259a6).[31] What might be read in later times as "engineering" feats can just as easily be in the realm of such clever demonstrations: Thales undertook to take Croesus across the Halys without building a bridge, by diverting the river, it is said (Hdt. 1.75). Notice that the performing sages often have a high-status audience, whether Greek or barbarian. Solon the Athenian played more to the democratic audience.

> Lest it should be thought that he had acquired Salamis by force only and not of right, he opened certain graves and showed that the dead were buried with their faces to the east, as was the custom of burial among the Athenians; further, that the tombs themselves faced the east, and that the inscriptions graven upon them named the deceased by their demes, which is a style peculiar to Athens. (Diog. Laert. 1.48)

We might call this deed that Diogenes records protoarchaeology; but it resembles silent rhetoric much more. It is an action that makes a point and proves the actor right.

Chilon was reported to have said in his old age that he was not aware of having ever broken the law, but conceded that once, in the case of a friend, he himself pronounced sentence, then persuaded his colleague to acquit the accused in order to maintain the law and yet not lose his friend (Diog. Laert. 1.71). Here the story shows the sage as a hypocrite, I suppose. Or, putting it more neutrally, as a superb actor (*hypokrites*). Pittakos was also clever in this mode of concealment. In a war between Mytilene and Athens he had the chief command on the one side, and Phrynon, who had won an Olympic victory in the pankration, commanded the Athenians. Pittakos agreed to meet him in single combat; with a net that he had concealed beneath his shield he entangled Phrynon, killed him, and recovered the territory (Diog. Laert. 1.74).

Another memorable gesture, barely verbal, occurs in the story in which a stranger from Atarneus in Mysia asked Pittakos whether he should marry a woman of his own status or one higher. The sage pointed with his staff to boys playing a game with tops, saying, "These will tell you all." On coming closer and hearing the boys shout, "Keep to your own path," the stranger divined that he should take the humbler bride (Callim. *Epigr.* 1). Similarly, it was told that, while Alyattes was besieging Priene, Bias fattened two mules and drove them into the camp, and that the king, when he saw them, was amazed that the good condition of the citizens extended to their beasts of burden. He decided to make peace and sent a messenger. Bias then piled up heaps of sand with a layer of corn on the top and showed them to the man. Confronted with this evidence of endless prosperity Alyattes made a treaty with the people of Priene (Diog. Laert. 1.83–4).

Periander of Corinth appears in the story in Herodotus that tells of a masterful example of the silent way of teaching. In Herodotus, he sends a messenger to the tyrant Thrasyboulos of Miletus to learn about governing. As Periander's messenger walked with the Milesian tyrant through a field, Thrasyboulos kept lopping off the heads of the tallest stalks of wheat, explaining nothing. But Periander, on being told of this odd behavior later, knew at once what it signified and proceeded to execute all the leading citizens. In this story, then, Periander emerges as the ideal audience for sage performances, a role on the opposite end of the spectrum.[32] Perhaps his cleverest personal performance, however, was his prearranged murder. There is a story that he did not wish the place where he was buried to be known, and so ordered two young men to go out at night by a certain road, which he pointed out to them; they were to kill the man they met and bury him. Then Periander ordered four more to go in pursuit of the two, kill them and bury them; finally, he dispatched a larger number in pursuit of the four. Having taken these measures, he himself went to meet the first pair and was slain (Diog. Laert. 1.96). Quite a grand finale.

Alongside the nonverbal performances of the sages are the more familiar things they said. I will not go through the long list of sayings of the sages. Let me point out simply that the context of these sayings usually involves a combination of action and utterance. We see this concern to enact words and deeds embodied in the content of the sages' remarks. Thus when the tyrant Peisistratos at Athens was already established in power, Solon, unable to move the people against him, piled his arms in front of the generals' quarters and exclaimed, "My country, I have served thee with my word and sword!" Having said this, he sailed to Egypt and to Cyprus (Diog. Laert. 1.50). According to another tradition, the son of Pittakos was killed by a smith with a blow from an ax while having his hair cut. When the people of Kyme sent the murderer to Pittakos, he, on learning the story, set him free and declared, "It is better to pardon now than to repent later." Notice that the saying can stand on its own, but the context gives it pungency and real point: Pittakos is no fool. Other stories of the sages are often stripped down to the bare verbal framework, with the articulate and nimble tongue of the wise man highlighted as the star performer. For instance, Thales, we are told, held that there was no difference between life and death. "Why then," said one, "do you not die?" "Because," said he, "there is no difference" (Diog. Laert. 1.35). Here I must point out that this verbal skill is part and parcel of the sages' roles as poetic performers; or to put it another way, the functions of the wise men as poets and as actors come together in their production of proverbial sayings. The comparatist Roman Jakobson once remarked that proverbs and sayings were "the largest coded unit occurring in our speech and at the same time the shortest poetic compositions." But, he stressed, they *are* pieces of verbal art.[33] The work of ethnographers in the past few decades has confirmed the view that proverbs are actually "performed" in traditional cultures. In his study of proverb use in New Mexican Spanish communities, Charles Briggs notes that the proverbs are framed by narratives, themselves artful performances, then foregrounded by citation devices ("Here's what he said . . . '') and carefully shaped and applied to the situation at hand. Like the oral art of epic verse making, proverbs are thus completely traditional and yet always innovated. They are embedded in situations in which the social use of artful speech and metaphor becomes a powerful tool for influencing events. Indeed, it is on metaphor that the issue hinges; for this can be either a verbal or nonverbal device, or both. It is at the heart of a poetics of performance.[34]

It is interesting in this regard that Bias, or Pittakos – Herodotus is unsure – advises Croesus not in direct terms, but by making a powerful metaphor, saying that the Greek islanders were raising "ten thousand horse" to attack Sardis. Croesus assumes that horses are horses; surely he will lick their cavalry, he says. But, of course, Bias means ships. When the truth sinks in, Croesus reacts with pleasure to the *performance* of the sage's wisdom (*epilogos*, Hdt. 1.27).[35]

Even without explicit "performance" factors mentioned, one can hear in the sages' sayings the poetic turn. Take Solon's "Speech is the mirror of action" (again, concerned with words and deeds); in another saying, Solon compared laws to spiders' webs, which stand firm when any light and yielding object falls upon them, while a larger thing breaks through them (as Diogenes explains). Secrecy Solon called the "seal of speech," and occasion the "seal of secrecy" (Diog. Laert. 1.58). (The latter, I believe, points specifically to the conditions of oral performance; it means, "You have to be there." Even if the "text" is transmitted, without knowledge of the occasion we cannot interpret it.) Solon also used to say that those who had influence with tyrants were like the pebbles employed in calculations; for "as each of the pebbles represented now a large and now a small number, so the tyrants would treat each one of those about them at one time as great, at another as of no account" (Diog. Laert. 1.59). Such proverbs can function as kernels of full-blown narratives.[36] They can be the kernels of dramatic performances as well. We can imagine Solon actually illustrating his pebble metaphor with rocks on the ground – or even just moving the pebbles, silently (like Thrasyboulos cutting the corn).

Given the emphasis on verbal skill, it is not surprising to find sayings that tell one how to behave verbally. Chilon, who had a style of speaking *named after him*, advised about speech acts, "Do not use threats against any one; for that is womanish" and, about speaking style, "Gesticulation in speaking should be avoided as a mark of insanity" (Diog. Laert. 1.70).

So outspoken was Anacharsis that he furnished occasion for a proverb, "To talk like a Scythian" (Diog. Laert. 1.101). Kleoboulos urged that one not laugh when other people were being bantered about. (This may have been hard to do in the male-symposium context that seems to have extended to many speaking situations in Greek social life.) The obscure sage Myson appears to have come up with the answer to the dilemma, if that is what the following story means: he was seen in Lakedaimon laughing to himself in a lonely spot, and when someone suddenly appeared and asked him why he was laughing when no one was near, he replied, "That is just the reason" (Diog. Laert. 1.108).

It is high time to put our composite sketch together and see what the sage resembles. One might say that our sages look most like early poets, but many archaic poets – Mimnermos, Kallinos, Archilochos – are never named as one of the sages. Then again, one could say that the sages were practical men, political advisers or tyrants, who had a flair for composing poetry. This neglects one aspect of the traditions – that their poetic productions are so wrapped up with their practical lives; Solon is no Gladstone or Disraeli. The real tip-off, I suggest, comes in the recurrent motif of the sages' "performances," whether verbal or gestural or both. Solon, again, provides a nice summing up: he performed his poem on Salamis while feigning madness (to avoid prosecution) in the assembly of the Athenians (Diog. Laert. 1.47). Poet, politician, and performer are one thing at one and the same time. Now we might think that to reconstruct all the sages on this model would be to generalize dangerously from one example. But there are two bodies of evidence to confirm that this composite picture of the sages as public, political, poetic performers has a basis in reality.

First, the evidence in a wide range of ethnographic literature indicates that in preliterate, traditional societies, the advising and decision making at top levels – by elders and the politically important – are done in an elaborate, ritualized context. A good example in our own hemisphere of how poetics combines with politics can be found in the "gathering" ceremonies of the San Blas Cuna of Panama. Village chieftains settle disputes at "talking" meetings; these alternate with frequent "singing" meetings at which one of the village chiefs sings, for several hours, mythic or "historical" narratives with a moral point directed at the community's present situation. At times, the chief sings highly personal, "dream" narratives or chants in an allegorical mode; the chant interpreter then explains his metaphors to the community. Every few weeks a group of chiefs from the region gather to perform these various sorts of instructional singing, on a larger basis.[37] Ronald Engard, who has done fieldwork in Cameroon, reports on what he calls the "aesthetics of power and obedience," which turn artistic events in which local kings act into an essential act of constitutional politics.[38] In these cultures, it appears that one reason people obtain and maintain power is their performance ability. Again, proverb performance is essential: "Political authority and proverbial authority have been allied since at least the time of Solomon," as a social historian notes.[39]

The second body of evidence is closer to home: to Greece, that is. In the poetry of Homer there are a number of depictions of social interaction. In these scenes, as I argue elsewhere, a "performer" justifies his *muthos* (a word I define as authoritative speech act) before a group of competing heroes. The best "performer" at such speech making is also the best all-around performer – Achilles.[40] Once again, if we did not have the comparative evidence from living oral cultures, the Homeric picture might be thought to be a poetic fantasy. As it happens, I believe

Homer can provide the confirmation we have been seeking – that the notion of a *group* of sages reflects the earliest formation of the Seven Sages stories, that Plato did not simply lump together some sages and call them the Seven.

From Homeric poetry, we see that speech making and fighting, first of all, are considered equivalent expressions of the strong personality. Achilles is reminded that the height of heroic behavior is to be a "speaker of words and doer of deeds." Furthermore, we see that all authoritative utterances are performed in a competitive situation. The idea of a critical, competitive audience is inherent in the world of Homeric speakers. This is particularly so in the political-military council we find in Homer, the *boulē*, at which the elders make their proposals in elaborately balanced form. Although this may represent a pure archaism in Homer's composition, it is more likely that the *boulē* structure is familiar to the epic composer from his contemporary milieu.

Given that the context of speech in Homer is inherently agonistic, I now propose that the sages, so like Homeric heroes in their self-presentation, concern for style, and functions in power management and advising, also operated agonistically. That is, one sage always sought to outdo the others, whether or not the others were present. In other words, *there had to be an idealized corporate body of sages for the very notion of archaic sage to make sense. One wise man doesn't work.*

At this point, we are in a position to understand the most famous story about the Seven Sages, the tale (or rather many tales) of the sages and the tripod. There are two main versions.[41] In one, certain Ionian youths, having purchased from Milesian fishermen their catch of fish, get involved in a dispute over a tripod, which was accidentally hauled up in the nets with the fish. Appealing to Delphi to find out who should get the tripod, they are told, "Whosoever is most wise."[42]

Accordingly they give it to Thales, and he to another, and so on until it comes to Solon, who remarks that *the god* was the most wise and sends it off to Delphi. A different version of the story says that Bathykles, an Arcadian, left at his death a drinking cup with the injunction that it "should be given to him who had done most good by his wisdom." So it was given to Thales, went the round of all the sages, and came back to Thales again. And he sent it to Apollo at Didyma (Diog. Laert. 1.28–32). Yet another version – arguably the oldest – says that Thales kept the tripod or cup.[43]

It is clear that there is some jockeying for position between the shrine of Apollo at Delphi and the ancient Ionic oracle of the god at Didyma.[44] Still other versions favor local sages like Chilon or Myson as the wisest. This is precisely what we would expect from an old oral tradition that has not had the kinks ironed out through the process of writing. Myths get transmitted in many versions for the same reason. What is most important for the moment is the very fact that wisdom is held up for participation and reward as if it were a competitive sport. As competition, moreover, it *requires* other players. That, I repeat, is why we must put back as early as the sixth century the tradition of Seven Sages.

One final point must be addressed. Why seven sages? Why not three, or nine, or five, or twelve – all perfectly respectable mystical numbers? Is seven just a lucky coincidence? After all, we have the Seven against Thebes, the Seven Wonders of the Ancient World. Is seven simply pulled out of the folkloric hat? My answer is yes, but I would add that the hat is very old indeed and fits the sages for quite specific reasons.[45]

We should look first to Near Eastern origins of the idea of seven wise men. The Ionian coast, after all, was in contact in the period we are discussing with points as far east as Babylon. Thales must have had access to Babylonian mathematical wisdom if he performed his memorable feat of predicting the eclipse of May 28, 585. Nothing indigenous to Ionia would have helped him. And sure enough, in Babylonian tradition there are Seven Sages. They are first mentioned in the epic of Gilgamesh, the hero of which is thought to have ruled the city of Uruk around 2500 B.C.E. In the epic, which contains elements as early as 2000 B.C.E. and as late as 1200 B.C.E., we are told that the walls of Uruk were built by seven wise men. Other sources depict these *apkallu* figures as having learned craft from the gods before the flood, having taught it to men, and being partially fish-shaped.[46] To my knowledge, we do not have sayings of these wise men or stories of competitions. In brief, the Mesopotamian tradition offers an intriguing but obscure parallel to Greek, but there is no evidence to date of direct influence.

Looking further east for hebdomads, we might find that ancient India offers us a closer parallel to the Greek tradition of the Seven Sages. In Sanskrit texts from the Vedas on, one can find fairly frequent mention of a group called the Seven Ṛṣis. The texts portray these men as both seers and poets, but also as creators, mystics, makers of sacrifice, and, in what seem to us stranger associations, stars – the Pleiades – and life breaths.[47] As in Greek tradition, the later literature inflates the number of sages from seven to dozens: there are subcategories of *Brahma ṛṣis, deva ṛṣis, raja ṛṣis, maharṣi,* as well as "sons of *ṛṣis*" and those with various claims to have contact with *ṛṣis*. Again, as in Greek tradition, many late texts contain quite ancient material along with later additions. And once more as in Greek, the set of seven, even when kept at that number, constantly varies. A final Indic phenomenon offers us a caution – although the names of the Seven Ṛṣis are found as early as the Vedas (1000 B.C.E.), complete lists, with the identification of a particular series as explicitly seven sages, occur first in the Sūtras – the earliest of which are at least four hundred years later than the youngest of the four Vedas. Earlier references than that are either to "the seven" or to individuals by name, but not in canonical groupings. Yet no one has proposed, to my knowledge, that the Seven Ṛṣis did not exist until the Sūtras.[48]

The *ṛṣis* are said to be rulers or to be the gurus of kings, in many texts. Again, they are associated with the composition of hymns to the gods and with foreseeing future events or having seer-like knowledge. Most important for my conclusion, they are associated regularly with the performance of sacrifice, at which they sometimes "see" the hymns they then compose – in other words, we get a bundling of features in the context of sacrifice, features that are attested separately as well in other stories not mentioning sacrifice.[49] I am drawn to mention here the clear connection between the Greek Seven Sages and religious activity. We have seen already that Thales and Solon dedicate tripods to Apollo – the god of oracles and seercraft. Furthermore, Thales is credited with foreseeing eclipses as well as good harvest years. Solon, we are told, wrote a poem foretelling the rise of the tyrant Peisistratos (Diog. Laert. 1.50). Both can be taken as stories of an almost Apolline foresight. In another tale, we see a more explicit connection: Herodotus relates that when Hippokrates was sacrificing at Olympia and his cauldrons boiled of their own accord, it was Chilon who advised him not to marry or, if he had a wife, to divorce her and disown his children (Hdt. 1.59). Here the sage functions as interpreter of signs at a sacrifice. It is perhaps not an accident that Chilon seems to be called (in a damaged text) a descendant of Branchos – the mythical founder of the temple of Apollo at Didyma near Miletus (Diog. Laert. 1.72). Most spectacular of the Seven Sages when it comes to religious activities is Epimenides, who is stated to have been the first who purified houses and fields and the first who founded temples. He was thought to have lived 154 years and slept for many of them (although some say, reports Diogenes, that he did not go to sleep but spent time in retirement gathering simples; Diog. Laert. 1.110–11).

Diogenes also reports a story that the Nymphs brought him food, which he kept in a cow's hoof; taking small doses of this, he sustained himself without appearing to eat (Diog. Laert. 1.114). This sort of behavior has an exact parallel in the ascetic activities attributed to the Seven Ṛsis, who fast and abstain. They even have rivalry matches, each trying to outdo the other in performing ascetic practices. In a description of one of these contests we hear that the sage Vasistha controlled a river, and that furthermore he owned a cow that granted his every wish.[50] Can we detect traces of the same activities in Thales' diverting the river Halys and Epimenides' cow hoof? I suspect that further work in Sanskrit will yield more. But even in Greek stories, we must acknowledge a fourth category for the sages, that of religious importance.[51]

A final parallel must be mentioned to round out the picture and perhaps explain an oddity in Greek: why do the sages pass around the tripod? If it is as a prize of contest, then we have a clear sign that the tradition contains early elements – for this practice is at home in Homer, and not in later literature. In the *Śatapatha Brāhmāṇa* there is cited a verse of an older text (ca. 1200–1000 B.C.E.), the *Atharvaveda* (10.8.9), reading, "There is a cup with its opening at the side and its bottom turned upwards, in which is placed the glory of all forms. There the seven Ṛsis are seated together, they have become the keeper of that great one." The interpreter of this passage proceeds to allegorize: the cup is the head, the sages are the "vital airs" (or *praṇas*) of the head.[52] But we can see that there is no need to find this in the actual Vedic text. We have simply seven men who together are responsible for an unusual vessel. Perhaps the vessel is of ritual significance; the text does not allude to any. But I wonder – do we have to do here, in Greek on the one hand and Vedic Sanskrit on the other, with a tradition not as young as Plato but rather as old as Indo-European antiquity?[53]

The Vedic evidence leads me to a final suggestion, one that would account for both the political and religious roles of the Seven Sages and may explain something of their association with Delphi. The institutions of the brahmans in ancient India and the pontifices of Rome present us with similar priestly collegia. The pontifices, as is well known, varied over time from three in number to fifteen; they were responsible for state cult and issued *decreta*, nonbinding decisions on religious matters. Recall, especially, that the pontifices conducted the sacred banquet for the Jupiter cult; after 196 such banquet preparations were carried out by Epulones (at one time three, later *Septemviri Epulones*). As for brahmanic activity, it centered primarily on sacrifice, which inevitably entails the preparation of sacred meals. One of the more striking features of Vedic sacrifice is its communal nature, as a cooperative enterprise that yet generates *competition* – or at least employs the rhetoric of agonal effort. An example comes at *Rig Veda* 10.71 (vv. 3 and 8):

> Through the sacrifice they traced the path of speech and found it inside the sages. They held it and portioned it out to many; together the seven singers [first seers] praised it.

> When brahmins perform sacrifices together as friends, some are left behind for lack of knowledge, while others surpass them with the power to praise.[54]

If we assume that archaic Greek peoples inherited, along with sacrificial practices, an Indo-European institution of the sacrificial collegium – a group of men learned not only in the craft of sacrifice but also in religious lore and precepts of all types – then the Seven Sages, in both their ritual and instructional roles, have the best claim to representing this archaic institution. In the process of being incorporated into the polis, the collegium might well have survived, in a modified form, within such civic bodies as the *gerousia* in Sparta or the *exēgetai* in Athens.[55] At the same time, an extrapolitical form of the institution could have *continued* to function at common sanctuaries such as Didyma and Delphi, in a form that emphasized sacrificial expertise and, hence, generalized "moral" teaching (a natural outgrowth of knowing what is "pleasing" to the gods ritually). The inherently localized political wisdom of the sages would necessarily drop away in the representation of their activity at Delphi, since no one sage could be an exponent of practical knowledge that would apply to all the various political structures of the Greek world. Gregory Nagy has shown how, in a different context, that of hero cult and epinikion, the polis differentiates its inherited tribal institutions by "absorbing the compatible aspects of this heritage and by internationalizing (that is, making inter-polis) the incompatible aspects."[56] To put this in our terms, the *competition* among sages (as local ritual experts) in a tribal context would have been incompatible with the ideological strains in the emerging polis that encouraged unification and hierarchy. Therefore, it could be "internationalized" into a long-distance competition between, for instance, the local "sages" such as Solon and Thales, who earlier had "competed" only with other wise men of their own region.[57] A model for such a projection of local phenomena onto the Panhellenic would have been available in existing networks of prestige gift exchange, I presume, a system clearly at work in organizing the tripod stories.[58]

The "sympotic" strain in the stories of the Seven Sages (as in the tale of their banqueting together) would not, then, be a recent invention, but a relic of a much older context. This is to say, the setting in Plutarch's *Banquet of the Seven Sages* may be an expression of a continuing tradition, not just Plutarch's innovation.[59] We can imagine that these learned specialists not only ate and drank but performed the sacrifice that began the meal. A communal, public form of the all-important sacrificial meal could, in turn, have been the original stage for the sages' "performance" of wisdom.

To summarize, if we look to the sages as exponents of early Greek notions of wisdom, it becomes clear that the practical skill of the wise person, the hallmark frequently mentioned as that which distinguishes archaic wisdom from later theoretical investigation, starting in the fifth century, is just one feature – and not the most important – in the representation of these figures. A unique and pungent eloquence, verbal or gestural, is even more characteristic, and ritual involvement counts for much, perhaps even offering the key to the antiquity of the sage concept. This combination of characteristics can be paralleled in living cultural traditions. Agonistic behavior, which I claim motivates the corporate representation of sages, can also be paralleled. Secularization and "internationalizing" trends transformed Greek sages by an evolution that never affected similar figures in ancient Rome and India, until they turned into philosophers. Socrates, then, provides a sort of endpoint. Against the background I have sketched, of sages who are performers in several spheres, we can certainly see continuities in Socrates' life, in the form of his relationship with Delphi, his role in politics, even his versifying of Aesopic fables. But as he is depicted, all these are marginal activities in Socrates' career. No archaic sage invented the *elenchos;* it was the speciality of a man who constantly broke the frame of the performance by confronting his audience in dialogue and refusing to rely on the power of emphatic, unidirectional self-presentation.

NOTES

1. Detienne and Vernant 1974: 42–3 recognize that Pittakos, one of the seven, fits the description of a trickster (citing Alc. fr. 69 V) and that Kleobouline (daughter of the sage Kleoboulos, nicknamed "Eumetis") has both the verbal and political skills characteristic of those who possess *mētis* (291–2).
2. See the sketch for such a method in Brillante 1990. My own analysis here owes a good deal also to folkloristics; see the representative approaches to similar problems in Dundes 1975.
3. On the problems related to the canonization of a particular set of seven sages, see Diog. Laert.1.13; Snell 1971:6–13; Barkowski 1972; Fehling 1985: 9–18, 39–48.
4. On the sources for Diogenes Laertius, especially in Book 1, see Wulf 1896: 7–12; Demoulin 1901: 12–50; Hope 1930: 37–97.
5. On this long tradition, see Blumenberg 1976: esp. 23–5.
6. Dicks 1970: 43–4 believes that Thales' scientific knowledge is highly overrated by the later sources, noting that he could not possibly have predicted the eclipse of May 28, 585 B.C.E. (reported in Hdt. 1.74; Diog. Laert.1.23). I share his skepticism.
7. Plutarch recognized the problem in chronology (*Solon* 21.1); see also Manfredini and Piccirilli 1977: 268–9; Fehling 1985: 91–3. On the saying, cf. Snell 1971: 102.
8. On the testimonium (*P. Ryl.* 18) that Chilon overthrew tyrannies (including that of Hippias!) with the general Anaxandridas, see A. Jones 1967: 45.
9. On early testimony to Pittakos' career, see Page 1955: 151–241. Humphreys 1983a: 248–9 notes that none of the sages was identified as a judge, but several had similar positions involving *arbitration*. I suggest that this term can be analyzed as a compound with verbal rection, from *aisa* and *humneo*, "one who declares formally the allotment." The denominative verb in the compound would then be continuing a sense that has merged in the simplex with more generalized senses of "declare" – but compare the function of formally stating divine *allotments*, as embodied in the genre called *hymnos*.

If this is the etymology, the dual function of sage as political figure and poet can be viewed as simply two aspects of one function: to state the way things should be in a formal manner. To understand such a combination we need to revise our notions of "song"; on this, see Nagy 1990b: 31–4 and later in this chapter on Cuna speech events.

10. Diogenes cites a verse from Hipponax regarding Bias' skill at pleading; this is one of the earliest attestations concerning a sage's activity (Hipponax fr. 123 W; cf. Demodokos fr. 6 W). His skill at words extended to diplomacy; he was renowned for arbitrating between Samos and Priene after the "Battle of the Oak" (Plut. *Quaest. Graec.* no. 20).

11. Kleobouline's riddle on the year is preserved at Diog. Laert. 1.91 and in *Anth. Pal.* 14.101.

12. On significant motifs in the description of Periander, see Gernet 1981: 295–7. Wagner 1828 collects the testimonia to his career.

13. On Anacharsis see Kindstrand 1981: esp. 33–50; Hartog 1988: 64–82.

14. In Diodorus Siculus (9.8) it is Solon who gets this reply on a visit to Myson. See Freeman 1926: 198.

15. See Oikonomides 1980, 1987. Defradas 1972: 272 dismisses the epigraphic lists as "dégradation du genre," unjustly, in my opinion.

16. Fehling 1985: 9–19. T. Brown 1989: 3 cites similar sentiments from Grote, while claiming that the notion of pre-Herodotean tales about the Seven Sages stems mainly from the work of Eduard Meyer. In favor of the alternative view, that a group identity was established quite early, is Snell 1954: 111, who cites a hexameter fragment apparently from a colloquy of the sages (*PSI* no. 1093 = Page *Gk. Lit. Papyri* no. 127), which he dates at least as early as the fifth century B.C.E. Wehrli 1973: 196 sees the sage collegium tradition as dating from the same early period as the *Contest of Homer and Hesiod* and Aesopica; Richardson 1981: 2 would put these traditions in the sixth century B.C.E. I thank the anonymous reader for Cambridge University Press for the following cogent suggestion: the syntax of Hdt. 1.29.1, "the wise men (*sophistai*) who happened to exist (*etunkhanon eontes*) at that time," with an imperfect indicative verb (rather than indefinite relative construction, "whichever . . . existed") implies that Herodotus thought the sages *were* actually all living at the same time.

17. Fontenrose 1988: 66 collects attestations of actual dedications of *phialai* at the Didymeion, but suggests that Thales' dedication, if it happened, was originally associated with the Delphinion of Miletus. For sixth-century dedicatory inscriptions in iambic trimeters (though not choliambic, as here), see P. A. Hansen 1983 (*CEG*): nos. 330 and 302. The unusual metrical form of the latter is discussed in Gallavotti 1977: 137–40; the text shows that creative innovation in favor of iambic metrical systems was going on in connection with politically important inscriptions in this crucial period.

18. Diog. Laert. 1.23 notes, however, that the work is really by Phokos of Samos. Plutarch (*De Pyth. or.* 18.402e) groups Thales with Hesiod and Eudoxos as an early composer of a poem on the stars, but adds, "*if* it is true that Thales wrote the *Astrologia* attributed to him."

19. The *Astronomia*, fr. 288–93 M–W; on the fragments, see Schwartz 1960: 248–52. Dicks 1970: 44 observes of Thales on historical grounds, "There is no reason to suppose that his astronomical knowledge was very different from that of Hesiod."

20. Hiller 1878 argued that Lobon is not only Diogenes' source but also the *author* of the poems ascribed to the Seven (as he certainly *was* author of the epigrams on poets, also preserved by Diogenes, and presented under his name as *Supp. Hell.* nos. 504–20). For other viewpoints, see Bergk 1882: nos. 968–71; Wilamowitz-Moellendorff 1925: 300–2; M. L. West 1972: 47; Lloyd-Jones and Parsons 1983: 255; Fehling 1985: 35–6.

21. Crönert 1911: 129–30 shows that the sages' *skolia* have thematic similarities with Attic

skolia of the fifth century, verses of Theognis, and even Euripidean lyrics. Metrically, they display interesting combinations of hexameters with ithyphallic, iambic, and hemiepes segments; see Gallavotti 1979: 118–19.

22. Manfredini and Piccirilli 1977: xxiii–xxiv. I can only hint here at what I see as the larger question regarding transmission of the sages' poetry and sayings: if Aristotle knows actual pieces of Solon's poetry, then can we not maintain that others in the Peripatetic school (Klearchos of Soli, Dikaiarchos, and Demetrios of Phalerum) had access to equally old and authentic sages' material for their collections? Or, put another way, if we do not believe *their* testimony, why should we trust Aristotle's? Linforth 1919: 7–13 offers a number of reasons for accepting Solon's poems as authentic, although admitting that the earliest evidence for a collection is from the mid-fifth century. Jaeger 1948: 454 believes Dikaiarchos stressed in the tradition the stories about sages that emphasized their political and legal expertise – but this is not to say he made the stories up.

23. See M. L. West 1972: 47.

24. On the pragmatics of similar dedications, see Svenbro 1988: 33–52. On the diction of the poem, see Markwald 1986: 34–83. Here, as in the stories of the sages' inscribing their maxims on Apollo's temple at Delphi and offering the tripod at an Apollo temple, there seems to be a link between poetry, wisdom, and dedication ritual. This highly conventionalized and powerful set of metaphors appears also in Pindaric poetry and has been fully explicated recently in the work of Kurke 1991: esp. 156–8, 188–96.

25. *PMG* 581; see Markwald 1986: 83 on whether Simonides' poem actually refers to this poem and on the ascription of the Midas epigram to Kleoboulos.

26. Diog. Laert. 1.97; for further testimonia on Periander as poet, see M. L. West 1972: 92.

27. On the recurrent pattern underlying such stories about legislators' leave taking, see Szegedy-Maszak 1978.

28. See Huxley 1962: 68–71 and Jones 1967: 45–6 on the complicated history of Chilon's ephorate.

29. For definitions of performance, with examples, see R. P. Martin 1989: 4–42. It is worth noting that in the diction of Herodotus the very action of giving advice, by Bias at the Panionion (1.170.1), was a "public presentation": the historian uses a verb (*apodexasthai*) that elsewhere denotes his *own* performed narrative. On the term and its significance, see Nagy 1990b: 217–24. I stress the appearance of two sages together at Hdt. 1.170 as an indication of agonistic context; see more later. I thank the anonymous Cambridge University Press reviewer for pointing out that Solon's advice to Croesus (Hdt. 1.30–3) also looks like it was given in a performative way and in an agonistic context, seeing that the other *sophistai* apparently gave advice to Croesus as well (cf.1.27).

30. For a fuller bibliography, see R. P. Martin 1989: 4–8.

31. On the further meanings of the anecdote, see Santoni 1983: 148–51.

32. Hdt. 5.92; Arist. *Pol.* 1284a26 has Periander giving the advice. On the variation, see Wehrli 1973: 201.

33. Jakobson 1966: 637.

34. See Briggs 1985 on proverb performance and Howe 1977 on metaphors.

35. Hdt. 1.27. As the citations in LSJ, s.v., make clear, the word applies to dramatic or rhetorical art. For collocation of similar performance language with "proverbial" sage advice, see Nagy 1990b: 219 n. 24, 239, 316 on *gnōmēn apophainesthai*.

36. Cf. Jakobson 1966: 638: "In many folklore patterns the proverb often appears to be a

moralizing envoy of an actual narrative. Or inversely a proverb seems a germ of a virtual fiction.''

37. Howe 1977: 133–6. See also the full-scale study of the institution by Sherzer 1983.
38. Engard 1989.
39. Obelkevich 1987: 45, who cites the modern example of the Merina of Madagascar, among whom the leaders are the best orators, who in turn are those most adept at proverbs.
40. R. P. Martin 1989.
41. Wiersma 1934 presents the versions in detail.
42. Wulf 1896: 12–20 collects eleven variants of the story; cf. Snell 1971: 114–27. Morgan 1990: 46 notes the increase in tripod dedication from external sources at Olympia in the eighth century and relates it to strategies by individuals for effective social display in the context of intracommunity rivalry at a state sanctuary, extended to communal sanctuaries. The provenance of tripod dedications at Delphi suggests they were prestige items circulating in an aristocratic gift-exchange network. I suggest such a network is represented in the tale of the sages.
43. On Thales keeping it, see Gernet 1981: 78–81, who compares stories of cult officials sequentially in charge of sacra. A variant of the ''cup'' version has Croesus donate a phiale (Plut. Sol. 4).
44. On Didyma's claims, see Parke 1985: 12–14.
45. Hirzel, cited by Wulf 1896: 9, had long ago suggested a Greek mythical precedent for the Seven Sages in stories about seven clever sons of Helios and the island/nymph Rhodes; the tale is alluded to by Pind. Ol. 7.71–6. Apart from the connection to Lindos (offspring of one of the Rhodian sons and city of the sage Kleoboulos), it is hard to see explicit links; it is possible, of course, that the myth reflects knowledge of an already established human institution.
46. See Reiner 1961; Burkert 1984: 106 connects them with traditions behind the ''Seven Against Thebes'' story.
47. Texts collected in Mitchiner 1982. He speculates (269) that the Indus Valley civilization acted as a conduit for a prehistoric notion of Seven Sages to enter Indic culture from Mesopotamia.
48. Mitchiner 1982: 4–6.
49. Mitchiner 1982: 193, 296–311; cf. Gonda 1975: 71.
50. Mitchiner 1982: 194.
51. Death stories reflect their status. For Bias the people of Priene dedicated a precinct that is called the Teutameum (Diog. Laert. 1.88). Chilon, according to the traveler Pausanias, was worshiped as a hero at Sparta (Paus. 3.16.4).
52. Mitchiner 1982: 7–8.
53. In the West, this tradition may underlie the ''cauldron of wisdom'' stories, which center on a contest over a magic vessel, found in the Mabinogion and in tales of Finn and Odin, on which see P. Ford 1977: 20. Yoshida 1965 adds to the dossier the Scythian cup, which is a sign of sacral kingship (cf. Hdt. 4.5–6), its modern reflex the magic cup of the Narts in Ossetic epic and the Holy Grail.
54. Translation by O'Flaherty 1981: 61–2. On brahmanic sacrificial roles, see Dumézil 1935, who compares the role of Roman flamen. On competition involving poets at sacrifice, see Gonda 1975: 80–1.
55. For what is known of the latter, see Oliver 1950.
56. Nagy 1990b: 143–5.
57. The analogy would be to athletic competition, which became institutionalized on the

Panhellenic level in the eighth century, but apparently existed before and after on the local level as well. Gernet 1981: 79 saw the athletic contests as a "spontaneous" model for the tripod story. On actual dedications of tripods, connected with early, *pre-Panhellenic* Olympics, see Lee 1988.

58. On the operation of this network, see Kurke 1991: 84–107.

59. Defradas 1954: 29 speculates that there were other such compositions before Plutarch's but concedes the lack of direct evidence. He would add to the indirect evidence the famous Ostia paintings depicting the sages accompanied by scatological sayings. These, Defradas suggests (34), may caricature a traditional theme (food) of sages' discussions, one that looms large in Plutarch's tale (158a–160c, Solon's talk with Kleodorus). I would note that the topic in that passage is tied to a discussion of what foods should be *dedicated at Delphi*.

PART THREE

Negotiating Civic Crisis

CHAPTER SEVEN

The Economy of Kudos

Leslie Kurke

THIS volume was organized (at least partly) to see if the methods and interests of the New Historicism could fruitfully be applied to the study of archaic Greece. "CULTURAL POETICS," the term Stephen Greenblatt coined to characterize his approach, aims to break down the barriers between literary text and cultural/historical context. It encourages us to "read" texts as context, and history itself as text, both informed by multiple, competing symbolic strategies and symbolic economies.[1] My aim in this essay is to develop a cultural poetics of athletic victory in the sixth and fifth centuries B.C.E., drawing on the "high art" of epinikion, but not depending on it exclusively to establish the circulation of powers and honors that subtended athletic success.

I begin with an observation and a question. The observation is the persistent connection between *kudos* and crowns in the diction of epinikion. For example, in *Olympian* 4 Pindar prays to Zeus:

> Οὐλυμπιονίκαν
> δέξαι Χαρίτων θ' ἕκατι τόνδε κῶμον,
> χρονιώτατον φάος εὐρυσθενέων ἀρετᾶν.
> Ψαύμιος γὰρ ἵκει
> ὀχέων, ὃς ἐλαίᾳ στεφανωθεὶς Πισάτιδι κῦδος ὄρσαι
> σπεύδει Καμαρίνᾳ. (*Ol.* 4.8–12)

> Receive this Olympic-victory *kōmos* by the grace of the Charites, the longest-lasting light of achievements broad in strength. For it comes from the chariots of Psaumis who, crowned with olive from Pisa, hastes to rouse *kudos* for Kamarina.

And in *Isthmian* 1, the poet intends to celebrate the Isthmus:

> ἐπεὶ στεφάνους
> ἐξ ὤπασεν Κάδμου στρατῷ ἐξ ἀέθλων,
> καλλίνικον πατρίδι κῦδος. (*Isthm.* 1.10–12)

since it bestowed six crowns from contests on
the people of Kadmos, victorious *kudos* for the
fatherland.

Nor is this association of *kudos* with the victor's crown limited to Pindar. Thus we
find in an address to the victor in Bacchylides:

ὁσσά⟨κις⟩ Νίκας ἕκατι
ἄνθεσιν ξανθὰν ἀναδησάμενος κεφαλάν
κῦδος εὐρείαις Ἀθάναις
θῆκας Οἰνείδαις τε δόξαν. (Bacchyl. 10.15–18)

however many times by the grace of Victory having
bound your blond head with flowers you established
kudos for broad Athens and glory for the Oineidai.[2]

The question is very simple – what does *kudos* mean in epinikion and why its
persistent connection with the victor's crown? Emile Benveniste once argued com-
pellingly from the Homeric evidence that *kudos* is not merely a synonym for *kleos*
(as it is often taken), but rather signifies special power bestowed by a god that
makes a hero invincible:

The gift of *kûdos* ensures the triumph of the man who receives it: in combat
the holder of *kûdos* is invariably victorious. Here we see the fundamental
character of *kûdos:* it acts as *a talisman of supremacy.* We use the term
talisman advisedly, for the bestowal of *kûdos* by the god procures an instan-
taneous and irresistible advantage, rather like a magic power, and the god
grants it now to one and now to another at his good will and always in order
to give the advantage at a decisive moment of a combat or some competitive
activity.[3]

Hermann Fränkel came independently to very similar conclusions. He observes in
a footnote to *Early Greek Poetry and Philosophy:*

Anthropologists have failed to notice that no Homeric word comes as close
to the widely discussed *mana* and *orenda* as κῦδος does. The traditional
rendering 'Fame' is false. κῦδος never signifies the fame which spreads itself
abroad. Fame (κλέος) is applicable even to the dead, but κῦδος belongs only
to the living (*Il.* 22, 435ff.). From Homer to late antiquity derivations of
κῦδος serve to designate the feeling of a man sure of himself and confident
of the future.[4]

Benveniste also notes that in Homer the formula *kudos aresthai,* "to win *kudos*"
is "often accompanied by a dative indicating the beneficiary": the Homeric warrior
wins *kudos* for his king or his people.[5] We might add that, in Homeric epic, only
two words take the epithet κυδιάνειρα, "bestowing *kudos* on men" – μάχη,
"battle," and ἀγορή, the "gathering place for assemblies and athletic contests."
To judge from the distribution of *kudos* in later texts and inscriptions, battle and
contests remain the arenas for the winning of *kudos.* Thus the term figures most

prominently in two classes of inscriptions: those commemorating war dead and those celebrating athletic victory.[6]

I

Given the continuity in the two spheres of *kudos,* does it retain any of its Homeric force (of talismanic power, or *mana*) in the fifth century? But before I can address the observation and the question, it is necessary to rehearse the evidence for the talismanic power of athletic victors in antiquity. This evidence is well known: the *mana* of athletes used to be a commonplace. It has now fallen into disrepute, however, because of its associations with the Cambridge anthropologists – James Frazer, Francis Cornford, and Jane Harrison.[7] But it should be possible to disengage "talismanic power" from the accoutrements of the Cambridge school – divine kingship, succession myths, and weather magic – defining it narrowly, with Benveniste, as magical potency in battle.

Consider the evidence. On a couple of occasions, Plutarch tells us that victors at the crown games were traditionally stationed beside the Spartan king when he went into battle:

ἐν δὲ Λακεδαίμονι τοῖς νενικηκόσι στεφανίτας ἀγῶνας ἐξαίρετος ἦν
ἐν ταῖς παρατάξεσι χώρα, περὶ αὐτὸν τὸν βασιλέα τεταγμένους
μάχεσθαι. (*Quaest. conv.* 2.5.2)

In Lakedaimon, there was a special place in the ranks for victors at the crown games, stationed to fight around the king himself.

And in the *Life of Lykourgos* (22.4):

ἐχώρει δὲ ὁ βασιλεὺς ἐπὶ τοὺς πολεμίους ἔχων μεθ' ἑαυτοῦ στεφανίτην
ἀγῶνα νενικηκότα.

The king used to go against the enemy having with him one who had won a crown contest.

Modern scholars have tended to follow Plutarch in giving this phenomenon a rationalistic explanation – it is because, they claim, athletics is such good training for war.[8] But two things should make us suspicious of such a rationalistic account. In the *Quaestiones convivales*, Plutarch uses the plural τοῖς νενικηκόσι στεφανίτας ἀγῶνας, which might suggest an elite corps of athletes as crack troops. But in the *Life of Lykourgos* the biographer uses a singular – στεφανίτην ἀγῶνα νενικηκότα. A single athletic victor hardly makes a swat team and suggests that he is not a fighting force so much as a talisman of victory (as the Spartan king himself was).[9] The other thing that should make us suspicious is that, in both passages, Plutarch specifies a victor at the *crown* games. If it were just a question of physical conditioning, surely any athletic victor would do, but instead we find a limitation that is inexplicable on purely rationalistic grounds.

In the same section of the *Quaestiones convivales*, Plutarch also reports that it is customary to tear down a part of the city wall for the entrance of athletic victors:

καὶ τὸ τοῖς νικηφόροις εἰσελαύνουσιν τῶν τειχῶν ἐφίεσθαι μέρος
διελεῖν καὶ καταβαλεῖν τοιαύτην ἔχει διάνοιαν, ὡς οὐ μέγα πόλει
τειχῶν ὄφελος ἄνδρας ἐχούσῃ μάχεσθαι δυναμένους καὶ νικᾶν.
(*Quaest. conv.* 2.5.2)

And the fact that, for the reentry of athletic victors, they bid them cast down
a part of the city wall has such an intent: that there is no great benefit of walls
for a city which has men able to fight and to win.

Plutarch's account (if not his rationale) is confirmed by the description of Nero's
triumphal return from Greece in Suetonius:

> Reversus e Graecia Neapolim, quod in ea primum artem protulerat, albis equis
> introiit disiecta parte muri, ut mos hieronicarum est; simili modo Antium,
> inde Albanum, inde Romam; sed et Romam eo curru, quo Augustus olim
> triumphaverat, et in veste purpurea distinctaque stellis aureis chlamyde co-
> ronamque capite gerens Olympiacam, dextra manu Pythiam, praeeunte pompa
> ceterarum cum titulis, ubi et quos quo cantionum quove fabularum argumento
> vicisset. (*Ner.* 25)

> Returning from Greece to Naples (because he had exhibited his skill there
> first), he entered with white horses where a part of the wall had been cast
> down, as is the custom for victors at the holy games; in a similar way [he
> entered] Antium, thence Albanum, thence Rome. But [he entered] Rome also
> in that chariot in which Augustus had once celebrated a triumph, and in a
> purple garment and a cloak decorated with gold stars, wearing on his head
> his Olympic crown, carrying his Pythian crown in his right hand, with a
> parade proceeding with the titles of all the rest [of the contests], where and
> whom he had beaten, by what song or plot of stories.

Suetonius adds an important detail when he notes, "ut mos hieronicarum est" –
"as is the custom for victors at the holy games."[10] The "holy games," as they
are defined from Pindar through agonistic inscriptions of the Hellenistic and Roman
periods, are the *crown* games – the games of the *periodos*.[11] Precisely the same
limitation seems to apply here as in the first case, the attendance on the Spartan
king. In this case, at least, a historian of Roman religion, H. S. Versnel, is willing
to countenance the possibility of talismanic power. He explains this strange practice,
which breaches the walls and then, immediately after the victor's entry, seals up
the gap, as a rite that symbolically seals the victor's power, his magical supremacy,
within the city.[12]

Finally, there is Diodorus Siculus' account of a battle between the Krotoniates
and the Sybarites in the sixth century B.C.E. According to Diodorus, the Sybarites
forced the Krotoniates into a war over suppliants to whom the Krotoniates had
given sanctuary. The Krotoniates engaged the Sybarites in battle, outnumbered
three to one:

> ... Μίλωνος τοῦ ἀθλητοῦ ἡγουμένου καὶ διὰ τὴν ὑπερβολὴν τῆς τοῦ
> σώματος ῥώμης πρώτου τρεψαμένου τοὺς καθ' αὑτὸν τεταγμένους. ὁ
> γὰρ ἀνὴρ οὗτος, ἑξάκις Ὀλύμπια νενικηκὼς καὶ τὴν ἀλκὴν ἀκόλουθον

ἔχων τῇ κατὰ τὸ σῶμα φύσει, λέγεται πρὸς τὴν μάχην ἀπαντῆσαι κατεστεφανωμένος μὲν τοῖς 'Ολυμπικοῖς στεφάνοις διεσκευασμένος δὲ εἰς 'Ηρακλέους σκευὴν λεοντῇ καὶ ῥοπάλῳ· αἴτιον δὲ γενόμενον τῆς νίκης θαυμασθῆναι παρὰ τοῖς πολίταις. (Diod. Sic. 12.9.5–6)

... With Milo the athlete commanding and, on account of the superabundance of his bodily force, first having turned those stationed against him. For this man, a six time Olympic victor and having the courage to go with his bodily nature, is said to have entered into battle crowned with his six Olympic crowns and wearing the garb of Herakles with lion skin and club. And [it is said] that he was marvelled at by his fellow citizens as being the cause of victory.

No rationalistic explanation can do justice to this passage – Milo goes into battle wearing his six Olympic crowns and single-handedly turns the enemy.[13] This account is intended to be a θαῦμα (a marvel), as Diodorus' last sentence signals. We must conclude that the Olympic victor in his Olympic crowns was believed to have magical potency on the battlefield.

But, it may be objected, all this evidence derives from very late sources – do we have any suggestion of a belief in the talismanic power of athletic victors in the sixth or fifth century B.C.E.? In light of these passages, it is worth looking carefully at Herodotus' account of the Elean seer Teisamenos (Hdt. 9.33–5). Consulting the Delphic oracle about offspring, Teisamenos is informed that he will "win five of the greatest contests" (ἀγῶνας τοὺς μεγίστους ἀναιρήσεσθαι πέντε). As a result, he goes into training and enters the Olympic pentathlon, missing the victory by a single fall. Thereupon, the Spartans realize that the oracle "refers not to athletic contests but to the contests of war" and attempt to recruit Teisamenos for the Spartan army:

Λακεδαιμόνιοι δὲ μαθόντες οὐκ ἐς γυμνικοὺς ἀλλ' ἐς ἀρηίους ἀγῶνας φέρον τὸ Τεισαμενοῦ μαντήιον, μισθῷ ἐπειρῶντο πείσαντες Τεισαμενὸν ποιέεσθαι ἅμα 'Ηρακλειδέων τοῖσι βασιλεῦσι ἡγεμόνα τῶν πολέμων. (Hdt. 9.33)

But the Lakedaimonians, having come to understand that the oracle referred not to athletic contests but to the contests of war, were attempting, having persuaded Teisamenos with a wage, to make him leader of wars together with their Heraklid kings.

But Teisamenos will join the Lakedaimonian forces only on terms of becoming a Spartan citizen. When the Spartans finally agree to his terms in fear of the Persian expedition, Herodotus concludes his story triumphantly:

συγχωρησάντων δὲ καὶ ταῦτα τῶν Σπαρτιητέων, οὕτω δὴ πέντε σφι μαντευόμενος ἀγῶνας τοὺς μεγίστους Τεισαμενὸς ὁ 'Ηλεῖος, γενόμενος Σπαρτιήτης, συγκαταιρέει. (Hdt. 9.35)

But when the Spartiates agreed also to these terms, thus indeed did Teisamenos the Elean, having become Spartan, take five of the greatest contests with them, serving as seer.

Herodotus' diction in this context bears striking similarities to the official victory announcement at the games. As R. W. Macan observes, "It marks the solemnity of the occasion with a quasi-heraldic flourish."[14] Herodotus' narrative confirms (even as it collapses) contests and war as two parallel spheres for the winning of *kudos*. It is as if Teisamenos, with the oracle's sanction, simply vaults over the intermediate step of athletic victory, moving straight to talismanic potency in battle. Indeed, the phrase Herodotus uses for his participation in battle, Τεισαμενὸν ποιέεσθαι ἅμα Ἡρακλειδέων τοῖσι βασιλεῦσι ἡγεμόνα τῶν πολέμων, suggests much more than the service of a seer. Commentators have expended a great deal of ingenuity to avoid the obvious meaning of the phrase,[15] but Teisamenos' close association with the Heraklid kings as "leader of wars" is explicable within the framework of talismanic power. Teisamenos, like the Spartan kings themselves, would be a leader by virtue of his charismatic authority, so that we need not assume that Herodotus said *hēgemōn* when he meant *mantis*.

The anecdotes of Plutarch and Diodorus Siculus are also very suggestive in general for the Greeks' predilection for crown victors as commanders in war and in the foundation of cities.[16] There are, in fact, a fair number of Olympic victors who act as oikists between the seventh century and the fifth.[17] The earliest is Chionis of Sparta, three-time Olympic victor, who, according to Pausanias, "had a share in the expedition with the Theraean Battos and founded Kyrene with that one" (Paus. 3.14.3).[18] Next is Phrynon, Olympic victor and leader of the Athenian expedition to Sigeum around 600 B.C.E.[19] Herodotus tells us of two Olympic victors who became oikists in the late sixth century: Philippos of Kroton, who accompanied the expedition of Dorieus in the 520s (Hdt. 5.47), and Miltiades, the son of Kypselos, whom the Dolonkoi took as their oikist to the Thracian Chersonese (Hdt. 6.36). The way in which Herodotus narrates the latter story suggests that there is an association in the mind of the historian between Miltiades' Olympic victory and his role as oikist: uncharacteristically for Herodotus, he does not mention that Miltiades was an Olympic victor when he is first introduced to the narrative; the Athenian aristocrat is characterized simply as ἐὼν οἰκίης τεθριπποτρόφου (of a household which kept four-horse chariots, Hdt. 6.35).[20] Instead, the fact of his Olympic victory is reserved for the quasi-heraldic announcement of his role as founder:

οὕτω δὴ Μιλτιάδης ὁ Κυψέλου, Ὀλύμπια ἀναραιρηκὼς πρότερον τούτων τεθρίππῳ, τότε παραλαβὼν Ἀθηναίων πάντα τὸν βουλόμενον μετέχειν τοῦ στόλου ἔπλεε ἅμα τοῖσι Δολόγκοισι καὶ ἔσχε τὴν χώρην. (Hdt. 6.36)[21]

Thus indeed Miltiades, the son of Kypselos, who was before this an Olympic chariot victor, at that time took every one of the Athenians who wanted to participate in the expedition and sailed together with the Dolonkoi and took the territory.

The last instance of a victor-oikist known to us from literary sources is Leon of Sparta, who won an Olympic chariot victory in 428 B.C.E.[22] This same Leon was probably one of the three commanders dispatched from Sparta to found Herakleia Trachinia in 426 B.C.E., as Thucydides tells us (Thuc. 3.92: οἰκισταὶ δὲ τρεῖς

Λακεδαιμονίων ἡγήσαντο, Λέων καὶ Ἀλκίδας καὶ Δαμάγων).²³ If it is characteristic of Herodotus to mention that an oikist is an Olympic victor, it may well be characteristic of Thucydides to suppress the fact. Simon Hornblower has argued that there may have been a religious element involved in the choice of Alkides as one commander of this expedition, for his name makes him an ideal candidate to found a colony named Herakleia in the neighborhood of Trachis. Yet, according to Hornblower, Thucydides consistently suppresses the religious element.²⁴ The same argument might be extended to Thucydides' failure to mention Leon's Olympic victory. If this is the case, Thucydides' silence tends to corroborate the claim that crown victors were believed to have special, talismanic power that contributed to the success of such colonial ventures.

Similarly, we know of several cases of victors at the great games serving as military commanders. Pausanias reports that Phanas of Messenia was an Olympic victor in the long race who commanded beside Aristomenes in the Second Messenian War (Paus. 4.17.9). Herodotus mentions Eualkides, crown victor and commander of the Eretrians during the Ionian Revolt (Hdt. 5.102).²⁵ In this light, it is worth considering Herodotus' account of another crown victor, Phayllos of Kroton. Right before the Battle of Salamis, the historian reports, "Of those living outside [Greece], the Krotoniates were the only ones who came to aid Greece when she was in danger with one ship, whose commander was Phayllos, three-time Pythian victor" (ἀνὴρ τρὶς πυθιονίκης Φάϋλλος; Hdt. 8.47). We might think one ship is very paltry aid, but the parallel of a *single* crown victor fighting beside the Spartan king should give us pause.²⁶ Perhaps the substantive aid was not the ship, but the man it carried, a talisman potent with three Pythian victories. Indeed, Herodotus himself offers an intriguing parallel for this one ship a few chapters later when he mentions that, after an earthquake, the Greeks at Salamis sent a ship to Aigina to fetch the Aiakidai (8.64, 8.83). According to Aiginetan tradition, it was this ship that initiated the battle (8.84). I suggest that there is a precise analogy between the one ship bearing the Aiginetan heroes and that which carried the crown victor – both contribute their talismanic power, their *mana,* to the fighting force.

II

Thus, there seems to be good evidence stretching back to the fifth century B.C.E. for the *mana* of crown victors. But as Benveniste and Fränkel have suggested, the Greek word for *mana* is *kudos.* To answer the question with which I began, I propose that we understand epinikian *kudos* as the civic adaptation of its Homeric precursor, with the city replacing the Homeric king as beneficiary of the victor's *kudos.* Consider in this light the first triad of *Olympian* 5:

Ὑψηλᾶν ἀρετᾶν καὶ στεφάνων ἄωτον γλυκύν
τῶν Οὐλυμπίᾳ, Ὠκεανοῦ θύγατερ, καρδίᾳ γελανεῖ
ἀκαμαντόποδός τ' ἀπήνας δέκευ Ψαύμιός τε δῶρα·
ὃς τὰν σὰν πόλιν αὔξων, Καμάρινα, λαοτρόφον,
βωμοὺς ἓξ διδύμους ἐγέραρεν ἑορταῖς θεῶν μεγίσταις
ὑπὸ βουθυσίαις ἀέθλων τε πεμπαμέροις ἁμίλλαις,

ἵπποις ἡμιόνοις τε μοναμπυκίᾳ τε. τὶν δὲ κῦδος ἁβρόν
νικάσας ἀνέθηκε, καὶ ὃν πατέρ᾽ Ἄ-
κρων᾽ ἐκάρυξε καὶ τὰν νέοικον ἕδραν. (Ol. 5.1–8)

Daughter of Ocean, receive with laughing heart the sweet peak
of highest achievements and crowns from Olympia, the gifts
of the untiring-footed chariot and of Psaumis. Exalting your
city which nurtures the people, O Kamarina, he honored the
six double altars at the greatest festivals of the gods with
sacrifices and the five-day competitions of contests, with horses
and mules and single-horse racing. And having won he dedicated to you luxurious *kudos,* and he heralded his father Akron
and his new-founded seat.

The poet begins by invoking the victor's city, Kamarina, and asking her to receive
"the sweet peak of achievements and Olympic crowns" (a typically Pindaric zeugma
of concrete and abstract; cf. *Pyth.* 8.19–20). He proceeds to assert that the victor
has dedicated *kudos* for his city (τὶν δὲ κῦδος ἁβρόν / νικάσας ἀνέθηκε). Notice
especially ἀνέθηκε here, which is the technical term for making a dedication.[27]
What the victor offers and what the city receives frame the triad, equating his *kudos*
with the proffered crown.

The same equation of *kudos* and crowns figures in agonistic inscriptions.[28] In the
inscriptions and elsewhere, "crowning the city" is a common formula for victory.
Thus in an epigram that Joachim Ebert dates to the first half of the fifth century
(Ebert 12 = *Anth. Pal.* 16.2):

Γνῶθι Θεόγνητον προσιδών, τὸν ὀλυμπιονίκαν
παῖδα, παλαισμοσύνας δεξιὸν ἡνίοχον,
κάλλιστον μὲν ἰδεῖν, ἀθλεῖν δ᾽ οὐ χείρονα μορφῆς,
ὃς πατέρων ἀγαθῶν ἐστεφάνωσε πόλιν.

Come to know Theognetos looking upon him, the boy
Olympic victor, skilled charioteer of the wrestling, most
beautiful to see, but in competing no worse than his form,
who crowned the city of good fathers.

Admittedly, this is a very ornate example, attributed in the *Palatine Anthology* to
Simonides. Ebert 35 (= *Anth. Pal.* 13.15) offers a somewhat less showy version
from the fourth century B.C.E.:

Εἰμὶ Δίκων υἱὸς Καλλιμβρότου, αὐτὰρ ἐνίκων
τετράκις ἐν Νεμέᾳ, δὶς Ὀλύμπια, πεντάκι Πυθοῖ,
τρὶς δ᾽ Ἰσθμῷ· στεφανῶ δ᾽ ἄστυ Συρακοσίων.

I am Dikon son of Kallimbrotos, and I was victorious
four times at Nemea, twice at Olympia, five times at
Pytho, and three times at the Isthmus. And I crown the
city of the Syracusans.[29]

"To crown the city" as a formula for victory points to a significant ritual event (a point to which I shall return). But it is worth noting that, on occasion, the verb κυδαίνω replaces στεφανόω. Thus in a late inscription from Ephesus (the last two lines after a long victory catalog):

> τοιγὰρ κυδαίνω γενέτην ἐμὸν Εἰρηναῖον
> καὶ πάτρην Ἔφεσον στέμμασιν ἀθανάτοις.
> (Ebert 76B.9–10 = *I. Olympia* 225, 49 C.E.)

> Accordingly, I bestow *kudos* upon my father Ei-
> renaios and my homeland Ephesus by means of
> immortal crowns.

Notice the instrumental dative στέμμασιν ἀθανάτοις: the inscription tells us explicitly that the victor's crowns are the means by which he bestows *kudos* on his city.[30] Furthermore, the functional equivalence of στεφανόω and κυδαίνω with the city as object bespeaks the same association that we find in Pindar and Bacchylides.

Other inscriptions clearly equate the victor's crown with *kudos* for his city. In a late inscription from Miletus, we read:

> Τηλεφίδαι σε ἔστεψαν ἀφ' Ἡρακλεῖος ἀγ[ώνων],
> Μίλητος δὲ τεᾶς κῦδος ἔδεκτο πάλα[ς]·
> (Ebert 74.1–2 = *Milet* III 164, after 129 B.C.E.)

> The Telephidai crowned you from the contests of Her-
> akles, and Miletus received the *kudos* of your wrestling.

And in an elegant dedicatory inscription preserved by Herodotus:

> Βόσπορον ἰχθυόεντα γεφυρώσας ἀνέθηκε
> Μανδροκλέης Ἥρῃ μνημόσυνον σχεδίης,
> αὑτῷ μὲν στέφανον περιθείς, Σαμίοισι δὲ κῦδος,
> Δαρείου βασιλέος ἐκτελέσας κατὰ νοῦν. (Hdt. 4.88)

> Having bridged the Bosphorus, full of fish, Mandrokles ded-
> icated to Hera a memorial of the bridge, having put a crown
> about himself and *kudos* about the Samians, when he ac-
> complished it according to the intent of King Darius.

This is not an athletic inscription, but a dedication to commemorate a different kind of remarkable achievement – the bridging of the Bosphorus for Darius' Scythian campaign. Still, the link between the individual's crown and *kudos* for his city is so compelling that it surfaces even here, where the crown is purely metaphorical.[31]

I suggest we read all these passages against the background of the rites that we know accompanied the victor's reentry to his city. The reentry itself was a very significant moment – we have one description in Diodorus Siculus of a fifth-century Akragantine victor escorted into the city by three hundred chariots drawn by white horses (Diod. Sic. 13.82.7–8). The crowds invoked blessings, pelted the victor with crowns, and bound *tainiai*, or fillets, about his head.[32] The procession went conspicuously through the main streets to the center of the city, where the victor was announced (just as he had been at the games).[33] The victor's crown was an important part of the ritual – indeed, as Louis Robert informs us, the technical term for the ceremony was εἰσάγειν τὸν στέφανον – to "bear in the crown."[34] After the announcement of the victor, the crown was often dedicated at the shrine of a local god or hero.[35]

This ritual practice, I believe, lies behind Pindar's request to Kamarina to receive the victor's crown in *Olympian* 5. We find the same request in other poems, addressed either to the city personified or to a local deity. Thus in *Pythian* 12:

Αἰτέω σε, φιλάγλαε, καλλίστα βροτεᾶν πολίων

. . .

δέξαι στεφάνωμα τόδ᾽ ἐκ Πυθῶνος εὐδόξῳ Μίδᾳ
αὐτόν τε νιν Ἑλλάδα νικάσαντα τέχνᾳ
(*Pyth.* 12.1, 5–6)

I ask you, shining one, most beautiful of mortal cities
. . . receive this crown from Pytho for glorious Midas,
and receive [the man] himself, who has beaten Greece
in his craft.

And again, in *Olympian* 13, the poet prays to Zeus:

δέξαι τέ οἱ στεφάνων ἐγκώμιον τεθμόν, τὸν ἄγει πεδίων ἐκ Πίσας,
πενταέθλῳ ἅμα σταδίου νικῶν δρόμον· (*Ol.* 13.29–30)

Receive for him the ordinance of crowns accompanied by the *kōmos,* which he leads from the plains of Pisa, winning the stadion race together with the pentathlon.

Notice especially στεφάνων ἐγκώμιον τεθμόν, τὸν ἄγει πεδίων ἐκ Πίσας. In this phrase, Pindar comes as close as he ever does to the technical term εἰσάγειν τὸν στέφανον. Some critics have preferred to understand the crown in these passages as a metaphor for the poet's song,[36] but there is much to be said for taking these injunctions literally – as references in epinikion to the victor's public dedication of his crown on his return home. *Olympian* 5 then adds the final term: by its equation of crowns received with the dedication of *kudos* for the city it suggests that the victor shares his talismanic power with his community by dedicating his victory crown. It is worth noting also that in all three of the passages with which I began, the poet's language transfers the victor's crown to the public sphere, identifying it with *kudos* for the city.[37]

Thus I would modify the thesis of Frank J. Nisetich, who argued that the moment of crowning at the games was so important that Pindar evokes it again and again in his verse. I would add that rituals involving the victor's crown punctuate *both* ends of his journey – first at the games and then on his return home.[38] Both moments are laden with *kudos* and the civic community participates in both – at the games, because the city also figures in the victory announcement; at home, because the ritual of reentry culminates in the *public* display and dedication of the crown. Both rituals are necessary to acknowledge the victory and to share the victor's talismanic power with his community.

Accordingly, we might describe all the rites involving the victor as an "economy of *kudos*" – a circulation of powers and honors whose goal is to achieve a harmonious sharing of this special commodity within the city. The victor invests the money and effort needed to train and to win, and then heralds his city at the moment of crowning (and, of course, he is not obliged to do so – he can announce a different city).[39] At home, he tenders the city his victory crown. The city, in response, rewards him for his victory with a lavish reentry rite, crowns and fillets, the lifelong privilege of eating in the prytaneion, large monetary awards, special front-row seats in the theater, and sometimes a statue set up at public expense in the city or at the site of the games.[40]

This symbolic economy of *kudos* is concretized as a circulation of crowns, whereby the crown itself becomes the bearer of *kudos* and its dedication the means of sharing that power with the city. For this reason, the link between the dictional evidence I have just reviewed and the anecdotal evidence considered earlier is the victor's *crown*. The association between *kudos* and crowns in epinikion and in the inscriptions explicates the strange limiting condition we observed in the later anecdotes: it is *only* crown victors who enter through a breach in the wall and crown victors who fight beside the Spartan king. Finally, remember Milo of Kroton marching out to battle wearing his six Olympic crowns.[41]

III

Within this economy of *kudos,* one particular form of honoring the victor deserves our closer attention: the victory statue. For on occasion, the epigrams that accompany such statues use the formula "the city crowned me winning with this image" (με . . . νικῶντα ἐστεφάνωσε εἰκόνι τῆιδε πόλις; *CEG* 855.1–2, cf. *CEG* 799 [both ca. 300 B.C.E.]). The language suggests that the victor's statue participates in the circulation of crowns that emblematizes the economy of *kudos*. How does the victor statue function within this symbolic economy? At the most obvious level, we can read the statue as recompense bestowed by the city for the victor's crown: a figurative exchange of crowns then motivates the diction of the inscriptions. Yet this reading hardly exhausts the statue's participation in an elaborate ritual economy. Just as the rites accompanying the victor's reentry to his city reenact his original coronation at the games, we might say that the statue group makes eternal the possibility of such reenactment. The inscriptions repeatedly emphasize the exact likeness of the statue to the victor, thereby confirming the tradition that victors had the privilege of erecting statues that were life-size but no larger.[42] For example, the earliest preserved inscription from an Olympic victor monument (*CEG* 394, first half of the sixth century B.C.E.) insists that the image is ϝίσο(μ) μᾶκός τε πάχος τε, "equal in height and thickness" to the victor.[43] Other inscriptions make it clear that the statue was not just like the victor, but like him at the moment of victory or return. In an Olympic inscription from around 300 B.C.E., for example,

Ὧδε στὰς ὁ Πελασγὸς ἐπ᾽ Ἀλφειῶι ποκα πύκτας
τὸμ Πολυδεύκειογ χερσὶν ἔφανε νόμον,
ἆμος ἐκαρύχθη νικαφόρος. ἀλλά, πάτερ Ζεῦ,

καὶ πάλιν Ἀρκαδίαι καλὸν ἄμειβε κλέος,
τίμασον δὲ Φίλιππον, ὃς ἐνθάδε τοὺς ἀπὸ νάσων
τέσσαρας εὐθείαι παῖδας ἔκλινε μάχαι.

(CEG 827 = Ebert 55)

Standing thus upon the Alpheios, the Pelasgian boxer
once showed forth the ordinance of Polydeukes with
his hands, when he was heralded victor. But, Father
Zeus, also again bestow noble glory on Arcadia, and
honor Philippos, who here leaned on four boys from
the islands with straight battle.

Here the inscription tells us explicitly that the statue re-creates the stance of the victor at the moment he won and was heralded.[44] And just as the statue replicates the victor as he was at the moment of victory, the words of the epigram reproduce the original victory announcement.

Several sources give us information about the form of the victory announcement. The oldest is a black-figure amphora of Panathenaic shape dated to the third quarter of the sixth century B.C.E., which depicts a herald before a victorious horseman, proclaiming ΔΥΝΕΙΚΕΤΥ:ΗΙΠΟΣ:ΝΙΚΑΙ (Δυνεικέτυ ἵππος νικᾷ – the horse of Duneiketos wins; Figure 29).[45] There is also a fragment of Timotheos, which according to Plutarch celebrates his victory over Phrynis:

μακάριος ἦσθα, Τιμόθε', ὅτε κᾶρυξ
εἶπε· νικᾷ Τιμόθεος
Μιλήσιος τὸν Κάμωνος τὸν ἰωνοκάμπταν,

(Timotheos fr. 26/802 PMG)

Blessed were you, Timotheos, when the herald
said, "Timotheos the Milesian beats the soft
Ionian-singing son of Kamon."

From much later sources we get somewhat more elaborate versions of the victory announcement. Thus Diogenes Laertius preserves an anecdote about Diogenes the Cynic that depends on the formula uttered by the Olympic herald, νικᾷ Διώξιππος ἄνδρας (Dioxippos beats the men; Diog. Laert. 6.43). Dio Cassius offers the most elaborate version of all in his account of Nero's victory announcement at all the chief games of Greece: τὸ δὲ δὴ κήρυγμα ἦν· Νέρων Καῖσαρ νικᾷ τόνδε τὸν ἀγῶνα καὶ στεφανοῖ τόν τε Ῥωμαίων δῆμον καὶ τὴν ἰδίαν οἰκουμένην (And the victory announcement was, "Nero Caesar wins this contest and crowns the Roman people and the inhabited world which is his own"; Dio Cass. 62.14).

With these announcements we might compare early inscriptions, both prose and verse. In a prose inscription from Olympia dated to the first third of the fifth century we find the elements of the victory announcement pared down to the barest possible form: Καλλίας Διδυμίο Ἀθηναῖος παγκράτιον· / Μίκων ἐποίησεν Ἀθηναῖος (Dittenberger and Purgold no. 146).[46] Some of the early verse inscriptions come close to the simplicity of their prose relatives – for example, a sixth-century in-

Figure 29. Herald announcing the victor in the horse race, as a youth approaches with tripod and crown. Black-figure amphora of Panathenaic shape, ca. 570 B.C.E. London, British Museum B144. (Photo courtesy of the Trustees of the British Museum.)

scription on a statue group of chariot, victor, and charioteer, as preserved for us by Pausanias:[47]

> Κλεοσθένης μ' ἀνέθηκεν ὁ Πόντιος ἐξ 'Επιδάμνου,
> νικήσας ἵπποις καλὸν ἀγῶνα Διός. (Paus. 6.10.6)

> Kleosthenes the son of Pontis from Epidamnos dedicated me when he won with the horses the noble contest of Zeus.

The only thing this couplet adds to the formula of the victory announcement (name of victor, patronymic, homeland, event, and site of games) is the fact of dedication, μ' ἀνέθηκεν.

Still other early inscriptions prefigure the more elaborate victory formula preserved by Dio Cassius. A late-sixth-century inscription recorded by Pausanias commemorates the victory of the racehorse Lykos:

> 'Ωκυδρόμας Λύκος 'Ισθμι' ἄπαξ, δύο δ' ἐνθάδε νίκαις
> Φειδόλα παίδων ἐστεφάνωσε δόμους. (Paus. 6.13.9)

> Swift-running Lykos, with victories once at the Isthmian games, and two here, crowned the houses of the sons of Pheidolas.

As in the inscription on the pseudo-Panathenaic amphora, the horse itself figures in the nominative, and as in the proclamation of Nero, by his victories he "crowns" the house of his masters. We have seen this same formula of crowning for the fifth-century victor Theognetos; we can now appreciate how this inscription re-creates the victory announcement in highly stylized form:

Γνῶθι Θεόγνητον προσιδών, τὸν ὀλυμπιονίκαν
   παῖδα, παλαισμοσύνας δεξιὸν ἡνίοχον,
κάλλιστον μὲν ἰδεῖν, ἀθλεῖν δ' οὐ χείρονα μορφῆς,
   ὃς πατέρων ἀγαθῶν ἐστεφάνωσε πόλιν. (Anth. Pal. 16.2)

Come to know Theognetos looking upon him, the boy Olympic victor, skilled charioteer of the wrestling, most beautiful to see, but in competing no worse than his form, who crowned the city of good fathers.

The inscription captures the moment when Theognetos was the object of all eyes – the moment he stood before the Olympic herald.[48] With elaborate poetic periphrases, it informs us of his victory, of the site of the games, of his age class (τὸν ὀλυμπιονίκαν παῖδα), of his event (παλαισμοσύνας δεξιὸν ἡνίοχον), and of his crown as a communal honor.[49]

To say that the monument makes possible the eternal renewal of the moment of victory is not merely to repeat the claim that it memorializes the athlete forever in an idealized form. Indeed, it is a truism that the victor statue immortalizes its model, preserving him precisely as he was in his moment of glory and even assimilating him to the divine.[50] What I have in mind is at once more concrete and more firmly rooted in ritual practices than that modern aestheticizing formulation allows. I would like to follow the lead of Joseph Day, who has recently proposed that, in the archaic period, funerary and dedicatory inscriptions functioned together with their monuments as substitutes for the original ritual event or "scripts" for its reenactment.[51] He has noted that such a model is also appropriate for epinikian inscriptions,[52] for the inscription traditionally contained some or all of the elements of the original victory announcement – the victor's name, his patronymic, his homeland, his event, and his age class. Therefore, when a passerby read the inscription aloud (and Jesper Svenbro has recently reminded us that reading in antiquity was almost exclusively reading aloud),[53] his voice was appropriated for the reenactment of the original herald's announcement of the victor.

We can take the argument for the monument's ritual reenactment yet a step further and suggest that the figurative references to crowning in the agonistic inscriptions evoke the original coronation of the victor. For we have evidence that the herald's public announcement of the victor's name, patronymic, and city took place *simultaneously* with his coronation by the Hellanodikas.[54] In this context, it is worth mentioning one of the more common types of victor statue, in which the victor stands at rest, wearing only a fillet.[55] Already by the Roman imperial period, it seems, this statue type was a source of puzzlement to viewers. Thus both Pausanias (6.14.6–7) and Philostratus (*Life of Apollonius* 4.28) offer somewhat fanciful explanations for the fillet depicted on an archaic statue of Milo of Kroton.[56] But in the archaic and classical periods, the fillet was the first token of victory, whether

Figure 30. Crowning of athletic victor wreathed in fillets. Black-figure amphora of Panathenaic shape. London, British Museum B138. (Photo courtesy of the Trustees of the British Museum.)

bound on by the victor himself (as in Polykleitos' famous statue)[57] or by others immediately after the contest (as in the case of the Spartan Lichas binding a fillet on his victorious charioteer; Paus. 6.2.2). The public announcement and coronation of the victor took place afterward,[58] so presumably the athlete came forward to receive his crown still wearing his victory fillet (Figure 30). If this was the case, the common type of the filleted athlete reproduced the victor just as he looked when he stood before the Hellanodikas to receive his crown. Thus the combination of epigram and victor statue elicited from its beholder a perfect re-creation of the original announcement and coronation. As the viewer lent his voice to the epigram that reconstructed the victory announcement, he stood in the position of the Hellanodikas and crowned the victor with his gaze.[59] Indeed, we know of at least one case in which the ritual reenactment seems to have gone even further: Pausanias tells us that even in his time, the victor statue of Oibotas at Olympia was periodically crowned with real wreaths (Paus. 7.17.4).[60]

It is perhaps in the context of this elaborate ritual reenactment that we should understand a formula preserved in two fourth-century B.C.E. inscriptions. In an inscription from Olympia whose first line is completely lost we read:

[   ]
ἔσταθι κυ[δαίνων τοῦδε π]οδῶν ἀρε[τάν]·
δὶς γὰρ ἄε[θλον ἐνεί]κα[το] Ὀλυμπίου ἐν Διὸς [ἄ]λ[σ]ε[ι]
πᾶχυν ὑπ[αὶ] χ[αλκέ]αν ἀσ[π]ί[δ]α ἐρεισ[άμενος]·
πρᾶτος δ[ὲ Κρ]ητῶν [πά]ντας [νίκασε Νέμεια]
καὶ δ᾽ ἐπ᾽ Ἀθαν[α]ί[α]ς [Π]αλλ[άδο]ς ἐσ[τέφετο]·
δὶς δὲ ὑπὸ Παρνασσοῖο φέρει κλέος, [ἔν τε] δι[αύλωι]
τέρμα καὶ ὁπλοφόρ[ο]υ πρῶτος ἑλὼν ἀ[έ]θ[λου]·
οὐδὲ μάταν ἐλαφροῖσι κ[ό]νιμ περι[. .]επ̣ε̣ι[. . .]αν
[π]ο[σ]σὶν Κασταλία[ς] θεῖον ἐνι[ψ]εν ὕ[δωρ]

(*CEG* 849 = Ebert 48)

Stand and bestow *kudos* upon the achievement of the feet of
this one. For twice he won the contest in the grove of Olympian
Zeus, leaning his arm under a bronze shield, and first of the
Cretans he beat all at Nemea and in [the festival] of Pallas
Athena he was crowned. And twice he bears glory from under
Parnassos, taking first place both in the diaulos and in the
hoplitodromos. And not in vain did he wash the dust from his
feet in the divine water of Kastalia.

And in a badly damaged inscription from Thebes that Ebert dates to the fourth or
third century B.C.E. on the basis of the letter forms:

[Ἴστα]σο κυδαίνων Λυσίξεν[ον, ὃς Νεμεαίωι]
[εἰν ἄλ]σει νίκαν ὠκέος ἐγ δολί[χου]
[ἄρατ᾽], ἐπεὶ παίδων τέλος ἔδραμ[εν· ἴσθ᾽ ὅτι Θήβας]
[ἁλικία] θείων οὐκ ἄμορος στεφ[άνων]

(*CEG* 790 = Ebert 57)[61]

Stand and bestow *kudos* upon Lusixenos, [who in the Nemean
grove won] victory from the swift long-race, when he out-
stripped the throng of boys. [Know that the youth of Thebes
is] not without a share of divine crowns.

In the first inscription, the formula ἔσταθι κυδαίνων prefaces an elaborate rendition
of multiple victories at different contests and in different events, while the later
inscription uses the same formula to commemorate a Nemean victor for a hometown
audience. In spite of the fragmentary condition of the two epigrams, they seem to
repeat the elements of the original victory announcements,[62] and in each case, they
mention the victor's crowns (ἐσ[τέφετο] *CEG* 849.6; θείων οὐκ ἄμορος
στεφ[άνων] *CEG* 790.4). Insofar as the passerby's reading aloud and gaze re-
create the original announcement and crowning of the victor, he can be said to
"stand and bestow *kudos* upon" the image, even as the original act endowed the
victor with talismanic power.[63] Thus the victory monument is doubly implicated in
the economy of *kudos,* for it looks backward, as an honor that recompenses the
victor's *kudos,* and forward, as the victor's talismanic double, perpetually regen-
erating his *kudos* in his absence.

For indeed, the absence of the victor – his eventual disappearance – is what the erection of the victory monument is predicated on. Because the victor will not always be available as bearer of *kudos,* the monument is fashioned to take his place. On a few occasions, the inscriptions themselves register the gap between the presence of the statue and the absence of the original victor.[64] Thus in a fifth-century distich from Olympia:

> Εὔθυμος Λοκρὸς Ἀστυκλέος τρὶς Ὀλύμπι’ ἐνίκων·
> εἰκόνα δ’ ἔστησεν τήνδε βροτοῖς ἐσορᾶν.
> (*CEG* 399 = Ebert 16)

> Euthymos of Lokris, son of Astykles, I won the Olympic
> games three times. And he set up this image for mortals
> to look upon.

The verb ἐνίκων in the first line makes the statue speak as the victor, Euthymos of Lokris, but the abrupt third-person verb ἔστησεν in the second line opens up a gap between the single past action of the now-absent victor and the eternal monument he set up.[65] In a more complex example from the early fourth century, the Spartan princess Kyniska shimmers in the play of presence and absence:

> Σπάρτας μὲν βασιλῆες ἐμοὶ| πατέρες καὶ ἀδελφοί,
> ἄρματι δ’ ὠκυπόδων ἵππων| νικῶσα Κυνίσκα
> εἰκόνα τάνδ’ ἔστασε μόναν| δ’ ἐμέ φαμι γυναικῶν
> Ἑλλάδος ἐκ πάσας τόν|δε λαβεῖν στέφανον.
> (*CEG* 820 = Ebert 33; *Anth. Pal.* 13.16)

> My fathers and brothers [are] the kings of Sparta, and
> winning with the chariot of swift-footed horses, Kyniska
> set up this image. And I affirm that I alone of women from
> all Greece took this crown.

Here the notice of the actual victory and erection of the monument – "Kyniska, winning with the chariot, set up this image" – interrupts a first-person discourse of eternal presence: "*My* fathers and brothers [are] the kings of Sparta . . . *I* affirm that *I* alone of women took this crown." As in the Euthymos inscription, the aorist third-person verb ἔστασε shatters the perfect identification of victor and image, calling our attention to the erecting hand, now absent, of the victor.[66]

This rift is felt even more profoundly in the few inscriptions that collapse the commemoration of victory and burial. One such inscription preserved by Pausanias (probably from the second half of the fourth century) reads:

> Μουνοπάλην νικῶ δὶς Ὀλύμπια Πύθιά τ’ ἄνδρας
> τρὶς Νεμέᾳ, τετράκις δ’ Ἰσθμῷ ἐν ἀγχιάλῳ,
> Χείλων Χείλωνος Πατρεύς, ὃν λαὸς Ἀχαιῶν
> ἐν πολέμῳ φθίμενον θάψ’ ἀρετῆς ἕνεκεν. (Paus. 6.4.6)

> Twice I win the men's single wrestling at Olympia and Pythia,
> three times at Nemea, and four times at the sea-girt Isthmus,
> Cheilon the son of Cheilon from Patrai, whom the Achaian

people buried for the sake of his achievement when he perished
in war.

The two distiches of the poem construct an elaborate opposition, juxtaposing the parallel realms of contests and wars, the eternal present νικῶ to the past event θάψ(ε), and the first person to the third. In the first two lines the statue speaks as the victor, but the ὅν clause in the third line modulates from identification to differentiation. The effect of this shift from first person to third and from present to past is to disengage the historic Cheilon, the man buried by the Achaians, from the eternal renewal of victory that the first distich enacts. It is the existence of the monument itself that enables the affirmation νικῶ.

A third-century funerary inscription from Miletus achieves a similar effect, while inverting the relation of first to third person:

> [Ἔστεφο]ν εὐθὺ νόμοισι πανήγυριν ἡνιοχοῦντε[ς]
> [Ἕλλησ]ι κλεινὴν πᾶσιν ᾿Ολυμπιάδα –
> [μάρτ]υρες ἀθάνατοι νίκης μνημεῖα σέβοντες –
> [ἀπτω]τεὶ νικῶντα πάλην παῖδας Κλεόνικο⟨ν⟩·
> [αὐτὰ]ρ ἐγὼ τόδε ἔτεοξα κασιγνήτωι μνημεῖον
> [. . .]ειδας, ξεστὸς δὲ κίων ⟨ἐ⟩πί σήματι ἄραρε
> [τέχν]ην ἀγγέλλων· μνήμην δ᾿ ἔχει῾Ελλὰς ἄπασα.
> (Ebert 65 = *Milet* 1238)

> Those who guide straight with their ordinances the Olym-
> pic Festival, glorious to all the Greeks, crowned – and
> the immortals who reverence the memorials of victory
> [are] witnesses – Kleonikos winning the boys' wrestling
> without a fall. But I, . . . eidas, set up this memorial for
> my brother, and the polished column is fixed upon his
> tomb announcing his skill. But all Greece holds
> remembrance.

As Ebert notes, the first four lines do not look like a funerary epigram – instead, they echo and elaborate traditional formulae of agonistic inscriptions. Only with lines 5–7, with the appearance of the victor's brother as "I," does the occasion of the epigram become clear. The brother's ἐγώ and his single past act of erecting the monument (ἔτεοξα) register with finality the victor's absence.

But again, this inscription reveals with particular clarity the function of the erected monument. The inscribed stone does not just mark the gap – the absence of the victor – it serves to replace him and renew his memory in a restored eternal present (notice the present participle ἀγγέλλων and the present verb ἔχει in the last line). Given what we have seen of the agonistic epigrams' re-creation of the original victory announcement, it is tempting to read ἀγγέλλων here in its technical sense. The monument appropriates the voice of the herald, to repeat in perpetuity Kleo-nikos' victory. Although this inscription is late and part of a funerary monument rather than a victor group, I suggest that its strategies are comparable to those of earlier victor statues and epigrams. We might say that the victor monument inserts itself into the gap between presence and absence as a *kudos*-producing machine.

All this suggests that the emphasis on the exact likeness of the statue to the victor (both in the inscriptions and in the construction of a life-size image) is more than aesthetic: the statue is fashioned as an exact replica of the victor, as his talismanic double. In this sense, we might extend the argument of Jean-Pierre Vernant from early Greek images of the gods and of the dead to victor statues, and see in them the "presentification of the invisible" rather than the secular "imitation of appearance":

> Figure of the gods, figure of the dead. In each case, the problem is the same: by means of localization in an exact form and a well-determined place, how is it possible to give visual presence to those powers that come from the invisible and do not belong to the space here below on earth? The task is to make the invisible visible, to assign a place in our world to entities from the other world. In the representational enterprise, it can be said that at the outset, this paradoxical aspiration exists in order to inscribe absence in presence, to insert the other, the elsewhere, in our familiar universe. . . . However the sacred power is represented, the aim is to establish a true communication, an authentic contact, with it. The ambition is to make this power present *hic et nunc,* to make it available to human beings in the ritually required forms.[67]

The ritual forms that surround the victor statue – the reenactment of the crowning and victory announcement it enables – confirm its participation in the symbolic economy of *kudos*. Indeed, the talismanic quality of the image as the victor's double figures most prominently in stories where the ritual norms are transgressed, and it is to these that we now turn.

IV

By scenes of transgression I refer to those cases in which victors are "canonized" as cult heroes, for the economy of *kudos* outlined here will help, in turn, to explain that phenomenon. The class of heroized victors, which has been the subject of a great deal of discussion recently, includes Philippos of Kroton, Hipposthenes of Sparta, Polydamas of Skotusa, Diognetos of Crete, Euthykles of Lokris, Oibotas of Dyme, Kleomedes of Astypalaia, Euthymos of Epizephyrian Lokris, and Theagenes of Thasos.[68] Fontenrose, who produced the most detailed collection of the victor-hero stories, explicates the phenomenon as the superimposition of a legendary hero type onto a historical (or quasi-historical) figure: "The hero-athlete tale, therefore, belongs to a wider type of hero legend, and the athlete is a special case of the legendary hero who was warrior, hunter, and athlete in one. The legend type tended to attach itself to famous athletes and shape them into legendary heroes."[69] Fontenrose's analysis offers us a descriptive paradigm for the assimilation of certain athletic victors to an ancient combat myth. What it does not provide is any motivation for this process – why should athletic victors in particular be available for such assimilation? That is to say, in what way were victors perceived by the Greeks as particularly like cult heroes? Nor does Fontenrose's model explain why only certain athletic victors achieved cult status. As E.N. Gardiner pointed out long ago, only a handful of the approximately eight hundred Olympic victors known to us from antiquity were worshiped as heroes.[70] Thus any explanatory model must account not only for what made certain athletes like cult heroes, but also for what made most unlike them.[71]

Furthermore, Fontenrose observes without being able to explain the prominence of victor statues in many of the athlete-hero legends he catalogs.[72] Thus in the stories of Theagenes, Euthykles, and Euthymos, it is something done to the victor's *statue* that precipitates heroization, while the statues of Theagenes and Polydamas were reputed to have healing powers long after their deaths (Lucian *Deor. conc.* 12). Finally, in the case of Oibotas (and perhaps Kleomedes), it is the lack of a statue and the honor it represents that provokes the anger of the athlete-turned-*daimōn*. All these story patterns become comprehensible once we situate the victor statue within the economy of *kudos*. As the victor's magical double, the statue continues to embody his talismanic power even after his disappearance and/or eventual death. In the case of athlete-heroes, where, as we shall see, there is a transgression or violation of the proper circulation of *kudos*, the statue functions as a kind of lightning rod, focusing and drawing off this imbalance of dangerous energy.[73]

Let us begin with the observation of François Bohringer that we can pinpoint the phenomenon of athletic heroization to a precise historical context: most of these athletes either belong to the first half of the fifth century or are eighth-century winners who seem to receive cult honors starting in the fifth century.[74] It is Bohringer's contention that what makes these athletes different from all the others is that their *cities* confront a period of crisis – either from internal stasis or from the threat of an external enemy.[75] As an example of the former he cites Theagenes of Thasos, whom Pouilloux argued was an active part of the pro-Athenian government of the city in the 450s and 440s.[76] The saga of his statue – that it was whipped nightly after his death by an enemy, until one night it fell on the enemy and killed him, then was cast into the sea, and miraculously recovered and restored by command of the Delphic oracle (Paus. 6.11.6–9) – maps in symbolic form the struggles for supremacy of the pro-Athenian faction against the opposition. As a parallel, we might think of the story recounted by Thucydides in which the Amphipolitans rejected Hagnon the Athenian as their oikist in the 420s, installing in his stead a cult of Brasidas, the victorious Spartan commander killed in the Battle of Amphipolis (Thuc. 5.11).

As an example of the second possibility – the threat of an external enemy – Bohringer cites the case of Euthymos of Lokris, reputed to be the son of the river Kaikinos, which marked the boundary between Lokris and Rhegion. We know that in the 470s, Rhegion was a very belligerent neighbor, threatening to expand into the territory of Lokris.[77] Under the circumstances, it was clearly advantageous for Lokris to claim a local hero whose river-god father circumscribed the limit of Rhegian territory. Or again, Bohringer suggests that the heroization of Oibotas sometime before 460 B.C.E. was the result of the annexation of his city, Paleia, by neighboring Dyme. Along with the city, the eighth-century athletic victor was also annexed, grafted onto a preexisting hero cult to legitimate the takeover.[78] This is not to suggest that these instances represent the cynical manipulation of cult for political ends: it seems rather that the political was still firmly embedded in a set of symbolic forms that included *kudos* and hero cult.

These, then, are the political conditions that can precipitate heroization. And we can say that athletes are available for heroization because they already participate in the realm of talismanic power. But if we ask how the Greeks themselves seem to have conceptualized and represented the process, it is as an imbalance in the economy of *kudos*. That is, those athletes become heroes who possess a superabundance of *kudos* or who suffered in life from a dearth of proper honors in response to their *kudos*.[79] In the first category, consider Philippos of Kroton, who died in the battle against Egesta in 520 B.C.E. Herodotus tells us, "And there died together with him Philippos the son of Boutakides, the Krotoniate, who was an Olympic victor and the most beautiful of the Greeks at his time (ἐών τε ᾿Ολυμπιονίκης καὶ κάλλιστος ῾Ελλήνων τῶν κατ᾽ ἑωυτόν). And because of his beauty, he received from the Egestans what no other [ever had]: over his tomb having established a heroön, they propitiate him with sacrifices" (Hdt 5.47). It appears that, in this narrative, his beauty *on top of* his Olympic victory stands as a sign of extraordinary divine favor and power.[80] A similar case is that of Polydamas of Skotusa. An Olympic pankration victor (408 B.C.E.), he is described by Pausanias as "the tallest of all men except those called heroes." Pausanias goes on to tell us that Polydamas (emulating Herakles) killed a lion with his bare hands, defeated three of the Persian immortals in single combat, and accomplished many other "marvels" (θαύματα) of strength (Paus. 6.5.4–8). Again, consider the stories that cluster around Euthymos of Epizephyrian Lokris. A boxer who won Olympic victories in 484, 476, and 472, he is said to have exorcised the Hero of Temessa, who haunted the city and exacted tribute of one local maiden a year (Paus. 6.6.4–11). According to Callimachus and Pliny the Elder, his two victory statues, one at Olympia and the other in Lokris, were struck by lightning on the very same day. The Delphic oracle, consulted about this marvel, bid the Lokrians sacrifice to Euthymos as a hero while he lived and as a god after his death.[81] We might describe lightning in this narrative as *kudos* made visible, a tangible sign from heaven singling out Euthymos for extraordinary, divine honors.[82]

The second category of victors comprises those who do not receive adequate acknowledgment and recompense for their *kudos* during their lifetimes. This failure of acknowledgment can take place either at the games or on their return home – the two nodes of significant ritual activity we identified earlier. For the individual, this breakdown in the economy of *kudos* means that the honor that is ultimately paid must be all the more extreme. For the victor's city, the circulation of *kudos* does not operate as it should, so that we might say that the only way the city can participate in the victor's power is by instituting cult. Consider first Kleomedes of Astypalaia, who killed his opponent in a boxing match at Olympia in 496 B.C.E. He was denied the victor's crown, returned home, and in a fit of insanity killed sixty local schoolboys by knocking down the pillar supporting the schoolhouse roof. When the Astypalaians pursued him to stone him, Kleomedes hid in a box in the temple of Athena.[83] Opening the container, his baffled fellow citizens found nothing and, consulting the Delphic oracle, were informed, "Kleomedes is the last of the heroes: honor him with sacrifices, since he is no longer mortal" (Paus. 6.9.6–8). Here it seems that, having been deprived of the normal victory and reentry rites, Kleomedes carries his *kudos* with him as a dangerous potency. A more extreme recompense is required to defuse that power and achieve the proper "circulation" of *kudos*.[84]

The story of Euthykles of Lokris provides another instance of a failure of honor that leads to a breakdown in the economy of *kudos*. According to Callimachus (frs. 84 and 85 Pfeiffer), Euthykles of Lokris won the Olympic pentathlon and some time thereafter was sent as ambassador to another city. He returned to Lokris with a set of mules (ἀπηναίους . . . ὀρῆ[ας) presented to him by a guest-friend. The demos of Lokris, "ever choked over the wealthy," interpreted the gift as a bribe and condemned Euthykles.[85] In addition, the Lokrians proceeded to mutilate his victor statue, which the city itself had erected. Thereupon, they suffered famine and consulted the Delphic oracle, who told them, ἐν τιμῇ τὸν ἄτιμον ἔχων τότε γαῖαν ἀρόσσεις (When you hold in honor the one without honor, then you will plow your land; Oinomaos of Gadara apud Euseb. *Praep. Evang* 5.34.15–16). When they understood the oracle, the Lokrians built an altar to Euthykles and honored his statue "like that of Zeus" (Callimachus fr. 85 [dieg. II 5] Pfeiffer).

The nearest parallel for the elements in this account is the story of Astylos of Kroton (see note 39), which also reveals what is at stake for the citizens of the victor's city. Recall that Astylos had himself "announced as Syracusan to gratify Hieron" (Paus. 6.13.1), whereupon the citizens of Kroton turned his house into a prison and tore down his local victor statue. In this instance, Astylos' use of the ethnic Syracusan in the victory announcement transfers his talismanic power to Hieron's city: under the circumstances, it is quite understandable that his fellow citizens should dismantle his victor statue, that *kudos*-producing machine. The parallel suggests that for the Lokrians also the issue of Euthykles' loyalty is an issue of who enjoys his special power: in the gift of the mules, we might say, the Lokrians read a competing economy of powers and honors. Indeed, the gift of mules and a car may itself be significant, since it allows Euthykles to reenact the *eiselasis* awarded to crown victors, but now under the auspices of another city. It turns out, however, that the Lokrians' suspicion is unjustified, and greater honor must be paid Euthykles as a result (notice the emphasis on τιμή and the pun on ἄτιμος in the oracle).

Finally, there is the example of Oibotas, eighth-century Olympic stadion victor. According to Pausanias, he was the first Achaian to win at Olympia, and yet he received "no special honor" (γέρας οὐδὲν ἐξαίρετον; 7.17.13) from the Achaians on his return home. Angered at this lack of proper acknowledgment, Oibotas cursed the Achaians, praying that they might never have another Olympic victor. Three centuries later, the Achaians finally consulted the Delphic oracle about "why they were always missing the mark of the crown at the Olympics" (στεφάνου τοῦ Ὀλυμπίασιν ἡμάρτανον; 7.17.13). The oracle informed them and they honored Oibotas with a statue at Olympia, whereupon an Achaian immediately won the stade race (in 460 B.C.E.).[86] After that, says Pausanias,

διαμένει δὲ ἐς ἐμὲ ἔτι Ἀχαιῶν τοῖς ἀγωνίζεσθαι μέλλουσι τὰ Ὀλύμπια
ἐναγίζειν τῷ Οἰβώτᾳ, καὶ ἢν κρατήσωσιν, ἐν Ὀλυμπίᾳ στεφανοῦν
τοῦ Οἰβώτα τὴν εἰκόνα. (Paus. 7.17.14)

Even to my time, those of the Achaians who are going to compete at the
Olympic games still make offerings to Oibotas, and, if they win, they crown
the statue of Oibotas at Olympia.

It is as if Oibotas has simply been inserted as an extra station in the Achaians'
circulation of *kudos*. With each new Achaian victory, his statue is recrowned and
his original talismanic power reactivated. And in this light, one other story Pausanias
tells about Oibotas is worth mentioning. He reports with disbelief what some of
the Greeks say: that although he won the Olympics in the eighth century, Oibotas
"fought together with the Greeks at the Battle of Plataea" (Paus. 6.3.8). This
anecdote (which Pausanias transmits without crediting) suggests the benefits thought
at an earlier time to accrue for the city that tapped into the *kudos* of a victor by
transforming him into a cult hero.

V

We have located the conceptual origin of athletic heroization in an imbalance in
the symbolic economy of *kudos*. But our analysis must still account for the temporal
localization of this phenomenon. Clearly, the first half of the fifth century was not
the only period of crisis or major danger for the Greek cities, so why was the
heroization of athletic victors generally restricted to this era? It is perhaps that the
late sixth and early fifth centuries saw a crucial conjunction of factors: on the one
hand, a period of great external threat and internal upheaval; on the other hand, a
serious bid for talismanic power by a beleaguered aristocracy. That is to say, perhaps
we must ground our cultural poetics in a politics and see the phenomenon of *kudos*
as an attempt by the aristocracy to lay claim to special power within the polis.
J. K. Davies has observed that aristocratic participation in chariot racing at the
great games increased dramatically in the sixth and fifth centuries B.C.E., and then
dropped off again in the fourth. He explains this phenomenon as the deployment
of property power as a substitute for the aristocracy's waning cult power within
the city, to be replaced, toward the end of the fifth century, by rhetorical skill. All
we need add to Davies's model is that charismatic authority is involved at least in
the first two forms of power.[87] Thus Max Weber himself mentions the hereditary
priesthoods of ancient Greece as a form of "charismatic blood relationship." As
this institutionalized form of charisma recedes in the face of the rational order of
the polis, aristocrats seek to renew their power and prestige within the city by
personal charisma won at the great games.[88]

Indeed, we can see this contested form of power, its lines of conflict, inscribed
in two of the most familiar texts of the fifth century – Herodotus' account of the
meeting of Solon and Croesus (Hdt. 1.30–3) and Xenophanes fr. 2 DK. In Herodotus, the encounter of the fabulously wealthy Lydian king and the Athenian sage

occupies a prominent place. In the famous anecdote, Solon answers Croesus' question, "Who is the most blessed (ὀλβιώτατος) of mortals?" by naming three Greek private citizens. To the relentless materialism of Croesus Solon opposes a symbolic economy of *kudos* in the two complementary realms of war and contests.[89] Though it is not often remarked (because Solon's paradigms are most often misread as a valorization of the simple life of the ordinary citizen), Tellos, as well as Kleobis and Biton, achieve extraordinary feats and enjoy extraordinary honor. Tellos the Athenian, whom Solon considers the most blessed of men, died a glorious death in battle after routing the enemy (τροπὴν ποιήσας τῶν πολεμίων ἀπέθανε κάλλιστα; I.30.5). The Athenians buried him "at public expense in the very spot where he fell and honored him greatly." Both his burial on the battlefield and Herodotus' expression ἐτίμησαν μεγάλως suggest that Tellos received cult honor after death (like those fallen and buried at Marathon and Plataea).[90]

As the complement to Tellos, Kleobis and Biton achieve an extraordinary feat in peacetime. Yet when we look closely at Herodotus' narrative, we discover that the shape of their story is the shape of athletic victory. We are told at the outset that the two had remarkable strength of body, and the proof is that both were "prizewinners" (ἀεθλοφόροι). Herodotus continues "and especially this story is told" (καὶ δὴ καὶ λέγεται ὅδε λόγος). καὶ δὴ καί in Herodotus conventionally adds the emphatic term to a series to which it belongs, so that here it situates the entire ensuing narrative under the sign of athletic victory.[91] And indeed, Kleobis and Biton are represented as engaged in a race, competing against the clock to bring their mother to the festival on time. When they reach the temple, the Argives surround them, "calling blessed the strength of the young men, and the Argive women blessing the mother for such children." Herodotus' narrative here evokes the *makarismos,* "the calling blessed," that traditionally accompanied the binding-on of fillets or the *phyllobolia* of the athlete immediately after the victory.[92] Finally, after their magical death, the Argives dedicate images of them at Delphi "on the grounds that they proved themselves to be the best men" (ὡς ἀνδρῶν ἀρίστων γενομένων). Here again, Herodotus' narrative replicates the conventions of athletic victory and its commemoration.

But Tellos and Kleobis and Biton are not only the embodiments of *kudos* in war and contests, respectively; they are also represented in Solon's discourse as aristocrats perfectly integrated into their civic communities. Again, because scholars tend to see the narrative as a valorization of the ordinary citizen, the aristocratic milieu of the story is rarely noted. But we are told that Tellos' children were καλοί τ' κἀγαθοί (gentlemen) and that his death was λαμπροτάτη (practically a buzzword in Herodotus and Thucydides for aristocratic display).[93] Kleobis and Biton, too, given that they were athletic victors, were likely to be aristocrats.[94] Yet these narratives strike a careful balance between the exceptional achievement of individual aristocrats and their participation in their civic communities. In the case of Tellos, it is easy to see how his death in battle functions as both a personal triumph and a civic good, but the treatment of Kleobis and Biton suggests that the civic advantages of athletic victory are somewhat more ambiguous. It is perhaps for this reason that all the elements of athletic victory are displaced in their story from agonistic competition itself to the transportation of their mother to a civic festival of Hera, for the latter stands unambiguously as the service of the common good.[95]

Once we discern in Tellos and Kleobis and Biton aristocratic embodiments of the economy of *kudos,* we can recognize that Herodotus' narrative participates in the "contest of paradigms" so characteristic of the late archaic period.[96] In setting these figures up as *paradeigmata* of human blessedness, the narrative attempts to make the values they represent into the only possible civic values. That these values are contested we can see from Xenophanes fr. 2 DK, a text that we must set in dialogue with Herodotus' account. In Herodotus, Solon opposes the purely material economy of Croesus with a symbolic economy of *kudos.* In the fragment of Xenophanes, the poet's voice espouses just the opposite: he rejects the symbolic economy that subtends athletic victory in favor of a material economy of civic acquisition. Xenophanes does not deny that athletic victors are possessors of *kudos,* for he begins his denunciation of athletics, "But if someone should win victory by the swiftness of his feet, or in the pentathlon, where the precinct of Zeus [is] beside the streams of Pisa in Olympia, or wrestling, or even having the grievous boxing, or the terrible contest which they call the pankration, then he would be more prestigious for his fellow citizens to look upon" (ἀστοῖσίν κ' εἴη κυδρότερος προσορᾶν; fr. 2.1–6).[97] Yet the poet resolutely refuses to engage the issue of athletics on the level of this symbolic economy. Instead, he shifts the terms in the last lines of the fragment, focusing on the city's "good government" and material prosperity: "For not even if a good boxer should be among the people, or one who is good at the pentathlon or wrestling or in the swiftness of his feet, the very thing which is most honored of all the works of strength of men in the contest, would the city on that account be more orderly. But there would be small joy for the city in this – if someone competing win beside the banks of Pisa – for these things do not fatten the city's coffers" (οὐ γὰρ πιαίνει ταῦτα μυχοὺς πόλιος; fr. 2.15–22). Certain modern scholars have read Xenophanes' poetry as an attack on aristocratic values, and we may apply that interpretation to fr. 2 as well.[98] In response to a serious aristocratic bid for renewed talismanic authority within the community, Xenophanes counters with a very different model of civic good, consciously rejecting charismatic power in favor of material well-being.

It is within this contest of paradigms that we must situate the victory odes of Pindar and Bacchylides. I began this essay by asking about the meaning of *kudos* within epinikion. If the economy of *kudos* does indeed have the political component I am suggesting, we should perhaps invert the priority of the terms: it is not *kudos* that resides within epinikion, but rather epinikion that functions within the economy of *kudos.* It is then no accident that epinikion as a genre appeared in the late sixth century and enjoyed its heyday in the first half of the fifth. Epinikion, victor statues, *and* the heroization of athletic victors proliferated in this period, all symptoms of an active negotiation between the aristocracy and the community at large over the forms of charismatic power. For all three – epinikion, victor statues, and athlete-hero cult – publicly restaged the original circulation of the crown in order to renew in perpetuity the victor's special power for his city.

NOTES

A shorter version of this essay was delivered at the 1990 American Philological Association Annual Meeting in San Francisco, and the section on victor statues was presented as a talk at Dartmouth College in October 1992. I owe thanks to Martin Bloomer, Tom Cole, W. R. Connor, Joseph Day, Crawford Greenewalt Jr., Tom Habinek, Paula Perlman, Seth Schwartz, Deborah Steiner, Kate Toll, and Emily Vermeule for reading and commenting on various versions. The contributions of Carol Dougherty to the essay's substance and organization require special thanks: even when the work has not been "officially" collaborative, she has made a tremendous difference.

1. See Greenblatt 1980, 1988b; Veeser 1989.
2. For other examples, see Pind. *Ol.* 5.1–8; Bacchyl. 1.155–65, 13.58–60. All quotations of Pinder are cited from Snell and Maehler 1980; those of Bacchylides from Snell and Maehler 1970.
3. Benveniste 1973: 348.
4. Fränkel 1973: 80 n. 14. For anthropological discussions of *mana* and *orenda*, see Lehmann 1915; Mauss 1972: 108–21.
5. Benveniste 1973: 351.
6. For the epithet κυδιάνειρα, see *Il.* 4.225, 6.124, 7.113, 8.448, 12.325, 13.270, 14.155, 24.391 (with μάχη) and *Il.* 1.490 (with ἀγορή). ἀγορή in Homer normally designates the assembly (as at *Il.* 2.144, 2.149; *Od.* 9.112), but on occasion it also functions as a substitute for ἀγών, the gathering place for contests (as at *Od.* 8.109). For *kudos* in athletic and military inscriptions, see *CEG* 4, 519, 657, 785, 790, 879, Ebert nos. 64, 69, 74, 75, 76, 78, 79, Peek no. 40. Notice also Pindar's formulation "whoever in contests or war wins luxurious *kudos*" (*Isthm.* 1.50).
7. See Frazer 1935: 89–105 and Cornford in Harrison 1912:212–59. More recently, Versnel 1970: 155–163 has revived the theory using the *mana* of iselastic victors as a parallel for the Roman triumph.
8. E.g., Lonis 1979: 27–35.
9. Cartledge 1987: 109–10, citing Weber 1978: 1285 and Taeger 1957: 33; cf. Versnel 1970: 158.
10. We should keep in mind that Suetonius was a serious scholar of things Greek (who wrote an antiquarian treatise *On Greek Games*) and Nero an obsessive Hellenizer (on Suetonius, see Wallace-Hadrill 1983: 44–8; on Nero, see Griffin 1984: 43–4, 85, 208–20). For the custom of breaking down a part of the wall, cf. the more skeptical report of Dio Cass. 62.20, and Vitr. 9, pref. 1; see also Sherwin-White 1966: 729 and P. Herrmann 1975: 156.
11. Cf. Pindar *Ol.* 8.64, *Ol.* 13.15, *Nem.* 6.59; Robert 1967: 16–18. Pleket 1975: 56–65 diverges somewhat from the traditional interpretation, defining the holy games as a larger category that includes but is not limited to "crown games." For a thorough discussion of the categories holy games, crown games, iselastic games, and thematic games, see Pleket 1975: 54–71.
12. Versnel 1970: 155–62. Gagé 1953: 177–9 aptly cites the Trojan horse as a parallel: recall that, in Vergil, the walls of Troy are breached to bring in the horse because it is believed by the Trojans to be a talisman of supremacy that will ensure their conquest of Greece (*Aen.* 2.189–94, 234–40). Martin Bloomer suggests to me that we should read the victor's crown as itself a metonymy for the circuit of the city walls, which can be brought into the city only through a break in this larger circuit.
13. The garb of Herakles is also significant in this context. In a sense, Herakles is the

talismanic hero par excellence, and as such he provides a model both for athletics (in Pindar [cf. Slater 1984: 249–64] and on the metopes of Zeus' temple at Olympia [cf. Raschke 1988: 43–8]) and for war. For evidence of Herakles as a talismanic hero in war, we should note that, according to Herodotus, two major battles of the Persian Wars were fought near precincts of Herakles (Marathon, Hdt. 6.108; Thermopylae, Hdt. 7.176; cf. Boedeker 1988: 46). As a parallel for Milo's assumption of the garb of Herakles for battle, cf. Diod. Sic. 16.44.3.

14. Macan 1908: 1.670. On the form of the victory announcement, see later.

15. Thus How and Wells 1928: 2.302: "This cannot mean that the seer was to share the actual command in war, for in comparison with this the grant of citizenship would be nothing. It seems to refer to the position of the kings as priests, since they offered sacrifice before all important undertakings. . . . Tisamenus was to act with them in this." Similarly Macan 1908: 1.667 (ad 9.33, l. 13); see also Fontenrose 1968: 94: "As *mantis*, and therefore as *hēgemōn,* he would be victorious in five great battles."

16. For the close connection between military expeditions and colonial ventures in this period, see Dougherty, Chapter 9, this volume.

17. See Hönle 1972: 47–8, 157–8.

18. Chamoux 1953: 123–4 takes Chionis as an official representative of Sparta, which, as the mother city of Thera, appropriately joined the colonial expedition to found Kyrene.

19. See Diog. Laert. 1.74; Strab. 599–600. Berve 1937: 28–9 argued quite plausibly that Phrynon's expedition only makes sense as a colonial venture. See also Hönle 1972: 47–8. The tradition of Phrynon's duel, one-on-one, with Pittakos (Diog. Laert. 1.74; Strab. 600; Suda s.v. Πιττακός; Plut. *malign. Herod.* 15; schol. ap. Aesch. *Eum.* 398) may also reflect a belief in the athlete's talismanic power.

20. For Herodotus' normal practice, see 1.31, 5.47.1, 5.71.1, 5.102.3, 6.103.2, 8.47.

21. Macan 1895: 1.296 (ad 6.36, l. 2) speculates that Herodotus is here reproducing the formulae of an inscription. If this is so, it suggests that a significant connection between Miltiades' athletic victory and his status as oikist was felt by the erectors of the monument that was Herodotus' source.

22. Moretti 1957: no. 332; date proposed by Hönle 1972: 157–8.

23. Thus Hönle 1972: 157–8.

24. Hornblower 1991: 506–7.

25. Other possible military commanders who were crown victors are Alkmeon of Athens (Moretti 1957: no. 81), Promachos of Pellene (Moretti 1957: no. 355), and Stomios of Elis (Moretti 1957: no. 404). There is, of course, a class issue here as well: in this period, victors at the Panhellenic games tended to be aristocrats (*pace* D. C. Young 1984), who also tended to be chosen military commanders. I will consider the overlap between these categories later.

26. In explaining the peculiarity of one ship, some modern scholars have tended to follow Pausanias, who claimed that Phayllos happened to be in mainland Greece when the Persian invasion occurred and that he responded by manning his own ship (Paus. 10.9.2; thus Macan 1908: 1.2.431–2). We should note, however, that there is no hint of this explanation in Herodotus, so that it may be a later conjecture, invented to rationalize the oddness of one ship.

27. See LSJ, s.v. ἀνατίθημι II.

28. Unfortunately, many of the early inscriptions are badly mutilated: the association of *kudos* and crowns may occur in *CEG* 834 (= Ebert 58) and Ebert 64.4.

29. Cf. Ebert 67 (*Anth. Pal.* 9.588); 71 (*SEG* iii 398); Moretti 1957: no. 38 (*IG* vii 530); *IG* xii suppl., 257; *Fouilles de Delphes* iii.2.67; *IG* ii² 3138.3–4; and "Demosthenes"

58.66: Ἐπιχάρης μὲν ὁ πάππος ὁ ἐμὸς Ὀλυμπίασι νικήσας παῖδας στάδιον ἐστεφάνωσε τὴν πόλιν (Epichares, my grandfather, having won the boys' stade race at the Olympics, crowned the city). See also Theotimos ap. schol. ap. Pind. *Pyth.* 5.34 (Drachmann 1964: 2.176) and Pliny *HN* 7.26, "more sacris certaminibus vincentium: neque enim ipsi coronantur, sed patrias suas coronant" (in the manner of those who win at the holy games: for they are not themselves crowned, but they crown their homelands); for more examples, Robert 1967: 19–23.

30. Although this inscription is very late, we find a close parallel for its diction in Pindar *Ol.* 10.66, ὁ δὲ πάλᾳ κυδαίνων Ἔχεμος Τεγέαν (Echemos bestowing *kudos* on Tegea in the wrestling), which answers the question τίς δὴ ποταίνιον ἔλαχε στέφανον (Who then was allotted a brand new crown?) at 60–1. See also Pind. *Pyth.* 1.31 (of Hieron's announcement of the newly founded city of Aitna at the Pythian games): κλεινὸς οἰκιστὴρ ἐκύδανεν πόλιν. This continuity, spanning five centuries, supports the contention of Pleket 1974: 79, 1975: 71–89 that the aristocratic *ideology* of the games endured (in spite of changes in the social status of competitors) well into the Roman period.

31. For a parallel instance of a metaphorical crown linked to *kudos,* see *Anth. Pal.* 7.251 (= Simonides 121D). Here the terms are reversed: those dead in battle "crown their homeland with unquenchable *kleos*" and thereby win *kudos* for themselves.

32. Cf. Thuc. 4.121.4, and the vase representations collected in Jüthner 1898. See also Gardiner 1910: 206; Slater 1984: 245–7.

33. As in the Ephesian inscription, Keil and Maresch 1960: no. 5 coll. 78–80, ll. 7–12 (ca. 300 B.C.E.): [ἔδοξε]ν τῆι βουλῆ(ι) καὶ τῶι δήμωι ... ἀναγγεῖλαι αὐτὸν ἐν τῆι ἀγοραῖ καθ[ά]περ οἱ ἄλλοι νικῶντες ἀναγγέλλονται (The Boule and the demos resolved to announce him in the Agora, just as the other victors are announced). See the discussion of Robert 1967: 14–17.

34. Or εἰσελαύνειν τὸν στέφανον, "to drive in the crown," from which the term "iselastic" derives: the iselastic games were those from which the victor had the privilege of reentering his city in a chariot. See Robert 1967: 17–18; Pleket 1975: 62–4.

35. See J. H. Krause 1838: 197–201; Stengel 1920: 210–11; Blech 1982: 114; Slater 1984: 245 with n. 24. For evidence for the dedication of the crown in Pindar, see *Ol.* 9.110–12; *Nem.* 5.50–4; *Nem.* 8.13–16 (*mitra*).

36. See esp. Nisetich 1975: 61–4.

37. For more extended discussion of these passages, see Kurke 1991: 203–9. Cf. *Pyth.* 8.5 (and as a parallel for Πυθιόνικον τιμάν as a periphrasis for the victor's crown, see *Pyth.* 5.30, ἀρισθάρματον ... γέρας). This interpretation may also apply to injunctions to "receive the *kōmos*" at *Ol.* 6.98, *Pyth.* 5.22, *Pyth.* 9.73, and *Nem.* 4.11, since, at *Ol.* 8.9–10, Pindar links the *kōmos* with the *stephanēphoria*. Thus *kōmos* and *stephanēphoria* may represent two parts of the ritual reentry, either one of which the poet can evoke as metonymy for the whole process. Cf. Heath 1988: 189–92.

38. Nisetich 1975. For the importance of both ends of the victor's journey, see Gagé 1953: 172–3.

39. Recall Astylos of Kroton, who, according to Pausanias (6.13.1), twice had himself "announced as Syracusan to gratify Hieron" (ἐς χάριν τὴν Ἱέρωνος ... ἀνηγόρευσεν αὑτὸν Συρακούσιον). The people of Kroton responded by turning his house into a prison and tearing down his statue in the temple of Hera Lakinia. I will consider later the importance of victor statues and the rituals that surround them; for now, I simply note that the severity of this punishment suggests there is a great deal at stake in the announcement of the victor's city. On punishments of athletes in general, see Forbes 1952.

158

40. For the privilege of eating in the prytaneion, see Xenoph. fr. 2 DK; Pl. *Ap.* 36d; *IG* i²
    77; *IG* xii, fasc. 5, 274, 281, 289 (Paros), and 1060 (Keos); for large monetary awards,
    see Plut. *Sol.* 23.5; Ath. 12.522a–d; Diog. Laert. 1.55; and Inscription from Ephesus
    (Keil and Maresch 1960: no. 5 coll. 78–80, where the monetary reward is specifically
    designated ἀργύριον εἰς τὸν στέφανον, "money for the crown"). Modern discussions
    of rewards for crown victors include J. H. Krause 1838: 199–201; Pleket 1974: 67,
    1975: 59; D. C. Young 1984: 128–33; Serwint 1987: 10–19.
41. This association of *kudos* and crowns may also explain why, for the Greeks, the crown
    games were the "holy games." Again, we may engage in the exercise of reading literally:
    the reason the holy games are holy is that winning marks the athlete out by bestowing
    on him special power. The crown of the crown games is the emblem of *kudos*.
42. Lucian *pro imag.* 11.
43. I follow Ebert's interpretation of this phrase; for discussion (with earlier bibliography),
    see Ebert 1972: 251–4.
44. Cf. *CEG* 862 (where the moment of return rather than that of crowning is highlighted),
    Ebert 56, 61 (*Anth. Pal.* 16.24), 67 (*Anth. Pal.* 9.588).
45. British Museum B144 (*ABV* 307, 59).
46. Cf. Dittenberger and Purgold 1896, nos. 143, 151, 152, 155, 158, 159, 162, 165, 167,
    168, 173. It is worth noting that the prose inscriptions become more detailed with time,
    just as the announcements preserved in literary sources do: cf. Dittenberger and Purgold
    1896, nos. 175, 177, 182.
47. Cf. Paus. 6.9.9 and *CEG* 399. I ignore here as anachronistic Pausanias' distinction
    between hippic dedications and gymnastic memorials (Paus. 5.21.1): see Gardiner 1922:
    123 and H.-V. Hermann 1972: 243 n. 436.
48. Cf. Pind. *Ol.* 8.17–20, *Ol.* 9.90–4, where the poet uses similar formulae to describe
    the beauty of a boy victor at the moment of crowning.
49. Noteworthy is the omission of the victor's homeland, for which Ebert 1972: 58 offers
    two possible explanations: (1) his homeland Aigina may have been recorded in a prose
    inscription added to the epigram, or (2) this epigram may have come originally from a
    statue of Theognetos set up in Aigina itself (in which case we cannot connect this
    epigram with the Olympic statue of Theognetos described by Pausanias at 6.9.1).
50. Thus, in different ways and to varying degrees, Hyde 1921: 71–99; Lattimore 1987;
    Serwint 1987: 18–24; Raschke 1988: 39–48; Vernant 1991: 159–63.
51. Day 1989a, 1989b.
52. Day 1989a.
53. Svenbro 1988: 9, 23–4, 43–4, 53–73, following Knox 1968. So also Ebert 1972: 22;
    Day 1989a.
54. See Gardiner 1910: 200–1, 205, 1955: 227–8; Nisetich 1975: 59, 64 with note 27.
    Nisetich adduces Eur. *Tro.* 220–3 and Paus. 8.40.2; he might have added a reference
    to the pseudo-Panathenaic amphora that we have already mentioned (Figure 29), for
    there a man approaches the victorious horseman bearing a tripod and a wreath as the
    herald announces the victory.
55. See Hyde 1921: 148–55. Hyde (155) notes that the fillet is a much more common feature
    than an actual sculpted crown. See also Serwint 1987: 112–16.
56. In Philostratus, Apollonius explains that Milo wears a fillet because he is represented
    as a priest of Hera. Pausanias' explanation of the fillet is much more far-fetched. He
    sees in it a representation of one of Milo's legendary feats of strength: "He would tie
    a cord round his forehead as though it were a ribbon or a crown. Holding his breath
    and filling with blood the veins on his head, he would break the cord by the strength
    of these veins" (Paus. 6.14.7, trans. W. H. S. Jones). As Scherer 1885: 23–4, Gurlitt

1890: 413, and Hyde 1921: 106–7 saw long ago, Pausanias' entire fanciful narrative derives from a misunderstanding of traditional archaic sculptural forms. For more recent discussions, see Lattimore 1987: 255; Serwint 1987: 103–4.

57. Cf. Paus. 6.4.5 and see Hyde 1921: 150–5 and Serwint 1987: 107–9 for discussion of the type.

58. It is not certain whether the coronation occurred immediately after the contest or on the last day of the festival at Olympia; for discussion, see Gardiner 1910: 200–1.

59. This reconstruction must remain largely speculative since we have very little solid evidence about which images went with which inscriptions. This aspect of ritual sheds new light on the observation of Nisetich 1975 that Pindar obsessively links crowns (real and metaphorical) with the naming of the victor in the odes. We can now link this practice with the victor monuments as ritual reenactments in different media; that is, both monuments and epinikion function to reanimate the victor's *kudos* by restaging the victory announcement and coronation.

60. See discussion on p. 153.

61. I accept Ebert's supplements; for a careful discussion of the merits and problems of other proposed supplements, see Ebert 1972: 173.

62. We must assume that the first line of Ebert 48 contained the victor's name, patronymic, and ethnic. See Ebert 1972: 152.

63. Cf. Ebert 1972: 152: "The passerby is supposed to announce the athletic fame of the one celebrated, which he does on the spot by reading aloud the epigram" (my translation).

64. Svenbro 1988: 49–52 identifies this gap as the enabling condition of the earliest Greek inscriptions and suggests that it accounts for the ἐγώ of the "oggetti parlanti" cataloged by Burzachechi 1962 and Häusle 1979. Cf. the discussion of D. C. Young 1983 on inscriptional ποτέ.

65. In this case, the oddness of the abrupt change from first to third person is palliated by the fact that the second half of the pentameter, τήνδε βροτοῖς ἐσορᾶν, is a revision that appears to postdate the original inscription: it stands in an erasure and is slightly longer than the original half-line would have been. Roehl 1882: 108–9, followed by Dittenberger and Purgold 1896; Hyde 1921: 38; Moretti 1953: 30–2, 1957: 86; Ebert 1972: 70–1; and Lattimore 1987: 250–1 conjecture that originally the city of Lokris or Euthymos' father had erected the statue, but that the Elean authorities "required the substitution of Euthymos as dedicant" (Lattimore 1987: 251; Roehl 1882: 108–9 suggested, *exempli gratia*, the supplements πατρὶς ἀγαλλομένη or παιδὶ φίλῳ γενέτωρ). In spite of these extenuating circumstances, I believe, the point stands: at least at the time when the inscription was altered, the shift from first to third person must have been perceived as acceptable. For a parallel (with no such curious history), see the Kyniska inscription (later in text).

66. I follow the reading of Ebert, who acknowledges the awkwardness of the shift from first to third person and back again, but is at a loss to explain it, except as the avoidance of an excessive frequency of *a*-sounds (1972: 112). Hansen (apud *CEG* 820) simply emends the stone's ἔστασε to ἔστασα, claiming that there are no good parallels for such a shift from first to third person within an epigram before 300 B.C.E. But as Hansen himself notes (1989: 229) aside from the anomalous *CEG* 399 (see note 65), *CEG* 493 and *CEG* 595 exhibit the same shift between first and third person. For the reasons stated in the text, I believe the third-person ἔστασε should be retained rather than normalized as Hansen does. We find a similar effect, without the change of person, in *CEG* 828 (= Ebert 38; 368 B.C.E.):

Ἑλλήνων ἦρχον τότε Ὀλυμπίαι ἡνίκα μοι Ζεύς
δῶκεν νικῆσαι πρῶτον Ὀλυμπιάδα

ἵπποις ἀθλοφόροις, τὸ δὲ δεύτερον αὖτις ἐφεξῆς
ἵπποις· υἱὸς δ᾽ ἦν Τρωίλος Ἀλκινόο.

I was Hellanodikas then when Zeus granted to me to
win the Olympics for the first time with prize-winning
horses, but the second time again in succession with
horses; and I was Troilos the son of Alkinoos.

As Ebert notes (1972: 129), the use of the imperfect ἦν in the last line of the inscription
need not indicate that the victor was already dead at the time the monument was erected;
it simply imagines the monument from the perspective of a future audience. Thus ἦν
too registers the absence of the victor and the presence of the image.

67. Vernant 1991: 153. Vernant himself acknowledges the applicability of this analysis to
victor statues: "If the archaic statue uses the human figure to convey this set of 'values'
that in their plenitude only belong to divinity and appear like a fragile reflection when
they gleam on the body of mortals, we can then understand how the same image, the
votive Kouros, can sometimes represent the god himself or sometimes a human person
who, *by virtue of his victory in the Games or through some other consecration,* is
revealed as 'equal to the gods' " (Vernant 1991: 161; my emphasis). Yet he also traces
a development whereby the image as a "copy that imitates a model" represents a new
state: "The human figure must have ceased to incarnate religious values; in its appearance, it must have become in and for itself the model to be reproduced" (Vernant 1991:
163). I am not so sure a clear evolutionary model is appropriate: it may be that the two
conceptions of figural art coexisted for a long time. As a parallel, see Mango 1963,
who discusses the reception of ancient statuary in the Byzantine era and notes the
coexistence in the sources of a belief in the magical power of statues and an interest in
their artistic, mimetic qualities (which he analyzes in terms of "popular" and "intellectual" responses respectively).

68. For discussions, see Gardiner 1916–17; Mylonas 1943–4; Pouilloux 1954; Fontenrose
1968; Hönle 1972: 98–106; Bohringer 1979; Crotty 1982: 122–31; Lattimore 1987;
Serwint 1987: 19–24. I follow Serwint's list rather than that of Fontenrose, who includes
many figures who fit his hero type, though they are not necessarily athletic victors. For
summaries of the stories attached to these victors, see Fontenrose, Crotty, and Serwint.

69. Fontenrose 1968: 87.

70. Gardiner 1916–17: 96, followed by Mylonas 1943–4: 289 and Serwint 1987: 19.

71. Nor does it solve the problem to claim, as Gardiner 1916–17: 96–7, Mylonas 1943–4:
284–9, and Serwint 1987: 19–24 do, that these athletes' "special recognition . . . had
nothing to do with their athletic victories" (Serwint 1987: 19). Such a claim smacks of
special pleading: it can hardly be a coincidence that all nine had some connection with
the great games. What these scholars' elaborate counterarguments do suggest is that
there was a complex interplay of factors involved in heroization, only one of which was
athletic victory.

72. Fontenrose 1968: 78. Note Fontenrose's characteristics (K), "The athlete had something
to do with rock and stone," and (M), "His statue was powerful or extraordinary."

73. I am indebted here to Vernant's discussion of the colossus as magical double: "[The
colossus] served to attract and pin down a double which found itself in abnormal
circumstances. It made it possible to reestablish correct relations between the world of
the dead and the world of the living. . . . The colossos fulfils several complementary
functions: it is a visible representation of the power of the dead man, it embodies the
active manifestations of it, and it regulates the relationship between it and the living"
(Vernant 1983: 314).

74. Bohringer 1979. Gardiner 1916–17: 97, Moretti 1957: 84, and Hönle 1972: 99 also note that this is predominantly a late-sixth- and early-fifth-century phenomenon.

75. Bohringer's model of crisis in fifth-century Greece corresponds well to Weber's general analysis of the origins of charismatic authority. As Weber observes: "All *extra*ordinary needs, i.e., those which transcend the sphere of everyday economic routines, have always been satisfied in an entirely heterogeneous manner: on a *charismatic* basis . . . the 'natural' leaders in moments of distress – whether psychic, physical, economic, ethical, religious, or political – were neither appointed officeholders nor 'professionals' in the present-day sense . . . but rather the bearers of specific gifts of body and mind that were considered 'supernatural' (in the sense that not everybody could have access to them)" (Weber 1978: 1111–12; see also 1148).

76. Pouilloux 1954: 72–7.

77. Cf. Pind. *Pyth.* 2.18–20 with scholia (Drachmann 1964: 2.37–8).

78. Bohringer 1979: 10–13. Pausanias notes and tries to rationalize the discrepancy between Oibotas' athletic inscription at Olympia (which designates Paleia as his hometown) and the tradition of his cult in Dyme (Paus. 7.17.6–7). For a different explanation of the discrepancy, see Ebert 1972: 85–6.

79. The analysis of Crotty 1982: 122–31 accounts for the second category as those who fail to achieve reintegration in their communities. The weakness of Crotty's model, however, is that it does not account for the first category of victors – those who do not seem to be alienated from their communities in any way.

80. For the pattern of heroizing a potent military enemy, see Visser 1982.

81. Callim. frs. 98–9 Pfeiffer; Pliny *HN* 7.152.

82. According to Plutarch, the bodies of those struck by lightning do not decay (*Quaest. conv.* 4.665c–d), while according to Artemidorus, to dream of lightning is fortunate for athletes, since it signifies victory (*Oneir.* 2.9). I owe both references to Serwint 1987: 51–52. Cf. Rohde 1925: 581–2: app. 1; A. B. Cook 1925: 2.1.9, 22–36.

83. Where perhaps, in the "normal" course of things, he might have dedicated his crown or set up a victory statue.

84. For another example of this pattern, we might cite Diognetos of Crete, a shadowy figure of whom we know only that he killed his boxing opponent Herakles (!) and so was denied the Olympic crown by the Elean authorities. Our only source, Ptolemy Hephaestion (ap. Phot. *Bibl.* 190. 151b) records that "the Cretans honor this Diognetos as a hero."

85. Euseb. *Praep. Evang.* 5.34.15–16 preserves the tradition that Euthykles was imprisoned and subsequently died. Callimachus appears to make no mention of the athlete, concentrating his attention entirely on the fate of Euthykles' statue.

86. In fact, this account ignores the fact that Achaians won at the Olympics in 688, 512, and 496 B.C.E.

87. Davies 1981: 88–131. Davies's model applies specifically to Athens, but we might extend it mutatis mutandis to aristocrats and others throughout the Greek world. Indeed, we can observe several different constituencies in different places seeking legitimacy or renewed talismanic authority through athletic victory. In western Greece, this is the period of intensive participation in the great games by tyrants; in Sparta, the kings and certain aristocrats who opposed the ephors were very active in chariot-racing competitions (on chariot racing as a significant political gesture by the Spartan aristocracy, see Hönle 1972: 146–59). In this context, it is worth noting that one of the latest-known victor-heroes is Kyniska of Sparta, daughter and sister of Spartan kings, who, according to Plutarch (*Ages.* 20), was encouraged in her horse-racing proclivities by her brother, King Agesilaos. Do her competition and heroization reflect a final bid for renewed

talismanic authority by the Spartan kingship in the face of the encroaching power of the Ephorate?

88. Quote from Weber 1978: 1137. According to the model of Weber (1978: 1111–1300), charisma always starts as personal and discontinuous (in contrast to patriarchal or bureaucratic authority). It can be institutionalized to support the claims of royal or aristocratic power, but eventually the institutionalized form gives way before the rational order of discipline and/or the worldly concerns of economics.

89. For a similar interpretation of Solon and Croesus, see Konstan 1983: 15–19; cf. Konstan 1987 (on the contrast Herodotus constructs between Greek and Persian notions of value in the *Histories*).

90. Cf. How and Wells 1928: I. 68; Loraux 1986: 38–42.

91. On Herodotus' use of καὶ δὴ καί, see Denniston 1954: 255–6; Erbse 1956: 215–16.

92. Cf. Bacchyl. 3.10; Pindar *Nem.* 11.11–12; Eur. *Bacch.* 1180, 1242–3; Timoth. fr. 26 *PMG.*

93. Also, according to the model of Loraux 1986: 42–56, the very fact that Tellos is remembered by name, rather than in an anonymous *dēmosion sēma,* harks back to an aristocratic paradigm of the "fine death."

94. Though D. C. Young 1984 has challenged the assumption that athletic victors of the archaic and classical periods were inevitably aristocratic, it is likely that Panhellenic victors at such an early date would have been upper class, since they alone had the necessary funds and leisure time for arduous training and competition. See Kyle 1985, Instone 1986, and Poliakoff 1989 for critiques of Young's argument.

95. For an expression of similar ambivalence about the communal value of athletic victory, cf. Tyrtaios fr. 12 W, ll. 1–16.

96. I borrow the phrase "contest of paradigms" from V. Turner 1974: 14. For more discussion of this phenomenon in the late archaic period, see Kurke 1991.

97. With this acknowledgment and subsequent rejection of talismanic power, we might compare Euripides' denunciation of athletic victors (from a fragment of the *Autolykos* preserved in Athenaeus). There, the unknown speaker insists that men who are "wise and good," "restrained and just" are more advantageous to the city than victorious athletes (Eur. fr. 282 Nauck²). Nonetheless, the speaker acknowledges that athletic victors go λαμπροὶ δ' ἐν ἥβῃ καὶ πόλεως ἀγάλματα (splendid in their youth and objects of admiration for the city). The designation of victors as ἀγάλματα is especially interesting in this context – we can understand the term etymologically as "objects of admiration," but its conventional meaning at this time is "a statue," especially "an image of a god."

98. See Mazzarino 1947; Bowra 1971: 115–21; Fränkel 1973: 328–330.

CHAPTER EIGHT

Hero Cult and Politics in Herodotus

The Bones of Orestes

Deborah Boedeker

RECENT studies of Greek hero cult have concentrated on two new emphases: on the one hand, the variety and multiplicity of phenomena that have been grouped under this rubric (a particular focus of Carla Antonaccio, Chapter 3, this volume),[1] and on the other, their complex connections to the development of the polis.[2] Several kinds of hero cults emerged together with the archaic city-state and contributed much to the expression of its identity and institutions. In addition to helping define a polis at an early stage of its existence, hero cults could also reflect its nature as it developed, geographically, politically, and ideologically in later periods. As Claude Bérard writes: "The city forms itself in a slow evolution, periodically marked by a series of ideological foundations."[3] In addition to cults of the "city founders," in whom Bérard is especially interested, new cults of heroes from the distant past were sometimes introduced in association with political changes; perhaps most familiar are the ten new Attic *phyle* heroes incorporated as part of the Kleisthenic reforms (Hdt. 5.66).[4] Assuming these two perspectives – the variety of hero cults and their relationship to political identity – this essay offers an expanded interpretation of a much-discussed passage in Herodotus: the translation of the bones of Orestes from Tegea to Sparta (1.66–8). Previous discussions of this incident, as we shall see, focus on its alleged propaganda value as an announcement that Sparta has changed its relationship to its neighbors. I will focus instead on three other aspects: first, and at greatest length, the "internal" meaning of Orestes at Sparta; second, the influence of a traditional story pattern on the making of "history" in this passage; finally, the function of the Orestes incident in the Herodotean narrative.

I

Once the worship of named heroes is established in Greek cities,[5] a new phenomenon appears: the translation of a hero to a different site. Our earliest example of this involves Kleisthenes, maternal grandfather of his Athenian namesake and tyrant of

Sikyon about 600–570 B.C.E., who during a conflict with Argos decides to oust the popular Argive hero Adrastos from the Sikyonian agora (Hdt. 5.67).[6] When he asks at Delphi if he may remove Adrastos, however, the Pythia responds that Adrastos was a king of Sikyon, whereas Kleisthenes is a mere "stone-thrower"; Adrastos must stay in Sikyon. Instead of getting rid of Adrastos, therefore, Kleisthenes decides to take less direct measures: he obtains from Thebes the hero Melanippos, Adrastos' bitter enemy, and installs him in the prytaneum in Sikyon. (Herodotus does not indicate why Thebes would agree to give up its hero or what form this transfer took.)[7] The honors previously paid to Adrastos are then redirected, some to the god Dionysos and others to the newly introduced hero.

Earlier in his work, Herodotus records another example of a city's attempt to procure and establish a new hero. This is the memorable story of the bones of Orestes and how their acquisition helped Sparta achieve its leading position in the Peloponnese. The incident can be dated to about 560 B.C.E., in the kingship of Anaxandrides and Ariston. At that time, says Herodotus, despite internal good order and general success in war, Sparta was long unable to conquer Tegea. Seeking advice at Delphi, the Spartans are told that they should bring Orestes to their own city. When they fail to locate the hero, the Spartans ask the Pythia where he is buried and receive a riddling answer. Eventually one Lichas, a Spartan *agathoergos*,[8] solves the riddle when he learns that a skeleton of heroic size is buried in a plot of land belonging to a certain Tegean ironsmith.[9] Back in Sparta, Lichas reports the situation. Then, with the collaboration of his fellow citizens, he returns to Tegea under the pretext that he has been exiled and needs a new place to live. With this ruse he is eventually able to rent the land from the smith, dig up the bones, and bring them to Sparta. According to Herodotus, from that time on Sparta was able to defeat Tegea in war (1.67–8).

Parallel though they are, the stories of Orestes and Melanippos nevertheless differ from each other in several respects. Whereas Kleisthenes the tyrant imports Melanippos on his own authority primarily to discomfit another hero, the Spartans more positively seek to propitiate a supernatural power in a common effort. Significantly, Herodotus reports Delphic disapproval of Kleisthenes' effort, at least insofar as it aims at damaging Adrastos, whereas the whole Orestes episode is directed by oracular responses. And in contrast to the limited success of Kleisthenes' attempt to discredit Adrastos, once the bones of Orestes arrive in Sparta the long-sought defeat of Tegea soon follows. Herodotus' account implies that the hero simply accomplishes what he was sought to do. Modern historians, nevertheless, skeptical about the military efficacy of bones even of heroic size, offer a more complex explanation.

According to a venerable scholarly tradition, with the bones of Orestes incident Sparta announces a change in its foreign policy.[10] Instead of pursuing absolute conquest it will now form alliances with other states, and to secure the goodwill of non-Dorians (especially Arcadians) Sparta will emphasize its Achaian heritage as heir of the Pelopids, perhaps at the expense of its Dorian identity. Indeed, this alleged political program has been dubbed the "bones of Orestes policy."[11] Bringing Orestes to Sparta is seen to mark a conscious change in the city's evolution: in the late eighth and seventh centuries Sparta conquered and helotized Messenia, but by the mid-sixth century it was content with a more or less friendly hegemony over Tegea and other Peloponnesian cities. Possession of Orestes is seen as the emblem of that relationship – and thus as marking the beginning of the Peloponnesian League.

D. M. Leahy pursues this notion most elaborately in two articles where he develops a theory about Sparta's use of heroic bones in foreign policy. In addition to finding in Orestes the "patron saint" of the new policy of alliance,[12] Leahy similarly interprets our meager evidence about a transferal of the bones of Orestes' son Teisamenos to Sparta from Achaian Helike on the north coast of the Peloponnese, presumably a little later than the Tegean affair.[13] Leahy argues that Sparta was trying here too to forge an alliance on the basis of a shared hero, who was now transferred to the dominant polis. He suggests that Sparta wanted to secure alliances because it feared a helot uprising and, in contrast to the common opinion that the legendary ephor Chilon was the architect of the new policy, posits one or both kings as the prime motivator.[14] In any event, the whole plan to achieve hegemony by importing non-Dorian hero cults into Sparta was abandoned, Leahy suggests, when Helike did not yield under the influence of such propaganda.[15]

For Leahy and most other scholars, the transferal of Orestes was clearly a propaganda maneuver. But as Ian Morris reminds us, such a skeptical assessment of ancient religious practices is in many cases unhistorical; we must beware of falling prey to an anachronistic "propagandistic fallacy."[16] Although Antonaccio argues in Chapter 3 that heroic remains were at times deliberately fabricated by early city-states, I find more persuasive Carol Dougherty's view (Chapter 9) that modern distinctions between sacred and secular (in this case, propagandistic) motives do not apply to archaic Greek use of religious conventions. Cynical manipulation of hero cult is unlikely for any sixth-century polis, I would argue, and especially for Sparta, whose "religiosity" is so abundantly documented.[17] The fact that a hero such as Orestes had a "political" significance does not mean that his remains were deliberately fabricated or his cult guilefully introduced.

Other considerations too suggest that the standard interpretation of the Orestes incident does not adequately explain its full significance. First, Sparta's interest in its pre-Dorian past by no means begins only with the war against Tegea. On the contrary, archaic Sparta had long acknowledged its Achaian antecedents.[18] As one example, the kings of Sparta were considered not Dorians like other Lakedaimonians, but Achaians by virtue of their descent from Herakles. And this belief long predates Kleomenes' famous declaration of Achaian identity when Athena's priestess tried to bar him, as a Dorian, from the Athenian Acropolis (Hdt. 5.72): it is reflected as early as a fragment of Tyrtaios, recalling how "Zeus gave this citadel to the Herakleidai, with whom we [the Dorians], leaving windy Erineos, came to the broad island of Pelops" (fr. 2.13–15 W).[19] Even more to the point, moreover, "Achaian" Tyndarids and Pelopids are attested in Lakonian cult long before the introduction of Orestes. A shrine of Menelaos and Helen was established on Mycenaean foundations at Therapnai by 700 B.C.E., and one of Agamemnon and Kassandra ("Alexandra") at Amyklai probably not much later.[20] Apparently there was an early cult of the Dioskouroi at Therapnai as well (Alkman fr. 5 PMG); these heroic twins (in what form we do not know) officially accompanied the Spartan kings into battle (Hdt. 5.75).

Panhellenic poetic traditions also attest the Pelopid association with Lakedaimon: Stesichoros, Simonides, and Pindar all locate Orestes and his family in the neighborhood of Sparta.[21] It seems unlikely that these poets varied the mythical topography merely to gratify one city's (supposedly) newly declared Achaian claims. Why would they do this? Pindar's testimony at least appears unmotivated by any special relationship to Sparta; none of his victory odes is even composed for a Spartan triumph. For Stesichoros there is indeed a tradition, suggested by the *Marmor Parium* and accepted by C. M. Bowra, that he visited Sparta; like many accounts of early Greek poets, however, this story very likely derives from passages in the poet's works that were later understood as biographical.[22] In any case we should not assume that an archaic poet would accept local innovations in a myth at the expense of his own aspirations to Panhellenic status.

Rather than looking for ad hoc reasons why a given poet should associate Orestes with Sparta, it is more in keeping with the evidence to conclude that, according to a widespread tradition, not only Menelaos but other Pelopids as well were at home in Lakonia. This variant may have left a trace even in Homeric epic: a passage in the *Odyssey* has Agamemnon blown off course as he sails around Cape Malea, the southeasternmost point in the Peloponnese and certainly not on the way from Troy to Mycenae (*Od.* 4.514–20); does this "slip" reflect a tradition that Agamemnon was actually on the way home to Lakedaimon, where perhaps he shared the kingship with Menelaos?[23] An anecdote in Herodotus suggests that, in the time of the Persian Wars, Spartans expected such a tradition to be familiar far from home: when he told Gelon that "Pelopid Agamemnon would groan" if he knew that the command of united Hellenic forces had been taken from Spartans by Syracusans (7.159), Syagros certainly meant to imply that Agamemnon himself came from Sparta.[24]

Besides the fact that the Pelopids were by no means new to sixth-century Lakonia, other reasons also argue against interpreting the translation of Orestes primarily as externally directed propaganda for Spartan hegemony. First, there is no evidence to suggest that the cult of Orestes, if indeed he had a continuing cult, was directed toward outsiders.[25] Then too, it is most unlikely that the Tegeans would have accepted Sparta's leadership on the grounds that it had stolen a hero's bones from them. Such relics were powerful, and a city that possessed them would not want them to fall into enemy hands.[26] Had the Spartans stolen the bones of a hero they honored, the Tegeans would surely not have meekly accepted the domination of their thievish neighbors.[27] But the bones of Orestes, according to Herodotus, were not even known to exist in Tegea before Lichas removed them.[28] Possession of Orestes might give the Spartans the *power* to defeat Tegea, but there is no reason to think it would have given them a *right* to hegemony *in the eyes of non-Spartans*. As George Huxley remarks, other poleis seem to have ignored Sparta's supposed political claims based on Orestes.[29]

Let us consider then what this new cult might have meant at Sparta itself. In discussing the importation of heroic remains, H. W. Parke and D. E. W. Wormell maintain that the "best spiritual help" might come not from native heroes, but that particularly in war, the enemy might be routed most effectively if their [i.e., the enemy's] own heroes were enshrined in the territory which they tried to conquer . . . [T]he Spartans on more than one occasion actually used the Delphic oracle as authority for the removal of the relics of a foreign hero to Sparta, and followed up this translation by claiming the sovereignty of the country and the hero's support in conquering it.[30]

Here Parke and Wormell are evidently referring to Orestes and Teisamenos – but from the Spartan perspective, these were not foreign heroes but native kings (e.g., Paus. 2.18.6). Now it is well known how important it was for kings, alive or dead, to remain in Sparta or return there. This concern, for example, apparently motivated the reburial of Leonidas in Sparta some forty years after the Battle of Thermopylae.[31] So too the remains of the fourth-century kings Agesilaos and Agesipolis, who died abroad: their bodies were carefully preserved and taken home for burial.[32] And conversely, when Demaratos left Sparta, even after he was deposed, the city was alarmed enough to pursue him vigorously (Hdt. 6.70).[33]

Our sources are silent about precisely why the kings' presence was so important to the polis; we are left to assume that their divine descent and permanent special status combined to charge them with daimonic power, not unlike the power attributed to heroes.[34] To what extent Spartan kings became "heroized" after death is a vexed question.[35] According to a problematic passage in Xenophon (Lak. Pol. 15.8–9), at their burials kings were honored like heroes rather than human beings, but Herodotus (6.58) compares their burial rites to the funerals of barbarian kings.[36] Unfortunately, we do not know whether Spartan kings received ongoing rites or whether (as seems more likely) they were treated "heroically" only at burial. The same ignorance prevails in the case of Orestes: whether he enjoyed continuing cult or just a memorial is nowhere documented. Like his Heraklid successors, however, this early king was conspicuously buried: Orestes in the agora itself,[37] the Agiads and Eurypontids separately in other public locations (Paus. 3.12.8, 3.14.2).

For other Greeks, Orestes' horrifying deeds may well have been the source of his religious power.[38] The crime of matricide with its ensuing pursuit, madness, and healing underlie his numerous memorials throughout the Peloponnese. "Back home" in Sparta, however, it seems that Orestes was valuable, especially as a former king. Why, though, at this moment in Spartan history?

The little we know about circumstances in early Sparta suggests several reasons for the "internal" importance of Orestes in the mid-sixth century. Although our evidence for the archaic period is sparse and inconsistent,[39] several traditions suggest that the Spartans not infrequently faced serious social and political problems. Factions were not unknown in the supposed city of "equals" (homoioi).[40] Early in this period, for example, apparently because of problems with their civic status, a group called the Partheniai were forced to leave Lakedaimon and establish Sparta's only colony, Tarentum.[41] Besides this more recent tradition, tales set in the more distant past may also reflect the conditions of a later period. In one such tale we hear of the Aigeidai, whom Herodotus calls (inappropriately in terms of Spartan ideology) a "great family" at Sparta.[42] Their ancestor Theras was said to have migrated to Thera when he could no longer serve as regent for his nephew, leaving behind at

Sparta a son he nicknamed significantly Oiolykos, "Sheep among Wolves" (as explained in Hdt. 4.147–9). Such traditions may suggest tensions between certain aristocratic families and the rest of the polis. On a larger scale, Plutarch's description of Lykourgos' land reforms depicts a great change from vastly unequal plots to allotments of "brotherly" size (*Lyk.* 8.1–4). These hints of earlier internal conflicts are supported by the cliché that Sparta enjoyed a change from worst to best government (e.g., Hdt. 1.65; cf. Thuc. 1.18).

Moreover, the time of Anaxandrides and Ariston (the Agiad and Eurypontid kings, respectively, when the bones of Orestes were recovered) was apparently beset with problems concerning the sovereignty itself. Herodotus records fascinating anecdotes about both kings, their several wives, and their sons (the Agiads Dorieus and Kleomenes, 5.39–41; the Eurypontid Demaratos, 6.61–6). Details in these stories suggest that there were conflicts between kings and ephors about the production of legitimate offspring and succession to the kingship. In the one case, the ephors mandated that the childless Anaxandrides take a second wife. In the other, when the (premature) birth of his son Demaratos was announced, Ariston declared in the presence of the ephors that the baby could not be his; later Demaratos was deposed because of his alleged illegitimacy. Whatever lies behind these Herodotean intrigues, such stories seem to reflect political and familial struggles within Sparta during the very generation that Orestes was imported into the city.

Besides the Orestes incident, other innovations affecting Spartan political identity may be dated to roughly the same time. M. I. Finley believes that the "constitutional" changes attributed to the legendary Lykourgos were actually introduced in the early sixth century.[43] Quite apart from the vexed questions of the historicity and date of the lawgiver, I accept Finley's careful argument that this period brought to Sparta many institutions designed, above all, to subordinate familial interests to those of the polis. Pavel Oliva, in contrast, sees the changes as attempts to resolve conflicts between the aristocracy (in which he includes kings and *gerousia*) and the people (represented by the Ephorate).[44] These two perspectives are by no means in conflict with each other: family identity and status are, above all, an aristocratic concern. It should be noted, however, that Finley also believes that Spartan "equality" in the context of intense competition and authoritarianism must have produced great tensions for individuals – both for those who wanted to excel and for those who did not, or could not. J.-P. Vernant, too, who calls Sparta "ahead of its time" in respect to its emphasis on political as opposed to familial identity, points out that even outstanding achievements like those of Aristodemos, the bravest Spartan in the battle of Plataea, could be publicly disregarded if they seemed too individualistic (Hdt. 9.71).[45]

Considered against this background, the translation of Orestes can be seen as a way to guarantee Spartan military superiority by installing a hero who transcended familial claims, in complete accord with the spirit of the "constitutional" reforms. It is an advantage for the troubled state that Orestes has no descendants at Sparta; he belongs to no family but to Lakedaimon as a whole.[46] (A similar tradition prevails for Lykourgos, said to have had but one son, who produced no further offspring; Plut. *Lyk.* 31.4.)

Like his fellow Pelopids and Tyndarids also honored at Sparta, Orestes transcends even the dual kingship – which at this time or shortly afterward, as we have seen, may have been in a state of contention with the ephors. So too, when the Tyndarid Dioskouroi accompany the Heraklid kings into battle (Hdt. 5.75), even royal authority seems dependent on ancient but nonancestral Lakedaimonian heroes. The possession of Orestes' remains thus marks *for Sparta* its right to "Pelopid" leadership of other states, while obviating any potential divisions within the polis.

The political character of the cult of Orestes is reflected also by the placement of his tomb in the agora, the city's premier public space. (Contrast, e.g., the shrine of the hero Astrabakos, which was situated more privately next to the house of the Eurypontid king Ariston; Hdt. 6.69.) Similarly, Pausanias reports that Teisamenos was buried near the buildings where Spartiates took their common meals (7.1.8). As Leahy suggests, it is not insignificant that such a figure was honored in a setting where the unity of Spartan *homoioi* was most distinctively marked.[47]

Orestes, brought back to Sparta by a state official, acting with the consent and collaboration of the whole polity, embodies Sparta's communal claim to the inheritance of the Pelopids. Herodotus' story about the bones of Orestes thus does not suggest an externally directed Lakedaimonian policy change from conquest to alliance and from Dorian to Achaian identification, as modern historians have claimed, so much as it affirms and effects for Spartans themselves the rightful dominance of their nonindividualistic polis of "equals."[48]

This interpretation of the significance of Orestes to Sparta implies a rather abstract idea of the state: Lakedaimon is Lakedaimon, whether under Pelopid or Heraklid kings. Such a concept is all the more noteworthy because, of course, the Spartans do not consider themselves autochthonous; they cannot claim descent from the old heroes associated with their land.[49] Orestes links Sparta, but no contemporary Spartans, with its heroic past and thereby helps dissipate competition for status among families that could otherwise have focused on their various ancestral heroes.[50]

To demonstrate further the "Spartan" character of the translation of Orestes it may be useful to compare briefly the translation of Theseus' bones from Skyros to his native Athens. The similarities between these traditions are apparent and have been pointed out since Pausanias (3.3.7),[51] but significant differences can also be discerned, especially in the relationships between the hero and his discoverer. Kimon's recovery of the bones of Theseus in the 470s brought home a powerful king who could also reflect contemporary Athenian political aspirations,[52] but this translation seems to have been in part a self-serving venture. Unlike Orestes, who was not claimed by any family at Sparta, Kimon cultivated a special relationship to Theseus – who, like Kimon's father Miltiades, was a hero of Marathon – and seems to have supported or initiated a campaign to publicize Theseus' exploits.[53] This standard interpretation could seem like another example of the modern "propagandistic fallacy" Ian Morris warns us about,[54] but the link with Kimon's popularity is actually established in the ancient tradition about the recovery of Theseus: according to Plutarch, Kimon's recovery of Theseus "made him very dear to the Athenian demos" (ἐφ' ᾧ μάλιστα πρὸς αὐτὸν ἡδέως ὁ δῆμος ἔσχεν; *Kim.* 8.6, cf. *Thes.* 36.2). The contrast with Orestes' discoverer Lichas (otherwise unknown) and the Spartan tradition is striking: the bones of Orestes benefit only the polis, no individuals or special groups within it.

II

For Sparta, I have argued, the importation of Orestes not only brings an old king back home, but also supports the ideology of the polis of equals. Herodotus himself, however, uses the Orestes tale primarily to show how Sparta became the Greek state selected by Croesus for alliance: now at last supremacy in war, due to Orestes, complements the city's political *eunomia,* due, of course, to Lykourgos. Remarkably, even Herodotus' reports of Lykourgos, set vaguely in the distant past,[55] are framed by his account of the Tegean Wars and the acquisition of Orestes. The story of Orestes' translation, it seems, has shaped the way Herodotus records what becomes for his readers the "history" of Sparta at this period. It will be worthwhile to look more closely at the structure and the force of this traditional plot.

The finding, moving, and honoring of heroic remains are phenomena frequently attested in Greek tradition and have a rich afterlife well into our own times.[56] For the archaic and classical periods, we hear of at least a dozen heroes who were thus recovered – always by or for a polis,[57] not an individual or family. Stories about such translations fall into a simple, well-defined pattern. First, a polis is confronted with a problem. Often this is a natural catastrophe such as plague (which motivates the installation of Hesiod in Orchomenos and Pelops' shoulder in Elis), although it could be merely a promise of better conditions (as with Hektor at Thebes, with whose worship the city will become rich).[58] In several cases besides that of Orestes, political and military concerns motivate new hero cults. The eponymous hero Arkas, for example, was translated to Mantinea in about 422, in connection with an attempt to establish an Arcadian league independent of Sparta.[59] Theseus was brought back by Kimon so that Athens could conquer Skyros (Paus. 3.3.7). Similarly, cults (although not involving the translation of heroic remains) were established in Attica for two Salaminian heroes at the time when Athens was competing with Megara for the possession of Salamis.[60] In a related tradition, before his mysterious disappearance at Colonus, Sophocles' Oedipus promises to protect Athens from future Theban attack (*Oed. Col.* 616–23).

Once the motivating problem is defined in a "translation" story, the affected city inquires at Delphi about a solution and is directed to find, relocate, and honor a particular named hero – usually one whose grave has not been recognized before. (This step is an important one; many of the "translation" stories are, like Herodotus' Orestes tale, effectively centered around an oracle, and this "kernel" may well be an important factor in the transmission of such stories.)[61] The discovery of the hero's grave is then described, frequently with some elaboration about the attendant difficulties. Then the hero is installed in his new home, and (at least implicitly) the problem is resolved. Very similar patterns underlie other Herodotean stories about newly established hero cults, which do not involve the translation of remains.[62]

The hero-translation plot, as we have noted, determines the structure of the entire Spartan passage here (1.65–8), incorporating even the material about Lykourgos.[63] This plot requires that the bones of Orestes be effective; *in this context,* Sparta's success is assured. In the Pythia's words, Sparta will become the "protector" (ἐπιτάρροθος; 1.67) of Tegea;[64] Herodotus further assures us that once it acquired

Orestes, Sparta was always able to defeat Tegea in battle (1.68; but no battles are reported). The translation story is over, ending neatly as its structure demands.

According to other traditions, however, also attested in Herodotus, Tegea was not dominated by Sparta quite to the (admittedly rather vague) extent implied here. Rather, as Immerwahr has noted, the two cities were involved in repeated hostilities. Sparta and Tegea united only against the Persians, and then only in a "kind of antagonistic cooperation."[65] Indeed, in Tegea Herodotus was shown the very fetters that Sparta had intended for Tegean enslavement; this hostile trophy, Fontenrose suggests, makes it seem unlikely that Sparta had a tight hold on Tegea before the late fifth century.[66] In the Orestes story, the requirements of the translation plot seem to have asserted themselves over the historical information at Herodotus' disposal. There is as always some discrepancy between story and history.

III

So far we have looked at the immediate context of the "bones of Orestes" story, where Sparta's military prowess is established. A somewhat broader perspective reveals that in this part of the *Histories* Herodotus is setting up a contrast between Athens and Sparta in the mid-sixth century, when Croesus was trying to determine which city he should choose as an ally (Hdt. 1.56–69).[67] What role does Orestes play in this larger narrative context?

Herodotus first describes what Croesus found in Athens: a city divided, with aristocratic families and their followers alternating wildly between alliances and hostilities. The result of this rampant factionalism was the tyranny of Peisistratos (1.59–64). This resourceful demagogue became tyrant no less than three times, once by a ruse that Herodotus brands as ridiculous, in which a mortal woman, the tall and beautiful Phye, actually fooled the usually clever Athenians when she impersonated Athena conducting Peisistratos into her city (1.60). In Chapter 4 of this volume, Rebecca Sinos offers a compelling interpretation of Herodotus' position here: he is opposed not to the possibility of divine intervention but to the idea that a god would support such an attempt at tyranny. (I would add that, at least for more recent history, all the "divine interventions" accepted by Herodotus are more subtle than this parade.)

In Herodotus' Sparta, Croesus observes a situation that is markedly different. At some earlier time, the mysterious Lykourgos had established his unique brand of *eunomia,* which changed Sparta from the most poorly governed city to the best (1.65). Now, thanks to Orestes, the city also enjoys virtually unchallenged military power, as we have seen, having finally succeeded in defeating its recalcitrant neighbor Tegea.[68] The Orestes–Lichas story provides a particularly specific counterpoint to the "Athena"–Peisistratos episode: in each case, a god or hero allegedly enters the city to establish political and military power. But whereas for Herodotus the Athenian episode is a mere sham concocted by a self-serving tyrant (a scheme even worse than the hero cults manipulated by Kleisthenes of Sikyon), the Spartan incident is directed by Delphi and carried out by an *agathoergos* who was serving only the interests of his city when he discovered how to bring home the bones of Orestes. As Herodotus arranges these traditions into a narrative structure and a time frame, Sparta is shown to be clearly a more stable power and a better ally for Croesus.

Stability and military might will come to Athens in Herodotus' narrative, but only when the tyranny is gone and *isonomia* established (cf. Hdt. 5.78).[69] At that point, let it be noted, new "political" hero cults are introduced to the city. In contrast to the transparent monarchical ploy of Peisistratos and his pseudo-Athena, Kleisthenes introduces ten new *phyle* heroes as protectors of the reorganized demos (5.66).

The translation of Orestes, in sum, not only serves Sparta's view of itself as heir to the Pelopid hegemony and strengthens the "Lykourgan" tendency to subordinate familial to a more abstract political identity. The story also functions as Herodotus' way to explain Lakonian superiority in the time of Croesus and to contrast Spartan *eunomia* with Athenian stasis. In Herodotus' narrative, as in historical Sparta, this translated hero supports and reflects positive political values.

NOTES

I thank Rebecca Sinos, Irad Malkin, Joseph Roisman, and Kurt Raaflaub for generous advice on an earlier version of this essay.

1. See also Whitley 1988 on opposing uses of hero cults in Attica and the Argolid; I. Morris 1988 on differing functions of hero cult; Kearns 1989 on the functions and origins of Attic hero cults.

2. E.g., Snodgrass 1982; Bérard 1983, esp. the programmatic statement on 43–4; de Polignac 1984: 127–51; Whitley 1988: 173–82; I. Morris 1988: 750–61. Malkin 1987: 262–6 suggests that Greek colonial cults of founding heroes were largely responsible for the development of "political" hero cults in the homeland. Kearns 1989: 44–63, 133–4, passim discusses functions of Attic heroes relative to the polis.

3. Bérard 1983: 57. See also de Polignac 1984: 139–40 for reinterpretations of the heroes Erechtheus and Theseus in changing political circumstances at Athens.

4. See Ober, Chapter 11, this volume, for a discussion of Kleisthenes and his reforms.

5. Early examples, attested archaeologically, include cults of Agamemnon at Mycenae and of Helen and Menelaos at Therapnai near Sparta. For discussion and references see Antonaccio, Chapter 3, this volume; also Snodgrass 1982: 112 and Huxley 1983: 7–9.

6. See also Bérard 1983: 45–6 on Kleisthenes' "manipulation" of hero cult.

7. Hdt. 5.77–81 relates another incident involving "movable" heroes, which must be dated to the late sixth century. When Athens defeated a Theban contingent shortly after the expulsion of the Peisistratids, Thebes asked Aigina for help in avenging itself. Aigina complied with this request by sending the Aiakids to Thebes. The gesture did not turn out to be very successful, it seems, because Thebes soon returned the heroes and requested men instead. Again, we do not know in what form the Aiakids were sent to Thebes, but the idea of borrowing heroes is surely related to the *permanent* transfer of heroic remains, as with Orestes and presumably with Melanippos.

8. I.e., one of several senior knights selected to "do good" for their city in various capacities for a year before retiring (Hdt 1.67).

9. Vandiver 1991: 34–8 discusses this episode from the perspective of the use in the Iron Age of heroes from an earlier and better era.

10. See Dickins 1912: 21–4, followed with varying emphases by subsequent historians of Sparta. Detailed discussions of this policy include Wade-Gery 1954: 565–7; A. H. M.

Jones 1967: 44–5 ("a great propaganda stroke"); Jeffery 1976: 121–2; Forrest 1980: 73–6, 79–83; O. Murray 1980: 247–8; Hooker 1989: 130–1; and esp. Leahy 1958 and Huxley 1979.

11. O. Murray 1980: 252.

12. Leahy 1958: 164. I agree that the story reported in Hdt. 1.66 indicates the Spartans planned to helotize Tegea as they had Messenia: the deceptive oracle suggests that they will "measure out" the land as if for *klēroi,* and the Spartans go to battle carrying the fetters with which they expect to bind their conquered enemies. Nevertheless, evidence apart from this narrative context suggests that, even before the defeats by Tegea, Sparta had begun to implement its policy of alliance, e.g., with the Skiritis. See Dickins 1912: 23; Michell 1952: 28–9; for the uncertain dating of the Skiritis alliance, de Ste. Croix 1972: 96 n. 13. Jeffery 1976: 114–15 argues that Spartan traditions suggest a perioikic policy as early as the eighth century, even before the helotization of Messenia.

13. Leahy 1955; the main source is Paus. 7.1.8. For other sources and variants of the Teisamenos tradition, see Leahy 1955: 30; J. Schmidt in Roscher 1916–24: 5.984–5.

14. Leahy 1955: 30, 37. Among those who attribute the alliance policy to Chilon are Dickins 1912: 24; Huxley 1962: 69; Forrest 1980: 76–7.

15. Leahy 1955: 34–5.

16. For criticism of what he names the "propagandistic fallacy" see Morris, Chapter 2, this volume. On Sparta specifically, see Immerwahr 1966: 294; Huxley 1983: 1; Parker 1989: esp. 157–61.

17. See Antonaccio, Chapter 3, and Dougherty, Chapter 9, this volume.

18. See further Calame 1987 on Spartan use of legendary genealogies.

19. The "Achaian" identity of its kings does not necessitate a depreciation of Sparta's Dorian heritage, as is often asserted: Kleomenes' own half-brother was named Dorieus. See also Hooker 1989: 130–1.

20. For a discussion of these cults see Cartledge 1979: 120–1 (note, however, that he suggests a mid-sixth-century date for the introduction of Agamemnon's cult at Amyklai [53]); Huxley 1983: 8–9; de Polignac 1984: 130–1 n. 12; Antonaccio, Chapter 3, this volume.

21. For Stesichoros (fr. 39 *PMG*) and Simonides, see schol. ap. Eur. *Or.* 46; Pind. *Pyth.* 11.16, 31–7; *Nem.* 11.34. For further testimony and discussion see Pfister 1909–12: 76–7, Nilsson 1932: 68–73, and Bowra 1961: 112–15, all of whom find in these passages evidence of Sparta's attempt "to change and reshape the myths in its own favor" (Nilsson 1932: 68). Kiechle 1963: 44, however, disagrees with Bowra on the idea of a Stesichorean innovation in this matter.

22. Bowra 1961: 107–19. See M. L. West 1969: 147–8, where Stesichoros *P. Oxy.* 2735.22–6 is read as a direct address by the poet to a Spartan prince; West concludes unnecessarily that Stesichoros must have performed this poem in Sparta itself. On biographies of Greek poets in general see Lefkowitz 1981.

23. See the succinct comments of S. West 1988: 224–5. For a different interpretation see Nilsson 1932: 71–3.

24. For more on this passage see Griffiths 1976, where it is argued that "Pelopid" should be replaced by "Pleisthenid" in Syagros' response, in order to restore a hexameter.

25. See Antonaccio, Chapter 3, this volume for a Durkheimian definition of cult. Elsewhere Antonaccio reports a possible externally directed political meaning for the cult of Menelaos at Therapnai – victory over Messenia – as well as suggesting a role for the Menelaos cult in the context of Spartan competition with Argos in the eighth century.

26. We can see this, e.g., in the case of Aigina, where the exact burial place of Aiakos was kept secret, most likely to keep him out of Athenian hands (Paus. 2.29.8). A similar

case involves the Palladion, stolen from Argos and brought to Sparta, then guarded by Odysseus, who was installed in a new cult for this purpose. For more examples see Kearns 1989: 46–8; Nagy 1990b: 178.

27. Similarly, Leahy 1955: 32: the bones of Teisamenos, if "stolen" from Helike, would presumably promote "not a ready acceptance of alliance but either protestations at the sacrilege or demonstrations of the falsity of the claim."

28. Centuries later, it is true, the Tegeans could show Pausanias an empty tomb outside their city, identifying it as the one from which Orestes had been stolen (Paus. 8.54.4), but this explanation is likely to stem from the famous story in Herodotus.

29. Huxley 1962: 67–8.

30. Parke and Wormell 1956: 1. 348.

31. Cf. Schaefer 1963: 323–36, who attributes to the fate of Leonidas, originally buried at Thermopylae, the report in Hdt. 6.58 that an image of a Spartan king would be ceremonially buried if the king fell in battle and (presumably) his body was not recovered and returned home. See further Connor 1979: 21–7, suggesting a contemporary political motive for the recovery of Leonidas.

32. For references see Rohde 1920: 145 n. 47.

33. Cf. Boedeker 1987: 197 n. 17.

34. Passages in *Od.* 19.109–14 and Hes. *Op.* 225–47 indicate that archaic poetry could attribute at least to living kings profound effects on the prosperity of their lands, far broader than merely the political results of their actions.

35. See most recently Parker 1988 and Cartledge 1988 on the question of heroization. Nagy 1990b: 152–3 argues that the Spartan kingship is an unusual case in which the "tribal" institution of ancestor worship (as opposed to hero worship) is retained in a polis.

36. See Hartog 1980: 166–70.

37. Paus. 3.11.10. On the significance of burying heroes in the agora, see Kearns 1989: 9.

38. See Dougherty, Chapter 9, this volume, for discussion of the daimonic power attributed to a (purified) murderer, including Orestes and other exiled killers of kinfolk.

39. See Starr 1965 for a critical evaluation of the sources.

40. Similarly, Forrest 1980: 50–1 suggests that the very name *homoioi* implies that at an earlier stage Spartiates had been notably *un*equal. For a detailed discussion of the evidence for seventh-century Sparta, see Kiechle 1963: 183–93.

41. On the relation between political problems at home and the colonization of Tarentum, dated to the late eighth or early seventh century, see, e.g., Kiechle 1963: 176–83; Forrest 1980: 61; O. Murray 1980: 107; Dougherty, Chapter 9, this volume.

42. On the Aigeidai and their position in Sparta see Michell 1952: 103–4 n. 3. For Spartan families who claimed special status as Heraklids, see Kiechle 1963: 134–5.

43. M. I. Finley 1968: esp. 148. This argument also reflects Plutarch's descriptions of the reforms of Lykourgos, most strikingly perhaps his remark concerning the education of boys not as the "private property of their fathers," but as the "common property of the city" (ἰδίους . . . τῶν πατέρων vs. κοινοὺς τῆς πόλεως; *Lyk.* 25.3). On Spartan traditions concerning the date of Lykourgos, see note 55.

44. Oliva 1971: 121–2, 132–6.

45. Vernant 1982 [1962]: 63–8.

46. Orestes' lack of descendants in Lakedaimon is perhaps all the more striking because he *was* considered an ancestor by other Greeks in the sixth century: the Penthilidai of Lesbos claimed descent from Agamemnon (Alc. fr. 70.6 V) via Penthilos, Orestes' son by Erigone. See further Huxley 1969: 88.

47. Cf. Leahy 1955: 29. On the ideals supposedly fostered by the *pheiditia* see also Plut.

Lyk. 12. In Chapter 3 of this volume, Antonaccio discusses other examples of communal meals at a tomb site.

48. This perspective on Orestes accords with the view expressed in Bérard 1982, 1983 that hero cults tend to support "democratic" rather than monarchical ideologies.

49. I. Morris 1988: 756 plausibly suggests that hero cult must have had a different significance for the "immigrant" Dorians than it did for "autochthonous" populations. Huxley 1983: 8–9 argues that, according to a tradition preserved in Apollod. 2.7.3, Herakles himself could be claimed as a king of Sparta; hence, he argues, the Heraklid kings could consider themselves natural heirs of their ancestor's throne. No evidence suggests that they did so, however; rather, Sparta based its claim to hegemony on nonancestral pre-Dorians such as Agamemnon, Menelaos, and Orestes.

50. Conversely, as Antonaccio argues in Chapter 3, this volume, in more overtly competitive communities "claims of descent from heroes . . . constituted a legitimating device that allowed such individuals ["big men"] to forge links with the past in a civic context."

51. Podlecki 1971: 142.

52. On Theseus as a political symbol see most recently Tausend 1989; Garland 1992: 82–98.

53. See Podlecki 1971: 143; Sourvinou-Inwood 1971: 108–9; Bérard 1983: 47–50; Vidal-Naquet 1986 [1967]: 313; Garland 1992: 84–5.

54. See note 16.

55. Lykourgos was by a Lakedaimonian account regent for his nephew Leobotes, who was eleven generations removed from Anaxandrides (cf. Hdt. 1.65, 7.204), the Agiad king at the time of the defeat of Tegea.

56. For ancient examples see Pfister 1909–12: 196–208; Rohde 1920: 122 with notes; Parke and Wormell 1956: vol. 1. For several modern examples cf. von Ungern-Sternberg 1985: 321–9. For an overview of the translation pattern see Fontenrose 1978: 75.

57. Three such heroes (Orestes, Teisamenos, and Leonidas) were brought back to Sparta; Pelops (his shoulder, at least) and Hippodameia were each transported to Olympia; no other city, as far as I know, engaged in this activity more than once through the fifth century.

58. For references see Parke and Wormell 1956: 1.395–6 (Hesiod), 349–50 (Pelops), and 349 (Hektor).

59. Parke and Wormell 1956: I.197–8.

60. Parke and Wormell 1956: I.110. See also Nilsson 1951a: 29–32; Kearns 1989: 46–7.

61. This step was omitted, it will be recalled, when the Sikyonian tyrant Kleisthenes imported Melanippos from Thebes. Lack of prior Delphic approval may explain the fact that the translation meets with only qualified success, at least as the episode is characterized by Herodotus. The translation of Orestes, like that of Melanippos, is one of many Herodotean stories that crystallize around an oracle – in this case, three oracles, two of them quoted fully in hexameters. Fontenrose 1978: 75, 81, 123–4 questions the historicity of these oracles; nevertheless, they form the kernel of the tradition Herodotus reports. For an interesting new theory on the use of oracles in Herodotus see Nagy 1990b: 321–33.

62. E.g., Onesilos of Cyprus (Hdt. 5.114) and the Phokaians who migrated to Corsica (Hdt. 1.167). For an elaboration of this pattern see Fontenrose 1968.

63. The impetus of the "translation" plot itself may also be seen in the varying amounts of detail recorded for different episodes in the story: the disastrous (for Sparta) "Battle of the Fetters" is reported with much more narrative elaboration (1.66) than the victories won subsequently: "And from this time on, whenever there was a trial between them, the Lakedaimonians were far superior in war" (1.68).

64. See Parke and Wormell 1956: 1.96; Huxley 1983: 6. I disagree with Huxley, however,

that the oracle suggests "Orestes will continue to protect the land of Tegea even if his bones are removed to Sparta." It is Sparta, not Orestes, that the Pythia calls ἐπιτάρροθος of Tegea.

65. Immerwahr 1966: 266, citing Hdt. 9.35.2, 9.37.3–4, 6.72.2, as well as the Orestes episode.

66. Fontenrose 1978: 124.

67. This contrast is apparently anachronistic, based on the status of the two cities at the time of the Persian Wars and afterward. Similarly, Nagy 1990b: 303. On the structure of this passage see Immerwahr 1966: 35–6, 86–8.

68. Herodotus mentions nothing at this point about the serious problems between Sparta and Argos, which would lead to the Battle of Champions in 546 B.C.E. (recounted in Hdt. 1.82). This gap suggests again how much his account of events in the archaic period is formed by preexisting story patterns such as the "translation story" described earlier.

69. For further discussion of parallels between Spartan *eunomia* and Athenian *isonomia* in this contest see Raaflaub 1988: 213.

CHAPTER NINE

It's Murder to Found a Colony

Carol Dougherty

A ETIOLOGICAL myths and legends – the births of heroes, cult origins, city foundations – have always fascinated the Greeks, and Plutarch sets the founding of Syracuse as the stage for the following drama of passion and politics:

> Melissos had a son named Aktaion, the most handsome and modest young man of his age. Aktaion had many suitors, chief among them Archias, a descendant of the Herakleidai and the most conspicuous man in Corinth both in wealth and general power. When Archias was not able to persuade Aktaion to be his lover, he decided to carry him off by force. He gathered together a crowd of friends and servants who went to Melissos' house in a drunken revelry and tried to take the boy away. Aktaion's father and friends resisted; the neighbors ran out and helped pull against the assailants, and, in the end, Aktaion was pulled to pieces and killed. The boys then ran away, and Melissos carried the corpse of his son into the marketplace of the Corinthians and displayed it, asking reparations from those who had done these things. But the Corinthians did nothing more than pity the man. Unsuccessful, Melissos went away and waited for the Isthmian festival at which time he went up to the temple of Poseidon and decried the Bakchiadai and reminded the god of his father Habron's good deeds. Calling upon the gods, he threw himself down from the rocks. Not long after this, drought and plague befell the city. When the Corinthians consulted the god about relief, the god told them that the anger of Poseidon would not subside until they sought punishment for Aktaion's death. Archias learned these things for he was one of those consulting the oracle, and he decided of his own free will not to return to Corinth. Instead he sailed to Sicily and founded the colony of Syracuse. There he became father of two daughters, Ortygia and Syrakousa, and was treacherously killed by Telephos, his lover who had sailed with him to Sicily, in charge of a ship. (*Mor.* 772e–773b)

This elaborate colonial account contains many intriguing narrative details – unrequited love, plague, suicide – but perhaps the most surprising is the element of

178

murder. Not all accounts of the founding of Syracuse, however, are equally colorful. Thucydides, in fact, gives a rather different, much less complicated version:

> Archias, one of the Herakleidai from Corinth, founded Syracuse, having first expelled the Sikels from the island where the inner city now is – though it is no longer surrounded by water. (6.3.2)

The basic facts of the settlement remain the same (Archias, Herakleidai, Corinth), but the discrepancies between the two accounts raise some interesting questions, and we might be tempted to ask which version preserves the "real story." If, on the one hand, Archias did kill Aktaion, why would Thucydides suppress that fact? Conversely, if there was no murder, why would Plutarch fabricate such a story? In addition, Thucydides mentions the expulsion of the native Sikels from the colonial site, a detail omitted from Plutarch's account. Given the scarcity and problematic nature of the sources available to us for studying the archaic colonization movement, we may never know "what really happened," but we can still learn a great deal about the ways in which the Greeks conceptualized colonization from the kinds of stories they told. We will see that Plutarch's version of the colonization of Syracuse is, in fact, part of a larger pattern of colonial representation, dating back to the Homeric poems, which omits mention of the bloodshed inherent in colonizing foreign lands and substitutes for it stories of Greek colonists as murderers.

If we return to Plutarch's account of the founding of Syracuse, we notice the pivotal role the Delphic oracle plays in the colonial narrative.[1] An act of murder precipitates civic pollution, which in turn prompts the consultation of the oracle. The recommended solution is that the murderer be sent into exile to expiate the crime; the exile begins as punishment for Aktaion's murder but then becomes Syracuse's founding expedition.[2] Why? What lies behind this narrative pattern? Callimachus, writing centuries after the archaic colonization movement, praises Apollo for helping men found cities in such a way that suggests a connection between the purification that murder demands and colonization. Apollo and his oracle at Delphi were especially instrumental in founding Callimachus' birthplace, the Theraean colony of Kyrene, and Callimachus tells the story of its foundation as part of his hymn to the god. When he invokes Apollo here as founder of cities, Callimachus calls him Phoibos; in fact, he emphatically refers to the god as Phoibos three times in three lines:

> Φοίβῳ δ' ἑσπόμενοι πόλιας διεμετρήσαντο
> ἄνθρωποι· Φοῖβος γὰρ ἀεὶ πολίεσσι φιληδεῖ
> κτιζομένῃσ', αὐτὸς δὲ θεμείλια Φοῖβος ὑφαίνει.
> (Callim. *Ap.* 55–7)

> Following Phoibos, men measured out their cities, for
> Phoibos always takes pleasure in the establishment of
> cities; Phoibos himself weaves their foundations.

Traditionally in Greek literature, as Phoibos, Apollo purifies humankind; he cleanses its houses and cities of pollution.[3] In this context, however, the choice of appellation is puzzling – why invoke a cathartic Apollo to build cities? Callimachus gently challenges us, I think, to make a connection between purification and colonization, and that connection is Phoibos Apollo, the god who weaves the foundations of cities.

Surely, as Irad Malkin has suggested, Apollo's role in Callimachus' hymn is metaphorical, but identifying the metaphor is only half the battle.[4] We must now ask how this metaphor works. Why is Phoibos Apollo, a purifying deity, an appropriate metaphorical guide for colonists? Literary theorists and anthropologists alike tell us that metaphors function as a conceptual framework for describing the unknown in terms of the known, and my plan is to unpack Callimachus' metaphor along these lines.[5] In this essay I will argue that the Greeks use Apollo and the purification process that murder demands as a conceptual analogy, a metaphor, to describe colonization. The second part of the essay will then show how this conceptual analogy in turn influences a narrative pattern in which a murderer consults Delphi and is told to found a colony. In conclusion, I will turn to Pindar's *Olympian* 7 and to a discussion of how the purification analogy and the narrative pattern of murderer-turned-founder operate in a specific literary context.

I

First, let us explore Apollo's role as a purifier of murderers and its relevance to describing the act of colonization. Apollo is an important civic deity for the Greeks, and he helps maintain a sense of cosmic and civic order by providing the necessary purification once a city is threatened by some sort of pollution or miasma. The concept of pollution is not so much a system of rationalization as a vehicle for the expression of social disruption: pollution represents chaos, and purification corresponds to the subsequent restoration of order to society.[6] It is especially the need for purification in cases of murder that demands Apollo's participation and provides the connection with colonization legends.[7]

As early as the epic poems, the threat to civic or community order that is caused by homicide is addressed by sending the murderer into exile.[8] Exile also appears in Drakon's code as the recommended punishment for homicide,[9] but we find the two most detailed discussions of murder and the pollution it causes in Antiphon's *Tetralogies* and Book 9 of Plato's *Laws*. In the *Laws*, Plato outlines the punishment for unintentional homicide (the murderer must go into exile for a year) and tells the following "ancient tale" (ἀρχαίων μύθων) as the rationale for this particular penalty:

> It is said that the man killed by violence, who has lived in a free manner, when newly dead is angry with his killer, and he himself is filled with dread and horror on account of the violence suffered; when he sees his own murderer going about in the very spots which he himself had frequented, he is terrified; and being disturbed himself, he disturbs the killer as much as possible (having memory as his ally) – both the man himself and all his doings. For this reason the killer must keep clear of his victim for all the seasons of an entire year and he must avoid the dead man's usual spots throughout his native country. (*Laws* 865d–e)

Similarly, in the *Third Tetralogy* attributed to Antiphon, the speaker for the prosecution argues that "the victim, robbed of the gifts bestowed by god upon him, naturally leaves behind him the angry spirits of vengeance, god's instruments of punishment" (I.3).

It was considered not just a personal matter between murderer and victim, but a civic responsibility to address cases of homicide, for if an act of murder was not avenged or acknowledged in some way, the whole community would suffer. For this reason, Plato explains that if a man kills a fellow tribesman with premeditation, he shall first of all be excluded from every place of lawful assembly; he shall be forbidden to pollute with his presence temples, markets, harbors, or other places of public assembly (*Laws* 871a). Following this same logic of contamination, the defendant in a speech of Antiphon claims as evidence of his innocence that he has never brought disaster to the community at large:

> I hardly think I need remind you that many a man with unclean hands or some other form of defilement who has embarked on shipboard with the innocent has involved them in his own destruction. Others, while they have escaped death, have had their lives imperiled owing to such polluted wretches. Many, too, have been proved to be defiled as they stood beside a sacrifice, because they prevented the proper performance of the rites. With me, the opposite has happened in every case. Not only have fellow-passengers of mine enjoyed the calmest of voyages; but whenever I have attended a sacrifice, that sacrifice has invariably been successful. (*On the Murder of Herodes* 82–3)

The *Tetralogies* resound with the constant refrain, expressed by the prosecution and defense alike, of the jurors' responsibility to convict and punish the killer. Failure to do so results in the pollution of the entire city.[10] In the *First Tetralogy,* the prosecution concludes its first speech with the reminder that it is against the public's interest to allow the polluted murderer to move about freely:

> οἰκείαν οὖν χρὴ τὴν τιμωρίαν ἡγησαμένους, αὐτῷ τούτῳ τὰ τούτου ἀσεβήματα ἀναθέντας, ἰδίαν μὲν τὴν συμφοράν, καθαρὰν δὲ τὴν πόλιν καταστῆναι. (I.11)

> And so you must hold the avenging of the dead a personal duty; you must punish the defendant himself for his impieties; you must see that the disaster is his alone and that the city is made pure.

In the prosecution's second speech, he expresses the connection between individual murderer and the whole city quite succinctly:

> ταῦτα οὖν εἰδότες βοηθεῖτε μὲν τῷ ἀποθανόντι, τιμωρεῖσθε δὲ τὸν ἀποκτείναντα, ἁγνεύετε δὲ τὴν πόλιν. (III.11)

> So with this in mind, help the victim, punish the killer and cleanse the city.

All three actions – helping the victim, punishing the killer, and purifying the city – are described as different aspects of the same process. Exile, the customary method of punishing a murderer, helps the victims by keeping the killer away from their homes, and it cleanses the city by ridding it of a defiled and potentially dangerous element.

The law demands that a murderer go into exile for a year, and Delphic Apollo and his oracle oversee this punishment. At this point, in some colonial tales, the murderer's exile overlaps with the start of a colonial expedition: a murderer consults Delphic Apollo to be purified and is sent into exile; this exile becomes the impetus to found a colony. Before we look at how a murderer in exile represents colonization, I want to introduce another type of colonial tale that, as we will see, works in the same way. This type describes its founders as political dissidents, forced to leave home in search of new territory as the losing party in a city's internal conflict or as victims of a new oppressive regime. The Partheniai, for example, were denied civic rights at home; they fled Sparta and founded Tarentum in southern Italy (Strab. 6.3.3).[11] According to Herodotus, the Phokaians set out on a colonial expedition to escape capture by the tyrant Harpagos (Hdt. 1.164–8). Menekles of Barka tells us that Battos founded Kyrene not because of a drought, as Herodotus says, but as a result of political upheaval in Thera (*FGrH* 270 F 6). I want to argue here that with respect to representations of colonization, the model of a political exile is structurally similar to that of the murderer who must flee his country. Plato, in fact, considers those who lead insurrections and stir up civil strife to be the moral equivalents of murderers – the actions of both are crimes against the state (*Laws* 856b). What we must remember is that for the Greeks political dissidence is not a purely secular problem; it threatens the state with religious pollution. Kylon's attempt at tyranny in Athens, for example, was enacted amid religious ritual and festivals, and in the end, the political coup demanded that Epimenides of Crete purify the city.[12] Just as an unpurified murderer poses a threat to the purity not just of an individual but of the whole city, a city's political problems can also bring plague upon it. In each case – murder or political stasis – the act of an individual or group of individuals threatens the stability and health of the city as a whole. As a result, those citizens must be expelled for the good of those who remain. It is the act of exile and the implicit threat to the well-being of the city if certain citizens are not exiled that are the critical narrative elements of the colonial account.

Now that we have established the civic nature of Apollo's role as purifier, we can return to our original question – why is it that once new colonies have been successfully established on foreign land, the Greeks choose to describe themselves to themselves as led by murderers? How does Apollo the purifier relate to Apollo the colonizer? Another way of posing the question is to ask what colonization and purification have in common as cultural systems. Using contemporary anthropological evidence to provide a framework for exploring the concepts of pollution and purification within the Greek world, we will see that there are three different ways in which purification rituals correspond to colonial activity. Mary Douglas's book, *Purity and Danger,* has been instrumental in describing the related phenomena of pollution and purification, and some of her observations will help us clarify the essential similarities between purification and colonization in archaic Greece.

First, the concept of purification in the Greek mind, as in many other cultures, consists of establishing categories and making divisions; a state of pollution occurs when these categories get confused.[13] Douglas argues that defilement is never an isolated event; it occurs only as part of a systematic ordering of ideas, one that depends on division. As a result, she warns us that "any piecemeal interpretation of the pollution rules of another culture is bound to fail. For the only way in which pollution ideas make sense is in reference to a total structure of thought whose keystone, boundaries, margins and internal lines are held in relation by rituals of separation."[14] Purification, then, allows a society to regulate the boundaries it has erected between what it considers sacred and profane, clean and polluted, beneficial and harmful. In Plato's *Sophist,* the interlocutors, Theaetetus and the stranger, discuss the art of division or discrimination (διακριτική), and they, too, conclude that the separation or division that "keeps the better and expels the worse" is called a kind of purification:

ΞΕ. Πᾶσα ἡ τοιαύτη διάκρισις, ὡς ἐγὼ ξυννοῶ, λέγεται παρὰ πάντων καθαρμός τις. (*Soph.* 226d)

Str. Every such discrimination, as I know it, is called by all a kind of purification.

Purification is the process of making divisions, and as we have seen, one way to purify a city entails the separation and expulsion of the negative element for the good of the whole citizen body. Similarly, mounting a colonial expedition involves choosing those citizens who will participate and those who will remain behind – another kind of division. And finally, the very process of establishing a new city on foreign territory depends upon acts of separation. The founder must divide the land itself into different civic components; he must determine that the proper boundaries between these components are distinguished and observed – boundaries between the sacred and profane, between individual members of the colony, and between the Greek inhabitants and their neighbors.

Second, the institution of purification unites individuals into groups; it provides those who have been expelled with the opportunity for a fresh start and, in this respect, has something in common with initiation rituals and rites of passage – both deal with issues of classification, boundary, and transition.[15] As in rites of passage, a group of colonists is identified that must be expelled from society; its members must cross boundaries, and thus they become dangerous or polluted in the eyes of those who remain at home. For example, those who were sent to colonize Kyrene were young men chosen from individual households in Thera. They were not allowed to return home when their first foundation attempt failed; instead, those who had stayed behind cursed the young men and pelted them with rocks, refusing to let them land (Hdt. 4.156). The colony, however, once successful, provided the Theraeans at home with relief from drought and the colonists themselves with a new identity as settlers of Kyrene.[16] Purification, then, a process of division, provides the mechanism whereby in initiation rituals the isolated group is first expelled and then reintegrated at a new level into its original society or, as in the case of colonization, the colonists are exiled from one city and reincorporated into Greek society as citizens of a new civic enterprise.

Finally, the transition from pollution to purification corresponds to the transformation of chaos and confusion into a state of order. Eliminating the dirt reorganizes the environment; it is a positive, creative act. In the same way, founding a colony creates a new civic entity out of the troubles and trauma of the mother city. The colonial legend records the natural imbalance that provoked the colonial expedition in order to highlight the order that is restored, both at home and abroad, precisely by the foundation of a new city.[17] As in the case of Kyrene or Tarentum, the motivation to colonize often comes from natural or political disaster. Drought or internal stasis forces a city to expel part of its population, thereby reorganizing the cosmic and civic environment and, in addition, creating a new city out of that which had to be discarded.

Rituals of purification, then, provide the Greeks with a conceptual model with which to describe colonization in terms of (1) the expulsion of part of its population, (2) its galvanization of individuals into a unified group, and (3) its creative role in founding a new city. A city's need to colonize appears to be very much like its need to be purified. Plato, in fact, in the *Laws,* draws together these concepts of pollution, political stasis, and colonization in a way that shows how Apollo's connection with purification rituals helps the Greeks represent the historical reality of founding a colony. He discusses political dissidents and measures to prevent revolutionary action. For Plato, colonization is the polite name for political exile:

ὅσοι διὰ τὴν τῆς τροφῆς ἀπορίαν τοῖς ἡγεμόσιν ἐπὶ τὰ τῶν ἐχόντων μὴ ἔχοντες ἑτοίμους αὑτοὺς ἐνδείκνυνται παρεσκευακότες ἕπεσθαι, τούτοις ὡς νοσήματι πόλεως ἐμπεφυκότι δι' εὐφημίας ἀπαλλαγὴν ὄνομα ἀποικίαν τιθέμενος, εὐμενῶς ὅτι μάλιστα ἐξεπέμψατο. (*Laws* 735e–736a)

People who, from want of the means of sustenance, show themselves ready to follow their leaders in an attack of the have-nots upon the haves, [these people] he [the legislator] sends abroad as a measure of relief, just as in the case of a deep-seated disease of the city, giving it the euphemistic name of colonization.

Plato provides us with valuable commentary on the choice of metaphor – the Greek way of representing the colonization movement both to themselves and to others, and we have reason to believe that the connection between the need to colonize and the demand for purification is not just a fiction of Plato's philosophical system. Plato characterizes the impetus for colonization and purification in the same terms – as a science of division. The negative element, a political dissident or murderer, is separated from the rest, purified, and given a fresh start. This is not to say that the Greeks cynically manipulated their religious traditions to justify sending a large number of their own people overseas to solve economic or political problems. Rather, as we saw earlier, in the archaic period religious ideology is firmly embedded in a political and historical context, and modern distinctions between the sacred and the secular are both irrelevant and misleading.[18]

We can now begin to see how the metaphor of purification, in addition to helping the Greeks conceptualize colonization, influences the shape of individual colonial tales. In a kind of narrative metonymy, the purification of an individual becomes a model for that of the city. A murderer consults Delphic Apollo to be purified and is sent out to found a colony. The myths of purification for murder by exile, as well as those concerning political dissidents, intersect with colonial traditions, and the point of contact, the common ground, is Delphic Apollo. The Apollo who purifies becomes the Apollo who colonizes.

II

Let us turn now to the narrative pattern itself.[19] First, I shall cite some additional examples: Pausanias relates a story about murder and the founding of a city in the territory of Megara. In Argos, during the reign of Krotopos, Psamathe, his daughter, gave birth to a son of Apollo's, which, fearing her father's anger, she exposed. The child was killed by Krotopos' dogs, and Apollo sent Poine, the personification of vengeance, to punish the Argives. A man named Koroibos killed Poine, but a second plague tormented the Argives. Consequently, Koroibos, of his own accord, went to Delphi to be punished for killing Poine. The Pythia would not allow him to return to Argos, but told him to take up a tripod, leave the sanctuary, and, wherever the tripod fell from his hands, build a temple to Apollo and live there himself. At Mt. Gerania, the tripod slipped, and Koroibos lived there in a village called Tripodiskoi, or "Little Tripods" (Paus. 1.43.7).[20]

Thucydides tells us that Alkmeon, son of Amphiareos, wandered for a long time after killing his mother and eventually founded Akarnania on the advice of the Delphic oracle. The oracle of Apollo is said to have told him there would be no release from his toils until he found a place "that at the time he killed his mother had not been seen by the sun and was not then land" (ἥτις ὅτε ἔκτεινε τὴν μητέρα μήπω ὑπὸ ἡλίου ἑωρᾶτο μηδὲ γῆ ἦν); the rest of the earth was polluted for him. At first he was at a loss, as they say, until he thought of the deposit of the Acheloos River, which was not piled up enough at the time of his mother's death to be called land – for he had been wandering a long time. He settled the land around Oineadai, ruled there, and named the place after his son, Akarnan (Thuc. 2.102.5–6). Apollonius of Rhodes plays upon this collocation of exile for murder and colonization in the *Argonautica*. When Herakles grows tired of their lengthy stay on the island of Lemnos, he asks Jason in frustration, "Are we exiled for manslaughter?" (*Argon.* 1.860).[21]

This particular pattern of colonial narrative is also influenced, at least in part, by the common mythological tale of a murderer sent into permanent exile. In the Homeric poems alone, Tlepolemos killed his uncle, left Argos, and settled the island of Rhodes (*Il.* 2.661–9); Patroklos killed a young boy in anger over a game of knuckle bones and fled with his father to Peleus (*Il.* 23.84–90); Theoklymenos fled from home and sought purification and sanctuary from Telemachos after killing a relative (*Od.* 15. 272–8). In Euripides' *Orestes*, Orestes must go into exile after killing his mother (1643–5), and the *Medea* closes with the heroine's flight from Corinth to Athens after the murder of Kreon's daughter and her own children. I would like to suggest, then, that the conceptual analogy of purification for colonization, together with this established narrative pattern of murderer-in-exile, generates the particular colonial narrative pattern of murderer-turned-founder. Once this particular pattern takes hold, it can shape the way "history" itself is represented and subsequently remembered. We can perhaps detect an example of this reshaping process at work in the divergent accounts of the founding of Syracuse as recorded by Thucydides and Plutarch. Thucydides describes a colonization expedition led by Archias of Corinth to Syracuse that expelled the native Sikels, while the tradition Plutarch records omits the Sikels and instead represents Archias as a murderer sent into exile. We should now explore why accounts such as that recorded by Plutarch (and others) come to be told. What is at stake?[22]

Colonial narratives such as these focus on the founder as murderer, and in addition to participating in the pollution analogy, this particular narrative strategy addresses two further aspects of the colonial process. First, commemorating a founding hero as a source of pollution and impurity contains within it the potential for annexing great power. To understand this apparent contradiction, we must realize that, in Greek thought, the concepts of purity and impurity are not mutually exclusive. In fact, the essential connection between the two phenomena is reflected in the etymological association between the Greek words ἄγος, traditionally translated as "pollution" or "defilement," and ἀγνός/ἅγιος, "holy" or "pure." The linguists Pierre Chantraine and Olivier Masson have shown that these terms are not diametrically opposed; they both refer to the forbidden aspect of the sacred.[23] The difference stems from the fact that the adjective ἀγνός refers to that element of the divine that separates mortals from gods; it presupposes a barrier that must not be crossed. The term ἄγος, then, designates the consequences of that same sacred power when, once the barrier has been crossed, it captures a man and delivers him to the divine.

The Greeks conceptualize defilement as the inversion of a positive religious value; it still carries religious force. Blood and dust can bring pollution, but they can also consecrate. That which is a source of pollution in one context becomes a source of religious power in another. Teiresias, for example, sees what is forbidden, Pallas Athena bathing; he has crossed the barrier between the human and the divine, and he must be punished. The punishment of blinding, however, contains aspects of the sacred, and he gains the power of prophecy.[24] Oedipus, murderer and committer of incest, the source of plague and disaster at Thebes, once exiled, carries a positive religious power to the land that accepts him, Athens. Mary Douglas, in her discussion of the African Lele culture, provides an interesting parallel; she describes the cult of the pangolin as one that, in a similar way, combines opposites as a source of power for good. The animal itself, a scaly anteater, is ambiguous:

> Its being contradicts all the most obvious animal categories. It is scaly like a fish, but it climbs trees. It is more like an egg-laying lizard than a mammal, yet it suckles its young. And most significant of all, unlike other small mammals its young are born singly. Instead of running away or attacking, it curls in a modest ball and waits for the hunter to pass.[25]

On the one hand, the pangolin transgresses most boundaries of animal categories so that normally it is considered taboo; on the other hand, its positive power is released in its dying. The pangolin is ritualized as a source of fertility; it is eaten in solemn ceremony by its initiates, who are thereby enabled to minister fertility to their kind. Not unlike the murderer in Greece who has transgressed sacred boundaries, this category-breaking animal provides a positive source of power to the Lele.[26]

Recognizing that, in the Greek system, pollution is inextricably linked to the sacred makes it easier to understand how individuals can be sources of both defilement and sacred power. Apollo himself personifies this ambiguity; he purifies murderers precisely because he himself has killed and undergone purification. Fragments of the Hesiodic *Catalogue of Women* refer to a myth in which Zeus kills Asklepios, Apollo's son, because he is jealous of Asklepios' success as a healer. Apollo, in revenge, kills the Kyklopes, for which he is forced to serve as a herdsman to Admetos for a year.[27] Pausanias tells us that Apollo had to go either to Tempe or to Crete to be purified after killing the Python at Delphi.[28] Both of these myths portray Apollo as a murderer, and although his were justifiable killings, he must seek purification. There is a presence in this god of two opposed qualities that are ultimately felt to be complementary.[29]

This interrelationship between the defiled and the sacred, a relationship personified in Phoibos Apollo, is quite useful to colonial discourse. By describing their origins as polluted and defiled, and themselves as murderers or political exiles, within the structure of the foundation legend, the colonists assume a new, positive and sacred value as founders of a new city. Following the lead of Mary Douglas, viewing the system as a whole, it is critical that we consider the figure of the colonist/murderer not as an isolated phenomenon, only as a source of pollution, but as part of a religious system that channels the religious power inherent in the defiled into a positive, consecrating force.[30]

Second, the narrative motif of founder as murderer addresses another important, if often overlooked, aspect of colonization: founding a colony overseas can be as dangerous and as violent as war. Thucydides, in fact, in Nikias' speech before the Sicilian expedition, inverts that metaphor; he describes the proposed all-out military enterprise in terms of colonizing foreign territory – each means a dangerous confrontation with hostile peoples and requires a large demonstration of force:

πόλιν τε νομίσαι χρὴ ἐν ἀλλοφύλλοις καὶ πολεμίοις οἰκιοῦντας ἰέναι, οὓς πρέπει τῇ πρώτῃ ἡμέρᾳ ᾗ ἂν κατάσχωσιν εὐθὺς κρατεῖν τῆς γῆς ἢ εἰδέναι ὅτι, ἢν σφάλλωνται, πάντα πολέμια ἕξουσιν. (6.23)

We must consider that we are like those going to settle a city among foreign and enemy peoples for whom it is necessary, on the very first day on which they land, straightway to conquer the land or know that if they fail, they will encounter complete hostility.

We know that the Greeks often settled territory occupied by native populations, and Thucydides shows us how dangerous and violent confrontations with local peoples could be; his account of the founding of Syracuse, we remember, mentioned the native Sikels, who had been expelled to make room for the Greeks.[31] Two poets, contemporaries of the archaic colonization movement, also mention confrontations between the Greek colonists and local populations. Mimnermos, in a fragment from the *Nanno,* describes the violence of the settlement of Kolophon and the *hybris* of the colonists:

ἡμεῖς αἰπὺ Πύλου Νηλήϊον ἄστυ λιπόντες
ἱμερτὴν Ἀσίην νηυσὶν ἀφικόμεθα.
ἐς δ' ἐρατὴν Κολοφῶνα βίην ὑπέροπλον ἔχοντες
ἑζόμεθ' ἀργαλέης ὕβριος ἡγεμόνες.
κεῖθεν δ' Ἀστήεντος ἀπορνύμενοι ποταμοῖο
θεῶν βουλῇ Σμύρναν εἵλομεν Αἰολίδα.

(Strab. 14.1.4)[32]

When we left the lofty city of Neleian Pylos, we came
by ship to the desired land of Asia; and having over-
whelming violence, we settled at lovely Kolophon,
leaders of terrible *hybris*. From there, we went forth
from beside the Asteis river and by the will of the gods
took Aiolian Smyrna.

Archilochos also recalls the hostility between Greeks and Thracians when Paros
colonized the island of Thasos.[33] Archeological evidence confirms the reports of
Thucydides and the contemporary poets; it shows precolonial native cultures at sites
such as Syracuse and Lokroi, and these natives cease to occupy the site shortly
after or at the time of colonization. Dunbabin argues that, although the first contacts
between Greeks and local populations were probably in part peaceful, when it came
to official colonial expeditions, the Greeks preferred the "sword to peaceful
penetration."[34]

In the literary traditions recording the archaic colonization movement, with the
few exceptions just mentioned, very little explicit attention is paid to the violent,
warlike confrontations that must have taken place between the Greek colonists and
the native peoples. Greek sources for archaic colonization tend to focus on the
metropolis and the leader of the expedition; they are far less informative about the
details of the colonists' destination. As a result, indigenous populations rarely appear
in Greek colonial accounts. Traces of their presence, however, particularly of their
confrontation with the colonists, emerge in the choice of narrative patterns and
metaphors. Colonial traditions that include murder displace the warlike violence of
the colonial expedition itself and relocate it within a religious system that can
address and expiate that violence. The murderous founder of the colonial legend
is made to shoulder the burden of the historical violence of settling foreign territory,
and his purification as the narrative unfolds prefigures that of the colonists
themselves.[35]

As the essays in this volume demonstrate, the archaic period was a time of great
and rapid change in Greece. As cities faced the challenges of overpopulation, land
shortage, economic developments, and political conflicts, overseas colonization
proved to be a productive and very successful solution. Representations of that
solution have been the focus of the first part of this essay. Access to objective
documentation for the archaic period is limited; instead, we have the myths and
legends that record the individual city foundations, and consequently we must be
aware of the many kinds of influences – political, historical, economic, religious,
literary – that can shape the form of the colonial (and other kinds of) narrative. I
have tried to tease out one such influence in this discussion of the founder as

murderer. This type of account describes overseas settlement by adapting the metaphor of purification to a colonial context and uses familiar narrative patterns to shape its narrative.[36]

III

My discussion up to this point has been largely schematic, and in conclusion, I would like to show how the collocation of murderer and city founder works in a specific literary context, namely Pindar's seventh *Olympian* ode. In this poem, which celebrates the victory of Diagoras of Rhodes in the boxing event at Olympia in 464 B.C.E., Pindar explains that he will sing the praises of Diagoras by celebrating the foundation of his native city. He tells the history of Rhodes in three triads, beginning and ending with Tlepolemos and his settlement of the island after being exiled from Argos for murder:

> ἐθελήσω τοῖσιν ἐξ ἀρχᾶς ἀπὸ Τλαπολέμου
> ξυνὸν ἀγγέλλων διορθῶσαι λόγον,
> Ἡρακλέος
> εὐρυσθενεῖ γέννᾳ. τὸ μὲν γὰρ
>   πατρόθεν ἐκ Διὸς εὔχονται· τὸ δ' Ἀμυντορίδαι
> ματρόθεν Ἀστυδαμείας. (20–4)[37]

> I wish, announcing from the beginning, from Tlepolemos, to straighten out the common account for the mighty race of Herakles. For they boast to descend on their father's side from Zeus, and on their mother's side, to be the sons of Amyntor through Astydameia.

This same Tlepolemos, murderer and colonial founder, appears in the *Iliad,* in the "Catalogue of Ships," leading the Rhodian contingent to Troy, and it may be this Iliadic passage (or one like it) that Pindar has in mind when he announces his desire to correct the common account (ξυνὸν ἀγγέλλων διορθῶσαι λόγον; 21).[38] To appreciate the nature of the correction it will be helpful to compare the two versions. First the Homeric account:

> Τληπόλεμος δ' ἐπεὶ οὖν τράφ' ἐνὶ μεγάρῳ εὐπήκτῳ,
> αὐτίκα πατρὸς ἑοῖο φίλον μήτρωα κατέκτα
> ἤδη γηράσκοντα Λικύμνιον, ὄζον Ἄρηος.
> αἶψα δὲ νῆας ἔπηξε, πολὺν δ' ὅ γε λαὸν ἀγείρας
> βῆ φεύγων ἐπὶ πόντον· ἀπείλησαν γάρ οἱ ἄλλοι
> υἱέες υἱωνοί τε βίης Ἡρακληείης.
> αὐτὰρ ὅ γ' ἐς Ῥόδον ἷξεν ἀλώμενος, ἄλγεα πάσχων·
> τριχθὰ δὲ ᾤκηθεν καταφυλαδόν, ἠδ' ἐφίληθεν
> ἐκ Διός, ... (2.661–9)

> Now when Tlepolemos was grown in the well-built mansion, he killed his own father's beloved uncle, Likymnios, scion of Ares, a man already aging. At once he put ships together

189

and assembled a host of people and fled across the sea, for the others threatened, sons and grandsons of the strength of Herakles. And he came to Rhodes a wanderer, having suffered troubles, and they settled there in triple divisions by tribes, beloved of Zeus, . . .

In *Olympian* 7, Pindar presents the following "corrected" version:

καὶ γὰρ Ἀλκμήνας κασίγνητον νόθον
σκάπτῳ θενών
σκληρᾶς ἐλαίας ἔκτανεν Τί-
  ρυνθι Λικύμνιον ἐλθόντ' ἐκ θαλάμων Μιδέας
τᾶσδέ ποτε χθονὸς οἰκι-
  στὴρ χολωθείς. αἱ δὲ φρενῶν ταραχαί
παρέπλαγξαν καὶ σοφόν. μαντεύσατο δ' ἐς θεὸν ἐλθών.
τῷ μὲν ὁ χρυσοκόμας εὐ-
  ώδεος ἐξ ἀδύτου ναῶν πλόον
εἶπε Λερναίας ἀπ' ἀκτᾶς
  εὐθὺν ἐς ἀμφιθάλασσον νομόν. . . . (27–33)

For he killed Likymnios, the bastard brother of Alkmene, striking him with a scepter of hard olive wood at Tiryns, as Likymnios was leaving the rooms of Midea, he, the founder of this land here – having been driven to anger. Disturbances of the mind cause even a wise man to wander astray. He went to consult the god, and the golden-haired one told him from his well-scented inner chamber to sail from the Lernean cape straight to a land surrounded by sea. . . .

The two accounts of the settlement of Rhodes obviously have much in common. In each, Tlepolemos, son of Herakles, kills Likymnios, his uncle. As a result, he immediately flees from home and settles Rhodes. There are, however, some important discrepancies as well. Most relevant to our current discussion, Pindar inserts Delphic Apollo into the colonization account. In the Homeric poems, we understand that it was fear of retribution from relatives that drove murderers, even in cases of justifiable killings, into exile. Accordingly, in the *Iliad*, Tlepolemos rounds up his companions and sails immediately to Rhodes without any divine consultation at all.[39] Once Apollo and the Delphic oracle become the accepted authorities in cases of the pollution resulting from murder, it is more often the case that the oracle itself directs the exile, and unlike the Homeric version, in *Olympian* 7 Tlepolemos does in fact consult Delphic Apollo after killing his uncle.

Furthermore, Pindar intensifies the importance of Delphi in his narrative by reminding his audience that Tlepolemos' role as founder of Rhodes is a direct consequence of his act of homicide. The word order makes it clear: Tlepolemos killed Likymnios, he, "the founder of this land, having been made angry" (τᾶσδέ ποτε χθονὸς οἰκιστὴρ χολωθείς; 30). Immediately following this mention of the angered oikist, Pindar interrupts his narrative with a gnomic passage: "Disturbances of the mind knock astray even the wise man" (αἱ δὲ φρενῶν ταραχαί/

παρέπλαγξαν καὶ σοφόν; 30–1). The gnome seems designed to explain the force of χολωθείς, "angered," and it is tempting to follow J. Defradas, who pursues the motif here as another Delphically influenced Pindaric correction. He suggests that by characterizing Tlepolemos' act as involuntary manslaughter, an act of passion rather than premeditated murder, Pindar specifically refers to the prominent role that Delphic Apollo and his oracle play in adjudicating such cases of murder.[40] Whether or not the motif is specifically Delphic, Pindar certainly does establish Delphi as the turning point in *Olympian* 7, the transition between the murderer's exile and the colonist's expedition.

We also recognize the narrative pattern; the murderer functions as an analog for the colonial founder, but in an epinikian context, this observation leads us to pose another question – why is a murdererous founder an appropriate model for an athletic victor? Indeed, Pindar's "corrected" version of the colonization of Rhodes led by a murderer in exile has seemed to some to be an unlikely source of praise for an Olympic victor, and scholars have tried to account for this apparent anomaly by saying that Pindar highlights the good that can come after a mistake is made.[41] While this interpretation is accurate to some extent, we can better understand this mythological parallel if we put the tale of Tlepolemos into the wider context of colonial discourse. As we have seen, the tendency to conflate a murderer in exile with an oikist who must lead a colony overseas reflects the Greek perception of an important similarity between purification through exile and colonization. Keeping this in mind, we gain new insight into Pindar's incorporation of Apollo and the Delphic oracle into his version of the colonization of Rhodes. But more important, we better understand Tlepolemos, the murderer, as an epinikian model for Diagoras, the victor in *Olympian* 7.

Elsewhere in the epinikian odes, Pindar tells a colonial tale in order to celebrate the athlete's victory; both *Pythians* 4 and 5, for example, employ Battos, the founder of Kyrene, as the model for praising King Arkesilaos, victor in the chariot race. In the odes that draw upon colonial traditions, Pindar suggests that there is an implicit similarity between colonization and victory in the Panhellenic games, and he develops this insight by juxtaposing the parallel careers of the founder and the victor. Both founder and victor must take risks and expend effort to be successful in their endeavors; as a result, Pindar describes the colony or victory that each gains in the end as a reward, or compensation, for his efforts. Each must leave home and travel to be successful; each gains his fame from excelling or being first. And finally, the founder and the victor both receive immortal honors from their respective cities. The founder is celebrated with the cult of the founder, and the victor enjoys the immortal fame of Pindar's song. Thus both a city founder and an athletic victor are valued, honored figures in their cities. One gives the city its name; he marks out civic boundaries and establishes the precincts of the gods. The other contributes to the continued glory of his city by causing its name to be called out in victory at Delphi or Olympia.

In *Olympian* 7 as well, Pindar uses the colonial founder of Rhodes, Tlepolemos, as the epinikian model for Diagoras, the boxing victor. But even more interesting, in this ode Pindar makes explicit the connection between purification and colonization discussed in the first part of this essay; he suggests that this model be extended to include Panhellenic victory as well. At the end of the three-part mythological section of *Olympian* 7, Pindar uses a locative adverb (τόθι) to return to Tlepolemos and Diagoras on Rhodes. The transition hinges upon Tlepolemos' compensation for the efforts of leading a colony:

> τόθι λύτρον συμφορᾶς οἰκτρᾶς γλυκὺ Τλαπολέμῳ
> ἵσταται Τιρυνθίων ἀρχαγέτᾳ,
> ὥσπερ θεῷ,
> μήλων τε κνισάεσσα πομπὰ
> καὶ κρίσις ἀμφ' ἀέθλοις. (77–80)

> Here, the sweet recompense for bitter sorrow was es-
> tablished for Tlepolemos of Tiryns, the founder, just
> as if for a god – a procession filled with the smoke of
> sacrificed sheep and athletic contests.

As the founder of the Argive colony of Rhodes, Tlepolemos receives heroic honors after death in the form of the founder's cult, and the specific nature of this cult is important here. The cult of the founder is a civic, not personal, celebration. This is the first independent cult of the new city – one not imported from the metropolis and therefore symbolic of the city's emerging self-identity.[42] The founder was buried in the agora and his cult was celebrated annually with sacrifices and athletic games. But because this colonial founder is also a murderer, in this poem Pindar presents Tlepolemos' posthumous transformation from colonial founder to civic hero as a kind of purification. The particular language used – ''sweet recompense for bitter sorrow'' (λύτρον συμφορᾶς οἰκτρᾶς γλυκὺ) – evokes Apollo's colonial role as purifier, and through chiastic word order Pindar suggests that the act of sweet purification (λύτρον . . . γλυκὺ) embraces and expiates the original crime of murder (συμφορᾶς οἰκτρᾶς). By commemorating a murderer as a founding hero, the new city thereby appropriates to itself the sacred power associated with the purification that murder demands. Pindar realizes this, and he specifically introduces Apollo's role as purifier into his account of Tlepolemos and the founding of Rhodes. After killing Likymnios, Tlepolemos consults Apollo's oracle at Delphi and then is pur-ified by setting out to found a colony. The emphasis is not on Tlepolemos as a polluted or defiled murderer, but on his positive and sacred value as a founder of a new city. By comparing Diagoras to Tlepolemos, Pindar suggests that a victorious athlete has similar powers to confer upon his city, and he thus deserves the reward of fame in return for the toils of victory in the boxing competition.

Pindar often draws parallels between the deeds of athlete and hero by describing each as toils or efforts. The resulting honors or celebrations received are corre-spondingly represented as compensation or rewards. At the very beginning of *Olympian* 7, Pindar refers to the song he sings in honor of Diagoras' Olympian victory as a πυγμᾶς ἄποινα (16) – a reward for boxing, and at the end of the mythological section, he similarly describes Tlepolemos' founder's cult as purifying compensation (λύτρον συμφορᾶς οἰκτρᾶς γλυκὺ).[43] The poet uses this same con-cept of compensation as purification (λύτρον) to describe the celebratory song and dance that accompany victory at the beginning of *Isthmian* 8 as well, and in this poem he combines both terms, which he uses separately in *Olympian* 7 to praise Diagoras and Tlepolemos:

Κλεάνδρῳ τις ἁλικίᾳ
   τε λύτρον εὔδοξον, ὦ νέοι, καμάτων
πατρὸς ἀγλαὸν Τελεσάρχου παρὰ πρόθυρον
ἰὼν ἀνεγειρέτω
κῶμον, Ἰσθμιάδος τε νί-
   κας ἄποινα (1–4)

Let someone, O young men, go to the glorious porch of his father Telesarchos and raise up the celebration for Kleander, in his youth, a glorious recompense for his efforts, the reward for an Isthmian victory.

As compensation for the risks and dangers of competition, compensation that is characterized in purificatory terms, Pindar offers the *kōmos* to the victor, a victory song and celebration.

To return to *Olympian* 7, the career of the oikist is a potent source of praise for the athletic victor. Furthermore, Tlepolemos' "shady" background as a murderer-turned-founder is not a liability but is, in fact, particularly relevant to Diagoras' role as victor. In Chapter 7 of this volume, Leslie Kurke discusses the talismanic power that a victorious athlete confers on his city, and this *kudos* is quite similar to the consecrating power associated with a purified murderer as founder of a new city. Athletes receive heroic honors under specific historical conditions – when a city suffers either an internal or an external crisis – and as Kurke has shown, the crisis that prompts the heroization of an athlete is represented as the transgression of proper ritual norms. We have seen that colonies, too, are said to be settled in response to civic crisis; colonial founders, especially those remembered as murderers, transgress boundaries as well, and as a result attain heroic status.[44]

In addition to the act of transgression, common to the ideology of athletics and colonization is the monstrous deed, the act of violence. Again we must remember that within this violence lies the potential for monstrous power. In this respect, the model of colonial murderer is useful within an epinikian context in another respect as well, for it addresses the violence of competition. Tlepolemos kills his uncle; Diagoras overcomes his opponent in a boxing match. In this sense, Pindar characterizes Tlepolemos' actions as a mythic exaggeration of what constitutes the violent sport of boxing. We saw earlier that within the narrative structure of colonization legends, the figure of the murderous founder acknowledges the bloodshed inherent in establishing new cities in foreign territories. Athletic competition as well provides a ritual context for the accommodation and expiation of the violence that forms a necessary part of any act of civilization.

In *Olympian* 7, Pindar includes the myth of Tlepolemos' murder and subsequent colonization of Rhodes as a model for the praise of Diagoras the Olympic boxing victor. The careers of both founder and boxer involve risk and violence; both combine individual achievement with glory for their cities. The talismanic power, or *kudos,* that the victorious athlete confers upon his native city is reinforced in this poem through the figure of Tlepolemos, a murderer transformed through purification into a city founder. Appropriately, crowns, the physical manifestation of that power which both athlete and founder bring to the city, also play a prominent role in *Olympian* 7; they concretize the link between Diagoras and Tlepolemos. At the beginning of the ode, Diagoras is crowned beside the Alpheos (στεφανωσάμενον; 15); he is crowned again at the end, twice at the games of Tlepolemos (ἐστεφανώσατο δίς; 81). Crowning imagery highlights the circular pattern of the narrative, the ring composition of the Tlepolemos myth.

The account of an angry murderer who then founds a colony no longer appears to be an unlikely source of praise for the very successful boxer Diagoras of Rhodes on the occasion of his Olympic victory. The myths and legends of the archaic colonial movement reveal a strong ideological link between purification and colonization, and we have seen that the key to this analogy lies not in the murder itself but in the two-step process of murder followed by purification. Just as the victorious athlete can bring talismanic power to his native city, the murderer is not only a source of pollution; once purified, he assumes a new constructive value as founder of the new city. In addition, accounts of purified murderers as colonial founders address the issue of transgression that is implicit in Panhellenic competition as well. In many ways, founding a colony is like being purified for murder, which in turn is like winning an Olympic victory. In exploring the metaphors, in determining what exactly these three institutions have in common, we gain a more precise picture of each.

NOTES

I thank Lisa Maurizio, Gregory Nagy, Emily Vermeule, and especially Leslie Kurke for their help and encouragement with this essay.

1. The god mentioned in this account is undoubtedly Delphic Apollo.

2. We should note here that Turner's model of social drama (breach, crisis, redressive action, reintegration or recognition of schism) precisely fits this narrative sequence. See V. Turner 1974: 23–59, esp. 37–42, for his definition of the four stages of a social drama.

3. Ruipérez 1953 shows that the title Phoibos is a *nomen agentis* derived from φοιβός, "purifier," which comes from a root meaning "to illuminate" or "shine bright." He notes a parallel relationship in Latin between *lux, luceo,* and *lustrare* and suggests that this might reflect early forms of purification through fire. Cf. Chantraine 1968–80: 1216–17. See also Versnel 1985–6: 135: "The word *Phoibos* is no longer interpreted as 'radiant' but rather as 'cathartic' or 'awful.' " For ancient etymologies along this line, see Plut. 393c; Macr. *Sat.* 1.17.33; Cornut. *theol.* 32.66.8; schol. ap. Ap. Rhod. 2.302.

4. Malkin 1987: 142–3 argues that although Callimachus may imply that the entire process of laying out the new city and apportioning the land is sanctioned or even directed by Apollo, we must not assume that the Greek colonists regarded their city plan as divinely ordained. His point is that the primary responsibility for organizing the new city belongs to the human founder. My point here is that the choice of Apollo as a metaphor is significant and needs to be explored further. See Lakoff and Turner 1989: 215, who argue that "poetic metaphor, far from being ornamentation, deals with central and

indispensable aspects of our conceptual systems. Through the masterful use of metaphoric processes on which our conceptual systems are based, poets address the most vital issues in our lives and help us illuminate those issues, through the extension, composition, and criticism of the basic metaphoric tools through which we comprehend much of reality.''

5. On the conceptual use of metaphor, see Geertz 1973, 1983; White 1973, 1978; V. Turner 1974; Lakoff and Johnson 1980; Sahlins 1981; Clifford and Marcus 1986; Lakoff and Turner 1989.

6. Apollo's prophetic powers and the advisory capacity of the Delphic oracle also help establish Apollo in the role of ritual purifier. If someone is sick or a plague attacks a region, the Greeks consistently consult the Delphic oracle as to the cause of the trouble. Cf. Burkert 1985: 147, who points out that in responding to pollution a person must discover the action that brought about the miasma. ''This, of course, requires super-human knowledge: the god of purifications must also be an oracle god.'' See the collections of Delphic responses collected by Parke and Wormell 1956 and Fontenrose 1978 for examples of consultations about plague.

7. Although, as Parker 1983 points out, Apollo has no cultic association with murder pollution (this is Zeus' territory), in myth and legend it is customary to consult Delphic Apollo to be purified for murder and to be sent into exile. See Parker's app. 7 (365–92) for a list of examples of the exile and purification motif pertaining to the killer in Greek myth.

8. Cf. Gagarin 1981: 10; he includes a list of all the homicides in the epic poems on 6–10.

9. *IG* i² 115 (i³ 104) ll. 10–12. Cf. Stroud 1968 for text, translation, and commentary on Drakon's homicide law.

10. Myth portrays the city of Thebes suffering a crippling plague because Laios' murderer has not been caught.

11. Ephoros tells us that the Lakedaimonians were at war with the Messenians and swore not to return home until they had destroyed Messene or were all killed. In the tenth year of the war, however, their wives were angry at having been abandoned to widowhood and complained that their country was in danger of lacking men. Their husbands then agreed to send the youngest men back home to cohabit with the unmarried women there. The children born of these unions were called the Partheniai.

12. For accounts of the Kylonian conspiracy, see Thuc. 1.126; Hdt. 5.71; for Epimenides' purification of Athens, see Arist. *Ath. Pol.* 1; Plut. *Sol.* 12. See Connor 1988b for a more general discussion of how arbitrary the distinctions are that we make on behalf of the Athenians between religious and secular events. Morris, Chapter 2, this volume, also discusses the Kylonian episode within this context.

13. Cf. Vernant 1988: 131–2: ''A 'besmirchment' seems to indicate some contact that is contrary to a certain order of the world in that it establishes communication between things that ought to remain quite distinct from each other.''

14. Douglas 1966: 41.

15. See Van Gennep 1960 for a general study of rites of passage. See Parker 1983: 22–3 for a discussion of how purification unites individuals into groups. On the similarities between initiation rites and purification rituals in cases of murder, see Burkert 1985: 81–2: ''A purification of this kind is clearly in essence a *rite de passage*. The murderer has set himself outside the community, and his reincorporation at a new level is therefore an act of initiation.''

16. Apollo has associations with the Athenian initiation of ephebes, and this connection has been brought to bear on his role as colonizer, for colonists are often young men crossing

the threshold into manhood. Cf. Harrison 1912: 439–44; Versnel 1985–6: 143–5. De Polignac 1984: 66–74 is also relevant here; he discusses initiation rites as integrative models in the birth of cities.

17. Cf. Vidal-Naquet 1986: 206. Talking about myths of origin, he says that "each city pictured for itself the transition 'in the beginning' from chaos to order and from Nature to Culture. The legendary tradition incorporates mythical elements but is felt and described as historical."

18. See Morris, Chapter 2, this volume, for further discussion of what he calls the "propagandistic fallacy."

19. Discussions of the historicity or literary nature of the colonial narrative fall outside the scope of this essay for two reasons. First, the Greeks did not make the same disciplinary distinctions favored by modern scholars between historical and literary treatments of the past (see Detienne 1986b; Brillante 1990; Calame 1990). Second, even if *we* insist on making these distinctions, we must refrain from privileging historical accounts of archaic colonization over literary accounts. Historical texts of any period are no less opaque, no less subjective in their use of metaphors and tropes, than are literary texts; they are equally available for narratological analysis. See, e.g., the essays collected in White 1978, especially "Historical Text as Literary Artifact," and Hunt 1989.

20. The story has obvious parallels with the *ver sacrum* legends (cf. Heurgon 1957); instead of following an animal, Koroibos carries a tripod. But the tripod marks the location of the new city and gives it its name. Pausanias goes on to say that Koroibos is buried in the agora of Megara (as is customary for city founders; Tripodiskoi is a village of Megara), and that the story of Psamathe and Koroibos is carved on his stele in elegiacs. There is also a visual representation of Koroibos killing Poine. Pausanias observes that these are the oldest stone images that he is aware of having seen. See *Anth. Pal.* 7.154 for the epigram.

21. Other examples of murderers as city founders include Aitolia: Apoll. 1.7.6; Athamantia: Apoll. 1.9.2; Argos Orestikos: Strab. 7.7.8; Magnesia: Parth. *Amat. Narr.* 5; Lipara: Diod. 4.67.4; Mycenae: Paus. 2.16.3; Rhodes: *Il.* 2.653–70; Pind. *Ol.* 7, Strab. 14.2.6; Zeleia: schol. ap. *Il.* 4.88.

22. It may be objected that this particular colonial motif is merely a Hellenistic invention, but as I will demonstrate in the final section of this essay, the story of Tlepolemos, murderer and founder of Rhodes, which first appears in the *Iliad* and which is later taken up by Pindar in *Olympian* 7, perfectly fits this model. As a general principle for scholars working on the archaic period, we must remember that the lateness of a source does not necessarily determine the antiquity (or lack thereof) of the account it records.

23. Chantraine and Masson 1954. Moulinier 1952: 296 rejects this etymological connection and makes a distinction between the two groups of words; see Vernant 1988: 135–7, however, for the problems with Moulinier's approach.

24. Vernant 1988: 138.

25. Douglas 1966: 168–9.

26. Douglas 1966: 169–70 interprets this cult as one of many "which invite their initiates to turn round and confront the categories on which their whole surrounding culture has been built up and to recognise them for the fictive, man-made, arbitrary creations that they are."

27. Euripides makes this legend the starting point for the *Alkestis* (1–8). Such a legend may suggest an underlying custom of making a murderer perform some menial service for a designated time among strangers in order to atone for his offense.

28. See Paus. 2.7.7 for Apollo's purification in Crete and see Frazer's 1898 note (vol. 3.53–7). The Tempe tradition seems to be aetiologically connected with the Septerion

festival at Delphi, and the Cretan version may be traced back to a time when the Cretans had a high reputation as ritual cleansers. In the *Homeric Hymn,* Apollo's priests come from Crete, and this narrative detail may represent the Cretan introduction of cathartic rites to Greece at Delphi. See Huxley 1975: 119–24. Similarly, as we saw earlier, Epimenides comes from Crete to purify Athens of the Kylonian plague.

29. Cf. Detienne 1986a.
30. We see this same principle at work in Sahlins's 1981 account of Cook's interaction with the Hawaiians. He argues that the historical event of Cook's arrival was interpreted by the Hawaiians within the ritual context of the Makahiki festival. A priest analyzing Cook's death at the hands of the Hawaiians explained that Cook had violated a Hawaiian taboo by removing wood from a temple. Sahlins shows (26) that this claim is historically inaccurate, but that within the larger mythic context, Cook becomes a taboo transgressor. This reanalysis is not intended as a justification of Cook's murder but rather signifies his present position as their divine guardian. In other words, Cook gains power and protective status for the Hawaiians precisely because he transgressed ritual norms.
31. For further examples, see Thuc. 6.1–5; cf. Diod. 8.21.3, for an oracle given to Phalanthos, the founder of Tarentum, telling him to be a "plague to the Iapygians."
32. Cf. Schmid 1947: 13–16.
33. Frs. 17, 18, 19, 88, 120 (Tarditi). Cf. Graham 1978: 61–98.
34. Dunbabin 1948: 43: "At least half the Greek colonies were built on sites previously occupied by native towns, and it is likely that most were. In every case of which we hear, the Greeks drove out the Sicels or Italians by force."
35. See Ober, Chapter 11, this volume, on Kleisthenes' role in the development of democracy in Athens, for a discussion of the similar tendency to attribute important historical events to a single man.
36. I should emphasize that the murderer/founder model discussed here is not the only one found in archaic colonization literature. For a discussion of other models and narrative patterns (marriage, riddles, athletic victory), see Dougherty 1993. In Chapter 8, this volume, Boedeker shows how a different kind of solution (transferal of a hero's bones) to civic crisis operates in a similar fashion. She develops the following pattern: civic crisis followed by consultation of the Delphic oracle, which then suggests finding, relocating, and honoring a particular hero. She shows how the representation of this solution, specifically in Herodotus' account of the Orestes' bones episode, is also influenced by a familiar narrative pattern. It becomes clear that colonization and transferal of a hero's bones are two alternative solutions to a similar problem: civic crisis. Kurke's essay on *kudos* (Chapter 7, this volume) also fits this pattern.
37. All quotations of Pindar are cited from Snell and Maehler 1980.
38. There has been much scholarly debate as to what διορθῶσαι means. I follow Defradas 1974 and translate it as "straighten out" in the sense of correcting a previous misunderstanding. D. C. Young 1968: 78 suggests "elevate to glory"; Norwood 1945: 258 n. 3 says "edit." The scholia gloss it variously as ἀκριβῶσαι or διασημῆναι; one scholiast suggests that Pindar wants to overapologize (ὑπεραπολογήσασθαι) for the exile of Tlepolemos.
39. There are, of course, other differences as well between the two accounts. For further discussion of Pindar's corrections, see Ruck 1968: 129–32; D. C. Young 1968: 82–3; Defradas 1974.
40. Defradas 1974. Unfortunately, as Parker (1983: esp. 138–43) has shown, the evidence is not as clear as Defradas would have us believe.
41. Gildersleeve 1890: 183, e.g., draws such a conclusion about all three myths in the poem: "In each of these three cases we have a good beginning followed by misfortune,

and yet a good ending crowns all.'' Cf. Norwood 1945: 138–45; Young 1968: 79–81 summarizes the bibliography.

42. For the literary and archeological evidence for the cult of the founder, see Malkin 1987: 189–240; for the burial of city founders in the agora, see Martin 1951: 197–201.

43. D. C. Young 1968: 77 n. 2 and Kurke 1991: 108–16 on ἄποινα here. See Nagy 1986: 92–4, 1990b: 136–45 for the chain of compensation that links hero and athlete.

44. See Kurke, Chapter 7, this volume, for examples of athletes who become city founders.

PART FOUR

The End of an Era

CHAPTER TEN

Thucydides' Solonian Reflections

Andrew Szegedy-Maszak

"By nature old Solon was a friend of the people" (ὁ Σόλων ὁ παλαιὸς ἦν φιλόδημος τὴν φύσιν), the thoroughly corrupted Pheidippides proclaims toward the end of Aristophanes' *Clouds* (1187), and he then explains to his father how they can exploit a "law" of Solon's, about the old and the new day, to dodge their creditors. Though obviously distorted for comic effect, this is one of the more substantial of the very few clues that we have to determine how Athenians of the fifth century regarded the political activities of their great statesman.[1] Research for this essay was originally begun with the intention of discussing Solon's role in the political discourse of the fifth century, but it soon became clear that he was not there, at least not *in propria persona*. In fact, direct fifth-century mentions of Solon are extremely sparse.[2] In addition to the brief, scattered references such as that in the *Clouds,* the only extended appearance he makes is in the pages of Herodotus, in the famous encounter with Croesus (1.29–34). The episode is so well known that it does not require retelling. Herodotus does allude to Solon's political activities in a brief introductory explanation (1.29): Solon removed himself from Athens for ten years because he had passed a code of laws for the Athenians and had extracted an oath from his fellow citizens that they would not change any of the statutes so long as he was away.[3] Herodotus uses the decidedly unhistorical meeting between Solon and Croesus to highlight certain thematic contrasts that are important throughout the *Histories:* between Greek and Asian, lawgiver and despot, quality and quantity, moderation and *hybris,* wisdom and folly. In other words, Herodotus gives Solon the role of a "wise adviser." Even though the contrast between ethics and politics was not as sharply drawn in the fifth century as it later was, it is indisputable that Solon's wise advice is completely ethical, not political.[4]

To a large degree, Solon's absence from this part of the historical record is due to the paucity of fifth-century theorizing about democratic institutions. In the words of Nicole Loraux, "It can be said with some semblance of certainty that Athens had no theory of democracy that was both *systematic* and *Athenian*." Despite such a lack, however, Loraux affirms that "we may gather together the scattered lineaments of a body of *democratic thought,* if not a systematic examination of the *theory of democracy,* for the fifth century."[5] In a splendid article, Kurt Raaflaub has recently outlined a method for discussing what evidence there is.[6] One of his basic principles is to avoid the more abundant fourth-century sources, except where the information in Aristotle's *Athenaion Politeia* is indispensable.[7] I have followed Raaflaub's lead despite the fact that virtually all modern discussions of Solon's position within Athenian democratic ideology are directed at his "afterlife" in the fourth century. So, for example, E. Ruschenbusch has argued that before 356 Solon was invoked as a poet, a lawgiver, and one of the Seven Sages, but not as the framer of a constitution.[8] While Ruschenbusch's contention is too stark, it does contain a large measure of truth. Instead of trying to define the dimensions of an absence or a negative space – that is, where does Solon *not* appear in fifth-century prose? – it seemed more feasible to borrow a leaf from American Studies. We may consider, for example, the following phrases: "Speak softly and carry a big stick," "the bully pulpit," "rough riders." All of them are still living elements within U.S. political rhetoric, and all originated with president Theodore Roosevelt. While they are easily identified as Roosevelt's, in the traces they carry of his personality and his approach to good government (another of his slogans), few Americans could identify the specific issues that first occasioned these phrases. My purpose in this essay is to suggest that the fifth-century Athenians could also practice the invocation of a historical figure by referring to one of his attributes, to a famous event in his life, or to one of his sayings, without assuming that the audience would be familiar with the details of his whole program, indeed without even using his name.[9] This assumption is not, of course, entirely novel. In his essay "Myth, Memory and History," M. I. Finley makes much the same claim: "The poets took care of the heroic past; for the rest, specific traditions, largely oral, were sufficient. In Athens, the Solonic codification, the tyrannicides, Marathon were the stock allusions of political orators and pamphleteers, and everyone knew all that anyone needed to know about them."[10] One might compare the deployment of such allusions to the vase painters' use of iconographic conventions. Such a repertoire of gestures and objects, however pared down and schematic they might be, allowed the viewers easily to identify specific mythological scenes and characters.

I propose to examine Thucydides as a test case, on the premise that although he never mentions Solon by name, motifs and slogans that are recognizably Solonian appear at a number of crucial places in his narrative. The value of identifying such Solonian resonances is that they can contribute to our understanding of Thucydides' attitude not only toward Athens' past but also toward the politics of his own day.

Thucydides' two digressions on Harmodios and Aristogeiton (1.20, 6.53.3–56.9) are sufficient evidence that he, and so presumably his audience, took a lively interest in the political history of the preceding century; they also show that Thucydides was aware of both the persistence and the limitations of popular tradition. He notes, with some annoyance, that while the Athenians of the late fifth century were anxious about the specter of tyranny, they were also "quite inaccurate in what they say about their own tyrants" (6.54.1). Thucydides uses the story of the tyrannicides to illustrate his own *akribeia* and the thoroughness of his research. Contesting the received version, Thucydides insists that Hippias, not the slain Hipparchos, was head of the tyrannical Peisistratid clan, and – most important – that the motives of Harmodios and Aristogeiton were personal rather than political. It is not my purpose here to discuss *why* Thucydides was so concerned to correct what he saw as errors in the popular opinion about the tyrannicides. The point is that he explicitly criticizes the kind of oral political lore that Finley describes in the passage just quoted.[11] Such criticism in turn gives rise to an inescapable dilemma in studying Thucydides' relation to Solon. In comments like the one about the tyrannicides, Thucydides claims for himself a more thorough knowledge of Athenian history than that possessed by the average citizen. There is, however, no way of telling how much familiarity Thucydides had with Solon's own language, whether poetic or legal/political; at the same time there can be no doubt that Thucydides was thoroughly acquainted with the work of Herodotus. To return to the tyrannicides, for example, it has been shown that Thucydides' account agrees on every important point with Herodotus' (though the latter has much less detail).[12] It is possible, then, that Thucydides' image of Solon was itself a simplified, or at least derivative, version that owed most of its major features to popular oral tradition and to Herodotus.[13] Given Thucydides' general erudition and sophistication, we can guess that he knew Solon's own words, but in the absence of concrete data, we cannot reach a definitive conclusion.[14] In the parts of my argument that depend on verbal correspondences, I have restricted the discussion to passages where parallels can be adduced from Solon's own poetry, so as to reduce some of the uncertainty. Nonetheless, much of what follows is necessarily speculative.

Preserved in a speech of Demosthenes is part of an elegy by Solon, a poem generally known as "Our City," that begins with the lines "Our city will never be destroyed by the plan of Zeus and the will of the blessed immortals." Solon then describes the catastrophes occasioned by political strife and concludes with a paian to *eunomia* – "which keeps all things in good order."[15] As already noted, we cannot be sure whether Thucydides knew this particular elegy, but there can be no doubt that he knew that Solon employed *eunomia* as "a programme for political action."[16] In Thucydides' history a form of *eunomia* occurs only once with complete certainty, at 1.18.1 when he connects the Spartan condition of *eunomia* with the disappearance of earlier stasis and with freedom from tyrants: " . . . of the Dorians, Sparta had stasis for the longest time of any we know (ἐπὶ πλεῖστον ὧν ἴσμεν χρόνον στασιάσασα), and yet at a very early period obtained good laws (ἐκ παλαιτάτου καὶ ηὐνομήθη) and was always free from tyrants (αἰεὶ ἀτυράννευτος ἦν); for it is for a period of slightly more than 400 years . . . that she has used the same *politeia* and held power over other cities." We do not have to concern ourselves with some troublesome aspects of the interpretation of this passage – such as whether Sparta's power was based on freedom from tyranny or on the durability of its constitution for 400 years[17] – but it is important to note the constellation of terms. Significantly, Spartan *eunomia* is identified both as an antidote to civil strife and as a protection against tyranny. This is strikingly close to the praise of *eunomia* composed by Solon. In the first part of the elegy "Our City" (fr. 4 W) Solon describes how the citizens themselves, driven by greed, are responsible for the troubles that befall them. Their leaders are no better. For a time, Justice has no hold over them, but eventually she wreaks vengeance in the form of stasis, warfare, evil conspiracies, or even slavery. *Eunomia,* in contrast, "straightens out crooked judgments given, gentles the swollen ambitions" – these are implicit references to tyranny – "and puts an end to acts of faction" (παύει δ' ἔργα διχοστασίης).

In Solon's vision, law and lawfulness serve as guardians for the whole society and every individual citizen. Martin Ostwald's brilliant analysis of the semantic field occupied by *nomos* and *eunomia* shows the nuances of the terms that take them far beyond a simple statutory sense, but he does not spend much time on their ideological implications. He consistently translates *eunomia* as "law and order." To some degree, of course, such a condition is a desideratum for all communities, ancient or modern. Still, to realize that this is not a mere truism or politically neutral formulation, we need think only of the use of the phrase "law and order" in contemporary U.S. political rhetoric. In the context of the Athenian democracy of the late fifth century, *eunomia* is part of an agenda of preserving traditional virtues. As it comes to be identified both with Sparta and with Solon, it stands in opposition to tyranny and stasis, and I think that, for Thucydides, it is also a counter to radical democracy.[18]

The other possible occurrence of the term is toward the end of the work as we have it. At 8.64.5, when Thucydides is recounting the events of 411, the Thasians are described as choosing for themselves a moderate government (σωφροσύνην) and its attendant freedom (ἐλευθερίαν) instead of accepting the sham *eunomia* offered to them by the Athenian oligarchs (τῆς ἀπὸ τῶν Ἀθηναίων ὑπούλου εὐνομίας). Ostwald argues that the latter text should have αὐτονομίας, primarily because the phrase then yields a more cogent irony, which Ostwald renders "self-determination imposed by the Athenians." Andrewes, however, rejects Ostwald's argument and retains εὐνομίας, concluding that "εὐνομίας is backed by impressive authority, and good sense can be made of it."[19] If Andrewes is correct, as I think he is, we have additional support for the schematic contrast in Thucydides' thinking that has been proposed here. Genuine *eunomia* is a force of moderation that preserves a state intact.

It may be objected that a single appearance (or, at most, a dual appearance) in a long text is a slender prop for such a large generalization about Thucydides' relation to Solon. Fortunately there is corroborating evidence, in the contrast between *eunomia* and *isonomia.*[20] The latter is the slogan adopted, and perhaps invented, by Kleisthenes to denote his new order, dedicated to the proposition that in Athens all free adult males were created equal. To sum up this section of my argument, in Thucydides, by contrast with *isonomia, eunomia* carries a positive tone that reflects its great proponent, Solon.

It *is* a matter of tone, of small signs rather than of systematic examination, but it is completely consistent with our general understanding of Thucydides' politics. Especially revealing is the absolutely consistent link in Thucydides between *isonomia* and *plēthos.* All four instances of the former are accompanied by the latter.[21] As Ostwald notes, "Thucydides, in all the *isonomia* passages, confines its meaning to a segment of the population, namely to the 'common people,' the 'broad masses.' "[22] Here Ostwald clearly outlines the ideological connotations of the term in Thucydides, but without drawing the conclusion that in Thucydides' overall analysis *isonomia,* linked as it consistently is to the *plēthos,* must have negative connotations. A salient example is to be found at 3.82.8, in the discussion of the stasis at Corcyra, which Thucydides says served as a model for civil strife in other cities. Indeed, the whole tone of the passage recalls Solon's fr. 4 W, in which the leaders of the people have an evil mind (ἄδικος νόος), and their great *hybris* is a prelude to much suffering.[23] According to Thucydides, the nearly personified acquisitiveness (πλεονεξία) and ambition (φιλοτιμία) spawn fanaticism (πρόθυμον). Moreover, and this is the significant point for our discussion, the leaders of two major factions always adopt fine slogans for their positions: "political *isonomia*" for the *plēthos* versus a "sensible government" (σώφρονος) for the aristocrats.[24] Both parties, needless to say, use such phrases to camouflage their own excesses. Even though it can be distorted by its use as a motto in bitter internecine struggle, σωφροσύνη, with its cognates, is otherwise a generally positive term in Thucydides' lexicon, identified with restraint and discipline in domestic politics.[25] In addition, it has a "loose association with *eunomia* as a condition" in the (admittedly uncertain) passage about the Thasians at 8.64.5.[26] By contrast, Thucydides displays a uniform suspicion of the mass of commoners, the *plēthos,* that occasionally flares into open hostility, as in the account of the defeat of the Spartans at Pylos, when he describes Kleon as a demagogue and "the most influential with the people" (τῷ πλήθει πιθανώτατος; 4.21.3).[27] That the despised Kleon exercised such power over the *plēthos* testifies, in Thucydides' view, to the degraded condition of Athenian democratic leadership after the death of Pericles.[28]

The reference to Pericles can serve as a bridge to a discussion of the general issue of Thucydides' concept of leadership. To pose the question more clearly: is it possible to see Solon as the implicit model for Thucydides' estimate of Pericles? In seeking an answer, our inquiry has to expand beyond the area of semantic resemblances to include broader biographical considerations.

There is some lingering uncertainty about the intent and many of the pragmatic details of Solon's reforms, but – thanks largely to the evidence provided by his own poetry – there is a fairly secure consensus about the outlines of his life and career.[29] Solon came from a well-to-do but not aristocratic family and rose to prominence when Athenian society was under severe strain from the antagonism between rich and poor, creditors and debtors. Resisting pressure from his supporters, he rejected the opportunity to take advantage of the turmoil in the polis and install himself as tyrant (fr. 32 W), preferring instead to serve in 594/3 as archon, with a special mandate to reform the constitution. To the disappointment of both the wealthy and the poor, he passed a measure for a one-time cancellation of debts and a perpetual abolition of debt bondage, but at the same time refused demands for redistribution of land. Thereafter, he reorganized the political structure of the state along economic lines, establishing four new property classes, which were granted differential degrees of access to political office. He also devised other important economic and political measures, like a restriction on certain exports and the right of appeal to a jury court, that do not concern us here. As has already been noted, he left Athens for a period after his reforms were in place.

Pericles' official power base was the generalship, which allowed for multiple reelections, so that he served as *stratēgos* for fourteen consecutive terms, from 443 until 429. In the estimate that Thucydides appends to his account of Pericles' "last speech" and death from the plague (in 427), we find the famous statement that, during Pericles' rule, Athens was nominally a democracy but in fact under the command of the first citizen (λόγῳ μὲν δημοκρατία, ἔργῳ δὲ ὑπὸ τοῦ πρώτου ἀνδρὸς ἀρχή; 2.65.9, cf. 1.139.4).[30] In comparing Solon's depiction of himself and Thucydides' depiction of Pericles, we may use, in a nontechnical sense, a set of overlapping Aristotelian categories: rhetoric, ethics, and politics. Before examining them, it would be well to address a possible objection. Solon and Pericles, as well as Thucydides, were doubtless influenced by, and acted on the basis of, broader ideological imperatives. It could be argued, therefore, that resemblances between Solon's depiction of his own activity and Thucydides' depiction of Pericles do not stem from conscious evocation on Thucydides' part but from the influence of an Athenian paradigm of excellent leadership. It seems to me, however, that within each of the three categories I have just named, there are analogies and symmetries that are too precise to be coincidental.

To begin with rhetoric, both Solon and Pericles were masters of public speaking. In the elegy on the "ages of man," Solon declares that at maturity a man is at his acme in intelligence and in the ability to speak (νοῦν καὶ γλῶσσαν... μέγ' ἄριστος; fr. 27.17 W). The two virtues, which are both personal and political, are indissolubly linked. Solon also reveals that his heart (*thumos*) commanded him to teach the people about the evils attendant on disorder (fr. 4.30 W). In this connection, it is worth stressing the importance of the fact that he could use verse both to promote and to commemorate his reforms and that he also had the ability to coin arresting political slogans. As Oswyn Murray notes, "Solon recited his words publicly, and intended them to be repeated by others – they were invested with the permanence and authority of poetry, but they were also meant to persuade."[31] Similarly, Thucydides calls Pericles the ablest man of his age in acting and speaking (λέγειν τε καὶ πράσσειν δυνατώτατος; 1.139.4) and has him deliver three brilliant speeches in the *History*.[32] In the encomium of Pericles in Book 2, Thucydides declares that his rhetorical power was such that he could control the disposition of the people, subduing them when they became overconfident and heartening them when they slipped into despondency (2.65.9). Just as Solon scolded his fellow citizens for their excesses, Pericles too could blame as well as praise.[33] Here we see a feature to which we shall return, the leader's ability to stand apart from the dominant mood. The main point, however, is that, like Solon, Pericles had peerless rhetorical skills that gave him an enormous and continuing advantage in defending his policies.[34]

By itself, however, speaking ability could be said to belong to any number of Athenian leaders, such as Kleon, who was "most influential with the people." In order to be a true virtue, eloquence has to be allied with personal incorruptibility and patriotism, and so we come to the second category, that of ethics. Here the main distinction is between public duty and private gain. In the elegy "Our City," Solon castigates those leaders who "grow rich pursuing unjust deeds" (πλουτοῦσιν δ' ἀδίκοις ἔργμασι πειθόμενοι; fr. 4.11 W). He repeatedly insists that wealth, when it is properly won, is a blessing, but a curse when it is obtained by dishonesty (e.g., fr. 13.7–8 W). It can lead to boundless greed (fr. 13.71–3 W). Among his proudest boasts, by contrast, are that he rejected the opportunity to make himself tyrant and never enriched himself at the expense of the public trust (e.g., frs. 32, 33 W).[35] In the Funeral Oration, Pericles praises the fallen Athenians in much the same terms, saying that, even if they had had some faults during their lives, they blotted out the evil with good; their public valor far outweighed their private flaws (κοινῶς μᾶλλον ὠφέλησαν ἢ ἐκ τῶν ἰδίων ἔβλαψαν; 2.42.3). He explains that the rich did not waver from fear of losing their wealth, nor did the poor from hope of escaping their poverty.[36] There is a Solonian echo here too. In verses that describe the human capacity for self-delusion, Solon speaks of someone without money, driven by the exigencies of poverty (πενίης δέ μιν ἔργα βιᾶται), who is always thinking of ways to gain great wealth (fr. 13.41–2 W). Such vain hopes are certain to be dashed by reality. When Pericles spoke of the selflessness of the wealthy, his audience might be expected to remember that he himself had displayed similar civic-mindedness. As a personal friend of the Spartan king Archidamos, he worried that the Spartans might spare his estates when they attacked the Athenian countryside. To avoid any suspicion of favoritism, he declared in the Assembly that his land and houses would become public property (2.13.1). In the encomium of Pericles, Thucydides says that he was powerful because of his reputation, intelligence, and manifest imperviousness to bribery (δυνατὸς ὢν τῷ τε ἀξιώματι καὶ τῇ γνώμῃ χρημάτων τε διαφανῶς ἀδωρότατος γενόμενος; 2.65.8).[37] The praise of Pericles is sharpened by contrast with his successors, whose self-promotion and self-enrichment (τὰς ἰδίας φιλοτιμίας καὶ ἴδια κέρδη; 2.65.7) ultimately led to the downfall of Athens.

We may conclude, then, with politics proper. Solon notably locates himself in the middle, between rich and poor. Several fragments of his poetry allude to this situation, which he insists he chose deliberately. He says that he set himself like a boundary stone in the "no man's land" between two armies (fr. 37.8–9 W) and that he held his strong shield over both factions alike, preventing an unjust victory by either side (fr. 5.5–6 W), and he even compares himself to a wolf surrounded by dogs (fr. 36.27 W). Loraux has produced a compelling analysis of this complex set of images, concluding that Solon's *mesotēs* is an ideological construction that is not to be identified with a pallid "moderation" but rather with a position of dominance within a struggle.[38] His refusal to identify himself with any faction stands in marked contrast to the behavior of his successors. Although the tyrant Peisistratos eventually became a moderate ruler who preserved constitutional forms and worked for the benefit of all Athenians, he began his career by actively taking sides in factional strife. The first step on the path that led to his successful seizure of power was leadership – perhaps creation – of the "Hill" party, composed largely of disaffected smallholders. Later, in the political struggles that followed the overthrow of the Peisistratids and the expulsion of Hippias, Kleisthenes, an Alkmeonid, triumphed over his rival Isagoras by abandoning his earlier allies and "adopting the demos as his party."[39] As we have seen, he went on to promulgate his reforms under the banner of *isonomia*. In his direct solicitation of the people, Kleisthenes can be seen as anticipating the tactics of those, like Kleon, whom W. R. Connor has labeled the "new politicians" of the fifth century.

Pericles' legendary aloofness had earned him the not entirely flattering nickname of "the Olympian," and as Thucycides saw it, one source of his great political strength was that he was not beholden to any particular group. Not surprisingly, Thucydides concentrates on freedom from control by the demos, noting specifically that Pericles was not led by the people but rather led them (2.65.8). As we have seen, he could be harsh when the situation called for it. At the same time, however, there is no hint that, as an Alkmeonid, he favored the members of his own aristocratic class.[40] Again, the contrast is drawn with his successors, who were more on a level with one another and, even when they were wellborn, were under some obligation to the people they were supposed to govern. Kleon, of course, is the most egregious example of a politician who depended on popular favor for his power, but the brilliant and treacherous Alkibiades is also culpable. Before his speech urging the Sicilian expedition, Thucydides describes him as exploiting his position among the people to augment his own power and wealth (6.15). Thucydides goes on to note somberly that Alkibiades' extravagance and self-promotion, which led to a suspicion that he was aiming at tyranny, contributed not a little to the ultimate collapse of Athens. The disparity with Pericles could not be clearer, or more damning.

Thucydides' analysis of the stasis at Corcyra (3.69–85) adds another dimension to our understanding of being "in the middle." When the forces of oligarchy and radical democracy collide in civil war, party allegiance assumes paramount importance. All other ties, even the most intimately personal or familial, become subordinate to party loyalty. In Thucydides' well-known formulation, "Words have to change their customary meaning" (3.82.4), for virtues and vices come to be defined solely as elements in a distorted political code. Under such circumstances, when "caution" equals "cowardice" and "irrational recklessness" constitutes "loyal courage," moderation is impossible, because it is merely a facade for weakness (τὸ δὲ σῶφρον τοῦ ἀνάνδρου πρόσχημα). Tellingly, the citizens who suffer most are those in the middle (τὰ δὲ μέσα τῶν πολιτῶν; 3.82.8), who come under destructive partisan fire from *both* sides, either because of their refusal to join in the fray (ἢ ὅτι οὐ ξυνηγωνίζοντο) or because of jealousy that they might survive. Scholars have long seen in the phrase about nonparticipation an echo of Solon's law forbidding neutrality during stasis.[41] *Mesotēs*, however, can also be seen applying specifically to Solon himself. One of his boasts is that his legislation, angering rich and poor alike, pleased no one but left him open to attacks from all: "In great matters, it is difficult to satisfy everyone" (fr. 7 W). Similarly Pericles himself acknowledges that his policies have aroused the ire of the Athenians (2.60), and Thucydides comments acerbically that it is the fickle nature of a mob to turn on its leaders and then restore them to power (2.65).

If Solon was "in the middle" of the battlefield, Pericles too was "in the middle," but above the fray. Despite the difference in elevation, both of them used their position to *restrain* the people under their command. In a noteworthy image, Solon writes that if another man had been handling the goad, he would not have been able to restrain the demos (οὐκ ἂν κατέσχε δῆμον; fr. 36.20–2 W, cf. fr. 5.1–4 W). After the passage quoted earlier about Pericles' incorruptibility, Thucydides concludes that, as a consequence, Pericles could restrain the people in freedom (κατεῖχε τὸ πλῆθος ἐλευθέρως; 2.65.8).[42] At first glance the phrase is almost an oxymoron, but in fact it is completely consistent with the rest of the evaluation. The adverb refers to Pericles' aforementioned power as an orator, specifically his ability to address the Athenians frankly, even reproachfully, without having to worry about their approval.[43] Pericles, like Solon, was unique for his time in combining the attributes we have discussed, and so was uniquely able to endow his city with good government. I have tried to show that both Thucydides' allusions to democracy and his portrait of Pericles owe several of their chief features to a Solonian model. Due to their command of language, their personal incorruptibility, and their location within the community, Pericles (as presented by Thucydides) and Solon (as presented by himself) share the ability to control the system they are ostensibly serving. To put it another way, the ideological implication is that a government may be of laws and not men, may be of the people, by the people, and for the people, but it needs a first citizen to make it work properly. In the absence of such a figure, the alternatives for the polis are grim: either tyranny or civil strife. By the late fifth century the Athenians had ample evidence of the devastating effects of stasis, and they also seem to have had a pervasive fear of conspiracies that would result in tyranny.[44]

To be even more speculative than I have been up to this point, I will conclude by suggesting that the evocations of Solon in Thucydides' text, in particular the parallels with Pericles, are signs of both Thucydides' attitude toward democracy and his pessimism, his sense of tragedy in history. In a famous aside (8.97), he expresses admiration for the "moderate polity" established late in 411, stating that during the rule of the five thousand Athens was especially well governed.[45] Moreover, as was discussed earlier, σωφροσύνη and its cognates, often linked to Sparta, are certainly positive terms in his political vocabulary. On the basis of such hints, some scholars have concluded that Thucydides was an oligarch or at least an oligarchic sympathizer.[46] The evocations of Solon, however, may suggest another, less drastic interpretation. Thucydides had ample reason to distrust and dislike Athenian radical democracy, not least because it sent him into exile, but he had no great fondness for the oligarchic alternative.[47] Instead, in the figure of Solon he could find an embodiment of a moderate democrat and in Solonian Athens a prefiguration of Periclean Athens, nominally a democracy but in fact under the rule of the first citizen. In both eras, the leader exemplified the paramount civic virtue of individual service within the context of communal law and order. If my analysis is correct, Thucydides bases his understanding of Athenian politics on an implicit set of paired oppositions: eunomia/isonomia//Solon/Kleisthenes//Pericles/Kleon (et al.). Within each pair, the second element represents a deterioration, or even an active corruption, of the first. Given his disparaging remarks about Pericles' political successors, and given what happened after Solon left office, Thucydides' prognosis for his fellow citizens can only be seen as bleak. He would find confirmation, if not solace, in Solon's words:

The leaders of the people are evil minded. The next stage will be great suffering, recompense for their violent acts, for they do not know enough to restrain their greed (κατέχειν κόρον) and apportion orderly shares for all as if at a decorous feast. (fr. 4.7–10 W, translated by R. Lattimore)

NOTES

1. For example, the only other appearance of Solon by name in Aristophanes occurs at *Av.* 1660, when Peisthetairos explains to Herakles that, in accordance with Solon's law, Herakles, as a bastard, will inherit none of his father's money. Aristophanes also uses *philodemos* one other time, at *Eq.* 787, when Demos gratefully compliments the Sausage-Seller, who has just provided him with a seat cushion. On the term *philodemos*, see Connor 1971: 99–108, esp. 101–2.

2. All the ancient sources have been assembled by Martina 1968; hereafter referred to as Martina with the citation number.

3. The lawgiver's departure from the polis after completing his code is a standard feature of such stories. See Szegedy-Maszak 1978.

4. "For Herodotus Solon apparently is the representative of Athens among the Seven Wise Men of Greece. . . . That Solon had given laws . . . was of course not forgotten in Athens, but there was no talk of a Solonian *politeia* until the opposition introduced the slogan of *patrios politeia*." Jacoby 1949: 29, quoted by Ruschenbusch 1958: 423 n 90. See also Immerwahr 1966: 156–8.

5. Loraux 1986: 202, 204, emphases in the original. M. I. Finley 1962: 9 made the same point even more forcefully: "I do not believe that an articulated democratic theory ever existed in Athens."

6. Raaflaub 1989; my debt to his insights and methods will be apparent throughout this essay.

7. I agree completely with Raaflaub 1989: 35 that "there is a substantial difference between the fifth and fourth centuries not only in the constitutional structure and in the working and spirit, but also in the perception of democracy."

8. Ruschenbusch 1958, who provides a thorough catalog of the sources; see esp. 407–8. See also Mossé 1979; M. H. Hansen 1989.

9. A crucial difference, of course, is that U.S. social myth has depended so heavily on diffusion through the technologies of various media. "Printed literature has been from the first the most important vehicle of myth in America, which sets it apart from the mythologies of the past" (Slotkin 1973: 19). This does not, however, affect my basic argument. It is worth noting that anthropologists have long recognized the coexistence and interplay of oral tradition and written history; see, e.g., Goody and Watt 1968: esp. 44–52.

10. M. I. Finley 1975: 29.

11. R. Thomas 1989 provides an extensive and thought-provoking analysis of the relation between the various literary accounts of the murder of Hipparchos and Athenian oral tradition, although it seems to me she disregards Thucydides' emphasis on the private nature of the quarrel that led to the murder (238–82; on Thuc., 242–5).

12. Contemporary discussion was initiated by M. Hirsch 1925. For a summary of the problems in the various accounts of the tyrannicides, see Fornara 1968.

13. The interrelationship between the two historians and its attendant complications are exemplified by the striking, well-documented correspondence between Solon's remarks in Herodotus 1.32.8–9 and a passage in Pericles' Funeral Oration dealing with autarky

(2.41.1); cf. Gomme 1956: 127; Loraux 1986: 153–4, 426 n 23. Thomas Scanlon provides an exhaustive analysis of the parallels between these passages in a forthcoming essay, "Echoes of Herodotus in Thucydides: Self-Sufficiency, Admiration and Law"; I am grateful to him for allowing me to read it in manuscript form. Although Scanlon is not as concerned as I am with Thucydides' evocation of the historical Solon, he reaches a conclusion similar to mine, that in Thucydides, "Pericles is . . . ennobled by being characterized as a second Solon."

14. For Herodotus the situation is clearer. As Chiasson 1986 points out, "That Herodotus knew at least some of Solon's poetry is beyond doubt, for at 5.113 he alludes to verses (fr. 19 West) in which Solon praises the Cypriote king Philocyprus" (249). Chiasson goes on to argue that in the speeches Herodotus ascribes to Solon in Book 1, "Herodotus consciously and explicitly evokes the memory of Solon's verse" (261).

15. Dem. 19.254 ff. = fr. 4 West; all subsequent references to the fragments of Solon's poetry will be to this edition. The most thorough and insightful study of the word *nomos* and the terms associated with it is still Ostwald 1969. Ostwald summarizes the meanings of *eunomia* in the sixth century: "As a quality it describes the behaviour of a normal and decent human being, and as a condition it characterizes a state which is well governed and in which justice, peace, and order prevail" (70).

16. Ostwald 1969: 64. In the same place, Ostwald says of fr. 4, "The definition of *eunomiē* as the condition of the society which [Solon] hopes to create by his reforms is couched in such lively and precise terms at the end of his poem 'Our City' that some modern scholars have dubbed the entire poem 'Eunomie,' even though there is no ancient warrant for this name."

17. Cf. Hdt. 1.65.6, a passage whose chronology is vexed but is significant in making a direct connection between Spartan *eunomia* and the Lykourgan reforms (which Thucydides does not mention); see also the comments of Gomme 1972: 128–31 and Ostwald 1969: 79–80.

18. In Ps.-Xenophon, *Ath. Pol.* 1.8–9, *eunomia* is unmistakably a conservative slogan. As Ostwald 1969: 83 says, "That *eunomia* denotes a condition, in this case [Ps.-Xenophon] the condition of a city in which the *ponēroi*, the common people, are kept in subjection, is obvious." Ps.-Xenophon, then, uses the term not in a broad sense of good order but "in a narrow political sense" (Ostwald 1969: 85). See also Ostwald 1986: 188–91.

19. Ostwald 1969: 176–7; Andrewes in Gomme, Andrewes, and Dover, 1981: 161; see also North 1966: 113; Edmunds 1975: esp. 76, 78; Connor 1985: 222 nn. 21, 22.

20. O. Murray 1980: 258 concisely sums up the distinction: "About this time [Kleisthenes' reforms] the old political ideal of *eunomia*, which had sufficed for Hesiod, Solon and the Spartans, acquired a competitor, *isonomia*: in contrast to 'good order' there was now also 'equal order'; the new word was the original word for democracy, supplanted only later by the more aggressive *demokratia*, 'people's power.' It is hard not to connect the new concept with the struggle in Athens between the Spartan-backed aristocrats and the newly democratic Kleisthenes, for *isonomia* is clearly a word formulated by analogy with the older *eunomia*, and perhaps in opposition to it."

21. The citations are: (1) 3.62.2, in a speech by the Thebans refuting the charge of medism; (2) 3.82.8, in the analysis of the stasis at Corcyra; (3) 4.78.2, on the good relations between the Thessalians and the Athenian people; (4) 6.38.5, in a speech by the Syracusan democratic leader Athenagoras.

22. Ostwald 1969: 115 and cf. note 2: "The idea of majority rule seems to inhere in all political uses of *plēthos* in Thucydides"; there follows a catalog of such instances, most of which simply equate the *plēthos* with a democratic assembly.

23. As Edmunds 1975: 88 notes, Solon fr. 4 W alludes to στάσιν ἔμφυλον πόλεμόν θ᾽

εὔδοντ': "where 'war' means 'civil war,' and the phrase is thus to some degree pleonastic after στάσιν ἔμφυλον, 'intestine discord.' For Thucydides, too, stasis is always at least dormant."

24. It is also worth noting that in the debate on constitutions (3.80.6) Herodotus has Otanes, the proponent of democracy, make the same link, in that *isonomia* is equated to rule of the *plēthos* and described as οὔνομα πάντων κάλλιστον. For the use of σώφρονος in Thucydides' description of the Corcyraean stasis, see North 1966: 108–9, 111–12.

25. See North 1966: esp. 110–15. She observes (112) that in Thucydides σωφροσύνη is "usually present . . . in discussions of the Spartan constitution, yet it might be used of any moderate form of government, especially one in which the power of the masses was in some way restricted." Hornblower 1987: 162 too makes the point that Thucydides' positive evaluation of σωφροσύνη stems from its being a guarantor of stability and a protection against stasis, "rather than [from] any doctrinaire conviction about the theoretically best form of government."

26. The quoted phrase is Ostwald's 1969: 176. His statement finds some comic corroboration in the *Birds*, wherein Basileia is said to control *euboulian, eunomian, sōphrosynēn*, along with *neōrias, loidorian, kōlakretēn, triōbola* (1537). See also North 1966: 113.

27. This recalls the description of Kleon before the debate on the fate of Mytilene, where he is described as "the most violent of the citizens and at that time by far the most influential with the demos" (βιαιότατος τῶν πολιτῶν τῷ τε δήμῳ παρὰ πολὺ ἐν τῷ τότε πιθανώτατος, 3.36.6). Nearly the same characterization is used of the Syracusan democratic leader Athenagoras (6.35.2). On the characterization, see Connor 1971: 132–3.

28. See Connor 1985: 79: "From a city adrift and leaderless to one driven by demagogues is but a small transition. The concern with the absence of effective leadership in Athens in the years following Pericles' pre-eminence naturally draws attention to the false leader, Cleon." Cf. M. I. Finley 1962; Ellis 1979; Cairns 1982; Raaflaub 1989: 54–60. Although she restricts her analysis to the terms *ochlos* and *homilos,* Hunter 1988 concurs in noting "Thucydides' disdain for the impulsive and irresponsible behavior displayed by the kind of mass audience addressed and manipulated by orators and other public speakers," such as "Cleon, whose posturing excites the crowd" (20, 25).

29. The most extensive ancient accounts of his life and work are Arist. *Ath. Pol.* 5–12, and Plut. *Sol.;* for the other sources, see Martina 1968. The most comprehensive recent discussion is Manville 1990: 124–56, and see also his index s.v. "Solon."

30. There had been a number of "first citizens" in the history of Athens, going back to Theseus in mythical times and including Drakon, Solon, Kleisthenes, and Themistokles. See Ruschenbusch 1958, who attempts to specify a date for the ascendancy of each leader to the position of "founder of the democracy" in the popular imagination.

31. O. Murray 1980: 174; see also Linforth 1919: 55. This is not to ignore the importance of the fact that Solon wrote down both his laws and his poetry. See Loraux 1988; at 125 n. 82, Loraux notes a resemblance between a saying Stobaeus attributes to Solon, about the best city being that in which there is the greatest competition for virtue (Martina 180), and a remark in Pericles' Funeral Oration (2.46.1). Because Stobaeus is so late, I have not put any emphasis on the parallel. Haslam 1990 points out that Pericles' remark at 2.61.2 – ἐγὼ μὲν ὁ αὐτός εἰμι καὶ οὐκ ἐξίσταμαι (I am the same and do not change my opinion) – is a trimeter and suggests that it may have been a proverbial expression, for which "the most probable source . . . is a tragedy, though one should not forget Solon."

32. Thuc. 1.139–44 (on the eve of the war); 2.35–46 (the Funeral Oration); 2.60–4 (the last speech). See also the description of Pericles before the Funeral Oration, in the explanation of how he was selected to give the speech: ἀνὴρ ᾑρημένος ὑπὸ τῆς

πόλεως, ὃς ἂν γνώμῃ τε δοκῇ μὴ ἀξύνετος εἶναι καὶ ἀξιώσει προήκῃ (a man chosen by the city, who seems to be not lacking in judgment and who excels in honor; 2.34.6). See Ober 1989: 87: "Pericles was surely not the first Athenian politician to have a way with words, but he seems to have paid more attention to the power of public speech than any Athenian public figure before him."

33. Pericles' critical stance is particularly notable in the last speech, as for example at 2.61.2: "It is because your own resolution is weak that my policy appears to you to be mistaken" (trans. Warner). On this type of behavior, see the illuminating remarks of Ober 1989: 318–24 (a chapter entitled "Leader, Critic, Opposer of the People's Will").

34. See also Connor 1962.

35. There is a later tradition that he even lost money due to his measure canceling all debts: Plut. *Sol*. 15.8–9 (Martina 282); Plutarch also records the countertradition that, by leaking news of the impending reform, Solon enabled a small group of wealthy friends to borrow money that they then did not have to repay (Plut. *Sol* 15.7–8). I have discussed elsewhere the consistent motif in the biographical tales of the lawgiver's obeying one of his own statutes at his own cost (Szegedy-Maszak 1978: 205–7).

36. As so often in Thucydides, the phrasing here is quite odd: πενίας ἐλπίδι, which Gomme 1956: 131 translates as "hopes concerned with poverty" and for which he would accept the explanation τῶν πενητῶν ἐλπίδι, "the poor man's [*sic*] hope." Gomme also notes the correspondence between this phrase and the passage from Solon fr. 13 W.

37. The linkage of *axiōma* and *gnōmē* echoes the description of "the man" chosen to deliver the Funeral Oration; cf. note 30.

38. Loraux 1984.

39. For Peisistratos, see Hdt. 1.59.3–64. For Kleisthenes, Hdt. 5.66–73. The quoted description is at 5.66.2: τὸν δῆμον προσεταιρίζεται. In his discussion of the latter phrase, Connor notes the odd usage of the verb, which occurs only two other times in Herodotus at 3.70.2 and 3 (1971: 90–1 and note 5); see also Ostwald 1969: 142–3 and Ober, Chapter 11, this volume.

40. On Pericles' ability to exploit an aristocratic style while espousing democratic ideals, see Connor 1971: esp. 119–28 and index s.v. "Pericles"; Ober 1989: 86–91.

41. Gomme 1956: 380 notes that *ta mesa* does not necessarily refer to the "middle class" (neither rich nor poor), but to neutrals in general, and concludes: "We should make the inevitable comparison with Solon's *nomos idios kai paradoxos*" with references to Plut. *Sol*. 20.1 and Arist. *Ath. Pol.* 8.5; see also Edmunds 1975 and Manville 1980: esp. 217–21.

42. Gomme 1956: 192 notes both the echo here of Pericles' language in the Funeral Oration (ἐλευθέρως . . . πολιτεύομεν; 2.37.1–2) and the contrast with the Thebans' description of their own oligarchy, which relies on force (κατέχοντες ἰσχύι τὸ πλῆθος; 3.62.4).

43. I follow here the analysis proposed by Edmunds and Martin 1977.

44. In addition to the popular anxieties about Alkibiades (Thuc. 6.15.4) see Thuc. 6.53.3, 60.1; Ar. *Lys.* 630–1; and esp. Ar. *Vesp.* 486–507.

45. The problems attendant on the interpretation of this passage are too numerous and ramified to discuss here; see Andrewes's comments in Gomme, Andrewes, and Dover 1981; cf. Connor 1985: 227–8 and most recently Hornblower 1987: 160–3. While Thucydides' praise of the five thousand cannot be dismissed as trivial, it is worth noting that his comments at 8.97 are cursory, particularly when compared to the extended encomium of Pericles in 2.65; cf. Connor 1985: 238.

46. E.g., McGregor 1956: 102 concludes, "[Thucydides] ended his life as he had begun it, a confirmed oligarch"; similarly, though less extreme, J. Finley 1942: 33 says that Thucydides became more conservative as he grew older; other references in Connor

1985: 237–8 and Pope 1988: 276. Although I disagree with many of Pope's analyses of Thucydides' methods and intentions, particularly his literalist interpretation of Thucydides' use of collective names in describing political behavior, his article does make a number of valuable observations.

47. Connor 1985: 237–42 argues persuasively that one aspect of the pervasive ambiguity in Thucydides is his deliberate subversion of the conventional antithesis between democracy and oligarchy.

CHAPTER ELEVEN

The Athenian Revolution of 508/7 B.C.E.

Violence, Authority, and the Origins of Democracy

Josiah Ober

THE periodization of history is, of course, a product of hindsight, and most historians realize that any past era can accurately be described as an "age of transition." The problem of fixing the end of the archaic period and the transition to the classical is thus a historiographic problem, one that reflects contemporary scholarly inclinations more than it does ancient realities. Nevertheless, since historians cannot work without periodization, and since English-language historiography seems to be entering a post-Annales phase characterized by a renewed interest in the significance – especially the symbolic and cultural significance – of events,[1] it may be worthwhile to look at a series of events that can be taken as the beginning of a new phase of Greek history. The events we choose to mark the transition will be different for any given region or polis, but for those interested in Athenian political history, the end of the archaic and the beginning of something new may reasonably be said to have come about in the period from ca. 510 to 506 B.C.E., with the revolutionary events that established the form of government that would soon come to be called *dēmokratia*.[2]

If the "Athenian Revolution" is a historically important event (or series of events), it is often described in what seem to me to be misleading terms. Historians typically discuss the revolution in the antiseptic terminology of "constitutional development" and their narrative accounts tend to be narrowly centered around the person and intentions of Kleisthenes himself. Putting Kleisthenes at the center of the revolution as a whole entails slighting significant parts of the source tradition. And that tradition, which consists almost entirely of brief discussions in Herodotus (5.66, 69–78) and the Aristotelian *Athenaion Politeia* (20–1), is scanty enough as it is. The reconstruction of the events of 508/7 offered here is simultaneously quite conservative in its approach and quite radical in its implications. I hope to show that by sticking very closely to the primary sources, it is possible to derive a plausible and internally coherent narrative that revolves around the Athenian people rather than their leaders. A close reading of the sources shows that the dominant role ascribed to elite leaders in modern accounts of a key point in the revolution is supplementary to the ancient evidence. All historians supplement their narratives with assumptions, models, and theories; supplementation of the source material, in order to fill in apparent gaps and silences, is an inevitable part of the process of even the most self-consciously narrative (rather than analytical) forms of historical writing. But such supplements (especially those that are widely accepted) must be challenged from time to time, lest they become so deeply entrenched as to block the development of alternative readings that may explain the source tradition as well or better.

Both of our two main sources state that during a key period of the revolution, Kleisthenes and his closest supporters were in exile and imply that the main Athenian players in the revolt were corporate entities: the Boule and the demos. The ascription of authoritative leadership in all phases of the revolution to Kleisthenes may, I think, be attributed to the uncritical (and indeed unconscious) acceptance of a view of history that supposes that all advances in human affairs come through the consciously willed actions of individual members of an elite.[3] In the case of other historical figures – for example, Solon – proponents of this elite-centered ''great man'' approach to history can at least claim support in the primary sources. But although he *is* regarded by the sources as the driving force behind important political reforms, Kleisthenes is not described in our sources as a Solon-style *nomothetēs*. The *Athenaion Politeia* (20.4) calls him τοῦ δήμου προστάτης (the leader who stands up before the people) and, while the label is anachronistic for the late sixth century, it seems to me a pretty reasonable description of Kleisthenes' historical role: like that of later Athenian politicians, Kleisthenes' leadership was not dependent on constitutional authority, but rather on his ability to persuade the Athenian people to adopt and to act on the proposals he advocated. In sum, I will attempt to show that while Kleisthenes was indeed a very important player in Athens' revolutionary dramas, the key role was played by the demos. And thus, *dēmokratia* was not a gift from a benevolent elite to a passive demos, but was the product of collective decision, action, and self-definition on the part of the demos itself.

Having advocated the study of historical events, and having simultaneously rejected the individual intentions of the elite leader as the motor that necessarily drives events, I shall go one step further out on the limb by suggesting that *the* moment of the revolution, the end of the archaic phase of Athenian political history, the point at which Athenian democracy was born, was a violent, leaderless event: a three-day riot in 508/7 that resulted in the removal of Kleomenes I and his Spartan troops from the soil of Attika.

In order to explain the events of 508/7 we need to review the revolutionary period that began in 510 B.C.E. – a fascinating few years characterized by a remarkable series of expulsions from the territory of Attika and returns to it. The series opened with the ouster of Hippias, son of Peisistratos. In 510 the Spartans, urged on by multiple oracles from Delphic Apollo, decided to liberate Athens from the rule of the Peisistratid tyrant. A preliminary seaborne invasion of Attika was repulsed by the tyrant's forces. King Kleomenes I then raised a second army, which he marched across the Isthmus into Athenian territory. This time Hippias' forces failed to stop the invasion. With the Spartans in control of Attika, the tyrant and his family were forced to retreat to their stronghold on the Acropolis. The Acropolis was a formidable obstacle, and the Spartan besiegers were initially stymied. Indeed, it looked as if they might abandon the attempt after a few days (Hdt. 5.64–5). But then Hippias made the mistake of trying to smuggle his sons past the besiegers and out of Athens. They were caught by the Spartans and held hostage. Hippias then surrendered on terms and was allowed to leave Athens with his family. Thus ended the tyranny.[4]

But the liberation raised more questions than it answered. Who would now rule Athens? One might suppose that the spoils of political authority would end up going to the victors. But as Thucydides (6.53.3; cf. Ar. *Lys.* 1150–6) pointed out, few Athenians had played much part in the expulsion. The victorious Spartans, for their part, had no interest in progressive political innovation. They surely intended Athens to become a client state, with a status similar to that of their allies in the Peloponnesian League. This would presumably mean that Athens would be governed by a rather narrow oligarchy, the form of government that (at least in the mid-fifth century; Thuc. 1.19) Sparta mandated as standard for all members of the League.[5] The Spartans did not permanently garrison Athens (this was not their style), but after withdrawing their forces they remained very interested in Athenian politics. In the aftermath of the "liberation," King Kleomenes, the dominant figure in late-sixth-century Sparta, encouraged attempts by Isagoras and other Athenian aristocrats to establish a government that would exclude most Athenians from active political participation.

In the period from 510 to 507 the political battlefield of Athens was not disputed between men who called themselves or thought of themselves as oligarchs and democrats, but rather between rival aristocrats. We cannot say exactly what sort of government Isagoras envisioned, but in light of subsequent developments it seems safe to assume that he intended to place effective control of affairs into the hands of a small, pro-Spartan elite. Isagoras' main opponent was Kleisthenes the Alkmeonid. Despite the fact that Kleisthenes himself had been willing to accept the high office of archon under the tyranny, some elements of the Alkmeonid family had probably been active in resistance to the tyrants.[6] Kleisthenes, obviously a leading figure among the Alkmeonids by 508/7, may have felt that his family's antityrannical activity had earned him a prominent position in the political order that would replace the tyranny. But that position did not come automatically. Indeed, Isagoras, with his Spartan connections, was gaining influence and was elected archon for 508/7 B.C.E.[7] Thus as Herodotus (5.66.2) tells us, Kleisthenes was getting the worst of it. In response Kleisthenes did a remarkable thing: τὸν δῆμον προσεταιρίζεται. I will leave this phrase untranslated for the time being, for reasons that will become clear later. At any rate, because he had in some way allied himself with the demos (the Athenian citizen masses) Kleisthenes now began to overshadow his opponents in the contest for political influence in Athens (Hdt. 5.69.2).

It is worth pausing at this point in the narrative to ask what the social and institutional context of the struggle between Isagoras and Kleisthenes would have been. Herodotus and the *Athenaion Politeia* employ the political vocabularies of the mid-fifth and late fourth centuries, respectively. But we must not apply the model of politics in Periclean or Demosthenic Athens to the late sixth century.

Isagoras and Kleisthenes had recourse to few if any of the weapons familiar to us from the political struggles of those later periods – ideologically motivated *hetaireiai*, ostracism, *graphē paranomōn*, and other public actions in the people's courts, finely honed orations by orators trained in the art of rhetoric. What shall we imagine in their place?

Late archaic Athens was surely more dominated by the great families than was the case in the fifth and fourth centuries. Yet it would be a serious mistake to suppose that the scion-of-a-great-family/ordinary-citizen relationship can be seen in fully developed patron/client terms – the model of Roman Republican politics is as anachronistic as that of democratic politics for late archaic Athens. The reforms of Solon had undercut the traditional authority associated with birth. The policies of the tyrants themselves had gone a long way in breaking down the traditional ties of dependence and obedience between upper- and lower-class Athenians. Moreover, Solon's creation of the formal status of citizen – a result of prohibiting debt slavery and of legal reforms that made Athenians potentially responsible for one another's welfare – had initiated a process whereby the demos became conscious of itself in forthrightly political terms. The tyrants had encouraged political self-consciousness on the part of the masses of ordinary citizens by the sponsorship of festivals and building programs. The upshot was that by 510–508 B.C.E. the ordinary Athenian male had come a long way from the status of politically passive client of a great house. He saw himself as a citizen rather than as a subject and at least some part of his loyalty was owed to the abstraction "Athens."[8]

And yet the political institutions in which an Athenian man could express his developing sense of citizenship were, in early 508, still quite rudimentary and were still dominated by the elite. We may suppose that the traditional "constitution," as revised by Solon, still pertained. Thus there were occasional meetings of a political assembly that all citizens had the right to attend. But it is unlikely that those outside the elite had the right or power to speak in that assembly; nor could they hope to serve on the probouleutic council of 400, as a magistrate, or on the Areopagos council.[9] Kleisthenes, as a leading member of a prominent family and as an Areopagite, surely did have both the right and the power to address the Assembly. It seems a reasonable guess that it was in the Assembly (although not necessarily uniquely here) that he allied himself to the demos, by proposing (and perhaps actually passing) constitutional reforms. The masses saw that these reforms would provide them with the institutional means to express more fully their growing sense of themselves as citizens. By these propositions and/or enactments Kleisthenes gained political influence and so Isagoras began to get the worst of it (Hdt. 5.69.2–70.1).[10]

But if Kleisthenes now had the people on his side, Isagoras was still archon and moreover he could call in outside forces. No matter what measures Kleisthenes had managed to propose or pass in the Assembly, a new constitutional order could become a practical political reality only if the Assembly's will were allowed to decide the course of events. Isagoras, determined that this not be allowed, sent word of the unsettling developments to Kleomenes in Sparta. Kleomenes responded by sending a herald to the Athenians, informing them that, ostensibly because of the old Kylonian curse, they were to expel (ἐξέβαλλε) Kleisthenes and many others from the city (Hdt. 5.70.2). Kleisthenes himself duly left (αὐτὸς ὑπεξέσχε; Hdt. 5.72.1).

Even after Kleisthenes' departure, Isagoras and/or Kleomenes must still have felt uneasy about the Athenian situation. A smallish (οὐ ... μεγάλῃ χειρί) mixed-nationality military force, featuring a core of Spartans and led by Kleomenes, soon arrived in the city (παρῆν ἐς τὰς 'Αθήνας; Hdt. 5.72.1). Kleomenes now, on Isagoras' recommendation, ordered further expulsions; Herodotus (5.72.1) claims that a total of seven hundred families were driven out (ἀγηλατέει). The archon Isagoras and his Spartan allies were clearly in control of Athens. That could have been the end of what we might call the progressive movement in Athenian politics. Athens might well have become another Argos – an occasionally restive but ultimately impotent client-state of Sparta. After all, the Spartans were the dominant military power in late-sixth-century Greece, while Kleisthenes and the other leading Athenians who opposed Isagoras were now powerless exiles.

But, of course, that was not the end of it. What happened next is the moment of revolution I alluded to earlier. According to Herodotus, Isagoras and Kleomenes next (δεύτερα)

> attempted to abolish the Boule (τὴν βουλὴν καταλύειν ἐπειρᾶτο),[11] and to transfer political authority to a body of three hundred supporters of Isagoras. But when the Boule resisted and refused to obey (ἀντισταθείσης δὲ τῆς βουλῆς καὶ οὐ βουλομένης πείθεσθαι), Kleomenes, together with Isagoras and his supporters, occupied the Acropolis (καταλαμβάνουσι τὴν ἀκρόπολιν). However, the rest of the Athenians ('Αθηναίων δὲ οἱ λοιποί), who were of one mind (τὰ αὐτὰ φρονήσαντες) [regarding these affairs], besieged them [on the Acropolis] for two days. But on the third day a truce was struck and the Lakedaimonians among them were allowed to leave the territory [of Attika]. (Hdt. 5.72.1–2)

In the aftermath of the expulsion of the Spartans, at least some of the non-Spartan members of Kleomenes' army (perhaps including Athenian supporters of Isagoras, although not Isagoras himself, who had been detained in Athens), were summarily executed (Hdt. 5.72.4–73.1). After these events (μετὰ ταῦτα) the Athenians re-called (μεταπεμψάμενοι) Kleisthenes and the seven hundred families (Hdt. 5.73.1). A new constitutional order (presumably resembling the order proposed by Kleisthenes or enacted on his motion before he was expelled) was soon put into place.[12]

Meanwhile, Kleomenes felt that the Athenians had "outraged" him "with words and deeds" (περιυβρίσθαι ἔπεσι καὶ ἔργοισι; Hdt. 5.74.1). I would gloss Herodotus' statement as follows: Kleomenes had been outraged by "the words" (of the *bouleutai* when they refused the dissolution order) and "the deeds" (of the demos in its uprising against the Spartans and the Athenian quislings). The Spartan king wanted revenge. He still planned to put Isagoras into power in Athens, but his counterattack of 506 fizzled owing to a lack of solidarity in the Peloponnesian ranks on the one side and Athenian unity and military discipline on the other (Hdt.

5.74–7). Within just a few years Athens had moved from the position of Spartan client-to-be to that of a powerful, independent polis. Athens twice had been occupied by an outside power and the Athenians had rejected the rule of a narrow elite in favor of a radical program of political reforms, risen up successfully against their occupiers when the reform program was threatened, institutionalized the reforms, defended the new political order against external aggression, and were on the road to democracy. It is an amazing story, and Herodotus (5.78) points out to his readers just how remarkable was the Athenian achievement. This, then, was the Athenian Revolution.

Herodotus' account is quite closely followed, and perhaps in a few places amplified, by the account of the Aristotelian *Athenaion Politeia.* I will focus on three aspects of the story that seem to me particularly notable. Two are familiar *topoi* of Kleisthenes scholarship; the third is not.

The first peculiarity is that Kleisthenes, an Areopagite and a leading member of a fine old family, was willing in the first place to turn to the demos – the ordinary people who, as Herodotus points out, "formerly had been held in contempt" (πρότερον ἀπωσμένον; Hdt. 5.69.2). The second striking thing is that, after his recall from exile, Kleisthenes *fulfilled* the promises he had made to the demos (in the form of proposals or enactments of the Assembly). He fully earned the trust they placed in him by establishing a form of government that, at least in the long run, doomed aristocratic political dominance in Athens. Much ink has been spilled over Kleisthenes' apparently peculiar behavior. Since Kleisthenes' actions seem to fly in the face of the aristocratic ethos (Thou shalt not mix with the lower sort) and to contradict a common assumption about human nature itself (Thou shalt always act in self-interest), sophisticated explanations have been devised to explain what he was up to. Among views of Kleisthenes in the scholarly literature, two dominate the field, at least in the English-speaking world. One, well represented by David M. Lewis's influential article in *Historia,* is what we might call the "cynical realist" view, which holds that Kleisthenes was no true friend of the Athenian demos, but instead he benefited (or at least intended to benefit) the Alkmeonids by extraordinarily clever gerrymandering in his establishment of the demes.[13] Lewis's "realist" view was advanced to counter the other dominant view – the "idealist" view of an altruistic Kleisthenes. This second viewpoint is perhaps best exemplified by the work of Victor Ehrenberg, who saw Kleisthenes as a selfless democratic visionary.[14]

I would not want to deny that Kleisthenes embraced a vision of a new society (discussed later) or that he hoped for a privileged place for his own family in that society. Yet neither the "realist" view of Kleisthenes the diabolically clever factional politician nor the "idealist" view of Kleisthenes the self-consciously altruistic Father of Democracy adequately accounts for the third peculiarity in Herodotus' story – the uprising that doomed Isagoras and his partisans by forcing the surrender and withdrawal from Attika of the Spartans. Although Herodotus' and *Athenaion Politeia*'s bare-bones accounts of the event do not give us a great deal to work with, it appears that a spontaneous insurrection against Isagoras and the Spartans followed in the wake of Kleomenes' attempt to abolish the Boule and his occupation of the Acropolis. Without the uprising, the Kleisthenic reforms would have remained empty words: proposals or enactments voided by the efficient use of force by an outside power.

We will probably never know the details of what actually happened between Kleomenes' attempt to dissolve the Boule and his surrender on terms, but we can at least say what did *not* happen, and this may be useful in itself. First, and perhaps foremost, we should not imagine the siege of the Spartans on the Acropolis as an organized military campaign. Whatever may have been the form of the pre-Kleisthenic Athenian military forces, there is no mention in Herodotus' or *Athenaion Politeia*'s accounts of the siege of military leaders or any sort of formal leadership – no reference to a polemarch or *stratēgoi*, no *naukraroi* calling in their clients from the fields. Now the silence of our sources is a notoriously slippery ground for argument, but (as demonstrated by their accounts of, e.g., Kylon and the *naukraroi*, Solon and the Eupatrids, and Peisistratos and the Alkmeonids) both Herodotus and the author of the *Athenaion Politeia* were very interested in aristocratic leadership – whether it was individual or collective and institutional. I find it hard to suppose that the identity of the aristocratic leaders of the insurrection could have been forgotten or fully suppressed in the sixty years between the revolution and Herodotus' arrival in Athens. Surely this brave resistance to the Spartan occupiers of the Acropolis is just the sort of thing that aristocratic families would remember for several generations. And it was just this sort of family tradition that formed the basis of much of Herodotus' Athenian narrative. One cannot, of course, rule out the possibility that Herodotus intentionally covered up the role played by leaders. But why would he want to do so? To further glorify the Alkmeonid Kleisthenes? Yet even if Herodotus did favor the Alkmeonids (which is far from certain), the hypothetical leaders would have been Alkmeonid allies, since Kleisthenes was immediately recalled and his constitutional reforms enacted.[15] In the end, positing aristocratic leadership for the action that expelled the Spartans is an *ignotus per ignotum* argument, a modern supplement which relies for its credibility on the unprovable (and elitist) assumption that aristocratic leadership in such matters would have been sine qua non. It seems to me preferable in this case to trust our only sources and suppose that Herodotus and *Athenaion Politeia* mention no leaders because Athenian tradition recorded none, and that Athenian tradition recorded none because there were none – or at least none from the ranks of the leading aristocratic families.

Moreover, there is no mention in Herodotus or *Athenaion Politeia* of Athenian hoplites at the siege of the Acropolis; according to Herodotus it is Ἀθηναίων οἱ λοιποί (the rest of the Athenians) who, united in their view of the situation, do the besieging. *Athenaion Politeia* 20.3 mentions *to plēthos* and *ho dēmos*. This does not, of course, mean that no men wearing hoplite armor took part in the siege – but it is noteworthy that there is no suggestion in either source that anything resembling a "regular" army formation was called up. This might best be explained by the hypothesis that no "national" army existed in the era before the carrying out of Kleisthenes' constitutional reforms. If there was no national army properly speaking, then archaic Athenian military actions were ordinarily carried out by aristocratic leaders (presumably often acting in cooperation with one another), men who were able to muster bodies of armed followers.[16] If this is right, the mass expulsion recommended by Isagoras and carried out by Kleomenes (which no doubt focused on aristocratic houses) would have completely disrupted the traditional means of mustering the Athenian army – and this may well have been among their motives for the expulsion. It is not modern scholars alone who doubt the ability of masses to act without orders from their superiors.

If we choose to stick with the two main sources, we may suppose that the action that forced the surrender of the Spartans was carried out in the absence of traditional military leaders and without a regular army. How, then, are we to visualize this action? The Athenian siege of the Acropolis in 508/7 is best understood as a riot – a violent and more or less spontaneous uprising by a large number of Athenian citizens. In order to explain Kleomenes' actions, we must assume that the riot broke out very suddenly and was of relatively great size, intensity, and duration.[17]

After their occupation of the Acropolis, Kleomenes and his warriors were barricaded on a natural fortress, one that had frustrated the regular Spartan army during the siege of Hippias only a couple of years earlier. Yet on the third day of the siege the royal Spartan commander agreed to a humiliating conditional surrender – a surrender that left his erstwhile non-Lakedaimonian comrades to the untender mercies of the rioters. Kleomenes' precipitous agreement to these harsh terms must mean that he had regarded the forces arrayed against him as too numerous (throughout the period of the siege) to contemplate a sortie. Why could the Spartans not simply wait out the siege, as Hippias had been prepared to do? Given the undeveloped state of archaic Greek siegecraft, it is unlikely that the Spartans feared a successful assault on the stronghold. It is much more likely that (unlike Hippias) they had not had time to lay in adequate supplies. This suggests that Kleomenes had occupied the Acropolis very quickly, which in turn probably means that he was caught off guard by the uprising. This inferential sequence supports a presumption that the uprising occurred quite suddenly. What, then, was the precipitating factor?

Herodotus' account, cited earlier, describes the action in the following stages:

1. Isagoras/Kleomenes attempts to dissolve the Boule.
2. The Boule resists.
3. Kleomenes and Isagoras occupy the Acropolis.
4. The rest of the Athenians are united in their views.
5. They besiege the Spartan force.
6. Kleomenes surrenders on the third day of the siege.

If we are to follow Herodotus, we must suppose that steps 1, 2, 3, 5, and 6 are chronologically discrete and sequential events. Step 4 cannot, however, be regarded as a chronological moment; word of events 1 through 3 would have spread through Athens through the piecemeal word-of-mouth operations typical of an oral society. Presumably those living in the city would have learned what was going on first, and the news would have spread (probably very quickly, but not instantaneously) to the rural citizenry.[18] Herodotus' language (τὰ αὐτὰ φρονήσαντες – "all of one mind") supports the idea of a generalized and quite highly developed civic consciousness among the Athenian masses – an ability to form and act on strong communal views on political affairs.

If we take our lead from Herodotus' account, two precipitating factors can be adduced to explain the crystallization of opinion and the outbreak of violent anti-Spartan action on the part of the Athenian demos. First, the riot may have been sparked by the Spartan attempt to dissolve the Boule and the Boule's resistance (thus the demos' action would have commenced as a consequence of steps 1 and 2, but before step 3). According to this scenario, Kleomenes and Isagoras were frightened by the sudden uprising into a precipitous defensive retreat to the nearby stronghold of the Acropolis. Alternatively, the riot might have broken out only after the Spartan occupation of the Acropolis (thus after step 3). On this reading of the evidence, the riot would have been precipitated by the Spartan's offensive (in both senses of the term) takeover of the sacred Acropolis. This second hypothesis would certainly fit in with Herodotus' (5.72.3–4, cf. 5.90.2) story of Kleomenes' sacrilegious behavior and disrespect for the priestess of Athena. Yet this scenario is not, to my mind, fully satisfactory. It does not explain why Kleomenes felt it necessary to bring his entire force up to the Acropolis. Why did Isagoras and his partisans (ὅ τε Κλεομένης καὶ ὁ Ἰσαγόρης καὶ οἱ στασιῶται αὐτοῦ; Hdt. 5.72.2) go up to the Acropolis with Kleomenes? And if the occupation of the Acropolis by Spartan forces was a deliberate and unhurried act of aggression, how are we to explain the failure to bring up enough supplies to last even three days?[19]

It is certain that the author of the *Athenaion Politeia* 20.3 saw Kleomenes' move to the Acropolis as a defensive response to a riot: when "the Boule resisted (τῆς δὲ βουλῆς ἀντιστάσης) and the mob gathered itself together (καὶ συναθροισθέντος τοῦ πλήθους), the supporters of Kleomenes and Isagoras fled for refuge (κατέφυγον) to the Acropolis."[20] Here the move to the Acropolis is specifically described as a defensive reaction to the Council's resistance and the gathering of the people. *Athenaion Politeia*'s statement has independent evidentiary value only if its author had access to evidence (whether in the form of written or oral traditions) other than Herodotus' account – on which he obviously leaned heavily. This issue of *Quellenforschung* cannot be resolved in any definitive way here, but it is not *a priori* unlikely that the author of *Athenaion Politeia,* who certainly had independent information on Kleisthenes' actual reforms, could have read or heard that Kleomenes and Isagoras fled to the Acropolis when a mob formed after the unsuccessful attempt to dissolve the Boule. At the very least, we must suppose that *Athenaion Politeia* interpreted Herodotus' account of the move to the Acropolis as describing a flight rather than a planned act of aggression.[21]

Finally, let us consider the only other classical source for these events: Aristophanes' *Lysistrata* (ll. 273–82). Here the chorus of Old Athenian Men, girding themselves for an assault on the Acropolis (held by a mixed-nationality force of women), urge one another on, "since when Kleomenes seized it previously, he did not get away unpunished, for despite his Lakonian spirit he departed giving over to me his arms, wearing only a little cloak, hungry, dirty, hairy-faced . . . that's how ferociously I besieged that man, keeping constant guard, drawn up seventeen ranks deep at the gates." This is not, of course, history, but a poetic and comic description. Kleomenes' surrender of arms and his hunger are plausible enough, but the overly precise reference to "seventeen ranks" is unlikely to reflect historical reality. Nevertheless, as Rosalind Thomas points out, the Aristophanes passage probably does represent a living popular tradition about the siege.[22] And that tradition evidently focused on the military action of the people rather than any doings of their leaders.

Although certainty cannot be achieved in the face of our limited sources, I think it is easiest to suppose that a spontaneous riot broke out when the Boule resisted. Caught off guard, Kleomenes and Isagoras retreated with their forces to the Acropolis stronghold to regroup. Rapidly spreading news of the occupation of the Acropolis further inflamed the Athenians and so the ranks of the rioters were continually augmented as rural residents took up arms and streamed into the city. From Kleomenes' perspective, the bad situation, which had begun with the resistance of the Boule, only got worse as time went on. Stranded on the barren hill without adequate food or water, and with the ranks of his opponents increasing hourly, Kleomenes saw that his position was hopeless and negotiated a surrender. This scenario has the virtue of incorporating all major elements of Herodotus' account and the two other classical sources for the events, explaining Kleomenes' behavior in rational terms and accommodating the means of news transmission in an oral society.

If, as I have argued, the Athenian military action that led to the liberation of Athens from Spartan control was a spontaneous riot, precipitated by the refusal of the *bouleutai* to obey Isagoras' or Kleomenes' direct order that the Boule dissolve itself in favor of the three hundred Isagoreans, how are we to explain the relationship between the Boule's act of defiance and the uprising itself? In the absence of direct textual evidence for either the motives of the *bouleutai* or their relationship to the demos, I offer, for comparative purposes, the example of another famous revolutionary refusal by a political body to dissolve when confronted with authority backed by force. Although such comparisons are supplementary, and not evidentiary in a formal sense, they are useful if they expand common assumptions about the limits of the possible, in this case by showing that an act of disobedience could indeed precipitate a revolution and that a successful uprising and siege could be carried out by a crowd without formal leaders or military training.

On June 17, 1789, the Representatives of the Third Estate of the Kingdom of France, a body originally called together by the king, declared themselves to be the National Assembly of France. This act of self-redefinition was not accepted as valid by the existing, and heretofore sovereign, authority of the kingdom. Six days later, on June 23, King Louis XVI surrounded the assembly hall with some four thousand troops and read a royal proclamation to the self-proclaimed assemblymen in which he stated that the Third Estate's act in taking the name "National Assembly" was voided; all enactments of the so-called National Assembly were nullified. Louis concluded his speech with the words "I order you, gentlemen, to disperse at once." But the National Assembly refused either to disperse or to renounce its act of self-naming.[23]

According to the brilliant interpretation of these events by Sandy Petrey, the Third Estate's renaming of itself and Louis's declaration that the renaming was void set up a confrontation between speech acts – both the Third Estate and Louis made statements that were intended to have material effects in the real world of French society – both sides were attempting to *enact* a political reality through the speech act of naming or (in Louis's case) "unnaming." In the normal environment of prerevolutionary France, the king's statement would have been (in the terminology of J. L. Austin's speech-act theory, on which Petrey's interpretation is based) "felicitous" or efficacious – the Assembly would *be* dissolved because a sovereign authority had stated that it was dissolved. Yet as Petrey points out, in a revolutionary situation speech acts are not, at the moment of their enunciation, either felicitous or infelicitous ipso facto. Rather their felicity or infelicity is demonstrated only in retrospect. In this case, the National Assembly did not dissolve when so ordered. By refusing to acknowledge the power of the king's speech to create real effects in the world, the Assembly contested the legitimacy of the king's authority.[24]

The confrontation of speech acts was not the end of the story. Louis subsequently attempted to enforce his will through the deployment of military force. This attempt was frustrated by the outbreak of riots in the streets of Paris. In the words of W. Doyle, in the weeks after the confrontation of June 23, "nobody doubted that the King was still prepared to use force to bring the Revolution to an end. The only thing that could prevent him was counter-force, and as yet the Assembly had none at its disposal. It was saved only by the people of Paris."[25] And thus the French Revolution was launched. Because the Revolution succeeded, it came to pass that the Third Estate's act of renaming had been felicitous and Louis's proclamation of nullification infelicitous; if the proof of the pudding is in the eating, the proof of the revolutionary speech act is in the rebellion.

Although the efficacy of its speech acts were as yet undemonstrated, the self-redefinition of the Third Estate as the National Assembly on June 17 and the refusal of the assemblymen of France to acknowledge the force of the king's proclamation of dissolution on June 23 helped to precipitate a revolution because they contested the "inevitability" or "naturalness" of the power of the king's speech to create political realities. Once the king's official proclamation was no longer regarded as an expression of sovereign authority, political discourse ceased to be a realm of orderly enactment and became a realm of contested interpretations. The success of any given interpretation was no longer based on its grounding in eternal and universally accepted truths about power and legitimacy; rather, success in interpretation was now contingent upon the subsequent actions of the French people acting en masse – in this case by rioting and besieging the Bastille.

The parallels between the early stages of the French and the Athenian revolutions are certainly not exact, but both similarities and differences may be instructive. First, it is much less clear in the Athenian case where, at any point in the story, sovereign authority lay – or indeed if we should be talking about sovereignty at all. Isagoras was archon in 508/7, and so the dissolution order issued to the Boule could be seen as carrying the weight of legitimately sanctioned authority. But the archon of Athens did not (I suppose) command the absolute sovereignty claimed by Louis XVI, and the perceived legitimacy of Isagoras' authority was probably not enhanced by his employment of foreign military support. What of the comparison

225

of the Athenian Boule to the National Assembly? This will depend on what body Herodotus meant by the word *boulē*. There are three choices (and all have had supporters among modern scholars) – the Areopagos Council, the Solonian Council of 400, or a newly established Council of 500. The parallel to the National Assembly is closest if we follow the hypothesis, recently revived by Mortimer Chambers, that the Boule in question was (perhaps a pro tem version of) the Council of 500, set up according to Kleisthenes' proposals and the Assembly's enactment before the arrival of the Spartans. This hypothesis would go far in explaining both Kleomenes' interest in eliminating the Council and the brave determination of the councilmen to resist. But Chambers' argument, based in part on his rejection of the existence of a Solonian Council of 400, must remain for the time being an attractive speculation.[26] In any event, we cannot be sure about exactly what powers the Boule claimed or its constitutional relationship to the archon.

Yet despite these caveats and uncertainties, several relevant factors in the French and Athenian cases seem quite similar. Herodotus' revealing comment that a king was "outraged by both words and deeds" (5.74.1) fits the French Revolution as well as the Athenian. In both cases, because of a verbal act of defiance by a political body, "official" political discourse – previously regarded by all concerned as authoritative and stable, as productive of acts of establishment, as a *thesmos* – became a battleground contested by two mutually exclusive interpretations of the source of legitimate public authority. Isagoras (or Kleomenes) said the Boule was dissolved. The *bouleutai* denied, by their resistance, the validity of this statement. As in the case of the French Revolution, it would be the actions of the ordinary people in the streets that would determine which of the opposed interpretations was felicitous and efficacious – rapidly evolving realities would decide whether the statement of Isagoras or that of the *bouleutai* conformed to reality. In both revolutions, the official authority's recourse to military force was stymied by superior unofficial force in the form of mass riots. Both revolutions featured short but decisive sieges (Acropolis and Bastille) by leaderless crowds of citizens; both sieges ended in a negotiated surrender by the besieged leaders of organized military forces.[27] Furthermore, both uprisings featured summary (and, I would add, morally reprehensible) killings of individuals identified as enemies of the revolution. The Athenian Revolution, no less than the French, was baptized in the blood of "counter-revolutionaries."[28] Yet the difference between Athens and France in this regard is also salient: the decade after 507 saw no equivalent to either Jacobinite Terror or Thermidorian reaction.

In terms of assigning credit (or blame) for the uprising and its aftermath, it is important to note that while the brave action of the bourgeois gentlemen of the Third Estate in naming themselves the National Assembly helped to foment the French Revolution, they did not take the lead in storming the Bastille,[29] and they were not able subsequently to control the direction of the Revolution. Nor were the *bouleutai* in control of the Athenian Revolution. Neither Herodotus nor *Athenaion Politeia* assigns the Boule a leadership role in the insurrection after its refusal to disperse. According to Herodotus, after the Boule refused to obey the dissolution order, Kleomenes and Isagoras occupied the Acropolis, and τὰ αὐτὰ φρονήσαντες, Ἀθηναίων οἱ λοιποί besieged the Acropolis – taken literally this comment would seem to exclude the *bouleutai* from any role at all. For *Athenaion Politeia* 20.3 it was when "the Boule resisted and the mob gathered itself together" that "the supporters of Kleomenes and Isagoras fled to the Acropolis," and subsequently it was the demos that besieged them. Both authors seem to agree on the importance of the Boule's act of defiance, but both also agree in seeing the key event as the uprising of the Athenian masses.[30]

Finally, how are we to interpret the political implications of this riotous uprising and its relationship to the subsequent Athenian political order – to the "constitution of Kleisthenes"? Once again, a comparative approach may offer some clues. The highly influential work of E. P. Thompson on food riots in eighteenth-century England and that of Natalie Z. Davis on religious riots in sixteenth-century France has led to the development of what seems to me a useful paradigm for the historical assessment of rioting. This model is discussed in some detail in a recent article by Suzanne Desan, who points out that, according to Thompson and Davis, violent collective actions in early modern England and France were not merely random outbreaks indicative of generalized popular dissatisfaction. Rather, these riots are best read as acts of collective self-definition, or redefinition. The English peasants were, for example, rioting in support of the reenactment of what Thompson described as a "moral economy" – a view of the world that was actually quite conservative in that it assumed the legitimacy of paternalistic (or at least clientistic) relations between peasantry and local aristocracy.[31]

The riot of 508/7 can thus be read as a collective act of political self-definition in which the demos rejected the archon Isagoras as the legitimate public authority. As Herodotus' account suggests, the riot was the physical, active manifestation of the Athenians having come to be "of one mind" about civic affairs. This reading clarifies the general role of Kleisthenes in the Athenian Revolution and the scope of his accomplishments. More specifically it helps to explain the relationship between Kleisthenes and the demos in the months before and after the definitive moment of the riot.

Let us return to the problems of the context and meaning of Herodotus' famous and problematic comment (5.66.2) that Κλεισθένης τὸν δῆμον προσεταιρίζεται. This phrase is often taken to be a description of a straightforward event with a straightforward subject and object. A. de Sélincourt's Penguin translation is typical: "Kleisthenes . . . took the people into his party." But we need not give the middle form προσεταιρίξεται quite such a clearly active force, nor need we imagine it as describing an event that occurred in a single moment. I would suggest as an alternative (if inelegant) translation: "Kleisthenes embarked on the process of becoming the demos' trusted comrade."[32] Herodotus' account certainly implies that Kleisthenes had developed a special relationship with the demos *before* his expulsion from Athens. That relationship, which I suggested earlier was characterized by proposals or enactments in the Assembly, was evidently the proximate cause of Isagoras' calling in of Kleomenes. But there is no reason to suppose that the process described by the verb προσεταιρίζεται was completed before Kleisthenes was expelled. In short, I would suggest that Kleisthenes himself did not so much absorb the demos into his *hetaireia*, as he *himself* was absorbed by an evolving, and no doubt somewhat inchoate, demotic vision of a new society, a society in which distinctions between social statuses would remain but in which there would be no narrow clique of rulers.

The sea change in Athenian political practice implied by Kleisthenes' new relationship with the demos was not signaled by an act of noblesse oblige – opening the doors of the exclusive, aristocratic *hetaireia* to the masses. Rather it was a revolution in the demos' perception of itself and of an aristocrat's perception regarding his own relationship, and that of all men of his class, to the demos. Kleisthenes acknowledged the citizens of Athens as equal sharers in regard to the *nomoi* and under the banner of *isonomia* the men of the demos became, in effect if not in contemporary nomenclature, Kleisthenes' *hetairoi*.[33] We must remember that Herodotus' terminology is that of the mid-fifth rather than the late sixth century. But in the fifth century, when Herodotus was writing his *Histories,* Athenian *hetairoi* were expected to help one another and to seek to harm their common enemies. The demos looked out for Kleisthenes' interests by attacking the Spartans and by recalling him immediately upon their departure. Political friendship was a two-way street, and Kleisthenes in turn looked after the interests of the demos by devising and working to implement (through enactments of the Assembly) an institutional framework that would consolidate and stabilize the new demotic vision of politics. That vision had grown up among the Athenian citizen masses in the course of the sixth century and had found an active, physical manifestation in the riot that occurred during Kleisthenes' enforced absence from the scene. The "constitution of Kleisthenes" channeled the energy of the demos' self-defining riot into a stable and workable form of government.

In sum, Kleisthenes was not so much the authoritative leader of the revolution as he was a highly skilled interpreter of statements made in a revolutionary context and of revolutionary action itself. This is not to deny any of his brilliance or even his genius. But it is to see his genius not in an ability to formulate a prescient vision of a future democratic utopia, nor in an ability to hide a selfish dynastic scheme behind a constitutional facade, but rather in his ability to "read" – in a sensitive and perceptive way – the text of Athenian discourse in a revolutionary age and to understand that Athenian mass action had created new political facts. Kleisthenes saw that the revolutionary action of the Athenian demos had permanently changed the environment of politics and political discourse. After the revolution there could be no secure recourse to extrademotic authority. If Athens were to survive as a polis, there would have to be a new basis for politically authoritative speech, but that basis must find its ground in the will of the demos itself. Having read and understood his complex text, Kleisthenes knew that there could be no turning back to rule by aristocratic faction – or at least he saw that any attempt to turn back the clock would bring on a bloodbath and make effective resistance to Sparta impossible. And so, acting as a good *hetairos,* well deserving the *pistis* placed in him (*Ath. Pol.* 21.1) by his mass *hetaireia,* Kleisthenes came up with a constitutional order that both framed and built upon the revolution that had started without him.

NOTES

This essay was revised in the summer of 1991, when I had the honor of being Visiting Fellow at the University of New England in Armidale, New South Wales. I owe thanks to many colleagues there, and especially to G. R. Stanton, whose detailed and insightful comments much improved a paper with whose fundamental tenets he still disagrees.

1. See introduction to Hunt 1989.
2. This is a traditional breaking point: Burn 1960: 324, e.g., ends his narrative of archaic Athenian history with the expulsion of Hippias. M. H. Hansen 1986 argues that *dēmokratia* was the name Kleisthenes used from the beginning. The relevant ancient sources are conveniently collected, translated, and annotated in Stanton 1990: 130–67.
3. For representative statements of the centrality of Kleisthenes' role, see Zimmern 1961: 143–4: "Cleisthenes the Alkmeonid, the leader of the popular party, . . . made a bid for power [after the Spartan intervention and the occupation of the Acropolis]. *Cleisthenes and the councillors* [my emphasis] called the people to arms and blockaded the rock . . . [upon the surrender of the Spartans] Cleisthenes was now master of the situation." O. Murray 1980: 254: "Kleisthenes 'took the people into his party' . . . proposed major reforms, *expelled Isagoras* [my emphasis], and in the next few years held off the attempts of the Spartans and their allies to intervene." Forrest 1966: 194: "Finally, with the *demos'* firm support, *he was able to rout Isagoras* [my emphasis] together with a Spartan force." Other textbooks do point out that Kleisthenes was in exile, e.g., Sealey 1976: 147; Bury and Meiggs 1975: 36; esp. M. Ostwald in *CAH²* (1988) 4.305–7. The modern account of the revolution closest in spirit to the one I offer here is perhaps Meier 1990: 64–6.
4. For the tyranny and its end, see D. M. Lewis in *CAH²* (1988) 4.287–302, with sources cited.
5. The government would not have been called oligarchy because the word had not yet been invented; for the history of the term, see Raaflaub 1983.
6. Accommodation and resistance of Alkmeonids to the tyranny: Lewis in *CAH²* (1988) 4.288, 299–301. But cf. the skepticism of R. Thomas 1989: 263–4, who argues that the Alkmeonids may have made up the tradition of their antityrannical activity and the story of their exile under the Peisistratids from whole cloth.
7. Isagoras as archon: *Ath. Pol.* 21.1. The attempt by McCargar 1974 to separate Isagoras, opponent of Kleisthenes, from the archon of 508/7 on the grounds that *some* archons in this period were evidently relatively young (perhaps not much over thirty) and Isagoras *may* have been relatively mature seems to me chimerical, especially in light of the extreme rarity of the name. *Ath. Pol.* 22.5 claims that after the institution of the tyranny, and until 487/6, all archons were elected (αἱρετοί). The tyrants had manipulated the elections to ensure that their own supporters were in office (see P. J. Rhodes 1981: 272–3); exactly how the elections would have been carried out in 509/8 (and thus what Isagoras' support consisted of) is unclear. We need not, anyway, suppose that Isagoras' election was indicative of a broad base of popular support; most likely his support was centered in the (non-Alkmeonid) nobility. On the power of the archaic archon, see *Ath. Pol.* 3.3, 13.2 with comments of P. J. Rhodes 1981.
8. See Ober 1989: 60–8; Manville 1990: 124–209; Meier 1990: 53–81. On the lack of formal patronage structures in classical Athens see Millett 1989.
9. On the Solonian constitution, see Ober 1989: 60–5, with references cited. For the Areopagos from the time of Solon to Kleisthenes, see R. W. Wallace 1989: 48–76.
10. Kleisthenes' connection with the demos is underlined by Hdt. 5.69.2: ὡς γὰρ δὴ τὸν

Ἀθηναίων δῆμον πρότερον ἀπωσμένον τότε πάντως πρὸς τὴν ἑωυτοῦ μοῖραν προσεθήκατο (the Athenian people, previously despised, he thus got entirely on his own side), and by *Ath. Pol.* 20.1: ὁ Κλεισθένης προσηγάγετο τὸν δῆμον, ἀποδιδοὺς τῷ πλήθει τὴν πολιτείαν (Kleisthenes brought the people over to himself by giving over political authority to the masses). Since Wade-Gery's seminal article (1933: 19–25), it has been widely accepted that the Assembly was the arena in which Kleisthenes won the favor of the people; cf. discussion by Ostwald 1969: 149–60.

11. The implied subject of the verb ἐπειρᾶτο is either Kleomenes or Isagoras. The grammar seems to point to Kleomenes, although presumably it was Isagoras (as archon) who gave the official order to the Boule. The point is in any case merely procedural: Herodotus' narrative demonstrates that Kleomenes and Isagoras were working hand in glove throughout.

12. Hdt. 5.66.2 implies that at least some of the reforms were put into place before Kleomenes' arrival; *Ath. Pol.* 20–1, discusses the reforms after giving the history of the revolution proper. I think it is most likely that some reforms were proposed and perhaps actually enacted by the Assembly before Kleomenes' arrival, but presumably there would not have been time for all the details of the new constitution to have been put into place. See later for the question of when the Council of 500 was established. For a review of the chronological issue, see Hignett 1952: 331–6; P. J. Rhodes 1981: 244–5, 249; Chambers 1990: 221–2.

13. D. M. Lewis 1963.

14. Ehrenberg 1973: 89–103: in 510 Kleisthenes was "a man of new and radical ideas" (89); in 508 he gained support "by revealing plans of a new democratic order" (90); "his reforms were . . . the first examples of democratic methods" (91). Kleisthenes was not primarily interested in personal power, rather "power was to him a means of creating the constitutional framework for a society on the verge of becoming democratic" (91). For Ehrenberg, then, Kleisthenes is both selfless and a strong leader whose place is "at the helm" (102). Cf. Ehrenberg 1950.

15. For a detailed discussion of the role of oral traditions (of family and polis) in Herodotus' construction of his account of the revolution and a vigorous attack on the hypothesis that Herodotus was an Alkmeonid apologist, see R. Thomas 1989: 144–54, 232–82.

16. Frost 1984.

17. I am assuming throughout that Kleomenes was an experienced and sane military commander and that his decisions were made accordingly. On the dubious tradition of the madness of Kleomenes, see Griffiths 1989. It is interesting to note how the demos' action simply disappears in some respectable scholarly accounts, e.g., Ehrenberg 1973: 90: "Cleomenes and Isagoras met, however, with the resistance of the council . . . which they had tried to disband and which was most likely the Areopagos. . . . The Spartans withdrew, Isagoras was powerless, and many of his followers were executed."

18. On how information was disseminated in Athens see Hunter 1990.

19. Herodotus' statement that Kleomenes seized the Acropolis and was subsequently thrown out along with the Lakedaimonians (ἐπεχείρησέ τε καὶ τότε πάλιν ἐξέπιπτε μετὰ τῶν Λακεδαιμονίων; 5.72.4) makes it appear likely that the whole force had gone up to the Acropolis together, had been besieged together, and had surrendered together. It is unlikely that a significant part of Kleomenes' forces joined him on the hill after the commencement of the siege, and Herodotus says nothing about any of his men being captured in the lower city before the surrender. It is worth noting that Kylon (Hdt. 5.71; Thuc. 1.126.5–11) and Peisistratos (twice: Hdt. 1.59.6, 60.5) had earlier seized the Acropolis, each time as the first stage in an attempt to establish a tyranny. Kleomenes' case is different in that his move came *after* he had established control of the city.

20. Stanton 1990: 142, 144 n. 6, translates συναθροισθέντος τοῦ πλήθους as "the common people had been assembled" on the grounds that "the verb 'had been assembled' is definitely passive." But I take the (morphologically) passive participle συναθροισθέντος as having a reflexive rather than a passive meaning; on the distinction see Rijksbaron 1984: 126–48. Reflexive meaning for the passive participle of συναθροίζω: Xen. An. 6.5.30; of ἀθροίζω: Thuc. 1.50.4, 6.70.4; esp. Arist. Pol. 1304b33.

21. For a discussion of the relationship between Herodotus' narrative and Ath. Pol. 20–1, see Wade-Gery 1933: 17–19 and P. J. Rhodes 1981: 240–1, 244, who argues that Herodotus was Ath. Pol.'s sole authority for 20.1–3. For general discussions of Ath. Pol.'s use of sources, see Chambers 1990: 84–91.

22. R. Thomas 1989: 245–7.

23. "Je vous ordonne, Messieurs, de vous séparer toute de suite." For the resolution of the Abbé de Sieyès renaming the Assembly, and the response of Louis at the "Royal Session" of June 23, see Wickham Legg 1905: 18–20, 22–33. For a narrative account of this stage of the Revolution, see Doyle 1980: 172–7.

24. Petrey 1988: esp. 17–51. Petrey's work is based on the ground-breaking linguistic theory of Austin 1975.

25. Doyle 1980: 177.

26. Chambers 1990: 222–3.

27. For the siege of the Bastille see Godechot 1970: 218–46. The Bastille was a formidable, if dilapidated fortress, guarded by a small force of eighty-four pensioners and thirty-two Swiss mercenaries. For the week before the assault of July 14, its commander, Governor de Launey, had refurbished the defenses to withstand an assault. Yet "he had only one day's supply of meat and two days' supply of bread, and moreover there was no drinking water inside the fortress . . . de Launey may . . . have thought that if he were attacked by an unarmed or ill-armed crowd the assault would not last longer that one day and that at nightfall the rioters would disperse" (219). It is tempting to suppose that Kleomenes thought along similar lines.

28. On the killing of Governor de Launey and seven other defenders of the Bastille on July 14, and of other agents of the Old Regime in the days thereafter, see Godechot 1970: 243–6. The Athenian killings have been questioned on the grounds of the wording of Ath. Pol. 20.3 (Κλεομένην μὲν καὶ τοὺς μετ' αὐτοῦ πάντας ἀφεῖσαν ὑποσπόνδους – they [the Athenians] released Kleomenes and all those with him under treaty), but as Ostwald 1969: 144 with n. 6 points out, this need only refer to the Lakedaimonian troops; cf. P. J. Rhodes 1981: 246–7.

29. For the composition of the crowd (mostly artisans from Paris) that stormed the Bastille and the absence of assemblymen or any other formal leaders, see Godechot 1970: 211, 221–6, 230, 237–9.

30. Cf., e.g., Hammond 1959: 185–6: "The Council resisted. It raised the people against Cleomenes and Isagoras, who seized the Acropolis and found themselves besieged"; Ostwald 1969: 144: "The Council refused to be intimidated and, with the support of the common people, besieged the acropolis"; Stanton 1990: 144 n. 6: the council in question must have been the Areopagos, since unlike the councils of 400 or 500 it "would have been sufficiently permanent and would have contained a sufficient accumulation of politically experienced men to organize resistance to a military force. A major thrust was the assembling of the common people . . . and this could have been achieved by the influence which ex-arkhon clan leaders in the Areopagos held over their retainers." The Areopagos leadership theory would need to explain how Kleomenes' force could be strong and decisive enough to "drive out" 700 families dispersed through

Attika (cf. Stanton 1990: 141 n. 14, who questions the number 700), but too weak to stop at most 100 to 200 men, who were presumably gathered in one place to hear the dissolution order, from organizing a resistance (number of Areopagites: R. W. Wallace 1989: 97 with n. 23; M. H. Hansen 1990, from which we must deduct those expelled with the 700).

31. Desan 1989.
32. It is important to keep in mind that the terminology is in any event Herodotus', not Kleisthenes'. It was probably not in use in Kleisthenes' day and reflects rather the political vocabulary of the mid-fifth century; Chambers 1990: 221.
33. On *isonomia* and its meaning, see Ober 1989: 74–5 with literature cited.

Bibliography

Abel, U. 1969. "Darstellung musischer Darbietungen auf attischen Vasen." M.A. thesis, University of Munich.

Abercrombie, N., S. Hill, and B. S. Turner. 1980. *The Dominant Ideology Thesis*. London: Routledge & Kegan Paul.

Abrams, P. 1972. "The Sense of the Past and the Origins of Sociology." *Past & Present* 55.18–32.

Ackerman, R. 1971. "Some Letters of the Cambridge Ritualists." *GRBS* 12.113–36.

———. 1972. "Jane Ellen Harrison: The Early Work." *GRBS* 13.209–30.

———. 1975. "Frazer on Myth and Ritual." *Journal of the History of Ideas* 36.115–34.

———. 1987. *J. G. Frazer: His Life and Work*. Cambridge: Cambridge University Press.

———. 1990. "J. G. Frazer." In *Classical Scholarship: A Biographical Encyclopedia*. Ed. W. W. Briggs and W. M. Calder III. New York: Garland. 77–83.

———. 1991a. "The Cambridge Group: Origins and Composition." In *The Cambridge Ritualists Reconsidered*. Ed. W. M. Calder III. Illinois Classical Studies suppl. vol. 2. Atlanta, Ga.: Scholar's Press. 1–19.

———. 1991b. *The Myth and Ritual School: J. G. Frazer and the Cambridge Ritualists*. New York: Garland.

Adler, F., et al. 1892. *Olympia*, vol. 2: *Die Baudenkmäler*. Berlin: Weidmann.

———. 1897. *Olympia*, vol. 1: *Topographie und Geschichte*. Berlin: Weidmann.

Africa, T. 1991. "Aunt Glegg Among the Dons or Taking Jane Harrison at Her Word." In *The Cambridge Ritualists Reconsidered*. Ed. W. M. Calder III. Illinois Classical Studies suppl. vol. 2: Atlanta, Ga.: Scholar's Press. 21–35.

Ahlberg, G. 1971a. *Fighting on Land and Sea in Greek Geometric Art*. Stockholm: Almqvist & Wiksell.

———. 1971b. *Prothesis and Ekphora in Greek Geometric Art*. SIMA 32. Göteborg: P. Astrom.

Alcock, S. 1991. "Tomb Cult and the Post-Classical Polis." *AJA* 95.447–67.

Alexandri, O. 1968. "Nykterini anaskaphi skammatos kata mikos tis Odos Kriezi." *AAA* 1.20–30.

Altherr-Charon, A., and C. Bérard. 1978. "Eretrie: L'organisation de l'espace et la formation d'une cité grecque." In *L'archéologie aujourd'hui*. Ed. A. Schnapp. Paris: Hachette Litterature. 229–40.

Anderson, P. 1983. *In the Tracks of Historical Materialism*. Chicago: University of Chicago Press.

Andrewes, A. 1957. *The Greek Tyrants*. London: Hutchinson's University Library.

———. 1982. "The Tyranny of Pisistratus." In *CAH²*, vol. 3, pt. 3. Ed. J. Boardman and N. G. L. Hammond. Cambridge: Cambridge University Press. 392–416.

Angiolillo, S. 1983. "Pisistrato e Artemide Brauronia." *PP* 38.351–4.

Ankersmit, F. 1989. "Historiography and Postmodernism." *History & Theory* 28.137–53.

Antonaccio, C. 1992. "Terraces, Tombs, and the Early Argive Heraion." *Hesperia* 61.85–105.

———. 1993. *An Archaeology of Ancestors: Hero and Tomb Cult in Early Greece.* London: Rowman & Littlefield, 1993.

Appadurai, A. 1981. "The Past as Scarce Resource." *Man* n.s. 16.201–19.

Auberson, P., and K. Schefold. 1973. Ερέτρια, ἀρχαιολογικὸς ὅδηγος [Eretria, archaeological guide]. Trans. P. Themelis. Athens.

Aupert, P. 1982. "Argos au VIIe siècle: Bourgade ou metropole?" *ASAA* 60.21–31.

Austin, J. L. 1975. *How to Do Things with Words,* 2d ed. Ed. J. O. Urmson and Martin Sbisà. Cambridge, Mass.: Harvard University Press.

Austin, M. M., and P. Vidal-Naquet. 1977. *Economic and Social History of Ancient Greece.* Berkeley and Los Angeles: University of California Press.

Back, F. 1883. *De Graecorum caeremoniis in quibus homines deorum vice fungebantur.* Berlin: G. Schade.

Baggley, J. 1988. *Doors of Perception.* London: Mowbray.

Bakir, G. 1981. *Sophilos.* Mainz: Philipp von Zabern.

Barkowski, O. 1972. "Sieben Weise." *RE* 2d ser., vol. 2 pt. 2, col. 2242–64. Munich: Alfred Druckenmüller.

Bazant, J. 1983. "War, Poetry, and Athenian Vases." *Listy Filologické* 106.203–9.

Beazley, J. D. 1922. "Citharoedus." *JHS* 42.70–98.

———. 1956. *Attic Black-Figure Vase-Painters.* Oxford: Oxford University Press.

———. 1963. *Attic Red-Figure Vase-Painters,* 2d ed. Oxford: Oxford University Press.

Beloch, J. 1890. "Wann lebten Alkaeos und Sappho?" *RhM* 45.465–73.

Bengtson, H. 1977. *Griechische Geschichte,* 5th ed. Munich: Beck.

Benson, J. 1970. *Horse, Bird, and Man.* Amherst: University of Massachusetts Press.

Benton, S. 1934–5. "Excavations in Ithaca, III: The Cave at Polis, I." *BSA* 35.45–73.

———. 1936. "A Votive Offering to Odysseus." *Antiquity* 10.350.

———. 1938–9. "Excavations in Ithaca, III: The Cave at Polis, II." *BSA* 39.1–51.

Benveniste, E. 1973. *Indo-European Language and Society.* Trans. E. Palmer. London: Faber & Faber.

Bérard, C. 1969. "Note sur la fouille au sud de l'héroôn." *AntK* 12.74–9

———. 1970. *Eretria,* vol. 3: *L'héroôn à la Porte de l'ouest.* Bern: Francke.

———. 1978. "Topographie et urbanisme de l'Eretrie archaïque: L'héroôn." *Eretria* 6.89–95. Bern: Francke.

———. 1982. "Récupérer la mort du prince: Héroïsation et formation de la cité." In Gnoli and Vernant 1982. 89–105.

———. 1983. "L'héroïsation et la formation de la cité: Un conflit idéologique." In *Architecture et société de l'archaïsme grec a la fin de la République romain.* Rome: Ecole française de Rome. 43–59.

Bergk, T. 1882. *Poetae Lyrici Graeci,* 4th ed., vol. 3. Leipzig: Teubner.

Berkhofer, R. F. 1988. "The Challenge of Poetics to (Normal) Historical Practice." *Poetics Today* 9.435–52.

Berve, H. 1937. *Miltiades: Studien zur Geschichte des Mannes und seiner Zeit.* Hermes Einzelschriften, vol. 2. Berlin: Weidmann.

Biersack, A. 1989. "Local Knowledge, Local History: Geertz and Beyond." In Hunt 1989. 72–96.

Binford, L. R. 1972. *An Archaeological Perspective.* New York: Seminar Press.

Binford, L. R., and S. R. Binford, eds. 1968. *New Perspectives in Archaeology.* Chicago: University of Chicago Press.

Bingen, J. 1965. "La Nécropole Ouest 4." In *Thorikos,* vol. 1: 1963. Brussels: Belgian Archaeological Mission to Greece. 19–29.

———. 1968a. "L'établissement géométrique et la Nécropole Ouest." In *Thorikos,* vol. 3: 1965. Brussels: Belgian Archaeological Mission to Greece. 31–56.

1968b. "Les établissements géométriques et la Nécropole Ouest." In *Thorikos*, vol. 4: 1966/7. Brussels: Belgian Archaeological Mission to Greece. 70–119.

Blech, M. 1982. *Studien zum Kranz bei den Griechen*. Berlin: Weidmann.

Bledstein, B. J. 1976. *The Culture of Professionalism: The Middle Class and the Development of Higher Education in America*. New York: Norton.

Blegen, C. 1937a. "Post-Mycenaean Deposits in Chamber-Tombs." *AE* 1937.377–90.

1937b. *Prosymna: The Helladic Settlement Preceding the Argive Heraeum*. 2 vols. Cambridge: Cambridge University Press.

Blegen, C., H. Palmer, and R. Young. 1964. *Corinth*, vol. 13: *The North Cemetery*. Princeton, N.J.: Princeton University Press.

Bloch, M. 1986. *From Blessing to Violence: History and Ideology in the Circumcision Ritual of the Merina of Madagascar*. Cambridge: Cambridge University Press.

Blumenberg, H. 1976. "Der Sturz des Protophilosophen: Zur Komik der reinen Theorie, anhand einer Rezeptionsgeschichte der Thales Anekdote." In *Das Komische* (= *Poetik und Hermeneutik*, vol. 7). Ed. W. Preisendanz and R. Warning. Munich: W. Fink. 11–64.

Boardman, J. 1967. *Greek Emporio*. London (*BSA* suppl. vol. 6).

1972. "Herakles, Peisistratos, and Sons." *RA* 57–72.

1975. "Herakles, Peisistratos and Eleusis." *JHS* 95.1–12.

1978. "Herakles, Delphi and Kleisthenes of Sicyon." *RA* 227–34.

1980. *The Greeks Overseas: Their Early Colonies and Trade*. New York: Thames & Hudson.

1982. "Herakles, Theseus and Amazons." In *The Eye of Greece*. Ed. D. Kurtz and B. Sparkes. Cambridge: Cambridge University Press. 1–28.

1983. "Symbol and Story in Greek Geometric Art." In Moon 1983. 15–36.

1984. "Image and Politics in Sixth-Century Athens." In *Ancient Greek and Related Pottery*. Ed. H. A. G. Brijder. Amsterdam: Allard Pierson Museum. 239–47.

1986. "Herakles in Extremis." In *Studien zur Ikonographie und Vasenmalerei*. Ed. E. von Boehr and W. Martini. Mainz: P. von Zabern. 127–32.

1988. "Sex Differentiation in Athenian Grave Vases." *AION ArchStAnt* 10.171–9.

1989. "Herakles, Peisistratos and the Unconvinced." *JHS* 109.158–9.

Boedeker, D. 1987. "The Two Faces of Demaratus." *Arethusa* 20.185–201.

1988. "Protesilaos and the End of Herodotus' Histories." *CA* 7.30–48.

Böhlau, J. 1887. "Frühattische Vasen." *JdI* 2.33–66.

Böhr, E. 1982. *Der Schaukel Maler*. Mainz: Philipp von Zabern.

Bohringer, F. 1979. "Cultes d'athlètes en Grèce classique: Propos politique, discours mythique." *REA* 81.5–18.

Bömer, F. 1952. *RE* 21.1878–1993. s.v. Pompa.

Bommelaer, J.-F. 1972. "Nouveaux documents de céramique protoargien." *BCH* 86.229–51.

Bothmer, D. von. 1951. "Attic Black-Figure Pelikai." *JHS* 71.40–7.

1960. "New Vases by the Amasis Painter." *AntK* 3.73–4, 80.

Bourdieu, P. 1977. *Outline of a Theory of Practice*. Trans. R. Nice. Cambridge: Cambridge University Press.

1984. *Distinction: A Social Critique of the Judgement of Taste*. Trans. R. Nice. Cambridge, Mass.: Harvard University Press.

Bourriot, F. 1976. "Recherches sur la nature du genos: Etude d'histoire sociale athenienne-periodes archaïque et classique," 2 vols. Ph.D. diss., University of Paris.

Bowersock, G. 1965. *Augustus and the Greek World*. Oxford: Oxford University Press.

Bowler, P.J. 1989. *The Invention of Progress*. Oxford: Oxford University Press.

Bowra, C. M. 1961. *Greek Lyric Poetry*, 2d ed. Oxford: Oxford University Press.

1971. "Xenophanes on the Luxury of Colophon." In *On Greek Margins*. Oxford: Oxford University Press.

Brady, I. 1991. *Anthropological Poetics*. London: Rowman & Littlefield.

Braudel, F. 1958. "Histoire et sciences sociales: La longue durée." *Annales ESC* 13.725–53.

Brelich, A. 1959. *Gli eroi greci: Un problema storico-religioso*. Rome: Edizioni dell' Ateneo.

Bremmer, J. 1983. *The Early Greek Concept of the Soul*. Princeton, N.J.: Princeton University Press.

———. 1987. "Greek Mythology: A Select Bibliography." In *Interpretations of Greek Mythology*. Ed. J. Bremmer. London: Croom Helm. 278–83.

Brickhouse, T. C., and N. D. Smith. 1988. *Socrates on Trial*. Princeton, N.J.: Princeton University Press.

Briggs, C. 1985. "The Pragmatics of Proverb Performance in New Mexican Spanish." *American Anthropologist* 87.793–810.

Brillante, C. 1990. "History and the Historical Interpretation of Myth." In *Approaches to Greek Myth*. Ed. L. Edmunds. Baltimore, Md.: Johns Hopkins University Press. 93–138.

Brookes, A. C. 1981. "Stoneworking in the Geometric period at Corinth." *Hesperia* 50.285–90.

Brouskari, M. 1979. *Apo to Athinaiko Kerameiko*. Athens: Ministry of Culture.

Brown, T. 1989. "Solon and Croesus (Hdt. 1.29)." *Ancient History Bulletin* 3.1.1–4.

Brückner, E., and A. Pernice. 1893. "Ein attischer Friedhof." *AM* 18.73–191.

Bundy, E. 1962. *Studia Pindarica*. Berkeley and Los Angeles: University of California Press. Repr. 1986.

Burkert, W. 1966. "Greek Tragedy and Sacrificial Ritual." *GRBS* 7.87–121.

———. 1979. *Structure and History in Greek Mythology and Ritual*. Berkeley and Los Angeles: University of California Press.

———. 1983. *Homo Necans*. Berkeley and Los Angeles: University of California Press.

———. 1984. *Die orientalisierende Epoche in der griechischen Religion und Literatur*. Heidelberg: Winter.

———. 1985. *Greek Religion*. Trans. J. Raffan. Cambridge, Mass.: Harvard University Press.

———. 1987. "The Making of Homer in the Sixth Century B.C.: Rhapsodes vs. Stesichorus." In *Papers on the Amasis Painter and His World*. Malibu, Calif.: J. Paul Getty Museum.

Burn, A. R. 1960. *The Lyric Age of Greece*. London: Edward Arnold.

Burr, D. 1933. "A Geometric House and a Proto-attic Votive Deposit." *Hesperia* 2.533–640.

Bury, J. B., and R. Meiggs. 1975. *History of Greece to the Death of Alexander the Great*, 4th ed. New York: St. Martin's.

Burzachechi, M. 1962. "Oggetti parlanti nelle epigrafi greche." *Epigraphica* 25.3–54.

Cabasilas, N. 1960. *A Commentary on the Divine Liturgy*. Trans. J. M. Hussey and P. A. McNulty. London: S.P.C.K.

Cairns, F. 1982. "Cleon and Pericles: A Suggestion," *JHS* 102.203–4.

Calame, C. 1977. *Les choeurs de jeunes filles en Grèce archaïque*, 2 vols. Rome: Edizioni dell' Atheneo.

———. 1987. "Spartan Genealogies: The Mythological Representation of a Spatial Organisation." In *Interpretations of Greek Mythology*. Ed. J. Bremmer. London: Croom Helm. 153–86.

———. 1990. "Narrating the Foundation of a City: The Symbolic Birth of Cyrene." In *Approaches to Greek Myth*. Ed. L. Edmunds. Baltimore, Md.: Johns Hopkins University Press. 277–341.

Calligas, P. 1984–5. Ἀνασκαφὲς στὸ Λευκαντὶ Ἀρχεῖον Εὐβοικῶν. [Excavations of ancient Lefkandi in Euboia]. Μελετῶν 26.253–69.

———. 1988. "Hero-Cult in Early Iron Age Greece." In *Early Greek Cult Practice* (Proceedings of the Fifth International Symposium of the Swedish Institute, Athens, June, 26–9, 1986). Ed. R. Hägg et al. Stockholm: Paul Astrom. 229–34.

Cambitoglou, A., et al. 1971. *Zagora*, vol. 1. Athens: Athens Archaeological Society.

———. 1988. *Zagora*, vol. 2. Athens: Athens Archaeological Society.

Carter, J. 1972. "The Beginning of Narrative Art in the Geometric Period." *BSA* 67.25–58.

Cartledge, P. 1977. "Hoplites and Heroes." *JHS* 97.11–28.

1979. *Sparta and Lakonia: A Regional History, 1300–362 B.C.* London: Routledge & Kegan Paul.

1985. "The Greek Religious Festivals." In Easterling and Muir 1985. 98–127.

1987. *Agesilaos and the Crisis of Sparta.* Baltimore, Md.: Johns Hopkins University Press.

1988. "Yes, Spartan Kings Were Heroized." *LCM* 13.3.43–4.

Catling. H. 1975. "Excavations at the Menelaion, 1973–1975." *LakSpoud* 2.258–69.

1976. "New Excavations at the Menelaion, Sparta." In *Neue Forschungen in griechischer Heiligtümern*. Ed. U. Jantzen. Tübingen: E. Wasmuth. 77–90.

1977a. "Excavations at the Menelaion, 1976–1977." *LakSpoud* 3.408–15.

1977b. "Excavations at the Menelaion, Sparta, 1973–76." *AR* 24–42.

1982–3. "Study at the Menelaion, 1982–1983." *LakSpoud* 7.23–30.

1988–89. "Olympia." *AR* 35.30.

1992. "Sparta: A Mycenaean Place and a Shrine to Menelaus and Helen." *Current Archaeology* 130.429–31.

Catling, H., and H. Cavanagh. 1975. "Two Inscribed Bronzes from the Menelaion, Sparta." *Kadmos* 15.145–57.

Catling, R. 1986. "Excavations at the Menelaion: 1985." *LakSpoud* 10.205–16.

Catling, R., and I. Lemos 1990. *Lefkandi*, vol. 2: *The Protogeometric Building at Toumba 1. The Pottery.* London: Thames & Hudson.

Cavanagh, R. 1991. "Surveys, Cities, and Synoecism." In Rich and Wallace-Hadrill 1991. London: Routledge & Kegan Paul.

Cavanagh, R., and R. R. Laxton. 1984. "Lead Figurines from the Menelaion and Seriation." *BSA* 79.23–36.

Chadwick, O. 1970. *The Victorian Church*, vol. 2. New York: Oxford University Press.

Chamay, J., and D. von Bothmer. 1987. "Ajax et Cassandre par le Peintre de Princeton." *AntK* 29.58–68.

Chambers, M., ed. 1990. *Aristoteles: Staat der Athener.* Aristotles Werke in deutscher Übersetzung, vol. 10.1. Berlin: Weidmann.

Chamoux, F. 1953. *Cyrène sous la monarchie des Battiades.* Paris: Bibliothèque des Ecoles françaises d'Athenes et de Rome. Fasc. 77.

Chantraine, P. 1968–80. *Dictionnaire étymologique de la langue grecque,* 4 vols. Paris: Klincksieck.

Chantraine, P., and O. Masson. 1954. "Sur quelques termes du vocabulaire religieux des Grecs: La valeur du mot ἄγος et ses dérivés." In *Sprachgeschichte und Wortbedeutung: Festschrift Albert Debrunner*. Bern: Francke. 85–107.

Chatzis, G. 1981–2. Η πρωτογεομετρικὴ ἐποχὴ στὴ Μεσσενίας. [The Protogeometric period in Messenia]. *Acts of the 2nd International Conference on Peloponnesian Studies*, vol. 2. 321–47. Athens.

Chiasson, C. 1986. "The Herodotean Solon." *GRBS* 27.249–62.

Clarke, D. L. 1968. *Analytical Archaeology,* 1st ed. London: Methuen.

Clifford, J., and G. Marcus, eds. 1986. *Writing Culture: The Poetics and Politics of Ethnography.* Berkeley and Los Angeles: University of California Press.

Cohen, G. 1978. *Karl Marx's Theory of History: A Defence.* Oxford: Oxford University Press.

Coldstream, J. N. 1968. *Greek Geometric Pottery.* London: Methuen.

1974. Review of G. Ahlberg, *Fighting on Land and Sea in Greek Geometric Art. Gnomon* 46.394–6.

1976. "Hero-Cult in the Age of Homer." *JHS* 96.8–17.

1977. *Geometric Greece.* London: E. Benn.

Connor, W. R. 1962. "Vim quandam incredibilem: A Tradition Concerning the Oratory of Pericles." *C & M* 23.23–33.

1971. *The New Politicians of Fifth-Century Athens.* Princeton, N.J.: Princeton University Press.

1979. "Pausanias 3.14.1: A Sidelight on Spartan History, c. 440 B.C.?" *TAPA* 109.21–7.

1985. *Thucydides,* rev. ed. Princeton, N.J.: Princeton University Press.

1987. "Tribes, Festivals and Processions: Civic Ceremonial and Political Manipulation in Ancient Greece." *JHS* 107.40–50.

1988a. "Early Greek Land Warfare as Symbolic Expression." *Past & Present* 119.161–88.

1988b. " 'Sacred' and 'Secular': Hiera kai hosia and the Classical Athenian Concept of the State." *Ancient Society* 19.161–88.

1989a. "City Dionysia and Athenian democracy." *C & M* 40.7–32.

1989b. "The New Classical Humanities and the Old." In *Classics: A Discipline and Profession in Crisis?* Ed. P. Culham, L. Edmunds, and A. Smith. Lanham, Md.: University Press of America. 25–38.

1991. "The Other 399: Religion and the Trial of Socrates." In *Georgica: Greek Studies in Honour of George Cawkwell.* London (*BICS* suppl. vol. 58). 49–56.

Contiades-Tsitsoni, E. 1990. *Hymenaios und Epithalamion: Das Hochzeitslied in der frühgriechischen Lyrik.* Stuttgart: Teubner.

Cook, A. B. 1925. *Zeus: A Study in Ancient Religion,* vol. 2: *Zeus God of the Dark Sky (Thunder and Lightning).* Cambridge: Cambridge University Press.

Cook, J. M. 1934–5. "Protoattic Pottery." *BSA* 35.165–219.

Cook, R. M. 1953a. "The Agamemnoneion." *BSA* 48.30–68.

——— 1953b. "The Cult of Agamemnon at Mycenae." In *Geras A: Keramopoullou.* Athens: Myrtide. 112–18.

——— 1969. "A Note on the Absolute Chronology of the Eighth Century B.C." *BSA* 64.13–15.

——— 1987. "Pots and Pisistratean Propaganda." *JHS* 107.167–9.

Cornford, F. M. 1912. *From Religion to Philosophy: A Study in the Origins of Western Speculation.* Cambridge: Cambridge University Press.

——— 1927. "The Origin of the Olympic Games." In J. Harrison, *Themis: A Study of the Social Origins of Greek Religion,* 2d ed. Cambridge: Cambridge University Press.

Coulson, W. 1988. "Geometric Pottery from Volimidia." *AJA* 92.53–74.

Coulson, W., and H. Kyrieleis, eds. 1992. *Proceedings of an International Symposium on the Olympic Games* (September 5–9, 1988). Athens: German Archaeological Institute.

Courbin, P. 1958. "Un fragment de cratère Protoargien." *BCH* 79.1–49.

——— 1966. *La Céramique géométrique de l'Argolide.* Paris: E. de Boccard.

——— 1974. *Tombes géométriques d'Argos,* vol. 1. Paris: J. Vrin.

——— 1977. Review of R. Hägg, *Die Gräber der Argolis,* vol. 1: *Revue Archéologique.* 326–30.

Couve, L. 1893. "Un vase proto-attique du Musée de la Société archéologique d'Athènes." *BCH* 17.25–30.

Crapanzano, V. 1980. *Tuhami: Portrait of a Moroccan.* Chicago: University of Chicago Press.

——— 1986. "Hermes' Dilemma: The Masking of Subversion in Ethnographic Description." In Clifford and Marcus 1986. 51–76.

Crawley, A. E. 1902. *The Mystic Rose: A Study of Primitive Marriage.* London: Macmillan Press.

Crönert, W. 1911. "De Lobone Argivo." In *XARITES: Friedrich Leo zum sechzigsten Geburtstag.* Berlin: Weidmann. 123–45.

Crotty, K. 1982. *Song and Action: The Victory Odes of Pindar.* Baltimore, Md.: Johns Hopkins University Press.

Darnton, R. 1985. *The Great Cat Massacre and Other Episodes in French Cultural History.* New York: Basic Books.

David, M. 1913a. Review of F. M. Cornford, *From Religion to Philosophy. L'Année Sociologique* 12.41–4.

——— 1913b. Review of J. E. Harrison, *Themis. L'Année Sociologique* 12.254–60.

Davies, J. K. 1981. *Wealth and the Power of Wealth in Classical Athens.* Salem, N.H.: Ayer.

Davison, J. A. 1955. "Pisistratus and Homer." *TAPA* 86.1–21.

    1958. "Notes on the Panathenaea." *JHS* 78.23–41.

    1962. "Addenda to 'Notes on the Panathenaea.' " *JHS* 82.141–2.

Day, J. W. 1989a. "Early Greek Dedicatory Epigrams as Substitutes for Ritual." Paper presented at the annual meeting of the American Philological Association, Boston, December 30, 1989.

    1989b. "Rituals in Stone: Early Greek Grave Epigrams and Monuments." *JHS* 109.16–28.

Defradas, J., ed. and trans. 1954. *Plutarque: Le banquet des Sept Sages*. Paris: Klincksieck.

Defradas, J. 1972. *Les thèmes de la propagande delphique,* 2d ed. Paris: Les belles lettres.

    1974. "ΔΙΟΡΘΩΣΑΙ ΛΟΓΟΝ: La Septième Olympique." In *Serta Turyniana: Studies in Greek Literature and Palaeography in Honor of Alexander Turyn*. Ed. J. Heller and J. K. Newman. Urbana: University of Illinois Press. 34–50.

Demakopoulou, K. 1968. "Μυκηναϊκὰ ἀγγεῖα ἐκ θαλαμοειδῶν τάφων περιοχῆς Ἁγίου Ἰωάννου Μονεμβασίας" [Mycenaean pottery from chamber tombs in the vicinity of Hagios Yiounnos, Monemvasia]. *ArchDelt* 23A. 145–94.

    1982. "Τὸ μυκηναικὸ ἱερὸ στὸ Ἀμυκλαῖο καὶ ἡ ΥΕ ΙΙΙ Γ περίοδος στὴ Λακωνία" [The Mycenaean Sanctuary at Amyklai and the LH III:C Period in Lakonia]. Ph.D. diss., University of Athens.

Demoulin, H. 1901. *Epimenide de Crète*. Brussels: Bibliothèque de la Faculté de philosophie et lettres de l'Université de Liège no. 12

Denniston, J. D. 1954. *The Greek Particles,* 2d ed. Oxford: Oxford University Press.

DePuma, R. D., and J. Penny Small, eds. Forthcoming. *Murlo and the Etruscans*. Madison: University of Wisconsin Press.

Desan, Suzanne. 1989. "Crowds, Community, and Ritual in the Work of E. P. Thompson and Natalie Davis." In Hunt 1989. 47–71.

Detienne, M. 1968. "La Phalange: Problèmes et controverses." In *Problèmes de la guerre en Grèce ancienne*. Ed. J.-P. Vernant. The Hague: Mouton. 119–42.

    1981a. *L'invention de la mythologie*. Paris: Gallimard.

    1981b. *The Gardens of Adonis*. Chicago: University of Chicago Press.

    1986a. "Apollo's Slaughterhouse." *Diacritics* 16.2.46–53.

    1986b. *The Creation of Mythology*. Trans. M. Cook. Chicago: University of Chicago Press.

Detienne, M., and J.-P. Vernant. 1974. *Les ruses de l'intelligence: La mètis des Grecs*. Paris: Flammarion.

Detienne, M., and J.-P. Vernant, eds. 1989. *The Cuisine of Sacrifice among the Greeks*. Chicago: University of Chicago Press.

Devillers, M. 1988. *An Archaic & Classical Votive Deposit from a Mycenaean Tomb at Thorikos* (Misc. Graeca Fasc. 8). Gent: Belgian Archaeological School in Greece.

Dickins, G. 1912. "The Growth of Spartan Policy." *JHS* 32.1–42.

Dicks, D. 1970. *Early Greek Astronomy to Aristotle*. Ithaca, N.Y.: Cornell University Press.

Diels, H., and W. Kranz, eds. 1951–2. *Die Fragmente der Vorsokratiker*. 6th ed. 3 vols. Zurich: Weidmann.

Dittenberger, W., and J. Purgold, eds. 1896. *Ausgrabungen von Olympia,* vol. 5. Berlin: Asher.

Donlan, W. 1981. "Scale, Value and Function in the Homeric Economy." *AJAH* 6.101–17.

    1982. "Reciprocities in Homer." *CW* 75.137–75.

    1989a. "The Unequal Exchange Between Glaucus and Diomedes in the Light of the Homeric Gift-Economy." *Phoenix* 43.1–15.

    1989b. "Homeric Temenos and the Land Economy of the Dark Age." *MH* 46.129–45.

Dörpfeld, W. 1935. *Alt Olympia,* vol. 1. Berlin: Mittler & Sohn.

Dorson, R. 1974. "The Eclipse of Solar Mythology." In *Myth: A Symposium*. Ed. T. Sebeok. Bloomington: University of Indiana Press. 25–63.

Dougherty, C. 1993. *The Poetics of Colonization: From City to Text in Archaic Greece*. New York: Oxford University Press.

Douglas, M. 1966. *Purity and Danger*. London: Routledge & Kegan Paul. Repr. 1985.

Doyle, W. 1980. *Origins of the French Revolution*. New York: Oxford University Press.

Drachmann, A. B., ed. 1964. *Scholia Vetera in Pindari Carmina,* 3 vols. Amsterdam: A. M. Hakkert.

Drews, R. 1983. *Basileus: The Evidence for Kingship in Geometric Greece*. New Haven, Conn.: Yale University Press.

Droop, J. P., et al. 1908–9. "I. Laconia: – I. – Excavations at Sparta, 1909. § 6. – The Menelaion." *BSA* 15.108–57

Duchemin, J. 1955. *Pindare: Poète et prophète*. Paris: Les belles lettres.

Dumézil, G. 1935. *Flamen-Brahman*. Paris: Geuthner.

Dunbabin, T. J. 1948. *The Western Greeks*. Oxford: Oxford University Press.

Dundes, A. 1975. *Analytic Essays in Folklore*. The Hague: Mouton.

Durkheim, E. 1912. *Les formes elémentaires de la vie religieuse*. Paris: F. Alcan. English trans. 1915.

Dwyer, K. 1982. *Moroccan Dialogues: Anthropology in Question*. Baltimore, Md.: Johns Hopkins University Press.

Dyer, R. 1969. "The Evidence for Apolline Purification Rituals at Delphi and Athens." *JHS* 89.38–56.

Eagleton, T. 1983. *Literary Theory: An Introduction*. Minneapolis: University of Minnesota Press.

Easterling, P. E., and J. V. Muir, eds. 1985. *Greek Religion and Society*. Cambridge: Cambridge University Press.

Ebert, J., ed. 1972. *Griechische Epigramme auf Sieger an gymnischen und hippischen Agonen*. Abhandlungen der sächsischen Akademie der Wissenschaften zu Leipzig, Phil.-hist. Kl. vol. 63, pt. 2.

Edelstein, E., and L. Edelstein. 1945. *Asclepius,* vols. 1 and 2. Baltimore, Md: Johns Hopkins University Press.

Edmunds, L. 1975. "Thucydides' Ethics as Reflected in the Description of Stasis (3.82–83)." *HSCP* 79.73–92

Edmunds, L., and R. Martin. 1977. "Thucydides 2.65.8: *Eleutherōs.*" *HSCP* 81.187–93.

Ehrenberg, V. 1950. "Origins of Democracy." *Historia* 1.515–48.

——— 1973. *From Solon to Socrates,* 2d ed. London: Methuen.

Ellis, J. R. 1979. "Characters in the Sicilian Expedition." *Quaderni di Storia,* Year 5. no. 10.39–69.

Else, G. F. 1957. "The Origin of ΤΡΑΓΩΙΔΙΑ." *Hermes* 85.27–34.

Engard, R. 1989. "Dance and Power in Bafut (Cameroon)." In *Creativity of Power*. Ed. W. Arens and I. Karp. Washington, D.C.: Smithsonian Institution Press. 129–62.

Engel, A. 1983. *From Clergyman to Don: The Rise of the Academic Profession in Nineteenth-Century Oxford*. Oxford: Oxford University Press.

Erbse, H. 1956. "Der erste Satz im Werke Herodots." In *Festschrift Bruno Snell*. Ed. H. Erbse. Munich: Beck. 209–22.

Eribon, D. 1991. *Michel Foucault*. Cambridge, Mass: Harvard University Press.

Euben, P., ed. 1986. *Greek Tragedy and Political Theory*. Berkeley and Los Angeles: University of California Press.

Evans-Pritchard, E. E. 1965. *Theories of Primitive Religion*. Oxford: Oxford University Press.

——— 1981. *A History of Anthropological Thought*. London: Faber & Faber.

Fagerström, K. 1988. "Finds, Function and Plan: A Contribution to the Interpretation of Iron Age Nichoria in Messenia." *OAth* 17.33–50.

Farnell, L. R. 1896–1909. *The Cults of the Greek States,* 5 vols. Oxford: Oxford University Press.

——— 1912. *The Higher Aspects of Greek Religion*. Oxford: Oxford University Press.

——— 1921. *Greek Hero Cults and the Ideas of Immortality*. Oxford: Oxford University Press.

——— 1934. *An Oxonian Looks Back*. Oxford: Oxford University Press.

Farrar, C. 1988. *The Origins of Democratic Thinking*. Cambridge: Cambridge University Press.

Fehling, D. 1985. *Die sieben Weisen und die frühgriechische Chronologie: Eine traditions-geschichtliche Studie*. Bern: P. Lang.

Ferguson, W. S. 1944. "The Attic Orgeones." *HTR* 37.61–130.

Finley, J. 1942. *Thucydides*. Cambridge, Mass.: Harvard University Press. Repr. 1963. Ann Arbor: University of Michigan Press.

Finley, M. I. 1952. *Studies in Land and Credit in Ancient Athens, 500–200 B.C.* New Brunswick, N.J.: Rutgers University Press. Repr. 1973. New York: Arno.

———. 1962. "Athenian Demagogues." *Past & Present* 21.3–24.

———. 1968. "Sparta." In *Problèmes de la guerre en Grèce ancienne*. Ed. J.-P. Vernant. Paris. 143–60. Repr. in Finley 1975. 161–77. Also in Finley 1981. 24–40.

———. 1975. *The Use and Abuse of History*. London: Chatto & Windus. Repr. 1986.

———. 1978. *The World of Odysseus*. London: Harmondsworth.

———. 1980. *Ancient Slavery and Modern Ideology*. London: Chatto & Windus.

———. 1981. *Economy and Society in Ancient Greece*. London: Chatto & Windus.

———. 1985. "Foreword." In Easterling and Muir 1985. xiii–xx.

Fish, S. 1989. "Commentary: The Young and the Restless." In Veeser 1989. 303–16.

Foley, A. 1988. *The Argolid, 800–600 B.C.: An Archaeological Survey*. SIMA 80. Göteborg: P. Astrom.

Foley, H. 1985. *Ritual Irony: Poetry and Sacrifice in Euripides*. Ithaca, N.Y.: Cornell University Press.

Fontenrose, J. 1968. "The Hero as Athlete." *CSCA* 1.73–104.

———. 1978. *The Delphic Oracle*. Berkeley and Los Angeles: University of California Press.

———. 1988. *Didyma: Apollo's Oracle, Cult, and Companions*. Berkeley and Los Angeles: University of California Press.

Forbes, C. A. 1952. "Crime and Punishment in Greek Athletics." *CJ* 47.169–73.

Ford, A. 1988. "The Classical Definition of ΡΑΨΩΔΙΑ." *CP* 83.300–7.

Ford, P., ed. and trans. 1977. *The Mabinogi and Other Medieval Welsh Tales*. Berkeley and Los Angeles: University of California Press.

Fornara, C. W. 1968. "The 'Tradition' about the Murder of Hipparchus." *Historia* 17.404–24.

Forrest, W. G. 1956. "The First Sacred War." *BCH* 80.33–52.

———. 1966. *The Emergence of Greek Democracy: The Character of Greek Politics, 800–440 B.C.* London: Weidenfeld & Nicholson.

———. 1980. *A History of Sparta, 950–192 B.C.*, 2d ed. London: Duckworth.

Foucault, M. 1972. *The Archaeology of Knowledge*. New York: Pantheon.

———. 1977. *Discipline and Punish: The Birth of the Prison*. Trans. A. Sheridan. New York: Pantheon.

Fowler, R. 1990. "Gilbert Murray." In *Classical Scholarship: A Biographical Encyclopedia*. Ed. W. W. Briggs and W. M. Calder III. New York: Garland. 321–34.

———. 1991. "Gilbert Murray: Four (Five) Stages of Greek Religion." In *The Cambridge Ritualists Reconsidered*. Ed. W. M. Calder III. Illinois Classical Studies suppl. vol. 2. Atlanta, Ga.: Scholar's Press. 79–95.

Fox, R. L. 1989. *Pagans and Christians*. New York: Viking.

Fox-Genovese, E. 1989. "Literary Criticism and the Politics of the New Historicism." In Veeser 1989. 213–24.

Fränkel, H. 1973. *Early Greek Poetry and Philosophy*. Trans. M. Hadas and J. Willis. New York: Harcourt.

Frazer, J. G. 1890. *The Golden Bough*, 12 vols. London: Macmillan Press.

———. 1898. *Pausanias' Description of Greece*, 6 vols. London: Macmillan Press.

———. 1935. *The Golden Bough*, part 3: *The Dying God*, vol. 4. New York: Macmillan.

Freeman, K. 1926. *The Work and Life of Solon, with a Translation of His Poems*. Cardiff: University of Wales Press.

French, E. 1989–90. "Olympia." *AR* 36.30.

——— 1990–1. "Olympia." *AR* 37.31.

Frödin, A., and A. Persson. 1938. *Asine: Results of the Swedish Excavations 1922–1930.* Stockholm: Generalstabens Litografiska Anstalts Forlag.

Frost, F. 1984. "The Athenian Military Before Cleisthenes." *Historia* 33.283–94.

——— 1985. "Toward a History of Peisistratid Athens." In *The Craft of the Ancient Historian.* Ed. J. Eadie and J. Ober. Lanham, Md.: University Press of America. 57–78.

Froude, J. A. 1871. *Short Studies on Great Subjects,* vol. 2. London: Longmans, Green.

Fustel de Coulanges, N. D. 1864. *La cité antique.* Eng. trans. 1873. Repr. 1980 with new introduction as *The Ancient City.* Baltimore, Md.: Johns Hopkins University Press.

Gagarin, M. 1981. *Drakon and Early Athenian Homicide Law.* New Haven, Conn.: Yale University Press.

Gagé, J. 1953. " 'Fornix Ratumenus': L'entrée 'iselastique' etrusque et la 'porta Triumphalis' de Rome." *Bulletin de la Faculté des Lettres de Strasbourg* 31.163–80.

Gallant, T. W. 1982. "Agricultural Systems, Land Tenure and the Reforms of Solon." *BSA* 77.111–24.

Gallavotti, C. 1977. "La dedica di Alcmeonide in Beozia e la cultura ateniese fra Solone e Tespi." *QUCC* 26.135–47.

——— 1979. *Metri e ritmi nelle iscrizioni greche* (= suppl. no. 2, *Boll. dei classici*). Rome: Accademia Nationale dei Lincei.

Gardiner, E. N. 1910. *Greek Athletic Sports and Festivals.* London: Macmillan Press.

——— 1916–17. "The Alleged Kingship of the Olympic Victor." *BSA* 22.85–106.

——— 1922. Review of W. W. Hyde, *Olympic Victor Monuments and Greek Athetic Art. JHS* 42.123–4.

——— 1955. *Athletics of the Ancient World,* 2d ed. Oxford: Oxford University Press.

Garland, R. 1985. *The Greek Way of Death.* London: Duckworth.

——— 1992. *Introducing New Gods: The Politics of Athenian Religion.* Ithaca, N.Y.: Cornell University Press.

Geary, P. 1978. *Furta Sacra.* Princeton, N.J.: Princeton University Press.

Gebhard, E., and F. Hemans. 1992. "University of Chicago Excavations at Isthmia, 1989: I." *Hesperia* 61.1–77.

Geertz, C. 1973. *The Interpretation of Cultures.* New York: Basic Books.

——— 1980. *Negara: The Theater State of Bali.* Princeton, N.J.: Princeton University Press.

——— 1983. *Local Knowledge: Further Essays in Interpretive Anthropology.* New York: Basic Books.

——— 1988. *Works and Lives: The Anthropologist as Author.* Stanford, Calif.: Stanford University Press.

Gellner, E. 1985. *Relativism and the Social Sciences.* Cambridge: Cambridge University Press.

Gentili, B. 1988. *Poetry and Its Public in Ancient Greece from Homer to the Fifth Century.* Trans. A. T. Cole. Baltimore, Md.: Johns Hopkins University Press.

Gerhard, E. 1843. *Etruskische und kampanische Vasenbilder.* Berlin: G. Reimer.

Gernet, L. 1932. *La génie grec dans la réligion.* Paris: La Renaissance du livre.

——— 1955. "Delphes et la pensée religieuse en Grèce." *Annales ESC* 10.526–42.

——— 1981. *The Anthropology of Ancient Greece.* Trans. B. Nagy and J. Hamilton. Baltimore, Md.: Johns Hopkins University Press.

Gero, J., and M. Conkey, eds. 1991. *Engendering Archaeology.* Oxford: Oxford University Press.

Giddens, A. 1977. *Durkheim.* Hassocks: Harvester.

——— 1981. *A Contemporary Critique of Historical Materialism.* Oxford: Oxford University Press.

Gilbert, F. 1965. "The Professionalization of History in the Nineteenth Century." In *History.* Ed. J. Higham, L. Krieger, and F. Gilbert. Englewood Cliffs, N.J.: Prentice-Hall. 320–39.

Gildersleeve, B. L., ed. 1890. *Pindar: The Olympian and Pythian Odes*. New York: American Book.

Gnoli, G., and J.-P. Vernant, eds. 1982. *La mort, les morts dans les sociétés anciennes*. Cambridge: Cambridge University Press.

Godechot, J. 1970. *The Taking of the Bastille, July 14, 1789*. Trans. J. Stewart. London: Faber & Faber.

Goldhill, S. 1986. *Reading Greek Tragedy*. Cambridge: Cambridge University Press.

Goldstein, J., and J. Boyer, eds. 1988. *University of Chicago Readings in Western Civilization, vol. 8: Nineteenth-Century Europe – Liberalism and Its Critics*. Chicago: University of Chicago Press.

Gomme, A. W. 1956. *A Historical Commentary on Thucydides*, vol. 2: *The Ten Years' War*, books II–III. Oxford: Oxford University Press.

———. 1959. *A Historical Commentary on Thucydides*, vol 1: *Introduction and Commentary on Book 1*. Oxford: Oxford University Press.

Gomme, A. W., A. Andrewes, and K. J. Dover 1981. *A Historical Commentary on Thucydides*, vol. 5: book VIII. Oxford: Oxford University Press.

Gonda, J. 1975. *Vedic Literature (Samhitas and Brahmanas)*. Wiesbaden: Harrassowitz.

Gooch, G. P. 1913. *History and Historians in the Nineteenth Century*. London: Longmans, Green. Repr. 1959. Boston: Beacon.

Goody, J. 1961. "Religion and Ritual – The Definitional Problem." *British Journal of Sociology* 12.142–64.

———. 1962. *Death, Property, and the Ancestors*. Stanford, Calif.: Stanford University Press.

Goody, J., and I. Watt. 1968. "The Consequences of Literacy." In *Literacy in Traditional Societies*. Ed. J. Goody. Cambridge: Cambridge University Press. 27–68.

Gould, J. 1985. "On Making Sense of Greek Religion." In Easterling and Muir 1985. 1–33.

Graham, A. J. 1964. *Colony and Mother City in Ancient Greece*. New York: Barnes & Noble.

———. 1978. "The Foundation of Thasos." *BSA* 73.61–98.

———. 1982. "The Colonial Expansion of Greece." In *CAH.²* vol. 3, pt. 3. Ed. J. Boardman and N.G.L. Hammond. Cambridge: Cambridge University Press. 83–162.

Greenblatt, S. 1980. *Renaissance Self-fashioning from More to Shakespeare*. Chicago: University of Chicago Press.

Greenblatt, S., ed. 1988a. *Representing the English Renaissance*. Berkeley and Los Angeles: University of California Press.

Greenblatt, S. 1988b. *Shakespearean Negotiations: The Circulation of Social Energy in Renaissance England*. Berkeley and Los Angeles: University of California Press.

Griffin, M. 1984. *Nero: The End of a Dynasty*. New Haven, Conn.: Yale University Press.

Griffiths, A. H. 1976. "What Syagrus Said: Herodotus 7.159." *LCM* 1.23–34.

———. 1989. "Was Kleomenes Mad?" In Powell. 1989. 51–78.

Gross, W.H. 1969. *Quas iconicas Vocant: Zum Porträtcharakter der Statuen dreimaliger olympischer Sieger*. Gött-Nachr. Phil-hist. Kl. 1969, no. 3. Göttingen: Vandenhoeck & Ruprecht.

Gurlitt, W. 1890. *Über Pausanias*. Graz: Leuschner & Lubensky.

Hägg, R. 1974. *Die Gräber der Argolis*, vol. 1 (*Boreas* 4.1). Stockholm: Almqvist & Wiksell.

———. 1982. "Zur Stadtwerdung des dorischen Argos." In *Paläst und Hütte*. Ed. D. Papenfuss and V. Strockas. Mainz: P. von Zabern. 297–307.

Hägg, R., ed. 1983a. *The Greek Renaissance of the 8th Century B.C.: Tradition and Innovation*. Stockholm: Svenska Institutet i Athen.

Hägg, R. 1983b. "Burial Customs and Social Differentiation in 8th-Cent. Argos." In Hägg 1983a. 27–31.

———. 1983c. "Funerary Meals in the Geometric Necropolis at Asine?" In Hägg 1983a. 189–94.

———. 1987. "Gifts to the Heroes in Geometric and Archaic Greece." In *Gifts to the Gods* (*Boreas* 15). Ed. T. Linders et al. Uppsala: Academia Ubsaliensis. 93–9.

Hägg, R., N. Marinatos, and G. Nordquist, eds. 1988. *Early Greek Cult Practice*. Stockholm: Svenska Institutet i Athen.

Hague, R. 1983. "Ancient Greek Wedding Songs: The Tradition of Praise." *Journal of Folklore Research* 20.131–43.

Hainsworth, J. 1987. "Classical Archaeology?" In *Studies in Mycenaean & Classical Greek Presented to John Chadwick (Minos 20–2)*. Ed. J. Killen et al. Salamanca: University of Salamanca. 211–20.

Hamilton, R. 1989. "Alkman and the Athenian Artkteia." *Hesperia* 58.449–72.

Hammond, N. G. L. 1959. *A History of Greece to 322 B.C.* Oxford: Oxford University Press.

Hansen, M. H. 1986. "The Origin of the Term demokratia." *LCM* 11.35–6.

——— 1989. "Solonian Democracy in Fourth-Century Athens." *C & M* 40.71–99.

——— 1990. "The Size of the Council of the Areopagos and Its Social Composition in the Fourth Century B.C." *C & M* 41.55–61.

Hansen, P. A. 1983. *Carmina Epigraphica Graeca (Saec. VIII–V)*. Berlin: de Gruyter.

——— 1989. *Carmina Epigraphica Graeca (Saec. IV A. Chr. N.)*. Berlin: de Gruyter.

Hanson, V. D. 1989. *The Western Way of War*. New York: Knopf.

Hanson, V. D., ed. 1991. *Hoplites: The Classical Greek Battle Experience*. London: Routledge & Kegan Paul.

Harrison, J. E. 1903. *Prolegomena to the Study of Greek Religion*. Cambridge: Cambridge University Press.

——— 1912. *Themis: A Study of the Social Origins of Greek Religion*. Repr. 1927. Cambridge: Cambridge University Press.

——— 1921. *Reminiscences of a Student's Life*. London: Hogarth. Repr. in *Arion* 4(1965). 312–46.

Hartog, F. 1980. *Le miroir d'Hérodote*. Paris: Gallimard.

——— 1988. *The Mirror of Herodotus: The Representation of the Other in the Writing of History*. Trans. J. Lloyd. Berkeley and Los Angeles: University of California Press.

Haslam, M. 1990. "Pericles poeta." *CP* 85.33.

Häusle, H. 1979. "ΖΩΟΠΟΙΕΙΝ – ΥΦΙΣΤΑΝΑΙ: Eine Studie der frühgriechischen inschriftlichen Ich-Rede der Gegenstände." In *Serta Philologica Aenipontana*, vol. 3. Ed. R. Muth and G. Pfohl. Innsbruck: Sprachwissenschaftliche Institut der Leopold-Franzens-Universität. 23–139.

Hawkes, C. F. C. 1954. "Archaeological Theory and Method: Some Suggestions from the Old World." *American Anthropologist* 56.155–68.

Heath, M. 1988. "Receiving the κῶμος: The Context and Performance of Epinician." *AJP* 109.180–95.

Herington, C. J. 1985. *Poetry into Drama*. Berkeley and Los Angeles: University of California Press.

Herman, G. 1987. *Ritualised Friendship and the Greek City*. Cambridge: Cambridge University Press.

Herrmann, H.-V. 1972. *Olympia: Heiligtum und Wettkampfstätte*. Munich: Hirmer.

——— 1980. "Pelops in Olympia." In Στέλε. Τόμος εἰς Μνήμην Ν. Κοντολέοντος. [Stele. Volume in memory of N. Kontoleon]. Athens: Association of the Friends of N. Kontoleon; 59–74.

Herrmann, P. 1975. "Eine Kaiserkunde der Zeit Marc Aurels aus Milet." *Istanbuler Mitteilungen* 25.149–66.

Heubeck, A., and A. Hoekstra. 1989. *A Commentary on Homer's Odyssey*, vol. 2: *Books ix–xxiv*. Oxford: Oxford University Press.

Heurgon, J. 1957. *Trois études sur le "ver sacrum."* Coll. Latomus 26. Brussels: Latomus.

Heyck, T. W. 1982. *The Transformation of Intellectual Life in Victorian England*. London: Croom Helm. Repr. 1989. Chicago: University of Chicago Press.

Hicks, R. D., ed. 1925. *Diogenes Laertius: Lives of Eminent Philosophers*, vol. 1. Cambridge, Mass.: Harvard University Press.

Hignett, C. 1952. *A History of the Athenian Constitution to the End of the Fifth Century B.C.* Oxford: Oxford University Press.

Hiller, E. 1878. "Die literarische Tätigkeit der sieben Weisen." *RhM* n.f. 33.518–29.

Hirsch, A. 1981. *The French New Left.* Boston: South End Press.

Hirsch, M. 1925. "Die athenischen Tyrannenmorder in Geschichtsschreibung und Volkslegende." *Klio* 20.129–67.

Hodder, I. 1986a. *Archaeology as Long-Term History.* Cambridge: Cambridge University Press.

——— 1986b. *Reading the Past: Current Approaches to Interpretation in Archaeology.* Cambridge: Cambridge University Press.

——— 1987. "The Contextual Analysis of Symbolic Meanings." In *The Archaeology of Contextual Meanings.* Ed. I. Hodder. Cambridge: Cambridge University Press. 1–10.

——— 1991a. "Interpretive Archaeology and Its Role." *AmAnt* 56.7–18.

——— 1991b. *Reading the Past,* 2d ed. Cambridge: Cambridge University Press.

Hodkinson, S. 1983. "Social Order and the Conflict of Values in Classical Sparta." *Chiron* 13.239–81.

Hoesterey, I., ed. 1991. *Zeitgeist in Babel.* Bloomington: University of Indiana Press.

Hollinger, D. A. 1991. "Postmodernist Theory and Wissenschaftliche Practice." *AHR* 96.688–92.

Hönle, A. 1972. *Olympia in der Politik der griechischen Staatenwelt von 776 bis zum Ende des 5. Jahrhunderts.* Bebenhausen: Lothar Rosch.

Hooker, J. T. 1985. "A Reading of the Seventh Olympian." *BICS* 32.63–70.

——— 1989. "Spartan Propaganda." In Powell 1989.122–41.

Hope, R. 1930. *The Book of Diogenes Laertius: Its Spirit and Method.* New York: Columbia University Press.

Hornblower, S. 1987. *Thucydides.* Baltimore, Md.: Johns Hopkins University Press.

——— 1991. *A Commentary on Thucydides, vol. 1: Books I–III.* Oxford: Oxford University Press.

How, W. W., and J. Wells. 1928. *A Commentary on Herodotus,* 2 vols. Oxford: Oxford University Press.

Howe, J. 1977. "Carrying the Village: Cuna Political Metaphors." In *The Social Use of Metaphor: Essays on the Anthropology of Rhetoric.* Ed. J. Sapir and J. Crocker. Philadelphia: University of Pennsylvania Press. 132–63.

Humphreys, S. C. 1978. *Anthropology and the Greeks.* London: Routledge & Kegan Paul.

——— 1980. "Family Tombs and Tomb Cult in Classical Athens: Tradition or Traditionalism?" *JHS* 100.96–126. Repr. Humphreys 1983b.

——— 1981. "Death and Time." In *Mortality and Immortality: The Anthropology and Archaeology of Death.* Ed. S. C. Humphreys and H. King. London: Academic Press. 261–83.

——— 1983a. "The Evolution of Legal Process in Ancient Attica." In *Tria Corda: Scritti in onore di A. Momigliano,* vol. 1. Ed. E. Gabba. Como: Edizioni New Press. 229–51.

——— 1983b. *The Family, Women, and Death.* London: Routledge & Kegan Paul.

Hunt, L., ed. 1989. *The New Cultural History.* Berkeley and Los Angeles: University of California Press.

Hunter, V. 1982. *Past and Process in Herodotus and Thucydides.* Princeton, N.J.: Princeton University Press.

——— 1988. "Thucydides and the Sociology of the Crowd." *CJ* 84.17–30.

——— 1990. "Gossip and the Politics of Reputation in Classical Athens." *Phoenix* 44.299–325.

Hurwit, J. 1985a. *The Art and Culture of Early Greece, 1100–480 B.C.* Ithaca, N.Y.: Cornell University Press.

——— 1985b. "The Dipylon Shield Once More." *CA* 4.121–6.

Huxley, G. 1962. *Early Sparta.* London: Faber & Faber.

——— 1969. *Greek Epic Poetry from Eumelos to Panyassis.* Cambridge, Mass.: Harvard University Press.

——— 1975. "Cretan Paiawones." *GRBS* 16.119–24.

——— 1979. "Bones for Orestes." *GRBS* 20.145–8.

245

1983. "Herodotos on Myth and Politics in Early Sparta." *Proceedings of the Royal Irish Academy* 1–16.

Hyde, W. W. 1921. *Olympic Victor Monuments and Greek Athletic Art*. Washington, D.C.: Carnegie Institution of Washington.

Iakovides, S. 1962. "I Mykinaiki Akropolis ton Athinon." Ph.D. diss., University of Athens.

Immerwahr, H. R. 1966. *Form and Thought in Herodotus*. Cleveland, Ohio: Press of Western Reserve University.

Instone, S. 1986. Review of D. C. Young, *The Olympic Myth of Greek Amateur Athletics*. *JHS* 106.238–9.

Jacoby, F. 1923. *Die Fragmente der Griechischen Historiker*. Berlin: Weidmann.

1949. *Atthis*. Oxford: Oxford University Press.

Jaeger, W. 1948. *Aristotle: Fundamentals of the History of his Development*, 2d ed. Trans. R. Robinson. Oxford: Oxford University Press.

Jakobson, R. 1966. *Selected Writings*, vol. 4: *Slavic Epic Studies*. The Hague: Mouton.

James, P., I. Thorpe, N. Kokkinos, R. Morkot, and J. Frankish. 1991a. *Centuries of Darkness: A Challenge to the Conventional Chronology of Old World Archaeology*. London: Cape.

James, P., et al. 1991b. "Review Feature: Centuries of Darkness." *Cambridge Archaeological Journal* 1.2.227–53.

Jameson, F. 1991. *Postmodernism, or the Cultural Logic of Late Capitalism*. Durham, N.C.: Duke University Press.

Jameson, M. H. 1965. "Notes on the Sacrificial Calendar from Erchia." *BCH* 89.154–72.

1986. "Sophocles, Antigone, 1005–1032: An Illustration." In *Greek Tragedy and Its Legacy*. Ed. M. Cropp, E. Fantham, and S. Scully. Calgary: University of Calgary Press. 59–65.

1988. "Sacrifice and Ritual: Greece." In *Civilization of the Ancient Mediterranean*, vol. 2. Ed. M. Grant and R. Kitzinger. New York: Scribner's. 959–79.

1990. "Perseus, Hero of Mykenai." In *Celebrations of Death and Divinity in the Bronze Age Argolid* (Proceedings of the Sixth International Symposium at the Swedish Institute at Athens June, 11–13, 1988). Ed. R. Hägg and C. Nordquist. Stockholm: P. Astrom. 213–223.

Jameson, M. H., et al. 1975. "Αρχαικαι Επιγραφαι εκ Τιρυνθος" [Archaic inscriptions from Tiryns] *AE*.150–205.

Jantzen, U. 1975. *Führer durch Tiryns*. Athens: Deutsches Archaeologisches Institut Athen.

Jeffery, L. H. 1976. *Archaic Greece: The City-States, c. 700–500 B.C.* London: Ernest Benn.

1990. *The Local Scripts of Archaic Greece*, 2d ed. Oxford: Oxford University Press.

Johansen, K. F. 1967. *"The Iliad" in Early Greek Art*. Copenhagen: Munksgaard.

Johnston, A. W. 1987. "IG II² 2311 and the Number of Panathenaic Amphorae." *BSA* 82.125–9.

Jones, A. H. M. 1967. *Sparta*. Oxford: Oxford University Press.

Jones, R. A. 1991. "La genèse du système? The Origins of Durkheim's Sociology of Religion." In *The Cambridge Ritualists Reconsidered*. Ed. W. M. Calder III. Illinois Classical Studies suppl. vol. 2. Atlanta, Ga.: Scholar's Press. 97–121.

Jüthner, J. 1898. "Siegerkranz und Siegerbinde." *Jahreshefte des Österreichischen Archäologischen Instituts in Wien* 1.42–8.

Kannicht, R. 1989. "Thalia – Über den Zusammenhang zwischen Fest und Poesie bei den Griechen." In *Das Fest*. Ed. W. Haug and R. Warning. Munich: Wilhelm Fink. 29–52.

Kearns, E. 1985. "Change and Continuity in Religious Structures after Cleisthenes." In *Crux: Essays Presented to G.E.M. de Ste. Croix*. Ed. P. Cartledge and F. D. Harvey. Exeter: Imprint Academic. 188–207.

1989. *The Heroes of Attica*. BICS suppl. 57. London: Institute of Classical Studies.

Keesing, R. 1987. "Anthropology as Interpretive Quest." *Current Anthropology* 28.161–76.

Keil, J., and G. Maresch. 1960. "Epigraphische Nachlese zu Miltners Ausgrabungsberichten aus Ephesus." *Jahreshefte Österr. Arch. Instituts* 45, Beiblatt, coll. 75–100.

Kellner, D. 1989. Ed. *Postmodernism: Jameson Critique.* Washington, D.C.: Maisonneuve Press.

Kertzer, D. 1988. *Ritual, Politics and Power.* New Haven, Conn.: Yale University Press.

Kiechle, F. 1963. *Lakonien und Sparta.* Munich: Beck.

Kindstrand, J. 1981. *Anacharsis: The Legend and the Apophthegmata.* Studia Graeca Upsaliensia 16. Uppsala: Almqvist & Wiksell.

Kirk, G. S. 1985. *"The Iliad": A Commentary.* Cambridge: Cambridge University Press.

Kleinknecht, H. 1937. "Zur Parodie des Gottmenschentums bei Aristophanes." *Archiv für Religionswissenschaft* 34.294–313.

Kloppenberg, J. T. 1989. "Objectivity and Historicism: A Century of American Historical Writing." *AHR* 94.1011–30.

Knox, B. M. W. 1968. "Silent Reading in Antiquity." *GRBS* 9.421–35.

Kolb, F. 1977. "Die Bau-, Religions- und Kulturpolitik der Peisistratiden." *JdI* 92.99–138.

Konstan, D. 1983. "The Stories in Herodotus' Histories: Book I." *Helios* 10.1–22.

——— 1987. "Persians, Greeks and Empire." *Arethusa* 20.59–73.

Kopff, E. C. 1990. "Paul Shorey." In *Classical Scholarship: A Biographical Encyclopedia.* Ed. W. W. Briggs and W. M. Calder III. New York: Garland. 447–53.

Korres, G. 1977. Τύμβοι, θόλοι, καὶ ταφικοὶ κύκλοι τῆς Μεσσηνίας [Mounds, tholoi, and funerary circles of Messenia]. In Acts of the First International Congress of Peloponnesian Studies, vol. 2. Athens. 337–69.

——— 1981–2. Η προβληματικὴ διὰ τὴν μεταγενεστέραν χρῆσιν τῶν μυκηναικῶν τάφων Μεσσηνίας [The problem of the later use of Mycenaean Tombs of Messenia]. In Acts of the Second International Congress of Peloponnesian Studies, vol. 2. Athens. 363–450.

Krause, C. 1972. *Eretria,* vol. 4: *Das Westtor. Ergebnisse der Ausgrabungen, 1964–68.* Bern: Francke.

——— 1981. "Zur städtebaulichen Entwicklung Eretrias." *ASAA* 69.175–85.

Krause, J. H. 1838. *Olympia.* Vienna: F. Beck.

Krauskopf, I. 1977. "Eine attische schwarzfigurige Hydria in Heidelberg." *AA* 92.13–37.

Kron, U. 1976. *Die zehn attischen Phylenheroen. Geschichte, Mythos, Kult und Darstellungen. AM* suppl. 5. Berlin: Mann.

Kübler, K. 1954. *Kerameikos.* vol. 5.1: *Ergebnisse der Aufgrabungen.* Berlin: de Gruyter.

Kuper, A. 1983. *Anthropology and Anthropologists,* 2d ed. London: Routledge & Kegan Paul.

Kurke, L. 1991. *The Traffic in Praise: Pindar and the Poetics of Social Economy.* Ithaca, N.Y.: Cornell University Press.

Kyle, D. G. 1985. Review of D. C. Young, *The Olympic Myth of Greek Amateur Athletics: Echos du Monde classique/Classical Views* 29 (n.s. 4).134–44.

——— 1987. *Athletics in Ancient Athens.* Leiden: E. J. Brill.

Kyrieleis, H. 1987. "Offerings of the 'Common Man' in the Heraion of Samos." In *Early Greek Cult Practice.* Ed. R. Hägg. Stockholm: P. Astrom. 215–21.

——— 1992. "Neue Ausgrabungen in Olympia." In Coulson and Kyrieleis 1992. 19–37.

La Fontaine, J. 1985. *Initiation.* Manchester: Manchester University Press.

Lakoff, G., and M. Johnson. 1980. *Metaphors We Live By.* Chicago: University of Chicago Press.

Lakoff, G., and M. Turner. 1989. *More Than Cool Reason: A Field Guide to Poetic Metaphor.* Chicago: University of Chicago Press.

Lalonde, G. 1968. "A Fifth Century Hieron Southwest of the Athenian Agora." *Hesperia* 37.123–33.

Lambert, S. D. 1986. "Herodotus, the Cylonian Conspiracy and the 'prytaneis ton naukraron.'" *Historia* 35.105–12.

Lamberton, R. 1983. *Porphyry on the Cave of the Nymphs.* Barrytown, N.Y.: Station Hill Press.

Lambrinoudakis, V. 1983. Ἀνασκαφαὶ Νάξου [Excavations on Naxos]. *Ergon* 77–9.
   1984. Ἀνασκαφαὶ Νάξου. *Ergon* 72–9.
   1985. Ἀνασκαφαὶ Νάξου *Ergon* 56–61.
   1987. "Veneration of Ancestors in Geometric Naxos." In *Early Greek Cult Practice.* Ed.
      R. Hägg. Stockholm: P. Astrom. 235–46.
Lang, A. 1898. *The Making of Religion,* 1st ed. London: Longmans, Green.
Langdon, M. K. 1976. *A Sanctuary of Zeus on Mt. Hymettos. Hesperia* suppl. vol. 16.
      Princeton, N.J.: American School of Classical Studies at Athens.
Lanza, D. 1977. *Il tiranno e il suo pubblico.* Turin: Einaudi.
Lattimore, S. 1987. "The Nature of Early Greek Victor Statues." In *Coroebus Triumphs:
      The Alliance of Sport and the Arts.* Ed. S. J. Bandy. San Diego, Calif.: San Diego
      State University Press. 245–56.
Lauter, H. 1985a. *Der Kultplatz auf dem Turkovuni. AM* suppl. 12. Berlin: Mann.
   1985b. *Lathuresa: Beiträge zur Architektur und Siedlungsgeschichte in spätgeometrischer
      Zeit.* Mainz: P. von Zabern.
Lavelle, B. M. 1991. "The Compleat Angler: Observations on the Rise of Peisistratos in
      Herodotus (1.59–64)." *CQ* 41.317–24.
Leahy, D. M. 1955. "The Bones of Teisamenos." *Historia* 4.26–38.
   1958. "The Spartan Defeat at Orchomenos." *Phoenix* 12.141–65.
Lee, H. 1988. "The 'First' Olympic Games of 776 B.C." In *The Archaeology of the
      Olympics.* Ed. W. Raschke. Madison: University of Wisconsin Press. 110–18.
Lefkowitz, M. 1981. *The Lives of the Greek Poets.* Baltimore, Md.: Johns Hopkins University
      Press.
Lehmann, F. R. 1915. "Mana: Eine begriffgeschichtliche Untersuchung auf ethnologischer
      Grundlage." Ph.D. diss., University of Leipzig.
Leighton, R. 1989. "Antiquarianism and Prehistory in West Mediterranean Islands." *AntJ*
      69.183–294.
Leisegang, H. 1950. *RE* 20.2, s.v. "Platon." Coll. 2342–2537.
Lesky, A. 1978. *RE* suppl. 11, s.v. "Homeros." Coll. 687–846.
Levine, P. 1986. *The Amateur and the Professional: Antiquarians, Historians and Archae-
      ologists in Victorian England, 1838–1886.* Cambridge: Cambridge University Press.
Lewis, D. M. 1963. "Cleisthenes and Attica." *Historia* 12.22–40.
Lewis, G. 1980. *Day of Shining Red.* Cambridge: Cambridge University Press.
Liddell, H. G., R. Scott, and H. S. Jones. 1940. *A Greek–English Lexicon.* 9th ed. Oxford:
      Oxford University Press.
Linforth, I. M. 1919. *Solon the Athenian.* Berkeley and Los Angeles: University of California
      Press.
Lloyd, G. E. R. 1979. *Magic, Reason, and Experience.* Cambridge: Cambridge University
      Press.
Lloyd-Jones, H., and P. Parsons. 1983. *Supplementum Hellenisticum.* Berlin: de Gruyter.
Lonis, R. 1979. *Guerre et religion en Grèce a l'époque classique: Recherches sur les rites,
      les dieux, l'idéologie de la victoire.* Centre de recherches d'histoire ancienne, vol. 33.
      Paris: Les belles lettres.
Loraux, N. 1981. *Les enfants d'Athéna.* Paris: F. Maspero.
   1984. "Solon au milieu de la lice." In *Aux origines de l'hellenisme: La Crète et la Grèce
      – Hommage à Henri van Effenterre.* Paris: Publications de la Sorbonne. 199–214.
   1986. *The Invention of Athens: The Funeral Oration in the Classical City.* Trans. A.
      Sheridan. Cambridge, Mass.: Harvard University Press.
   1987. *Tragic Ways of Killing a Woman.* Trans. A. Forster. Cambridge, Mass.: Harvard
      University Press.
   1988. "Solon et la voix de l'écrit." In *Les pouvoirs de l'écriture.* Ed. M. Detienne. Lille:
      Presses universitaires de Lille. 95–129.
Lorimer, H. L. 1903. "The Country Cart of Ancient Greece." *JHS* 23.132–51.
Lyotard, J.-F. 1984. *The Postmodern Condition.* Minneapolis: University of Minnesota Press.

Macan, R. W., ed. 1895. *Herodotus: The Fourth, Fifth, and Sixth Books,* 2 vols. London: Macmillan Press.

1908. *Herodotus: The Seventh, Eighth, and Ninth Books,* 2 vols. London: Macmillan Press.

MacKinnon, C. A. 1989. *Toward a Feminist Theory of the State.* Cambridge, Mass.: Harvard University Press.

Maine, H. 1883. *Dissertations on Early Law and Custom.* London: J. Murray.

Malkin, I. 1987. *Religion and Colonization in Ancient Greece.* Leiden: E. J. Brill.

Mallwitz, A. 1972. *Olympia und seine Bauten.* Munich: Prestel.

1981. "Kritisches zur Architektur Griechenlands im 8. und 7. Jhs." *AA* 599–642.

1988. "Cult and Competition Locations in Olympia." In *The Archaeology of the Olympics.* Ed. W. Raschke. Madison: University of Wisconsin Press. 79–109.

Manfredini, M., and L. Piccirilli. 1977. *La vita di Solone.* Verona: Mondadori.

Manganaro, M., ed. 1990. *Modernist Anthropology: From Fieldwork to Text.* Princeton, N.J.: Princeton University Press.

Mangelsdorff, E. 1913. *Das lyrische Hochzeitsgedicht bei den Griechen und Römern.* Hamburg: Druck der Druckerei-Gesellschaft Hartung.

Mango, C. 1963. "Antique Statuary and the Byzantine Beholder." *Dumbarton Oaks Papers* 17.53–75.

Manville, P. B. 1980. "Solon's Law of Stasis and Atimia in Archaic Athens." *TAPA* 110.213–21.

1990. *The Origins of Citizenship in Ancient Athens.* Princeton, N.J.: Princeton University Press.

Marett, R. R. 1909. *The Threshold of Religion.* London: Methuen.

Marinatos, S. 1953. Περὶ τοὺς νέους βασιλικοὺς τάφους τῶν Μυκηνῶν [Concerning the new royal tombs of Mycenae]. In *Geras A. Keramopoullou.* Athens: Myrtide. 54–88.

Markwald, G. 1986. *Die homerischen Epigramme: Sprachliche und inhaltliche Untersuchungen.* Königstein/Ts.: Hain.

Martin, R. 1951. *Recherches sur l'agora grecque: Etudes d'histoire et d'architecture urbaines.* Paris: E. de Boccard.

1975. "Problèmes de topographie et d'évolution urbaine." In *Contribution à l'étude de la société et de la colonisation eubéennes.* Cahiers du Centre J. Bérard no. 2. Naples: Centre Jean Bérard. 48–52.

Martin, R. P. 1989. *The Language of Heroes: Speech and Performance in the "Iliad."* Ithaca, N.Y.: Cornell University Press.

Martina, A. 1968. *Solon, Testimonia Veterum.* Rome: In Aedibus Athenaei.

Marx, K. 1977a. "Preface to *A Critique of Political Economy.*" 1859. Trans. in *Karl Marx: Selected Writings.* Ed. D. McLellan. Oxford: Oxford University Press. 388–92.

1977b. "Towards a Critique of Hegel's Philosophy of Right." 1844. Trans. in *Karl Marx: Selected Writings.* Ed. D. McLellan. Oxford: Oxford University Press. 63–73.

Mauss, M. 1972. *A General Theory of Magic.* Trans. R. Brain. New York: Norton.

Mayor, A. 1989. "Paleocryptozoology: A Call for Collaboration Between Classicists and Cryptozoologists." *Cryptozoology* 8.12–26.

Mazarakis, A. 1985. "Contribution à l'étude de l'architecture religieuse grecque des âges obscurs." *AC* 54.5–84.

1987. "Geometric Eretria." *AntK* 16.1–10.

Mazzarino, S. 1947. *Fra oriente e occidente: Ricerche di storia greca archaica.* Florence: La Nuove Italia.

McCargar, D. J. 1974. "Isagoras, Son of Teisandros, and Isagoras, Eponymous Archon of 508/7: A Case of Mistaken Identity." *Phoenix* 28.275–81.

McDonald, W., et al. 1983. *Excavations at Nichoria in Southwest Greece,* vol. 3: *Dark Age and Byzantine Occupation.* Minneapolis: University of Minnesota Press.

McGregor, M. 1956. "The Politics of the Historian Thucydides." *Phoenix* 10.93–102.

McLellan, D. 1973. *Karl Marx: His Life and Thought.* London: Macmillan Press.

McLennan, J. F. 1876. *Studies in Ancient History*. London: Bernhard Quadritch.
   1885. *The Patriarchal Theory*. London: Macmillan Press.
Megill, A. 1991. "Fragmentation and the Future of Historiography." *AHR* 96.693–8.
Meier, C. 1990. *The Greek Discovery of Politics*. Trans. D. McLintock. Cambridge, Mass.: Harvard University Press.
Metzger, H. 1975. "Ekphora, convoi funèbre, cortège de dignitaires en Grèce et à la périphérie du monde grec." *RA* 209–20.
Meuli, K. 1975. "Griechische Opferbräuche." In *K. Meuli, Gesammelte Schriften*, vol. 2. Basel: Scwabe. 907–1021.
Michell, H. 1952. *Sparta*. Cambridge: Cambridge University Press.
Millett, P. 1989. "Patronage and Its Avoidance in Classical Athens." In *Patronage in Ancient Society*. Ed. A. Wallace-Hadrill. London: Routledge & Kegan Paul. 15–47.
   1991. *Lending and Borrowing in Ancient Athens*. Cambridge: Cambridge University Press.
Mitchiner, J. 1982. *Traditions of the Seven Ṛṣis*. Delhi: Motilal Banarsidass.
Momigliano, A. 1977. *Essays in Ancient and Modern Historiography*. Oxford: Oxford University Press.
Momigliano, A., and S. C. Humphreys. 1980. "Foreword." In Fustel de Coulanges [1864] 1980. ix–xxiii.
Moon, W., ed. 1983. *Ancient Greek Art and Iconography*. Madison: University of Wisconsin Press.
Moretti, L. 1953. *Iscrizioni agonistiche greche*. Rome: A. Signorelli.
   1957. *Olympionikai, i vincitori negli antichi agoni olimpici*, ser. 8, vol. 8, fasc. 2. Rome: Accademia nazionale dei Lincei.
Morgan, C. A. 1988. "Corinth, the Corinthian Gulf and Western Greece During the Eighth Century B.C." *BSA* 83.313–38.
   1990. *Athletes and Oracles: The Transformation of Olympia and Delphi in the Eighth Century B.C.* Cambridge: Cambridge University Press.
Morgan, C. A., and T. Whitelaw. 1991. "Pots and Politics: Ceramic Evidence for the Rise of the Greek State." *AJA* 95.79–108.
Morris, I. 1986. "The Use and Abuse of Homer." *CA* 5.81–138
   1987. *Burial and Ancient Society*. Cambridge: Cambridge University Press.
   1988. "Tomb Cult and the Greek Renaissance: The Past in the Present in the 8th C." *Antiquity* 62.750–61.
   1989a. "Attitudes Toward Death in Archaic Greece." *CA* 8.297–320.
   1989b. "Circulation, Deposition and the Formation of the Greek Iron Age." *Man* n.s. 24.501–19.
   1991a. "The Archaeology of Ancestors: The Saxe–Goldstein Hypothesis Revisited." *Cambridge Archaeological Journal* 1.2.147–69.
   1991b. "The Early Polis as City and State." In Rich and Wallace Hadrill 1991. 25–57.
   1992. *Death Ritual and Social Structure in Classical Antiquity*. Cambridge: Cambridge University Press.
   Forthcoming. "Burning the Dead in Archaic Athens: Animals, Men and Heroes." In *Culture et cité: L'avènement de l'Athènes archaïque*. Ed. D. Viviers and A. Verbanck-Pierard. Brussels: Free University of Brussels.
Morris, S. P. 1984. *The Black and White Style*. New Haven, Conn.: Yale University Press.
Mossé, C. 1979. "Comment s'élabore un mythe politique: Solon 'père fondateur' de la démocratie athénienne." *Annales ESC* 34.425–37.
Moulinier, L. 1952. *Le pur et l'impur dans la pensée des Grecs d'Homére à Aristote*. Paris: C. Klincksieck.
Müller, F. M. 1878. *Lectures on the Origin and Growth of Religion*. New York: Scribner.
   1882. *Introduction to the Science of Religion*. London: Longmans, Green.
Murdoch, I. 1968. *The Nice and the Good*. London: Chatto & Windus.
Murray, G. 1912. *Four Stages of Greek Religion*. Oxford: Oxford University Press.
Murray, O. 1980. *Early Greece*. Brighton: Harvester.

Mylonas, G. 1943–4. "Athletic Honors in the Fifth Century." *CJ* 39.278–89.

1958. *O Protoattikos Amphorefs tis Elefsinos*. Athens: Archaiologikes Hetareias.

1972–3. Ο ταφικὸς Κῦκλος Β τῶν Μυκηνῶν [Grave Circle B at Mycenae]. Athens: Archaiologikes Hetareias.

1975. *To Dytikon Nekrotapheion tis Elefsinos*, 3 vols. Athens: Archaiologikes Hetareias.

Nagy, G. 1979. *The Best of the Achaeans*. Baltimore, Md.: Johns Hopkins University Press.

1986. "Ancient Greek Epic and Praise Poetry: Some Typological Considerations." In *Oral Tradition in Literature*. Ed. J. Foley. Columbia, Mo.: University of Missouri Press.

1989. "Early Greek Views of Poets and Poetry." In *The Cambridge History of Literary Criticism*, vol. 1: *Classical Criticism*. Ed. G. A. Kennedy. Cambridge: Cambridge University Press. 1–77.

1990a. *Greek Mythology and Poetics*. Ithaca, N.Y.: Cornell University Press.

1990b. *Pindar's Homer: The Lyric Possession of an Epic Past*. Baltimore, Md.: Johns Hopkins University Press.

Nauck, A., ed. 1889. *Tragicorum Graecorum Fragmenta*. 2d ed. Leipzig: Teubner.

Nilsson, M. P. 1932. *The Mycenaean Origin of Greek Mythology*. Berkeley and Los Angeles: University of California Press.

1951a. *Cults, Myths, Oracles, and Politics in Ancient Greece*. Lund: Skrifter utgivna av Svenska institutet i Athen, no. 8. Repr. 1986. Gote: P. Astrom.

1951b. "Die Prozessionstypen im griechischen Kult." *Opuscula selecta* 1.166–214.

Nisetich, F. J. 1975. "Olympian 1.8–11: An Epinician Metaphor." *HSCP* 79.55–68.

Nock, A. D. 1944. "The Cult of Heroes." *HTR* 37.141–74.

1972. "Deification and Julian." 1957. In *Essays on Religion and the Ancient World*. Ed. Z. Stewart. Oxford: Oxford University Press. 833–46.

North, H. 1966. *Sophrosyne: Self-knowledge and Self-restraint in Greek Literature*. Ithaca, N.Y.: Cornell University Press.

Norwood, G. 1945. *Pindar*. Berkeley and Los Angeles: University of California Press.

Novick, P. 1988. *That Noble Dream: The "Objectivity Question" and the American Historical Profession*. Cambridge: Cambridge University Press.

1991. "My Correct Views on Everything." *AHR* 96.699–703.

Nylander, C. 1962. "Die sog. mykenischen Säulenbasen auf der Akropolis." *OAth* 4.31–77.

Oakley, J., and R. Sinos. 1993. *The Wedding in Ancient Athens*. Madison: University of Wisconsin Press.

Obelkevich, J. 1987. "Proverbs and Social History." In *The Social History of Language*. Cambridge Studies in Oral and Literate Culture, vol. 12. Ed. P. Burke and R. Porter. Cambridge: Cambridge University Press. 43–72.

Ober, J. 1989. *Mass and Elite in Democratic Athens: Rhetoric, Ideology, and the Power of the People*. Princeton, N.J.: Princeton University Press.

O'Flaherty, W. D. 1981. *The Rig Veda: An Anthology*. Harmondsworth: Penguin.

Ohly, D. 1953. *Griechische Goldbleche des 8. Jahrhunderts vor Christus*. Berlin: Mann.

1961. "Die Chimären des Chimärasmalers." *AM* 76.1–11.

Oikonomides, A. 1980. "The Lost Delphic Inscription with the Commandments of the Seven and P. Univ. Athen. 2782." *ZPE* 37.179–83.

1987. "Records of the 'Commandments of the Seven Wise Men' in the 3rd c. B.C." *Classical Bulletin* 63.67–76.

Oliva, P. 1971. *Sparta and Her Social Problems*. Amsterdam: Hakkert.

Oliver, J. 1950. *The Athenian Expounders of the Sacred and Ancestral Law*. Baltimore, Md.: Johns Hopkins University Press.

Osborne, R. G. 1984. "The Myth of Propaganda and the Propaganda of Myth." *Hephaistos* 5/6.61–70.

1987. "The Viewing and Obscuring of the Parthenon frieze." *JHS* 107.98–105.

1988. "Death Revisited, Death Revised: The Death of the Artist in Archaic and Classical Greece." *Art History* 11.1–16.

1989. "A Crisis in Archaeological History? The Seventh Century B.C. in Attica." *BSA* 84.297–322.

1991. "Whose Image and Superscription Is This?" *Arion* 3d. ser. 1.255–275.

Ostwald, M. 1969. *Nomos and the Beginnings of Athenian Democracy*. Oxford: Oxford University Press.

1986. *From Popular Sovereignty to the Sovereignty of Law*. Berkeley and Los Angeles: University of California Press.

Overbeck, J. 1980. "Some Recycled Vases in the West Cemetery at Eleusis," *AJA* 84.89–90.

Page, D. L. 1955. *Sappho and Alcaeus: An Introduction to the Study of Ancient Lesbian Poetry*. Oxford: Oxford University Press.

Page, D. L., ed. 1962. *Poetae Melici Graeci*. Oxford: Oxford University Press.

Papademetriou, I. 1952. "Ἀνασκαφαὶ ἐν Μυκηναῖς" [Excavations at Mycenae]. *PAE* 456–72.

1955. "Ἀνασκαφαὶ ἐν Μυκηναῖς." *PAE* 218–23.

Parke, H. W. 1985. *The Oracles of Apollo in Asia Minor*. London: Croom Helm.

Parke, H. W., and D. E. W. Wormell. 1956. *The Delphic Oracle*. 2 vols. Oxford: Oxford University Press.

Parker, R. 1983. *Miasma: Pollution and Purification in Early Greek Religion*. Oxford: Oxford University Press.

1988. "Were Spartan Kings Heroized?" *LCM* 13.1.9–10.

1989. "Spartan Religion." In Powell 1989. 142–72.

Parsons, T. 1937. *The Structure of Social Action*, 2 vols. New York: Free Press.

Patzer, H. 1962. "ΡΑΨΩΔΙΟΣ." *Hermes* 80.314–25.

Pax, E. 1962. *Reallexikon für Antike und Christentum*. 5.832–909. s.v. "Epiphanie."

Peacock, S. J. 1988. *Jane Ellen Harrison: The Mask and the Self*. New Haven Conn.: Yale University Press.

1991. "An Awful Warmth about Her Heart: The Personal in Jane Harrison's Ideas about Religion." In *The Cambridge Ritualists Reconsidered*. Ed. W. M. Calder III. Illinois Classical Studies supp. vol. 2. Atlanta, Ga.: Scholar's Press. 167–84.

Pecora, V. 1989. "The Limits of Local Knowledge." In Veeser 1989. 243–76.

Peek, W. 1955. *Griechische Versinschriften*, vol. 1: *Grabepigramme*. Berlin: Akademie.

Pembroke, S. 1970. "Locres et Tarente: Le rôle des femmes dans la fondation de deux colonies grecques." *Annales ESC* 5.1240–70.

Perdrizet, P. 1905. "Attikon aggeion meta parastaseos pompes gamou." *AE* 209–14.

Petrey, S. 1988. *Realism and Revolution: Balzac, Stendhal, Zola and the Performance of History*. Ithaca, N.Y.: Cornell University Press.

Pfister, F. 1909–12. *Der Reliquienkult im Altertum*. 2 vols. Gießen: A. Topelmann.

1924. *RE* suppl. 4.277–323. s.v. "Epiphanie."

Pfuhl, E. 1900. *De Atheniensium pompis sacris*. Berlin: Weidmann.

Pleket, H. W. 1974. "Zur Soziologie des antiken Sports." *Medelingen van het Nederlands Institut te Rome* 36 (n.s. 1).57–87.

1975. "Games, Prizes, Athletes and Ideology: Some Aspects of the History of Sport in the Greco-Roman World." *Stadion* 1.49–89.

Plommer, H. 1960. "The Archaic Acropolis." *JHS* 80.127–59.

Podlecki, A. 1971. "Cimon, Skyros and 'Theseus' Bones.' " *JHS* 91.141–3.

Poliakoff, M. 1989. Review of D. C. Young, *The Olympic Myth of Greek Amateur Athletics*. *AJP* 110:166–71.

Polignac, F. de. 1984. *La naissance de la cité grecque*. Paris: Decouverte.

Pope, M. 1988. "Thucydides and Democracy." *Historia* 37.276–96.

Popham, M. 1981–2. "Lefkandi: Toumba." *AR* 28.15–17.

1982–3. "Lefkandi: Toumba." *AR* 29.12–15.

Popham, M., et al. 1982a. "Further Excavation of the Toumba Cemetery at Lefkandi, 1981." *BSA* 77.213–48.

1982b. "The Hero of Lefkandi." *Antiquity* 56.169–75.

1988–9. "Further Excavation of the Toumba Cemetery at Lefkandi, 1984 and 1986: A Preliminary Report." *AR* 35.117–29.

Pouilloux, J. 1954. "Recherches sur l'histoire et les cultes de Thasos de la fondation de la cité à 196 avant J.-C." Ph.D. diss., University of Paris.

Poulsen, F. 1905. *Die Dipylongräber und die Dipylonvasen.* Leipzig: Teubner.

Powell, A., ed. 1989. *Classical Sparta: Techniques Behind Her Success.* London: Routledge.

Preisshofen, F. 1977. "Zur Topographie der Akropolis." *AA* 74–84.

Preziosi, D. 1989. *Rethinking Art History.* New Haven, Conn.: Yale University Press.

Price, S. 1984. *Rituals and Power: The Roman Imperial Cult in Asia Minor.* Cambridge: Cambridge University Press.

Pritchett, W. K. 1979. *The Greek State at War,* vol. 3. Berkeley and Los Angeles: University of California Press.

Protonotariou-Deilaki, E. 1992. "Skepseis yia tin Katagogi ton Agonon: Schesi Epitymvias Latreias – Ekecheirias Agonon." In Coulson and Kyrieleis 1992. 167–71.

Qviller, B. 1981. "The Dynamics of the Homeric Society." *SO* 56.109–55.

Raaflaub, K. 1983. "Democracy, Oligarchy, and the Concept of the 'Free Citizen' in Late Fifth-Century Athens." *Political Theory* 11.517–44.

1987. "Herodotus, Political Thought, and the Meaning of History." *Arethusa* 20.221–48.

1988. "Athenische Geschichte und mündliche Überlieferung." In *Vergangenheit in mündlicher Überlieferung.* Ed. J. von Ungern-Sternberg and H. Reinau. Colloquium Rauricum 1.197–225.

1989. "Contemporary Perceptions of Democracy in Fifth-Century Athens." *C & M* 40.33–70.

Rabinow, P. 1977. *Reflections on Fieldwork.* Berkeley and Los Angeles: University of California Press.

Radcliffe-Brown, A. R. 1952. *Structure and Function in Primitive Societies.* London: Cohen & West.

Raschke, W. J. 1988. "Images of Victory: Some New Considerations of Athletic Monuments." In *The Archaeology of the Olympics: The Olympics and Other Festivals in Antiquity.* Ed. W. J. Raschke. Madison: University of Wisconsin Press. 38–54.

Raubitschek, A. 1949. *Dedications on the Athenian Akropolis.* Cambridge, Mass.: Archaeological Institute of America.

Redfield, J. M. 1975. *Nature and Culture in the "Iliad."* Chicago: University of Chicago Press.

1983. "The Economic Man." In *Approaches to Homer.* Ed. C. Rubino and C. Shelmerdine. Austin: University of Texas Press. 218–47.

1986. "The Growth of Markets in Archaic Greece." In *The Market in History.* Ed. B. Anderson and A. Latham. London: Croom Helm. 29–58.

1991. "Classics and Anthropology." *Arion* 3d ser. 1.2.5–23.

Rée, J. 1991. "The Vanity of Historicism." *New Literary History* 22.961–84.

Reese, D. 1985. "Fossils and Mediterranean Archaeology." Abstract. *AJA* 89.347–8.

Reiner, E. 1961. "The Etiological Myth of the 'Seven Sages.' " *Orientalia* 30.1–11.

Renfrew, A. C. 1972. *The Emergence of Civilisation.* London: Methuen.

Rhodes, P. J. 1981. *A Commentary on the Arisotelian Athenaion Politeia.* Oxford: Clarendon Press.

1991. "The Athenian Code of Laws, 410–399 B.C." *JHS* 111.87–100.

Rhodes, R. F. 1987. "Early Stoneworking in the Corinthia." *Hesperia* 56.229–32.

Rich, J., and A. Wallace-Hadrill, eds. 1991. *City and Country in the Ancient World.* London: Routledge & Kegan Paul.

Richardson, N. 1981. "The Contest of Homer and Hesiod and Alcidamas' Mouseion." *CQ* 31.1–10.

Richter, G. M. A., and L. F. Hall. 1936. *Red-Figured Athenian Vases in the Metropolitan Museum of Art.* New Haven, Conn.: Yale University Press.

Rihll, T.E. 1989. "Lawgivers and Tyrants (Solon, FRR. 9–11 West)." *CQ* n.s. 39.277–86.

Rijksbaron, A. 1984. *The Syntax and Semantics of the Verb in Classical Greek.* Amsterdam: J. C. Gieben.

Robert, L. 1967. "Sur des inscriptions d'Ephèse." *Revue de Philologie* 3d ser. 41.7–84.

Robertson, N. 1978. "The Myth of the First Sacred War." *CQ* 28.38–73.

1990a. "The Laws of Athens, 410–399 B.C.: The Evidence for Review and Publication." *JHS* 110.43–75.

1990b. "Some Recent Work in Greek Religion and Mythology." *EMC/CV* 9.419–42.

1991. "Some Recent Work in Greek Religion and Mythology (continued)." *EMC/CV* 10.57–79.

Robinson, H. S. 1976. "Excavations at Corinth: Temple Hill, 1968–1972." *Hesperia* 45.203–39.

Roehl, H., ed. 1882. *Inscriptiones Graecae antiquissimae praeter Atticas in Attica repertas.* Berlin: G. Reimer.

Rohde, E. 1920. *Psyche: The Cult of Souls and Belief in Immortality among the Ancient Greeks,* 8th ed. Trans. W. B. Hills. New York: Harcourt, Brace, Jovanovich.

Rolley, C. 1974. "Fouilles à Erétrie, archéologie, histoire et religion," *RA* 7th ser. 2.307–11.

Rombos, T. 1988. *The Iconography of Attic Late Geometric II Pottery.* SIMA Pocketbook no. 68. Partille, Sweden: P. Astrom.

Roscher, W. H. R. 1873. *Apollon und Mars.* Leipzig: W. Engelmann.

Roscher, W. H. R., ed. 1916–24. *Lexikon der griechischen und römischen Mythologie,* 2d ed. 6 vols. and suppl. Leipzig: Teubner.

Rose, H. J. 1940. "Some Herodotean Rationalisms." *CQ* 45.78–84.

Rösler, W. 1980. "Ein Gedicht und sein Publikum. Überlegungen zu Sappho fr. 44 LP." *Hermes* 103.275–85.

Ross, D. 1991. *The Origins of American Social Science.* Cambridge: Cambridge University Press.

Rothblatt, S. 1968. *The Revolution of the Dons: Cambridge and Society in Victorian England.* London. Repr. 1981. Cambridge: Cambridge University Press.

Rougé, J. 1970. "La colonisation grecque et les femmes." *Cahiers d'Histoire* 15.307–17.

Roussel, D. 1976. *Tribu et cité: Annales littéraires de l'Université de Besançon,* vol. 193. Centre de recherches d'histoire ancienne, no. 23. Paris: Les belles lettres.

Ruck, C. 1968. "Marginalia Pindarica." *Hermes* 96.129–42.

Ruipérez, M. 1953. "Etymologica: Φοῖβος 'Απόλλων." *Emerita* 21.14–17.

Ruschenbusch, E. 1958. "Patrios Politeia: Theseus, Drakon, Solon und Kleisthenes in Publizistik und Geschichtsschreibung des 5. und 4. Jahrhunderts v. Chr." *Historia* 7.398–424.

1966. *Solonos Nomoi.* Historia Einzelschrift 6. Wiesbaden: F. Steiner.

Sackett, H. 1986. "The Burial Building at Lefkandi: Evidence for Euboean Leadership and Overseas Enterprise during the 'Dark Age.'" Paper delivered at the 88th Annual Meeting of the Archaeological Institute of America. San Antonio, Tex., December 28, 1986. Abstracts 11:1.

Säflund, G. 1965. *Excavations at Berbati, 1936–1937.* Stockholm: Almqvist & Wiksell.

Sahlins, M. 1981. *Historical Metaphors and Mythical Realities.* Ann Arbor: University of Michigan Press.

1985. *Islands of History.* Chicago: University of Chicago Press.

Ste. Croix, G. E. M. de. 1972. *The Origins of the Peloponnesian War.* Ithaca, N.Y.: Cornell University Press.

Sakellariou, M. 1989. *The Polis-State: Definition and Origin.* MELETHMATA 4.1989. Athens: Research Centre for Greek and Roman Antiquity, National Hellenic Research Foundation.

Salapata, G. 1990a. "Lakonian Plaques and Their Relation to the Stone Reliefs." *Akten des*

XIII internazionalen Kongresses für klassische Archäologie (Berlin 1988). Mainz: P. von Zabern. 525.

1990b. "Pausanias 3.19.6: The Sanctuary of Alexandra at Amyklai." Paper presented of the 92nd Annual Meeting of the Archaeological Institute of America, San Francisco, December 30, 1990. Abstracts 14.78–9.

Salmon, J. 1972. "The Heraeum at Perachora, and the Early History of Corinth and Megara." *BSA* 67.159–204.

1984. *Wealthy Corinth*. Oxford: Oxford University Press.

Sansone, D. 1988. *Greek Athletics and the Genesis of Sport*. Berkeley and Los Angeles: University of California Press.

Santoni, A. 1983. "Temi e motivi di interesse socio-economico nella leggenda dei 'Sette Sapienti'." *ASNP* (ser. 3.13.1)91–160.

Schachter, A. 1981. *Cults of Boiotia*, vol. 1: *Acheloos to Hera. BICS* suppl. 38.1. London: University of London.

Schaefer, H. 1963. "Das Eidolon des Leonidas." In *Probleme der alten Geschichte: Gesammelte Abhandlungen und Vorträge*. Ed. U. Weidemann and W. Schmitthenner. Göttingen: Vandenhoeck & Ruprecht. 323–36.

Schauenburg, K. 1979. "Herakles Mousikos." *JdI* 94.

Schefold, K. 1978. *Götter- und Heldensagen der Griechen in der spätarchaischen Kunst*. Munich: Hirmer.

Scheliha, R. von. 1987. *Vom Wettkampf der Dichter*. Amsterdam: Castrum Peregrini Presse.

Scherer, C. 1885. "De olympionicarum Statuis." Inaug. diss., University of Göttingen.

Schilardi, D. 1988. "The Temple of Athena at Koukounaries." In R. Hägg, N. Marinatos, and G. Nordquist 1988. 41–8.

Schlesier, R. 1990. "Jane Ellen Harrison." In *Classical Scholarship: A Biographical Encyclopedia*. Ed. W. W. Briggs and W. M. Calder III. New York: Garland.

Schliemann, H. 1881. *Orchomenos*. Leipzig.

Schmemann, A. 1990. "The Liturgical Revival and the Orthodox Church." In *Liturgy and Tradition*. Ed. T. Fisch. Crestwood, N.Y.: Vladimir's Seminary Press.

Schmid, P. B. 1947. *Studien zu griechischen Ktisissagen*. Freiburg: Paulusdruckerei.

Schneider, L., and C. Höcker. 1990. *Die Akropolis von Athen*. Cologne: DuMont Buchverlag.

Schusky, E. 1972. *Manual for Kinship Analysis*. New York: Holt, Rinehart, and Winston.

Schwartz, J. 1960. *Pseudo-Hesiodea: Recherches sur la composition, la diffusion et la disparition ancienne d'oeuvres attribuées à Hésiode*. Leiden: E. J. Brill.

Seaford, R. 1987. "The Tragic Wedding." *JHS* 107.107–30.

Sealey, R. 1957. "From Phemios to Ion." *REG* 70.312–55.

1976. *A History of the Greek City States, ca. 700–300 B.C.* Berkeley and Los Angeles: University of California Press.

de Sélincourt, Aubrey, trans. 1954. *Herodotus: The Histories*. Middlesex: Penguin Books.

Senjak, R., ed. 1990. *Fieldnotes: The Making of Anthropology*. Princeton, N.J.: Princeton University Press.

Servais, J. 1968. "Les fouilles sur l'haut de Vélatouri." In *Thorikos*, vol. 3: 1965. Brussels: Comité des fouilles belges en Grèce. 127–41.

Serwint, N. J. 1987. "Greek Athletic Sculpture from the Fifth and Fourth Centuries B.C.: An Iconographic Study." Ph.D. diss., Princeton University (DA order no. 8724798).

Shapiro, H. A. 1989. *Art and Cult under the Tyrants in Athens*. Mainz: P. von Zabern.

1992. "*Mousikoi Agones:* Music and Poetry at the Panathenaic Festival." In *Goddess and Polis: The Panathenaic Festival in Ancient Athens*. Ed. J. Neils. Princeton, N.J.: Princeton University Press. 53–75.

Shaw, B. D., and R. P. Saller. 1981. "Editors' Introduction." In M. I. Finley, *Economy and Society in Ancient Greece*. London: Chatto & Windus. ix–xxvi.

Sheedy, K. 1990. "A Prothesis Scene by the Analatos Painter." *AM* 105.117–51.

Sheridan, A. 1980. *Michel Foucault: The Will to Truth*. London: Tavistock.

Sherwin-White, A. N., ed. 1966. *The Letters of Pliny*. Oxford: Oxford University Press.

Sherzer, J. 1983. *Kuna Ways of Speaking: An Ethnographic Perspective*. Austin: University of Texas Press.

Simon, E. 1954. "Zur lekythos des Panmalers in Tarent." *ÖJh* 41.77–90.

———. 1983. *The Festivals of Attica*. Madison: University of Wisconsin Press.

Skias, A. N. 1912. "Neoterai anaskaphai en ti panarchia Elefsiniaki nekropolei." *AE*.1–39.

Slater, W. J. 1984. "Nemean One: The Victor's Return in Poetry and Politics." In *Greek Poetry and Philosophy: Studies in Honour of Leonard Woodbury*. Ed. D. E. Gerber. Chico, Calif.: Scholar's Press. 241–64.

Slotkin, R. 1973. *Regeneration through Violence*. Middletown, Conn.: Wesleyan University Press.

Smith, M. 1991. "William Robertson Smith." In *The Cambridge Ritualists Reconsidered*. Ed. W. M. Calder III. Illinois Classical Studies suppl. vol. 2. Atlanta, Ga.: Scholar's Press. 251–61.

Smith, W. R. 1889. *Lectures on the Religion of the Semites*. London: A. & C. Black.

Snell, B. 1954. "Zur Geschichte vom Gastmahl der sieben Weisen." In *Thesaurismata (Fst. Kapp)*. Ed. O. Hiltbrunner et al. Munich: Beck. 105–11.

———. 1971. *Leben und Meinungen der sieben Weisen*, 4th ed. Munich: Heimeran.

Snell, B., and H. Maehler, eds. 1970. *Bacchylidis Carmina cum Fragmentis*. 10th ed. Leipzig: Teubner.

———. eds. 1980. *Pindarus*, part 1: *Epinicia*. 6th ed. Leipzig: Teubner.

Snodgrass, A. 1971. *The Dark Age of Greece: An Archaeological Survey of the Eleventh to the Eighth Centuries B.C.* Edinburgh: Edinburgh University Press.

———. 1980a. *Archaic Greece: The Age of Experiment*. Cambridge: Cambridge University Press.

———. 1980b. "Toward the Interpretation of the Geometric Figure Scenes." *AM* 95:90–8.

———. 1982. "Les origines du culte des héros dans la Grèce antique." In Gnoli and J.-P. Vernant. 1982. 107–19.

———. 1986. "Interaction by Design: The Greek City-State." In *Peer Polity Interaction and the Development of Socio-Cultural Complexity*. Ed. A. C. Renfrew and J. F. Cherry. Cambridge: Cambridge University Press. 47–58

———. 1987. *An Archaeology of Greece*. Berkeley and Los Angeles: University of California Press.

———. 1988a. "The Archaeology of the Hero." *AION ArchStAnt* 10.19–26.

———. 1988b. *Cyprus and Early Greek History*. Nicosia: Bank of Cyprus Cultural Foundation.

Sourvinou-Inwood, C. 1971. "Theseus Lifting the Rock and a Cup Near the Pithos Painter." *JHS* 91.94–109.

Spencer, H. 1882. *Principles of Sociology*, vol. 1. London: Williams & Norgate.

Stahl, M. 1983. "Tyrannis und das Problem der Macht." *Hermes* 111.202–20.

Stanton, G. R. 1990. *Athenian Politics ca. 800–500 B.C.: A Sourcebook*. London: Routledge & Kegan Paul.

Starr, C. 1961. *The Origins of Greek Civilization*. New York: Knopf.

———. 1965. "The Credibility of Early Spartan History." *Historia* 14.257–72.

———. 1977. *Economic and Social Growth of Early Greece, 800–500 B.C.* Oxford: Oxford University Press.

Stavropoullos, P. 1958. "Anaskaphi arkhaias Akadimeias." *Praktika* 5–13.

Stengel, P. 1920. *Die griechischen Kultusaltertümer*, 3d ed. Munich: C. H. Beck.

Stewart, J. 1959. *Jane Ellen Harrison: A Portrait from Letters*. London: Merlin Press.

Stone, L., ed. 1975. *The University in Society*. Princeton, N.J.: Princeton University Press.

Straten, F. T. van. 1976. "Daikrates' Dream: A Votive Relief from Kos and Some Other kat'onar Dedications." *BABesch* 51.1–38.

Stroud, R. 1968. *Drakon's Law on Homicide*. Berkeley and Los Angeles: University of California Press.

Sutton, R. 1981. "The Interaction Between Men and Women Portrayed on Attic Red-Figure Pottery." Ph.D. diss., University of North Carolina.

Svenbro, J. 1988. *Phrasikleia: Anthropologie de la lecture en Grèce ancienne*. Paris: Decouverte.

Szegedy-Maszak, A. 1978. "Legends of the Greek Lawgivers." *GRBS* 19.199–209.

Taeger, F. 1957. *Charisma: Studien zur Geschichte des antiken Herrsherkultes*, 2 vols. Stuttgart: W. Wohlkammer.

Tankard, E. 1956. *Panathenaic Amphorae Made in Athens in the Sixth Century B.C.* Liverpool: Liverpool Public Museums.

Tarditi, G., ed. 1968a. *Archilochus*. Rome: In Aedibus Athenaei.

Tarditi, G. 1968b. "Sull' origine e sul significatio della parola rapsodo." *Maia* 20.137–45.

Tausend, K. 1989. "Theseus und der delisch-attische Seebund." *RhM* 132.225–35.

Thomas, B. 1991. *The New Historicism and Other Old-Fashioned Topics*. Princeton, N.J.: Princeton University Press.

Thomas, R. 1989. *Oral Tradition and Written Record in Classical Athens*. Cambridge: Cambridge University Press.

1990. "Ancient Greek Family Tradition and Democracy." In *The Myths We Live By*. Ed. R. Samuel and P. Thompson. New York: Routledge & Kegan Paul. 203–15

Thompson, E. P. 1963. *The Making of the English Working Class*. London: V. Gollancz.

Thompson, H. A. 1940. *The Tholos of Athens and Its Predecessors*. *Hesperia* suppl. vol. 4. Princeton, N.J.: Princeton University Press.

Thomson, G. 1941. *Aeschylus and Athens: A Study of the Social Origins of Drama*, 1st ed. London: Lawrence & Wishart.

Tilly, C. 1984. *Big Structures, Large Processes, Huge Comparisons*. New York: Russell Sage Foundation.

Tillyard, E. M. W. 1923. *The Hope Vases*. Cambridge: Cambridge University Press.

Tiverios, M. 1989. *Perikleia Panathinia*. Athens: Andromeda Books.

Tod, M. N., and A. J. B. Wace. 1906. *A Catalogue of the Sparta Museum*. Cambridge: Cambridge University Press.

Touchais, G. 1982. "Chronique des fouilles." *BCH* 106.588–92.

Touloupa, E. 1972. "Bronzebleche von der Akropolis in Athen: Gehämmerte geometrische Dreifüsse." *AM* 87.57–76.

Travlos, I. 1983. "I Athina kai i Elefsina ston 8o kai 7o p. Chr. aiona." *ASAA* 61.323–38.

Trendall, A. D. 1948. *Handbook to the Nicholson Museum*. Sydney: University of Sydney.

Trigger, B. 1989. *A History of Archaeological Thought*. Cambridge: Cambridge University Press.

Turner, F. M. 1981. *The Greek Heritage in Victorian Britain*. New Haven, Conn.: Yale University Press.

Turner, V. 1969. *The Ritual Process*. Ithaca, N.Y.: Cornell University Press.

1974. *Dramas, Fields, and Metaphors: Symbolic Action in Human Society*. Ithaca, N.Y.: Cornell University Press.

1981. "Social Dramas and Stories about Them." In *On Narrative*. Ed. W. J. T. Mitchell. Chicago: University of Chicago Press. 137–64.

Ungern-Sternberg, J. von. 1985. "Das Grab des Theseus und andere Gräber." In *Antike in der Moderne*. Ed. W. Schuller. Konstanzer althistorische Vorträge und Forschungen 15.321–329.

Vanderpool, E. 1955. "Newsletter from Greece." *AJA* 59:266.

Vandiver, E. 1991. *Heroes in Herodotus: The Interaction of Myth and History*. Frankfurt: P. Lang.

Van Gennep, A. 1960. *The Rites of Passage*. London: Routledge & Kegan Paul.

Veeser, H. A., ed. 1989. *The New Historicism*. New York: Routledge & Kegan Paul.

Verdenius, W. J. 1976. "Pindar's Seventh Olympian Ode: Supplementary Comments." *Mnemosyne* 4th ser. 29.43–53.

1987. *Commentaries on Pindar*, vol. 1: *Mnemosyne* suppl. vol. 97. Leiden: E. J. Brill.

Vermeule, C. C., and D. von Bothmer. 1959. "Notes on a New Edition of Michaelis: Ancient Marbles in Great Britain. Part Three: 1." *AJA* 63.

Vernant, J.-P. 1980. *Myth and Society in Ancient Greece*. Brighton: Harvester.

———. 1981. "Preface." In Gernet 1981. vii–xi.

———. 1982. *The Origins of Greek Thought*. Ithaca, N.Y.: Cornell University Press.

———. 1983. *Myth and Thought Among the Greeks*. London: Routledge & Kegan Paul.

———. 1988. *Myth and Society in Ancient Greece*. New York: Zone Books.

———. 1989. "At Man's Table: Hesiod's Foundation Myth of Sacrifice." In Detienne and Vernant. 1989. 21–86.

———. 1991. *Mortals and Immortals*. Ed. F. Zeitlin. Princeton, N.J.: Princeton University Press.

Vernant, J.-P., and P. Vidal-Naquet. 1981. *Myth and Tragedy in Ancient Greece*. Chicago: University of Chicago Press.

Versnel, H.S. 1970. *Triumphus: An Inquiry into the Origin, Development, and Meaning of the Roman Triumph*. Leiden: E. J. Brill.

———. 1985–6. "Apollo and Mars One Hundred Years after Roscher." *Visible Religion: Approaches to Iconography*. 4.134–67.

———. 1987. "What Did Ancient Man See When He Saw a God? Some Reflections on Greco-Roman Epiphany." In *Effigies Dei: Essays on the History of Religion*. Ed. D. van der Plas. Leiden: E. J. Brill. 42–55.

Vian, F. 1963. *Les Origines de Thèbes: Cadmos et les Spartes*. Paris: C. Klincksieck.

Vidal-Naquet, P. 1968. "La tradition de l'hoplite athénien." In *Problèmes de la guerre en Grèce ancienne*. Ed. J.-P. Vernant. The Hague: Mouton. 161–81.

———. 1986. *The Black Hunter: Forms of Thought and Forms of Society in the Greek World*. Trans. A. Szegedy-Maszak. Baltimore, Md.: Johns Hopkins University Press.

Villard, F. 1954. *CVA Louvre 11*. Paris: E. Champion.

Visser, M. 1982. "Worship Your Enemy: Aspects of the Cult of Heroes in Ancient Greece." *HTR* 75.403–28.

———. 1984. "Vengeance and Pollution in Classical Athens." *Journal of the History of Ideas*. 193–206.

Viviers, D. 1987. "La conquête de la Sigée par Pisistrate." *AC* 56. 5–25.

Vliet, E. van der. 1986. " 'Big-Man,' Tyrant, Chief: The Anomalous Starting Point of the State in Classical Greece." In *Private Politics: A Multi-Disciplinary Approach to 'Big-Man' Systems*. Ed. M. A. van Bakel et al. Leiden: E. J. Brill. 117–26.

Voigt, E.-M., ed. 1971. *Sappho et Alcaeus*. Amsterdam: Polak & Van Gennep.

Von der Mühll, P. 1963. "Weitere pindarische Notizen." *MH* 20.4.197–202.

Vos, M. F. 1986. "Aulodic and Auletic Contests." In *Enthousiasmos: Fst. Hemelrijk*. Amsterdam: J. C. Gieben. 122–30.

Wace, A. 1932. *Chamber Tombs at Mycenae. Archaeologia* 82.

———. 1949. *Mycenae: An Archaeological History and Guide*. Princeton, N.J.: Princeton University Press.

Wade-Gery, H. T. 1933. "Studies in the Structure of Athenian Society: II. The Laws of Kleisthenes." *CQ* 27.17–29.

———. 1954. "The Growth of the Dorian State." *CAH* 3.527–70.

Wagner, K. 1828. *De Periandro corinthiorum tyranno septem sapientibus adnumerato*. Darmstadt.

Wallace, P. 1985. "The Tomb of Hesiod and the Treasury of Minyas at Orkhomenos." In *Proceedings of the 3rd International Conference on Boiotian Antiquities*. McGill University Monographs in Classical Archaeology and History, no. 2. Ed. J. M. Fossey and H. Giroux. Amsterdam: J. C. Gieben. 166–78.

Wallace, R. W. 1989. *The Areopagos Council, to 307 B.C.* Baltimore, Md.: Johns Hopkins University Press.

Wallace-Hadrill, A. 1983. *Suetonius: The Scholar and His Caesars*. London: Duckworth.

Walters, R. 1980. "Signs of the Times: Clifford Geertz and Historians." *Social Research* 47.537–56.

Waterhouse, H., and R. Hope Simpson. 1961. "Prehistoric Laconia: Part II." *BSA* 56.114–75.

Weber, M. 1974. "Zu frühen attischen Gerätfiguren." *AM* 89.27–46.

1978. *Economy and Society: An Outline of Interpretative Sociology*. Ed. G. Roth and C. Wittich. Berkeley and Los Angeles: University of California Press.

Webster, T. B. L. 1955. "Homer and Attic Geometric Vases." *BSA* 50.38–50.

1972. *Potter and Patron in Classical Athens*. London: Methuen.

Wehrli, F. 1973. "Gnome, Anekdote und Biographie." *MH* 30.193–208.

Weinberg, S. 1974. "KTL from Corinth." *Hesperia* 43.522–34.

Weisz, G. 1983. *The Emergence of Modern Universities in France, 1863–1914*. Princeton, N.J.: Princeton University Press.

West, M. L. 1969. "Stesichorus Redivivus." *ZPE* 4.135–49.

1972. *Iambi et Elegi Graeci*, vol. 2. Oxford: Oxford University Press.

West, S. 1988. *Book IV: Commentary*. In *A Commentary on Homer's "Odyssey,"* vol. 1. Ed. A. Heubeck, S. West, and J. B. Hainsworth. Oxford: Oxford University Press. 192–245.

White, H. 1973. *Metahistory: The Historical Imagination in Nineteenth-Century Europe*. Baltimore, Md.: Johns Hopkins University Press.

1978. *Tropics of Discourse: Essays in Cultural Criticism*. Baltimore, Md.: Johns Hopkins University Press.

1989. "New Historicism: A Comment." In Veeser 1989. 293–302.

Whitley, J. 1988. "Early Greek States and Hero Cults: A Reappraisal." *JHS* 108.173–82.

1991a. "Social Diversity in Dark Age Greece." *BSA* 86.341–65.

1991b. *Style and Society in Dark Age Greece*. Cambridge: Cambridge University Press.

1993. "Protoattic Pottery: A Contextual Approach." In *Classical Greece: Ancient Histories and Modern Archaeologies*. Ed. I. Morris. Cambridge: Cambridge University Press.

Wickham Legg, L. G., ed. 1905. *Select Documents Illustrative of the French Revolution*. Oxford: Oxford University Press.

Wide, S. 1893. *Lakonische Kulte*. Leipzig: Teubner.

Wiersma, W. 1934. "The Seven Sages and the Prize of Wisdom." *Mnemosyne* 3.150–4.

Wilamowitz-Moellendorff, U. 1922. *Pindaros*. Berlin: Weidmann.

Williams, C. K. II. 1982. "The Early Urbanization of Corinth." *ASAA* 60.9–21.

Williams, F. 1978. *Callimachus: Hymn to Apollo*. Oxford: Oxford University Press.

Winkler, J. J., and F. Zeitlin, eds. 1990. *Nothing to do with Dionysos?* Princeton, N.J.: Princeton University Press.

Wood, D. K. 1990. "Francis Cornford." In *Classical Scholarship: A Biographical Encyclopedia*. Ed. W.W. Briggs and W. M. Calder III. New York: Garland. 23–36.

Wright, J. C. 1982. "The Old Temple Terrace at the Argive Heraeum and the Early Cult of Hera in the Argolid." *JHS* 102.186–201.

Wulf, H. 1896. *De fabellis cum collegii septem sapientium memoria coniunctis quaestiones criticae*. Halle: E. Karras.

Yoshida, A. 1965. "Sur quelques coupes de la fable grecque." *REA* 67.31–6.

Young, D. C. 1968. *Three Odes of Pindar: A Literary Study of Pythian 11, Pythian 3, and Olympian 7*. Leiden: E. J. Brill.

1983. "Pindar Pythians 2 and 3: Inscriptional ποτέ and the 'Poetic Epistle.' " *HSCP* 87.31–48.

1984. *The Olympic Myth of Greek Amateur Athletics*. Chicago: University of Chicago Press.

Young, R. S. 1942. "Graves from the Phaleron Cemetery." *AJA* 46.23–57.

Zimmern, A. 1961. *The Greek Commonwealth*, 5th ed., rev. Oxford: Oxford University Press.

Zschietschmann, W. 1930. "Homer und die attische Bildkunst un 560 v. Chr." *JdI* 45.45–60.

Index

Abrams, Philip, 17
Achilles, 119–20
Acropolis, 12, 36, 42 n92, 61, 73, 80, 166,
  217, 219, 221–3, 227
Adrastos, 165
Aeschylus, 80
Agamemnon, 54, 57, 166–7
Agamemnoneion, 55
agathoi, 34–5
Aigisthos, 50
Alcock, Susan, 54
Alkaios, 110
Alkibiades, 208
Alkmeon, 185
Alkmeonids, 23, 207–8, 217, 220–1
Amyklai, 54, 57, 166
Anacharsis the Scythian, 109, 111–12, 115, 118
Anakreon, 92
Anaximenes, 114
ancestor, 8–9, 35, 46–70; *see also* kinship
Andrewes, A., 204
Antiphon, 180–1
Aphrodite, 79
Apollo, 19, 74; at Didyma, 113, 120–2
Apollonius of Rhodes, 185
Arcadia, 57
Archias, 178–9, 186
Archidamos, 79
Archilochos, 119, 188
Argos, 33–4, 36, 49–50, 55, 58–62, 103, 165,
  185, 189, 219
Ariadne, 81–2
Aristagoras, 87
aristocracy, 6, 11, 24, 64, 136, 153–5, 157 n25,
  158 n30, 169, 172, 205, 208, 217, 220–2,
  227–8

aristoi, 64–5
Aristogeiton, 202–3
Aristophanes, 201, 223–4
Aristotle, 20, 36–7, 109, 111, 114, 202
Artemis, 74, 80, 83
Asine, 50–1, 59–60
Asklepios, 80, 187
Assembly, 218, 220, 227–8
Athena, 9, 23, 36, 55, 61, 73–4, 78–83, 85–8,
  99, 100–1, 146, 166, 172–3, 186, 223
Athenaion Politeia, 215–17, 220–3, 226–7
Athens, 9–10, 12, 16, 21, 23, 29, 30–2, 34–7,
  52, 57, 59, 61–4, 78, 80–3, 85–8, 92, 104,
  110–11, 116–17, 123, 170, 172–3, 182, 185–
  6, 201–32
athletics, 52, 85, 93, 131–63, 189–94, 197 n36;
  victory announcement, 136, 138, 140, 142–6
Attika, 31, 33, 37, 52, 55, 57–9, 61–2, 171,
  216, 220
audience, 7, 9, 12, 73–4, 83–5, 88, 100–1, 104,
  116–17, 120, 124, 202; *see also* drama;
  performance
Augustus, 24, 134
Austin, J. L., 225
autochthony, 62–3, 170

Bacchylides, 132, 139, 155
Battos, 136, 182, 191
Bauman, Richard, 116
Beazley, John, 101
Benveniste, Emile, 132–3, 137
Bérard, Claude, 164
Berbati, 49–50, 59, 64
Bergk, Theodor, 113
Bias, 109–10, 117–18
Biton, 154–5

261

Boardman, John, 81
Böhr, Elke, 101
Bohringer, François, 150
Bothmer, Dietrich von, 100–1
Boule, 216, 219–27
Bourriot, François, 63–4
Bowersock, Glen, 24
Bowra, C. M., 167
Brahman, 121–4
Briggs, Charles, 118
Bronze Age, 26, 47–8, 50, 52, 54–7, 59–63, 65
burial practices, 9, 26, 29–37, 46–70, 116, 147, 168, 170–1, 192; reuse, 49, 56–7, 60–1, 64–5
Burkert, Walter, 35, 104

Cabasilas, Nicholas, 85
Callimachus, 113, 150, 152, 179–80
Cambyses, 86
ceremony, 4–7, 9, 48, 73, 83, 85; victory ceremony, 11, 140
Chambers, Mortimer, 226
Chantraine, Pierre, 186
chariots, 74–8, 81, 83, 88, 139, 143, 152, 191
Chilon, 109, 115–16, 118, 120, 122, 166
Chios, 104
citizens, 27, 33–4, 104, 114, 117, 154–5, 165, 183, 203, 206, 209, 218, 222, 226; see also demos
city-state, see polis
civil war, see stasis
coinage, 10
Coldstream, Nicholas, 35, 52
colonization, 3, 10–11, 35, 168, 178–98; colonial founder, 8, 10, 11, 47, 52, 64, 136–7, 150, 164, 182–3, 186–94
Comte, Auguste, 17
Connor, W. R., 4, 23–4, 27, 83, 208
Cook, Captain, 5–6
Corcyra, 111, 205, 208
Corinth, 34, 36, 111, 117, 178–9, 185–6; Corinthia, 33
Cornford, Francis, 21, 133
Crawley, A. E., 19
cremation, 30–1, 34–6, 51; see also burial practices
Croesus, 86–7, 110, 115–16, 118, 154, 171–3, 201
crowns, 8, 131–63, 194
cult, 9, 24, 33, 80, 178; ancestor cult, 46–70; founder's cult, 70 n91, 191–4; hero cult, 9, 11, 26, 46–70, 123, 149–51, 154, 164–77; tomb cult, 46–70
Cyprus, 52, 110, 117

Dark Age, 25, 30, 35–57
Davies, J. K., 153
Davis, Natalie Z., 227
Day, Joseph, 144
dedications, 34, 128 n59, 139, 153; dedicatory inscriptions, 144; tripods, 121; victory dedications, 138, 140, 143
Defradas, J., 191
Delphi, 124; oracle, 3, 11, 23, 36, 79, 87, 120, 122, 135–6, 150–2, 165, 168, 171–2, 178–80, 182, 185, 190–2, 216; temple at, 112, 123
Delphic Apollo, 11, 120–1, 179–82, 184–5, 187, 190–2
Delphic games, see Panhellenic games
democracy, 3, 12, 37, 113, 116, 197 n35, 201–2, 204–6, 208–9, 215–32
demos, 6, 12, 23, 36, 64–5, 152, 170, 173, 207–9, 215–32
Demosthenes, 203, 217
Desan, Suzanne, 227
Detienne, Marcel, 25
Diagoras, 189, 191–4
Diodorus Siculus, 85, 134, 136, 139
Diogenes Laertius, 93, 109, 112–16
Dionysus, 79, 85, 165
Dioskouroi, 57, 79, 86, 166, 170; Polydeukes, 142
Dipylon cemetery, 29–31
Dipylon Master, 29
Dipylon shield, 30
Dipylon vase, 8, 28–32
Dorians, 6, 165–6, 170, 203
Douglas, Mary, 182–3, 186–7
Doyle, W., 225
Drakon, 36, 180, 212 n30
drama, 3, 4, 7–10, 79, 83–6, 101, 118, 141, 178; see also performance; tragedy
Dumézil, Georges, 25
Dunbabin, T. J., 188
Durkheim, Emile, 20–2, 25, 48, 52

Ebert, Joachim, 138, 146, 148
Edelstein, E., and L. Edelstein, 80
Egypt, 31, 52, 86
Ehrenberg, Victor, 220
Eleusis, 28, 31, 57, 61
elite, 7, 36, 56, 61, 216, 218–19; see also aristocracy
Else, Gerald, 3–4
Engard, Richard, 119
Ephesus, 80
Epimenides, 23, 36, 109, 112, 122, 182
epinikion, 8, 11, 123, 131–2, 140–1, 155, 191
epiphany, 9, 10, 73, 79–80, 83, 86

Eretria, 58
Euboia, 51, 58
eunomia, 12, 171–2, 203, 205, 209
Euripides, 79, 185
Evans-Pritchard, Edward, 18, 22
exile, 165, 179–87, 189–91, 216, 219

Farnell, Lewis, 22–3, 48, 52
Fehling, Detlev, 112–14
Ferguson, W. S., 59
Finley, Moses, 22, 24–5, 169, 202–3
Fish, Stanley, 33
Fontenrose, Joseph, 149, 172
Foucault, Michel, 7, 27
Fränkel, Hermann, 132, 137
Frazer, James, 19, 22, 25, 133
French Revolution, 224–6
Froude, J. A., 17
Fustel de Coulanges, N. D., 18–20, 22, 25

Gardiner, E. N., 149–50
Geertz, Clifford, 4–6, 8, 27–8, 32, 108
Gellner, Ernest, 21
Gerhard, Eduard, 98
Gernet, Louis, 22, 25
Goffman, Erving, 116
Goody, Jack, 28
Gorgons, 28, 31–2
Gould, John, 23
Green, J. R., 17
Greenblatt, Stephen, 7, 131
Grote, George, 20

Harmodios, 202–3
Harrison, Jane, 21–2, 133
Hawkes, C. F. C., 25
Hegel, 26
Hektor, 171
Helen, 57, 86, 166, 173 n5
Hera, 33, 61, 85, 155
Heraion (Argive), 34, 60–1
Herakleidai, 135–6, 166, 168, 170, 178–9
Herakles, 31, 52, 81–2, 111, 135, 151, 162 n84, 166, 185, 189–90
Hermes, 25, 74
hero, 10–11, 31, 47, 51–2, 61, 64, 76–9, 82, 85, 87–8, 119, 132, 149–50, 164–78; age of, 35, 54; hero-athlete, 11, 70, 91, 149–55; hero's bones, 23, 61–3, 164–77; founding hero (*see* colonization)
Herodotus, 4, 8, 11, 23, 35, 73–4, 79–80, 83, 86–8, 103–4, 110, 113, 118, 122, 135–7, 139, 153–5, 164–77, 182, 201, 215, 217, 219, 220–3, 226–8
Herzfeld, Michael, 116

Hesiod, 25, 35, 52, 76, 113, 171, 187
Hestia, 25
hetaireia, 227–8
Heyck, T. W., 17
Hipparchos, 10, 92–3, 98, 101, 103, 202
Hippias, 23, 92, 202, 207, 216, 221
Hodder, Ian, 46
Homeric poems, 3, 10, 24, 35, 51–2, 54, 57, 61–2, 64–5, 76, 79, 92–3, 96, 103–4, 119–20, 122, 132–3, 137, 167, 179, 180, 185, 189–90; *Iliad*, 10, 92, 103–4, 189–90; *Odyssey*, 10, 34, 55, 80, 92, 103–4, 167
hoplite warrior, 35, 41 n68, 75–80, 85, 221
Hornblower, Simon, 137
Humphreys, Sally, 18, 24–5, 46–7, 64–5
Huxley, George, 167
Hyakinthos, 57

Immerwahr, H. R., 172
inhumation, 30–1, 34, 36–7, 51; *see also* burial practices
Ionia/Ionians, 6, 87, 114–15; Ionian revolt, 137
Iron Age, 9, 46, 48–9, 52, 55–8, 60, 62, 64–5
Isagoras, 23, 207, 217–27
isonomia, 173, 204–5, 208–9, 228
Isthmia, 33
Isthmian games, *see* Panhellenic games
Ithaka, 54, 62

Jakobson, Roman, 116, 118
James, Michael, 25

Kassandra, 54, 57, 166
Kearns, Emily, 59
Keesing, Roger, 27
Kerameikos, 29–30, 58–9, 63, 79
Kimon, 58, 170–1
kinship, 46–9, 54, 63–4
Kleisthenes of Athens, 12, 64, 164, 197 n35, 204, 207–9, 212 n30, 215–32
Kleisthenes of Sikyon, 103, 164–5, 172, 176 n61
Kleobis, 154–5
Kleoboulos, 109, 111, 114–15, 118
Kleomenes, 12, 23, 87, 169, 216, 218–19, 221–4, 226
Kleon, 12, 205–6, 208–9
Klytemnaistra, 50
kudos, 11, 131–63, 193–4
Kylon, 36, 182, 219, 221
Kyrene, 136, 179, 183–4, 191

Labov, William, 116
Lakonia, 54–8, 61, 167

Lang, Andrew, 19
lawgiver, 110, 169, 201, 213 n35, 216
Leahy, D. M., 166, 170
Lefkandi, 50–2
Lévi-Strauss, Claude, 25, 109
Lewis, David M., 220
literacy, 3, 10
Lloyd-Jones, Hugh, 114
Lobon, 113–14
Loraux, Nicole, 25, 201, 207
Lykourgos, 82, 86–7, 169, 171–3
Lyotard, Jean-François, 27, 32
lyric, 6, 9, 77, 79, 92, 104, 113–15, 131–2,
    137–8, 140, 142, 155, 157–8, 160 n59, 166–
    7, 189–94; see also epinikion

Macan, R. W., 136
Malinowski, Bronislaw, 24–5
Malkin, Irad, 180
Manville, Brook, 27
Marathon, 57, 59, 79, 170, 202
Marett, R. R., 19
marriage, 25, 197 n36; see also wedding
Marx, Karl, 20, 22, 25; Marxism, 15, 16, 21,
    24, 26; Marxists, 16, 20, 27
Masson, Olivier, 186
Mauss, Marcel, 24–5
McLennan, John F., 19
Megakles, 73
Megara, 33, 36, 171, 185
Menelaion, 54, 57, 60, 62
Menelaos, 57, 166–7, 173 n5
Menidhi, 57, 59
Messenia, 55–7, 61–2
metaphor, 4–5, 8, 10–11, 80, 118–19, 180,
    184, 189, 194
Meyerson, Ignacy, 25
Miletus, 87, 115, 117
Miltiades, 136, 170
Mimnermos, 114, 119, 187–8
Minos, 82
model, 6–9, 86; see also paradigm
Momigliano, Arnaldo, 25
Moulinier, Louis, 23
mousikoi agones, 10, 93, 98–100, 103
Müller, Max, 19–21
Murdoch, Iris, 15
Murray, Gilbert, 21–2
Murray, Oswyn, 206
Mycenae, 34, 50, 53–5, 59, 61–2, 167
Myson, 109, 115, 119–20

Nagy, Gregory, 35, 123
Nemean games, see Panhellenic games
Nero, 134, 143

Nessos Painter, 31
New Historicism, 7, 8, 65 n3, 131
Nisetich, Frank J., 140
Nock, Arthur Darby, 24, 59
Novick, Peter, 16, 28

Odysseus, 55, 80, 104, 108
Oedipus, 171, 186
oikist, see colonization
oikos, 28, 47, 49
Oliva, Pavel, 169
Olympia, 62
Olympic games, see Panhellenic games
Olympus, 81
Orestes, 11; bones of, 11, 63, 164–77
Osborne, Robin, 28, 31–32
Ostwald, Martin, 204

Paiania, 9, 73
Pan, 80
Panathenaia, 10; festival, 92–3, 95–6, 100–1;
    games, 37; vase 98–100
Panhellenic games, 3, 36, 116, 131–63, 189;
    see also athletics
Panhellenism, 3, 10, 31, 35, 54, 56, 62, 93,
    123, 167, 191–2, 194
paradigm, 4, 10, 26, 76, 79, 149, 155, 206,
    227; see also model
Pareto, Vilfredo, 21
Paris, 104
Parke, H. W., 167–8
Parson, Peter, 114
Parsons, Talcott, 20–2
Partheniai, 168, 182
Pausanias, 54, 83, 85, 137, 143, 145, 147,
    152–3, 179, 185, 187
Pecora, Vincent, 26
Peisistratos, 8–10, 23, 37, 73, 78–83, 85–8, 92–
    3, 103, 117, 121, 172–3, 203, 207, 216
Pelopeion, 62
Pelopids, 165–7, 169, 170, 173
Pelops, 62, 171
Penelope, 80
performance, 4, 8–10, 73, 77, 83, 86–8;
    rhapsodic performance, 92–107; ritual
    reenactment, 83–5, 88, 141, 144–5, 149;
    sages as performers, 115–19
Periander, 109, 111–12, 115, 117
Pericles, 12, 205–7, 209, 217
Persian Wars, 86, 88, 167, 172
Petrey, Sandy, 224
Phaiakians, 80
Phaleron, 31
Pheidippides, 80
Phye, 8–10, 82, 172

Pindar, 77, 131–2, 134, 139, 167, 180, 189–94
Pittakos, 109–10, 114–17
Plato, 40 n46, 92, 96, 101, 111–12, 114, 120, 180, 182, 184
Plutarch, 37, 79, 82, 114, 123, 133–4, 142, 169–70, 178–9, 186
Polanyi, Karl, 24–5
Polignac, François de, 33
polis, 3, 9, 11, 25–6, 33, 35, 37, 43 n112, 47, 62, 64–5, 123, 153, 164, 166–71, 205, 215, 220, 228
Polis (cave at Ithaka), 54–5
pollution, 23, 178–98
Polyneikes, 80
Polyphemos vase, 28, 31–2
Poseidon, 178
Pouilloux, J., 150
Priam, 104
Price, Simon, 24
procession, 9, 52, 73, 76, 80–1, 83–4; chariot procession, 74–5, 77–8; victory procession, 10, 78, 139–41, 152; wedding procession, 75–6, 85
Prosymna, 50, 59–60
proverbs, 118–19
purification, 11, 23, 25, 41 n68, 175 n38, 178–98

Raaflaub, Kurt, 202
Radcliffe-Brown, Alfred, 21–2, 24
Redfield, James, 25
relics, 62, 167–8
rhapsode, 10, 92–107
rhetoric, see speaking skill
Rhodes, 189–94
rites of passage, 183
ritual, 3–7, 9–10, 15–45, 47–8, 50, 52, 54, 74, 76–8, 83–5, 123, 140–1, 144, 149, 151, 182, 186, 193; see also purification
Robert, Louis, 140
Rohde, Erwin, 52, 62
Rousseau, Jean-Jacques, 21
Roussel, Denis, 64
Ruschenbusch, E., 202

sacrifice, 34–6, 38 n3, 41 n68, 52, 121–3, 181, 192
sage, 10, 108–28; Seven Sages, 10, 12, 108–28, 202
Sahlins, Marshall, 5–7, 11
Salamis, 119, 171; battle of, 79, 137
Sapir, Edward, 116
Sappho, 79
Schmemann, Father Alexander, 84
Sealey, Raphael, 104

Seeley, John, 18
Sélincourt, Aubrey de, 227
Shorey, Paul, 22
Sikyon, 165
Simonides, 92, 114–15, 138, 167
slavery, 41–2 n86, 204, 218
Smith, H. R. W., 101
Smith, W. Robertson, 18–19, 22, 35
Snodgrass, Anthony, 3, 26, 30–1
Socrates, 23–4, 92, 96, 123
Solon, 12, 36–7, 93, 109–11, 114–23, 154–5, 201–14, 218, 221
Sophocles, 171
Sparta, 11, 23, 54, 57, 61–2, 79, 85–6, 115, 123, 133, 135–7, 147, 164–77, 182, 203–4, 216–24, 226, 228
Spartan kings, 57, 62, 133, 136–7, 141, 162 n87, 166–9, 207
speaking skill, 8, 110–11, 115–20, 124, 126, 153, 206, 209, 224–6
speech act, 10, 118–20, 225
Starr, Chester, 26
stasis, 9, 25, 29, 36, 110, 150, 169, 172, 182, 184, 193, 204–5, 208, 227
statues, 154; victor statues, 141–52
Stesichoros, 167
Suetonius, 134
Svenbro, Jesper, 144
symposium, 118–19, 123
Syracuse, 178–9, 186–8

Tarentum, 168, 182, 184
Tegea, 164–7, 171
Teiresias, 186
Teisamenos, 168, 170
Tellos, 154–5
Thales, 109–10, 113–17, 120–3
Theagenes, 149–50
Thebes, 31, 165, 171
Thera, 182
Therapne, 54, 86, 166, 173 n5
Theras, 168
Theseion, 58
Theseus, 23, 59, 79, 81–2, 170–1, 173 n3, 212 n30
Thessaly, 36, 52
Thomas, Rosalind, 224
Thompson, E. P., 227
Thorikos, 57, 59
Thrasyboulos, 115, 118
Thucydides, 3, 12, 36, 104, 136, 150, 154, 179, 186–8, 201–14
Tilly, Charles, 26
Tiryns, 60–1
Tlepolemos, 189–94

Toumba, 51–2

tragedy, 3–4, 38 n3

transgression, 149–52, 168, 186–7, 193–4

Trojan War, 19

Troy, 31, 104, 167, 189

tyrant/tyranny, 3, 6, 10, 36, 64, 74, 85, 87, 92, 98, 110–13, 115, 117–18, 121, 162 n87, 164, 172–3, 182, 202–5, 207–8, 216–18

Vernant, Jean-Pierre, 23, 25–6, 35, 149, 169

Versnel, H. S., 134

victor, 8, 10–11, 77–8, 131–63, 189–94; *see also* athletics

Vidal-Naquet, Pierre, 25

Wace, Alan, 50

Walters, Ronald, 27

warfare, 10, 23, 29–30, 35, 57, 61, 66 n15, 76, 79–80, 87, 89 n8, 132–7, 139, 141, 149–51, 153–4, 165, 168, 171–3, 179, 187–8, 193, 204, 216–17, 221–4; *see also* hoplite warrior

Weber, Max, 21, 24–5, 37, 153

wedding, 76–8, 85; *see also* marriage

White, Hayden, 16, 28

Whitley, James, 31

Wilamowitz-Moellendorff, U. von, 114

wisdom, 10, 86, 108–28

Wormell, D. E. W., 167–8

Xenophanes, 154

Zeus, 36, 85, 87, 131, 142, 146, 152, 189, 203